WIDE
OPEN
TOWN

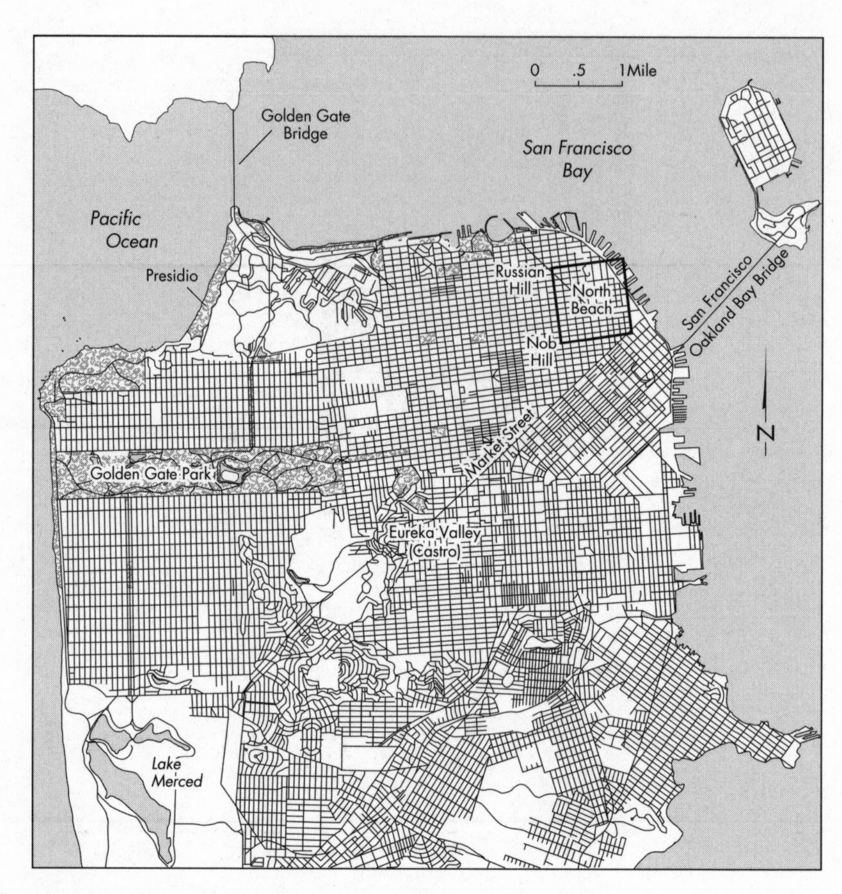

City of San Francisco, c. 1940.

UNIVERSITY OF CALIFORNIA PRESS
Berkeley Los Angeles London

University of California Press
Berkeley and Los Angeles, California

University of California Press, Ltd.
London, England

Library of Congress Cataloging-in-Publication Data

Boyd, Nan Alamilla, 1963–
Wide-open town : a history of queer San Francisco to 1965 / Nan Alamilla Boyd.
p. cm.
Includes index.
ISBN 0-520-20415-8 (cloth : alk. paper)
1. Gays—California—San Francisco—History.
I. Title.

HQ76.3.U52S2635 2003
305.9'0664'0979461—dc21 2002151314

Manufactured in the United States of America
13 12 11 10 09 08 07 06 05 04
10 9 8 7 6 5 4 3 2 1

The paper used in this publication is both acid-free and totally chlorine-free (TCF). It meets the minimum requirements of ANSI/NISO Z39.48–1992 (R 1997) (*Permanence of Paper*). ♾

To Reba Hudson and Rikki Streicher

Contents

Acknowledgments

This book is dedicated to Reba Hudson and Rikki Streicher. Lifelong friends, Reba and Rikki were part of a queer bar scene that flourished in San Francisco's North Beach district during the 1940s and 1950s. Through their stories as well as those of the forty others I interviewed for this book, San Francisco's queer history came vividly to life. The interviews unlocked what seemed to me to be a secret past, a history where gay men and lesbians socialized together in bars that were central to San Francisco's growing tourist economy. More importantly, through the assertion of the right to be different, they described a world that, in the end, became important to social change. I want to thank Reba, Rikki, and the others who agreed to let me interview them for this project. Their stories inspired me, and their histories frame this book.

This book began over ten years ago with the support of two key figures, Henry Abelove and Mari Jo Buhle, who encouraged me to develop a dissertation in U.S. lesbian and gay history. At the time, the infant field of queer studies was growing, and, in the tradition of women's history, community studies based on oral history research seemed an important first step in creating a discourse about lesbian and gay history. I also want to thank Anne Fausto-Sterling, Jacqueline Jones, and Robert Lee, who warmly guided me through graduate school and impressed me with their commitment to teaching. I also thank my graduate peers for their unswerving political commitments and general good sense: Gail Bederman, Laura Briggs, Oscar Campomanes, Peter Cohen, Krista

Comer, Ann DuCille, Elizabeth Francis, Kevin Gaines, Jane Gerhard, Linda Grasso, Bill Hart, Matt Jacobson, Melani McAlister, Bob McMichael, Louise Newman, Donna Penn, Tricia Rose, Laura Santigian, Jessica Shubow, and Lauri Umansky.

In San Francisco, as I started my research, I attached myself to the Gay, Lesbian, Bisexual, Transgender Historical Society of Northern California, where I found a vibrant research culture and a new academic home. Allan Bérubé encouraged me unfailingly. He taught me the basics of oral history research and inspired me with his friendship. Eric Garber, Paula Jabloner, Terence Kissack, Ruth Mahaney, Gayle Rubin, and Susan Stryker helped me in large and small ways, mostly through their dedication to local history. More than anyone else, though, I want to thank the indomitable Willie Walker. His quirky style and passion for San Francisco's queer history made every trip to the archives a pleasure.

Two grants, a Community Service Fellowship from Brown University's Center for Public Service and a pre-doctoral fellowship from the Women's Studies Department at the University of California at Santa Barbara, helped me through the difficult first years of research. Later, a job at the University of Colorado at Boulder brought me in contact with a new circle of scholars and friends. I want to thank my colleagues in the Women's Studies Program, Jo Belknap, Mary Churchill, Michiko Hase, Janet Jacobs, Alison Jaggar, Kamala Kempadoo, Susan Kent, Lisa Sun-Hee Park, Anne Marie Pois, and Marcia Westkott, who generously supported my work. The administrative staff in Women's Studies, Jeanie Lusby and Anna Vayr, aided my progress in uncountable ways. I also thank those at Boulder who have encouraged me with their friendship and support: Jo Arnold, Emilio Bejel, Irene Blair, Kathleen Chapman, Bud Coleman, Michael du Plessis, Maria Franquiz, Jane Garrity, Donna Goldstein, Julie Green, Karen Jacobs, Suzanne Juhasz, Patricia Limerick, Meg Moritz, Lisa Peñaloza, Michelene Pesantubbee, Terry Rowden, Jan Whitt, Marcia Yanamoto, and Margie Zamudio.

At Boulder, I also had the support of students who shared my enthusiasm for queer studies: Jami Armstrong, Davida Bloom, Keri Brandt, Matt Brown, Deanne Buck, Jamie Coker, Carey Gagnon, Evalie Horner, Ben Humphreys, Carl Nash, Cathy Olson, Louisa Pacheco, Mary Romano, Elisabeth Sheff, Sarah Sturdy, Stacey Takaki, and Jill Williams. Tea de Silvestre and Robin Schepps helped transcribe some of my oral history tapes. Abby Coleman, Kris Gilmore, Evalie Horner, and Carl Nash also worked as research assistants in the final stages of completing the manuscript.

In 1995–1996, my research was supported by a Rockefeller Fellowship in the Humanities from CLAGS, the Center for Lesbian and Gay Studies at the City University of New York Graduate Center. While I was in New York, my work benefited from the insights of Jeffrey Edwards, Jeffrey Escoffier, Elizabeth Freeman, Judith Halberstam, Jacob Hale, Henry Rubin, and Ben Singer, whose work in queer and transgender studies has had a great impact on my own. Finally, without the work of other queer historians, this book could not exist. I am deeply indebted to Allan Bérubé and John D'Emilio for their early work on San Francisco's queer history. I am also indebted to the work of Brett Beemyn, Alex Chasin, George Chauncey, Martin Duberman, Lisa Duggan, Estelle Freedman, Katie Gilmartin, Ramón Gutierrez, John Howard, Miranda Joseph, Jonathan Ned Katz, Elizabeth Lapovsky Kennedy, Martin Meeker, Joanne Meyerowitz, Esther Newton, Will Roscoe, Leila Rupp, Siobhan Somerville, Marc Stein, and Jennifer Terry.

There were many research and reference librarians who helped me along the way. Paula Jabloner, an archivist at the Gay, Lesbian, Bisexual, Transgender Historical Society, offered assistance at crucial moments. Susan Goldstein and Roberto Landazuri, at the San Francisco Archives of the San Francisco Public Library, helped me decipher the problem of police records and walked me through their labyrinthine clipping file collections. Keith Gresham helped secure important holdings in U.S. lesbian and gay history for the University of Colorado libraries. Reference librarians at the California State Archives provided access to the records of the California Alcoholic Beverage Control Board, and archivists at the Bancroft Library helped me locate the rare "hotel magazines" that ran advertisements for San Francisco's early queer establishments. I also thank Polly Thistlethwaite for her enthusiasm for this project and her countless hours of support, research- and otherwise.

For the past two years (2000–2002), my work has been supported by the Stanford Institute for Research on Women and Gender. I warmly thank the IRWG staff, particularly Amita Kumar and Sally Schroeder, and the cadre of junior and senior scholars whose biweekly presentations have kept me stimulated. Also, in the last few years there have been a handful of precious friends who read drafts of the manuscript and offered critical insight. Rickie Solinger read several final chapters and enthusiastically encouraged me. Lee Bernstein read the entire final draft of the manuscript and provided crucial insight into restructuring the book. Susan Lee Johnson and Camille Guerin-Gonzales have continuously supported my work. My editors at the University of California Press, particularly Naomi Schneider and Jan Spauschus, have been wonderful. The four outside readers for the press, Susan Cahn, Leila Rupp, Mary Ryan, and Marc Stein, offered criticisms that have enabled the book to become much better than it might have been. Most importantly, Elizabeth Lapovsky Kennedy has been an extraordinary mentor and friend. She read multiple drafts of the manuscript, attended many conference presentations, and truly encouraged my research and writing.

Finally, I warmly thank my long-term friends who gave me every reason to continue when I doubted that I would finish this book—Mary Beth Abella, John Bouffard, Marjorie Bryer, Carmen Cortez, Michelle Davey, Sven Davis, Heidi Doughty, Rebekah Eppley, Alex Harris, Karen Henry, Tiffany López, Lisa Martin, Melissa Murphy, and Karen Wolfe. Pamela Rosenblum guided me through the last few years with warmth and wisdom. My parents, Marion Bowman and Donald Boyd, have enthusiastically encouraged my academic work. My sister, Erika Boyd, and her husband, David DeAndreis, generously put me up for months at a time when I returned each summer to San Francisco to "finish the book." Finally, I thank my beautiful family, Brenda Buenviaje and Max Leone Buenviaje-Boyd for, most simply, the largeness of their love.

INTRODUCTION

San Francisco Was a Wide-Open Town

> I think it's important to realize that San Francisco did not happen after New York or after Stonewall. . . . This was something that developed in San Francisco and evolved because there were a large number of Gay people who just did the traditional American thing of organizing—organizing around people's interests.
>
> *Larry Littlejohn, interview, 1990*

San Francisco is a seductive city. Perched on the edge of a continent, its beautiful vistas, eccentric characters, and liberal politics reflect both the unruly nature of its frontier-town beginnings and the sophisticated desires of an urban metropolis. Sociologists Howard Becker and Irving Horowitz call San Francisco a culture of civility, noting that "deviance, like difference, is a civic resource, enjoyed by tourist and resident alike."[1] But while the strength of the city's queer communities is world renowned, there are few texts devoted to San Francisco's gay and lesbian history.[2] What follows, as a result, charts new ground. It asks the question "Why San Francisco?" Why do so many people associate San Francisco with homosexuals and homosexuality? In my research—and casual conversations—many answers have emerged. There are the same-sex dances of the Gold Rush era, the city's location as an international seaport, the homosocial entertainments of the city's Barbary Coast, the artistic revivals of the turn of the twentieth century, the tradition of vigilante law and order, the persistence of civic graft, the strength and diversity of the city's immigrant communities, the staunch resistance to anti-sex and anti-alcohol ordinances, the military presence of two world wars, and the bohemian, Beat, and hippie cultures that flourished in the postwar generations.[3] But, by and large, when asked "Why San Francisco?" most people refer to San Francisco's history of sexual permissiveness and its function as a wide-open town—a town where anything goes. These powerful (and sexual) metaphors frame the chapters that follow. What does it mean for San Francisco to be wide open? What impact did this have on the growth and development of the city's queer cultures and communities? Why does San Francisco remain so enigmatically attached to a sexually permissive and queer sensibility?

San Francisco is a queer town not simply because it hosts disproportionately large gay, lesbian, bisexual, and transgender communities but because a queerness is sewn into the city's social fabric. From its earliest days, sex and lawlessness have been fundamental to San Francisco's character. The Gold Rush of 1849, for instance, transformed San Francisco into a vibrant and opulent city with a reputation for licentious entertainment and vigilante government. Prior to that time, San Francisco had been a frontier town on the far reaches of overlapping empires. Still, its early history of shifting colonial rule and international commerce reveals a web of alliance and exploitation that would be its legacy. In 1776, when Spanish settlers constructed a mission and presidio—the twin pillars of Spanish-American colonization—near the territories of the Coast Miwoks, Wintuns, Yokuts, and Costanoans, they did so with Indian labor, luring Indian settlers into a colonial township at the northern edge of a tenaciously expanding Spanish empire. With Mexican independence from Spain in 1821, however, Yerba Buena village (as San Francisco was then called) became part of Mexico's northern territory and barely governable as the port secularized and became increasingly active for ships seeking commerce with traders and trappers. By the mid-1840s, as Mexico braced for war with the United States, Yerba Buena's population grew as foreign-born (Anglo-American) merchants moved into town and married the daughters of Mexican landowners and civic leaders, using sexual and familial connections to create wealth, social standing, and political alliances. Thus, in 1848, when the United States acquired California through the Treaty of Guadalupe-Hidalgo and Yerba Buena was renamed San Francisco, the city's population of Indians, *Californios* (Mexican ranchers), Anglo-American settlers, and their children—a total of just over eight hundred—reflected San Francisco's colonial history as well as its frontier-town ethics.[4]

The discovery of gold in the California foothills coincided with California's transfer from Mexican to U.S. authority, and these events dramatically altered San Francisco's economic development: almost overnight, San Francisco became a booming commercial center.[5] In 1848,

San Francisco had the best port in California, and the cargo ships that served the west coast docked there. As a result, San Francisco became a home base for the thousands of fortune seekers who passed through the town on their way to the gold fields. Miners who needed tools and provisions purchased these goods from San Francisco's growing class of merchants and shopkeepers. Later, as vast fortunes in gold and silver moved back through the city for trade or investment, San Francisco became a banking and financial stronghold. By 1868, ten insurance companies managed almost $6 million in capital, and by 1887, twenty-six banks controlled almost $150 million in assets.[6] In addition to its function as a financial center, San Francisco became a conduit for international trade. As agriculture and manufacturing developed through the 1860s to meet the needs of California's booming population, surplus goods traveled through the port of San Francisco, and investors secured lucrative global markets. For instance, along with Spanish-colonial trade routes to South America (particularly Chile and Peru), the Caribbean, and the eastern ports of North America, San Franciscan investors developed trade relationships with Japan and China and secured a virtual monopoly with the Hawai'ian Islands and the Philippines.[7] By 1890, the city's merchants handled an astonishing 99 percent of the coast's imports and 83 percent of its exports.[8] By the turn of the century, San Francisco had become the economic capital of the Pacific coast.

The consolidation of U.S. national authority and the growth of San Francisco's economy stimulated a vast in-migration of miners, merchants, and adventurers. By 1850, just a year after the Gold Rush officially started, San Francisco counted 35,000 residents. The city's exponential growth continued through the end of the century, its population jumping from 57,000 to 149,000 between 1860 and 1870, and by the turn of the century, San Francisco was the eighth largest city in the United States, with a population of almost 343,000.[9] Contrary to the traditional story of "the west," San Francisco's swelling population and vast economic growth were not due to the migration of Anglo-Americans who traveled the overland trails or braved the long sea passage around the Cape of Good Hope—though there were many who traveled these paths. In the years between 1850 and 1860, the majority of San Franciscans were foreign born (the average in other U.S. cities at the time was 10 percent).[10] The first wave of gold miners came from Valparaiso, Chile, and Lima, Peru—two South American port cities with a history of gold mining and long-established trade relations with San Francisco.[11] Chilean gold miners brought tools and technology, notably the *arrastra,* a large circular drag mill that extracted gold from crushed rocks.[12] An abundance of gold seekers also came from South China's Guangdong province—they came initially as temporary workers sent to augment their families' household income, but many stayed, carving out a new life for themselves in Gam Saan or Gold Mountain, the Cantonese term for California.[13] And while many African Americans traveled to California with "gold fever," many migrated west to escape southern slavery and the Fugitive Slave Law of 1850.[14]

San Francisco's overlap of cultures and communities, foreign and native born, contributed to a live-and-let-live sensibility, but it was the city's early history of lawlessness, boss politics, and administrative graft that solidified its reputation as a wide-open town. Prostitution and gambling quickly became big business in San Francisco, and for the right price the possibilities for sex and gaming seemed endless. In fact, at the start of the Gold Rush, a colony of Mexican and South American prostitutes settled on the southeastern slopes of Telegraph Hill, forming the nucleus of what would become the city's North Beach district.[15] A decade later, the Barbary Coast emerged in the degenerated storefronts on what was San Francisco's most important commercial thoroughfare. This was Pacific Street, or Terrific Street, as it was called in the 1890s, between the waterfront and Kearny Street. The Barbary Coast came to be known as San Francisco's roughest vice district, "the haunt of the low and the vile of every kind," an indignant historian reported in 1876. "The petty thief, the house burglar, the tramp, the whoremonger, lewd women, cut-throats, murderers, all are found here."[16] To sustain its reputation, the Barbary Coast hosted a battery of cheap amusements: groggeries with sawdust-covered floors, wine and beer dens (also known as "deadfalls"), melodeons (liquor dens with mechanical music boxes), dance halls, and concert saloons.

Through the second half of the nineteenth century, however, periods of flamboyant economic growth coincided with anti-vice campaigns that displayed the tension between San Francisco's reputation for vice and the reality of periodic purges. The most famous manifestation of these campaigns were the Vigilance Committees of 1851 and 1856, which followed on the heels of Gold Rush prosperity, price inflation, and exponential population growth.[17] Arguing that city police could not protect citizens' "security to life and property" and promising that "no thief, burglar, incendiary or assassin, shall escape punishment," the Vigilance Committee of 1851 executed three men during its ten-day tenure.[18] It also demanded heightened regulation of the in-migration of "undesirables," linking law and order with border control. The revival of the vigilantes in 1856 stemmed more directly from an association of sex with lawlessness. The 1856 Vigilance Committee took shape, initially, to insure the speedy trial and execution of two men accused of killing James King, the owner of an anti-vice daily, *The Evening Bulletin.* Before his death, King had crusaded against police corruption in his daily editorials, but he aimed his most caustic attacks at gambling and prostitution. Although formal vigilante action diminished after the 1850s, San Francisco's history repeats a pattern of anti-vice crusades, particularly during election time, that called for the protection of property (through the regulation of borders) and the control of sexual capital (through the regulation of brothels). Ironically, periods of anti-vice activism—the 1850s, 1870s, 1910s, and 1950s—produced a wealth of print material that advertised and drew international attention to San Francisco's vice districts, particularly its infamous Barbary Coast and, later, its North Beach and Tenderloin districts.[19] San Francisco's reputation for vice thus became its calling card. Despite periodic anti-vice crusades, a wide range of adventure-seekers, homosexuals among them, made their way through the Golden Gate.

Though a legacy of sex and lawlessness frames San Francisco's early history, San Francisco's queer history—its history of publicly visible queer cultures and communities—blossomed in 1933 with the repeal of Prohibition and the emergence of queer entertainments in the city's tourist-district nightclubs, bars, and taverns. Through the 1930s, 1940s, and 1950s, tourist-based queer cultures mutated and exploded, shooting off in multiple directions. Queer communities took up residence in waterfront bars, in the theater district, along Market Street, among labor activists and communists, in Chinatown, along the old Barbary Coast, among the city's Beat artists and poets, in bohemian bars and taverns, and as part of a fledgling civil rights movement called the homophile movement.[20] With little more than same-sex attraction and/or gender-transgressive behavior to bind them together, the queer communities that existed in San Francisco during these years did not form a cohesive whole. They did not recognize each other, in the words of Benedict Anderson, as part of a "deep horizontal comradeship."[21] Instead, there were multiple cultures and communities that overlapped and, at times, commingled in the intimate spaces of bars and baths, dances and house parties. Sometimes the differences between queer communities overwhelmed the possibility of forging a larger collectivity, but at other times—during a bar raid, perhaps—a larger sense of community seemed on the brink of articulation. Because there is no way to contain the many histories of San Francisco's queer cultures and communities to a single narrative, this book offers a partial and subjective look at the evolution, from the 1930s through the 1960s, of two competing social worlds: bar-based cultures and, later, homophile communities. The period studied ends in 1965 with the New Year's Day raid on a costume ball sponsored by the Council on Religion and the Homosexual in San Francisco's California Hall. The raid and its aftermath can be seen as the last of a series of events that fundamentally altered the relationship between queer communities and the police. These events demonstrated, first, the growing political strength of what was increasingly known as the city's "gay community" and, second, the growing coordination of lesbian, gay, queer, and homophile organizations.[22] In other words, by 1965, the queer communities that had evolved through the 1930s, 1940s, and 1950s had acquired both the ability to negotiate directly with police, civic leaders, and lawmakers *and* the ability to work together as a coherent social and political constituency.

In the pages that follow, I use the term "queer" alongside the terms "lesbian," "gay," and "homosexual" to describe individuals who engaged in same-sex sexual behaviors and activities. Unlike "lesbian," "gay," and "homosexual," however, the term "queer" was not a common mode of self-identification in the 1930s, 1940s, and 1950s. More often, it was a derogatory term used to stigmatize and humiliate sexual outsiders. Nevertheless, in the spirit of reclamation, I use "queer" to signify behaviors or cultures that were marked by a combination of sexual, gender, and, at times, racial transgression.[23] In effect, I use the term to describe the quality of one's sexual being that was unique, different, or stood in contrast to an accepted norm (such as the vigilant intraracial heterosexuality of the post–World War II era). However, because many people in the early to mid–twentieth century identified their sexuality in different ways (using terms such as "butch," "dyke," "fairy," or "queen")—or not at all—I use "queer" to include individuals who did not identify themselves as gay or lesbian but whose behaviors, activities, and/or attitudes reflected a resistance to what Michael Warner calls "heteronormativity," the persistence of heterosexual dominance and privilege.[24] Queer thus functions as an umbrella category, a wider category of social identification than lesbian, gay, or homosexual, and, in the tradition of queer theory, it functions as shorthand to identify multiple meanings, associations, and identifications.[25] Along the same lines,

I use the term "gender-transgressive" alongside "transgender" to describe queer behavior or activities (such as cross-gender entertainments) that involved non-normative gendered expression, performance, or display. At the midcentury, however, the term "transgender" took on a new meaning with the articulation of transsexual identities and communities. As a result, while I use the terms "gender-transgressive" and "transgender" to describe a range of queer behaviors and activities, they also flag the roots of an emergent transsexual and transgender community in San Francisco that has its own history, one linked to, but, in important ways, unique from the history of lesbians and gay men.

In this book I also use a number of different terms to characterize social groups and associations. I take for granted that queer communities existed in opposition to mainstream society—though, as this book will reveal, to varying degrees. For this reason, I use the terms "culture," "subculture," "community," and "social world" somewhat interchangeably to describe San Francisco's many queer social groups. While the term "community" has functioned in much sociological discourse as distinct from "culture" in its dependence on kinship and family, in this study "community" loses its association to kinship and becomes very similar to "culture."[26] Also, when modified by the oppositional term "queer," the distinction between "culture" and "subculture" tends to fade, so I use the simpler term "culture" to signify social groups and practices that "deviated from the normative ideals of adult [heterosexual] communities."[27] However, I do use the term "culture" in the traditional sense of "subculture" to signify the character of certain social groups, typically urban youth, who expressed their opposition to mainstream social structures in their use of public space and in their desire to "appropriate parts of the city for their street (rather than domestic) culture."[28] As a result, at times, I differentiate between culture and community, attaching a greater degree of oppositional character to cultures than communities (as in the phrase "queer cultures and homophile communities").

Research for the book began with forty-five oral history interviews, some of which I quote from at length in the pages that follow. The oral histories were collected by what ethnographers call the snowball method, in which interviewees were asked to identify others who, like themselves, had been living in San Francisco and participating in some aspect of the city's queer social or political life prior to 1965. I made an effort to balance the number of interviewees by several factors. I tried to find participants who were living in San Francisco in the 1940s (roughly one-third fall into this category). Also, because the stories of homophile activists had, at the time that I was doing my research, become more familiar to readers of lesbian and gay history than the story of bar-based communities, I gave priority to interviewees who had spent a lot of time in bars during the 1940s and 1950s. In the end, the number of interviewees with a high level of participation in gay bars roughly equaled those who had been active in homophile organizations—though of course there was a great deal of overlap between bar life and homophile activism. The final collection of interviews is also gender balanced and diverse by class, race, and ethnicity (approximately one-third of the interviewees are Latino, Asian American, Native American, or African American, and a significant number identified themselves as working class).

Many of the interviews have been transcribed, and they are available for consultation at the Gay, Lesbian, Bisexual, Transgender (GLBT) Historical Society in San Francisco. Other research sites include the manuscript and periodical collections at the GLBT Historical Society and the Lesbian Herstory Archives in New York City. The collections in the San Francisco history room at the San Francisco Public Library were also useful, particularly the clippings files on neighborhoods and the extensive collection of tourist guides. I also spent time at the University of California's Bancroft Library looking through tourist magazines, and I spent several weeks leafing through the records of California's Alcoholic Beverage Control Board in the California State Archives in Sacramento. There are many other sources that have been vital to the story I am about to tell, but the voices that most influenced me were those of the individuals I had the honor of interviewing. It is these voices that I hope are most vividly reflected in the pages that follow.

Of the scholarly books that address San Francisco's gay and lesbian history, most have focused on the impact of World War II or the influence of the city's homophile organizations on gay and lesbian social movements. Allan Bérubé's pioneering study of the social world of lesbians and gay men during World War II, *Coming Out under Fire,* addresses a wider terrain than San Francisco, but it has much to say about the impact of the war's military presence on the development of San Francisco's queer and gender-transgressive nightlife. Bérubé argues that World War II had an unprecedented influence on the function of San Francisco's gay and lesbian communities. Bars proliferated in order to serve the vast influx of gay and lesbian military personnel, social networks expanded, and policing took on a whole new quality. For better or worse, World War II seemed to fundamentally change the quality of queer life in San Francisco.[29] John D'Emilio's work on San Francisco extends this argument to suggest that World War II was a turning point in the city's gay and lesbian history. In a foundational article on San Francisco's gay and lesbian history, he argues that the war—particularly its demographic changes—set the stage for the emergence of gay and lesbian social and political movements in the 1950s and 1960s.[30] While *Wide-Open Town* is indebted to the work of scholars who set World War II at the center of their analysis, it takes as its point of departure a rethinking of this fundamental concern. Was World War II a turning point in San Francisco's gay and lesbian history? What kind of queer social worlds preceded the war, and how much continuity was there between pre–World War II cultures and the social movements that followed in their wake? This project pushes the scope of San Francisco's queer history beyond World War II to look at the more fundamental impact of tourism and nightclub entertainment on the growth and development of the city's gay and lesbian communities. Clearly, World War II had a tremendous impact on the city's queer entertainments and the state's methods of policing. But, as the following chapters will illustrate, World War II functioned to elaborate and extend the tourist-based cultures that emerged in the post-Prohibition era, rather than to fundamentally alter them.

A second framing paradigm in U.S. lesbian and gay history that this project addresses is the impact of homophile movements on mid-twentieth-century social and political activism. The most important studies in this field are John D'Emilio's *Sexual Politics, Sexual Communities: The Making of a Homosexual Minority in the United States, 1940–1970* and Marc Stein's *City of Sisterly and Brotherly Loves: Lesbian and Gay Philadelphia, 1945–1972*.[31] Published in 1983, D'Emilio's scrupulously researched text takes as its starting point the seeming invisibility of pre-Stonewall homosexual communities and the puzzling eruption of gay liberation movements in the months following New York City's 1969 Stonewall Riots. "Isolated men and women do not create, almost overnight, a mass movement premised upon a shared group identity," he argues.[32] In a search for the roots of the gay liberation movement, D'Emilio discusses the handful of homophile organizations that emerged in the postwar era and fought for civil rights in the decades preceding Stonewall. Despite his emphasis on national organizing, D'Emilio has much to say about San Francisco's queer history. Many of his oral history interviewees are San Franciscans, and the focus on homophile organizing often places San Francisco at the center of his analysis. Although he is mindful of the impact of bar-based subcultures, D'Emilio argues that homophile organizations, namely the Mattachine Society and the Daughters of Bilitis, set the stage—both organizationally and ideologically—for the mass movements that emerged in the 1970s. Central to this argument are two crucial elements: the importance of Stonewall as a turning point in gay and lesbian history and the linear progression of homophile-to-liberation-movement activism.

Stein's more recent work complicates D'Emilio's argument by focusing on the relationships between gay men and lesbians in pre- and post-Stonewall Philadelphia. Stein casts a somewhat more critical gaze on homophile organizing—he, too, analyzes the impact of bar-based cultures—but his narrative maintains both the centrality of Stonewall and the function of homophile activists as the primary agents of social change. Were homophile organizations a necessary pre-condition for liberation movement activism? Were there other influences in the social organization of gay and lesbian resistance? What impact did bar-based cultures have on the development of lesbian and gay social and political movements? This book asserts that while homophile organizations were important to the emergence of social and political movements, they were only part of the story of queer mobilization and emancipation. In San Francisco, the roots of queer activism are more fundamentally found in the less organized (but numerically stronger) pockets of queer association and camaraderie that existed in bars and taverns. Queer social movements in San Francisco, as a result, functioned more broadly than formal, membership-driven organizations. They sprang from a variety of influences. Moreover, while Stonewall remains a crucial part of east coast gay and lesbian history—it operates as a key turning point—it did not function as a mobilizing factor in San Francisco's queer social history. In fact, many of the demands articulated through the Stonewall Riots had already been addressed in San Francisco by 1965.[33]

This project is a community study and, as such, it raises the issue of social geography. It examines the function of cultural resistance and the evolution of social movement activism by looking closely at one site or spatially defined environment: San Francisco. This book does not attempt to compare San Francisco to other large cities in any depth. Rather, its close analysis and detailed attention to the function of municipal government and micro-level policing allow for a deeper appreciation of the wide variety of queer urban experiences. For instance, San Francisco's history evidences a unique response to post-Prohibition liquor control. While other studies, like George Chauncey's *Gay New York: Urban Culture and the Making of the Gay Male World, 1890–1940,* argue that the repeal of Prohibition and the development of new methods of policing shut down gay and lesbian public entertainments, in San Francisco repeal seemed to stimulate the development of queer and gender-transgressive entertainments.[34] In post-Prohibition California, the state's liquor control administration was placed within the state's tax board (the State Board of Equalization), so there was less emphasis, at the state level, on vice control than on the financial management of liquor production and distribution. This, combined with San Francisco's traditionally hostile approach to liquor control, allowed the city's post-Prohibition tourist and entertainment districts to develop in ways that were physically impossible in locations that had experienced widespread social and political support for Prohibition. San Francisco, as a result, stands out as a uniquely queer environment in the post-Prohibition era.

Community studies also allow for a closer look at the process of identity formation. They trace the impact of environment or social geography on the development of group identity and political consciousness. How, for instance, did same-sex behaviors translate into coherent or intelligible public identities? What was the relationship between identity formation, community articulation, and political mobilization? In their 1993 study of Buffalo, New York's lesbian history, *Boots of Leather, Slippers of Gold: The History of a Lesbian Community,* Elizabeth Kennedy and Madeline Davis explore the relationship between culture and politics—or lesbian cultural visibility, social identity, and political power. They explore this relationship by identifying the "prepolitical" consciousness of working-class lesbians in post–World War II Buffalo. While Kennedy and Davis borrow the term "prepolitical" from Eric Hobsbawm to distinguish between political actions that "are part of distinctly defined political institutions" and "social acts of resistance that haven't yet crystallized into political institutions," the term functions within lesbian and gay historiography to highlight the impact of culture, particularly bar culture, on social and political movements.[35]

The term "prepolitical" destabilizes formal, membership-based political movements as the central focus of lesbian and gay history and identifies instead the possibilities of bar-based cultural resistance. For instance, the puzzle of Stonewall lies in the myth that "post-Stonewall" gay liberation movements erupted out of nowhere. D'Emilio explains this contradiction by highlighting the heretofore uncelebrated work of homophile organizations.[36] Yet, in a location that sustained little to no homophile activism, Buffalo, Kennedy and Davis explain the prepolitical impact of bar culture on post-Stonewall liberation movements as a function of social self-awareness: "Without the support and strategy of a political movement, late-1950s rough and tough butches were not able to immediately achieve their goal of creating a better world for lesbians and gays. They did, however, succeed in forging the consciousness that was to become, a decade later, central to gay liberation. . . . This consciousness in the larger lesbian and gay subcultures throughout the country provided an environment for the rapid spread of gay liberation and in many cases actually provided some of the impetus for the movement."[37] In this way, the identities forged outside of formal social movements such as homophile organizations were, perhaps, essential to the *kind of resistance* that sustained gay liberation movements. Identity formation, as such, becomes less central to the emergence of political movements than social consciousness—and a culture of resistance.

While Kennedy and Davis make a case for the impact of bar-based cultural resistance on the eventual successes of the gay and lesbian liberation movements, their book stresses other forms of resistance as well. Kennedy and Davis introduce the butch-fem culture of Buffalo bar life, a style of self-representation and social organization that relied on a loosely mimetic but innovative form of masculine and feminine (butch and fem) lesbian gender roles. Through butch-fem culture, Kennedy and Davis argue, working-class lesbians in postwar Buffalo resisted male and heterosexual dominance. They expanded the opportunities for female sexual autonomy. And they augmented the function of queer visibility. As a result, Kennedy and Davis suggest that Buffalo's working-class lesbians existed as "strong and forceful participants in the growth of gay and lesbian consciousness and pride."[38] The cultural expressions upon which butch-fem communities emerged carved out social spaces that allowed new, and I would argue "political," sensibilities to emerge. Bar life, as a result, remains "prepolitical" only in the sense that it laid a foundation for homophile movements to develop, but bar life can also be seen as "political" in that it opened up the possibility for new modes of social resistance. For instance, as lesbian cultures emerged in San Francisco's North Beach district, they had a political function beyond their foundation for future political movements.[39] San Francisco's lesbian bar life can be seen as part of a larger queer public culture that interacted with homophile organizations such as the Daughters of Bilitis, but its mode of expression and social integrity remained distinct from those of the formal political organizations that emerged in the postwar era. The experiences and activities of women who engaged in same-sex sexual relations and interacted with or participated in any number of public environments, including bars and taverns, framed a cultural politic—a politic of lesbian visibility and queer social resistance in San Francisco that stressed their differences from members of mainstream heterosexual society, rather than their similarities to them.

The function of social and cultural resistance is made more explicit in the work of George Chauncey. Chauncey locates the heroes of his community study, *Gay New York,* within New York City cafes, speakeasies, and drag balls.[40] Chauncey's attention to the social geography of working-class culture enables him to construct a new historical paradigm—one that refigures the relationship between sexual behavior, identity, and community in light of the urban environments gay men traversed:

> [The] project of the book, then, is to reconstruct the topography of gay meeting places, from streets to saloons to bathhouses to elegant restaurants, and to explore the significance of that topography for the social organization of the gay world and homosexual relations generally. It analyzes the cultural conditions that made it possible for some gay meeting places to become well known to outsiders and still survive, but it pays more attention to the tactics by which gay men appropriated public spaces not identified as gay—how they, in effect, reterritorialized the city in order to construct a gay city in the midst of (and often invisible to) the normative city.[41]

Through an analysis of New York City's turn-of-the-twentieth-century sexual topography, Chauncey suggests that there are significant differences in the meaning and social organization of homosexual behaviors, and that those differences are a product of gender and class. For instance, he distinguishes between "fairies," effeminate homosexual men, and "queers," gender-normative men who practiced same-sex sexuality. Arguing that the sexual difference most salient to early-twentieth-century working-class urban environments depended more on gender than sexual practice, Chauncey explains that the sexual topography fairies traversed (the "lost gay world") functioned to clarify "the boundaries that distinguished the men of that world from other men in a culture in which many more men engaged in homosexual practices than identified themselves as queer."[42] In other words, the sexual topography or urban spaces fairies occupied (or reterritorialized) facilitated the development of identities that did not function within a homo/hetero binary, the sexual regime now hegemonic in American culture. As a result, the constituents of "gay New York" did not express the same *kinds of identities* that, later, defined the world inhabited by homophile activists.

Wide-Open Town builds on the insights of D'Emilio, Stein, Kennedy, Davis, and Chauncey to address the social geography of San Francisco's queer communities. It challenges the linear relationship between behavior, identity, community, and activism in that the social worlds—the pockets of cultural resistance—that evidenced the greatest amount of community interaction and mounted the heaviest challenge to mainstream law and order were not factions that clearly articulated same-sex sexual identities or aligned themselves with overtly political organizations. Instead, they were queer and gender-transgressive groups that occupied the social world of bars and taverns. These groups expressed multiple and overlapping social identities based on class, race, and gender. They fought to secure public space for themselves, and they worked to protect that space from hostile outsiders. In the 1950s, however, as homophile activists began to articulate new social identities (i.e., as sex variants, homophiles, homosexuals, and lesbians), they distanced themselves from the working-class and transgender culture of queer bars and taverns. With monthly publications, they promoted gender-normative identities and worked to connect homophile communities to a practice of political integration and social assimilation. While this book in no way seeks to minimize the importance of homophile movements, it attempts to complicate the story of social movement activism by tracing the urban landscapes queer San Franciscans traversed as well as those they claimed for themselves. It argues that the act of traversing landscapes and claiming space had a political momentum of its own, outside the paradigm of identity politics, and the culture of queer bars and taverns was not important simply as a stepping-stone for the more important project of homophile activism. Instead, this study argues that the communities forged inside bars and taverns functioned politically and, ultimately, offered practical and ideological responses to policing that were distinct from those of San Francisco's homophile (or lesbian and gay civil rights) organizations.

The chapters that follow are organized both chronologically and thematically, and as such, they use different modes of investigation and analysis. Each chapter is introduced by an oral history interview that grounds the historical narrative that follows in a first-person account of some of the events that chapter describes. The first two chapters provide a cultural analysis of San Francisco's early queer history—they emphasize the impact of arts and entertainment on the emergence of publicly visible gay and lesbian communities. The first chapter, "Transgender and Gay Male Cultures from the 1890s through the 1960s," describes the evolution of female impersonation in the burlesque and vaudeville traditions of the American stage. It documents the overlap between female impersonation, queer style, and a culture of prostitution that often circulated in and around urban theater districts. It then traces the impact of early-twentieth-century anti-prostitution and anti-alcohol movements on San Francisco's entertainment districts, explaining why San Francisco was a fertile ground for the emergence of queer and gender-transgressive entertainments in the post-Prohibition era. In San Francisco, queer entertainments emerged in the intimate space of nightclubs, where, because of the dark and protected atmosphere, female impersonation made a revival in the 1930s. Finally, this chapter traces the career of two popular nightclubs, Finocchio's and the Black Cat, that used the theatrical quality of female impersonation to sustain a queer and bohemian clientele through the 1930s and 1940s. In the 1950s, as theater-based queer clubs gave way to a proliferation of gay bars, nightclubs like the Black Cat continued to frame the notion of queer community in the context of sex transgression and gender transgression. In this way, the gay bar became a public institution—a legitimized public space—without forfeiting its history of difference and defiance.

The second chapter, "Lesbian Space, Lesbian Territory: San Francisco's North Beach District, 1933–1954," mirrors the first chapter in its emphasis on queer theater and performance. It describes the nightclubs lesbians frequented in San Francisco's post-Prohibition era, particularly Mona's, and it traces the careers of a cohort of male impersonators who entertained at several North Beach nightspots through the 1930s, 1940s, and 1950s. Chapter 2 then describes the overlap of sex tourism and race tourism in San Francisco's North Beach district, drawing a parallel between the development of sex-tourist venues like Mona's and the transformation of Chinatown into a tourist destination in the late 1930s. Sex tourism and race tourism generated a new kind of tourist economy for the city; they showcased difference and, in doing so, generated a permissive quality of same-sex and cross-race sexual display. As sexualized entertainments became part of San Francisco's allure, tourist industry dollars cast a thin veneer of protection around the city's queer entertainments. Meanwhile, the lesbians who frequented North Beach bars and taverns often shared these spaces with prostitutes and sex workers. Like prostitutes, the lesbians who left their homes at night to frequent bars and taverns in the post-Prohibition era were often treated as outlaws. They were harassed, policed, and prosecuted on the same terms as prostitutes, and they learned from prostitutes how to traverse the extralegal world of nighttime entertainments. As a result, a publicly visible lesbian culture emerged in San Francisco's North Beach district at the conjunction of tourist industry protections and a sex-based street culture that often left lesbians at the mercy of the police. The chapter concludes with the 1954 police raid on Tommy's Place, a butch-fem bar that became the focus of a citywide scandal and, later, a U.S. Senate subcommittee investigation on juvenile delinquency. Like the butch bartenders arrested at Tommy's Place, publicly visible lesbians remained vulnerable to the whims of politics and police even as they learned to translate their cultural capital (tourist appeal) into a legitimate business enterprise (gay- and lesbian-owned bars).

The third chapter, "Policing Queers in the 1940s and 1950s: Harassment, Prosecution, and the Legal Defense of Gay Bars," steps away from the history of gay and lesbian bar life to investigate the social history of policing in San Francisco. It starts with the impact of World War II on San Francisco's queer social worlds and argues that the militarization of San Francisco enabled municipal, state, and federal policing agencies to coordinate their efforts in new ways. As federal agencies, specifically the Armed Forces Disciplinary Control Board, targeted gay bars over other areas of what they called "disease and disorder" (such as prostitution zones), they drew local police and the state's alcohol control agencies with them. In the period between 1942 and 1951, the State Board of Equalization, California's tax and alcohol control agency, became more vigilant in policing bars and taverns. Even though tourism remained important to San Francisco's queer and transgender nightlife, the gay bar became increasingly vulnerable to surveillance and regulation. But as owners of gay bars were increasingly cited with infractions, forced to attend hearings, and threatened with the revocation of their liquor licenses, they developed legal strategies to defend themselves. Several bar owners hired lawyers to argue their cases, and in 1951, Sol Stouman, the owner of the Black Cat bar, won a state supreme court case against the State Board of Equalization that affirmed the right to serve alcohol to homosexuals. Explicit in this decision was the right to public association, a conclusion that overturned the most effective tool of local policing agencies: the presumed illegality of gay bars and taverns. In the years following the Black Cat decision, policing agencies found themselves unable to disrupt the growth and development of San Francisco's gay nightlife, and gay bars enjoyed a brief but vibrant period of reestablishment. In 1955, however, partly in response to *Stouman v. Reilly,* the California State legislature created a new agency, the Alcoholic Beverage Control Board (ABC). Using undercover agents and dubious state regulations, the ABC vigorously attacked gay bars, but the bars fought back with a number of lower-court cases that confirmed the legality of *Stoumen* and the right to public association. In constant negotiation with multiple policing agencies, the communities that formed inside gay and lesbian bars took on a siege mentality. As they fought to defend their territory from police intrusion, they came to understand the power of collective action. Their choice to legally defend themselves with the right to (group) public association rather than (individual) privacy rights inserted new ideas and new language into a nascent movement for lesbian and gay civil rights.

The fourth chapter, "'A Queer Ladder of Social Mobility': San Francisco's Homophile Movements, 1953–1960," takes its name from a chapter of Daniel Bell's 1960 publication, *The End of Ideology.* Seeking to explain the insights and failures of Marxism, Bell argues that crime syndicates, like suburban businessmen, often expressed a "hunger for the forbidden fruits of conventional morality."[43] Similarly, in an attempt to communicate directly with mainstream society and break through the stereotypes and assumptions that shrouded their humanity, members of homophile organizations sought new modes of social and political representation. The chapter begins with a look at the birth and evolution of two homophile organizations, the Mattachine Society and the Daughters of Bilitis. By 1955, both organizations made San Francisco their home, and through monthly publications they pushed new images of homosexual subjectivity into the public sphere. The Mattachine Society and the Daughters of Bilitis fought censorship, organized against police harassment, and worked with professionals and scientific experts to increase the visibility of gay men and lesbians in mainstream society. While bar-based communities used the First Amendment right to assembly to protect the queer use of bars and taverns, homophile organizations stressed individual rights based on the Fourteenth Amendment's due process clause to lobby for their own protection. Homophile activists sought to improve conditions for homosexuals by participating legitimately in the realm of mainstream political action, thus distancing themselves from the outlaw behavior of bar-based communities. They particularly eschewed the gender-transgressive behavior of bar-based societies, aligning themselves instead with a notion of citizenship that projected middle-class and corporate values. Homophile attitudes were easily digested by scholars and researchers eager to translate a sympathetic view of homosexuals to the world around them, and the Mattachine Society and the Daughters of Bilitis found themselves interviewed and analyzed by a small army of academics. Popular and academic publications often exaggerated homophile attitudes, however, exploiting the seeming pathology of bar-based communities for a sympathetic picture of homophile citizenship and subjectivity. The chapter ends with an examination of the ideological standoff between bar-based cultures and homophile communities. While both sought to improve the condition of urban life for San Francisco's lesbian and gay populations, it seemed that homophile activism, at times, functioned at the expense of bar cultures and communities.

Chapter 5, "Queer Cooperation and Resistance: A Gay and Lesbian Movement Comes Together in the 1960s," documents the transformation, between 1960 and 1965, of a fractured and divisive community into a cooperative enterprise. Picking up where chapter 4 leaves off, it describes a series of public events that brought San Francisco's queer communities into the public eye and forced bar-based and homophile movements to work together. It also documents the birth, between 1961 and 1964, of four new organizations: the League for Civil Education, the San Francisco Tavern Guild, the Society for Individual Rights, and the Council on Religion and the Homosexual. The combination of publicity and organizational development restructured San Francisco's queer communities' relationship to the public sphere and the popular press. As a result, a new discourse of resistance emerged on the border between San Francisco's queer-bar cultures and its homophile communities. Meanwhile, as the African American civil rights movement began to successfully press for rights based on the Fourteenth Amendment's equal protection clause, gay and lesbian activists followed suit. Gay and lesbian activists framed a politic that asserted the notion of homosexuals as an oppressed minority, and a rhetoric of equal protection and minority group rights brought bar-based and homophile activists together. Bar-based and homophile activists rallied against police harassment; they joined forces to raise funds; and, in the spirit of radical cooperation, they began to articulate a "gay" sensibility. Thus, in early 1965, when a police dragnet attempted to shut down a community-sponsored benefit for San Francisco's Council on Religion and the Homosexual, gay organizations launched a multi-dimensional protest that forever changed the character of San Francisco's queer communities. In 1965, at the height of the civil rights era—and well before New York's Stonewall Riots—what was increasingly called a "gay community" in San Francisco began to look and act like a formidable political constituency.

ORAL HISTORY

José Sarria

I was born in San Francisco at the St. Francis hospital. San Francisco wasn't as complex then, nor big or modern. It was a very quiet city. Those were good days, before the Depression. We had a nice home on Broderick and California Streets. I had a good childhood. I went to kindergarten at the Emerson School there on California Street. Then I was put in private schools because I spoke Spanish. Later, I learned English. My mother was forever and a day hassling me because she didn't want me to forget the Spanish. And I was kind of troublesome. I didn't like private schools—you had to dress in uniforms. In those days you had the Buster Brown style, big bows and things. I was very stylish. Then came the Depression, and I was put in public schools.

During the Depression there were food lines. But then with Roosevelt coming in in 1932, I believe, people began to work. You had the Works Progress Administration, WPA. Libraries were being built, the Hetch Hetchy dam was being dug, and roads were being repaired. Everybody worked but they didn't make a lot of money. And you stood in line to get food. I remember my mother would go with a bag and they'd shovel in some potatoes and carrots and turnips. You got some butter, you got some things. One place was located, I can always remember it, at the corner of Mission and South Van Ness Avenue. If you look at the building, you'll see where people would line up for vegetables. And back then you didn't have television, you had picture shows. And before the war, they had bingo nights. If you got bingo, you got bags of food: turkey, a ham, all kinds of things. We would always go. You got two movies and a chance at bingo. My mother was very lucky, so I loved that. It was good amusement.

My family used to go downtown, and once in a while I'd dress up. Later, we went to places like the Paper Doll, which was not gay gay gay as per se,

José Sarria, interviewed by Nan Alamilla Boyd, tape recording, San Francisco, 15 April 1992, Wide Open Town History Project, GLBT Historical Society. This interview has been edited by the author.

but once in a while I would go as a girl. I didn't really do that until in the 1950s. My mother would take me out and we'd go, just to be crazy, just for the hell of it. There was no argument about it. I did go to the Avalon Theater one New Year's and there this guy wanted to pick me up, so we had to get out of there fast. I was having too many people chase me, and it was getting to be a ruckus. The Avalon Theater is now the theater at Sutter and Van Ness Avenue. They had a beautiful ballroom.

I really didn't have any problems until I got arrested during my last year of college. It was kind of a disaster. It was a secret—all the family has gone to the grave never knowing what happened. It was brought out after I ran for public office in 1961 because they wanted to discredit me so that no gay person would ever run for office again—it wasn't until ten years later when you had Harvey Milk run for office—but in 1961 I fought them when they tried to discredit me.

I was arrested in the all-men's bar in the St. Francis Hotel, the Oak Room. It was more or less a trumped-up charge. It got to be that the hotel was getting very notorious, so they had to make some arrests. It was the same way all during that period. When the parks got too overcrowded, they would have police raids to quiet everybody down and satisfy the public. I was arrested and, well, when you were arrested you had to then carry a card. Oh, it was a mess. I had a college education, spoke languages, but where are you going to get a job? There was a bar called Pearl's in Oakland on Twelfth Street. The "Toonyville Express" was what they called the streetcars that used to run across the bridge at that time, so you got off, went up the fire escape, went in the back door to Pearl's. Michelle was performing there—she told me about it.

Michelle was a boy. He was a boy. He won first place at an amateur show, so I went to my mother's dressmaker for a dress. I borrowed my mother's charge account, charged what I needed, and I went to Pearl's. I won second place, which was two weeks' engagement at fifty dollars a week, so I thought, "I might be able to make a living this way." I came back to the city to a place called the Beige Room. I entertained as what they called the intermission person. I sang two numbers during the intermission of the Lynne Carter Revue, Lynne Carter and the Four Cartiers. Then there was a competition for Finocchio's. At that time, the lead Mexican singer at Finocchio's had died, so they came to the Beige Room. They were looking for a Mexican person. There was another boy, can't think of his name, and myself, both Latino, and I had a better voice but was not known. The other boy was known, so Finocchio's took her, that person. He stayed at Finocchio's until he retired.

Around that time I started going to the Black Cat. It had to be the '50s, the early '50s. But I had been to the Black Cat before. I had been going to the

Black Cat since I came back from overseas. I got out of the service in '47, and at that time I was going to the Black Cat as a customer because it was a fun place to go. Also, the hungry i, the Purple Onion, those bars. Broadway was quite alive with big entertainment. And that's how it happened, that's how I started working at the Black Cat. I just got up and sang a song.

I have a very nice tenor voice. I could reach high C in a normal voice, which was unusual. Of course as a youngster I took all the various things that young children at that age took: ballet dancing, tap dancing. These were supposed to be the amenities that gave you poise and character, so I had all of that. I walked rather straight. I had a lot of things on my side. So when I'm asked to sing, I get up and sing. To work at the Black Cat, I had to be a little bit different, so I'd put on a little bit of makeup. Short hair was in style for women, not long hair, and I would dress in basic black and pearls. I wore men's slacks, a leotard type of top, and I would borrow my mother's earrings. They all were legitimate things. My mother always said if you're going to wear jewelry, make sure it's good. My eyebrows were plucked in those days. I didn't look like a clown—I was neither there nor here. You could say I was a boy, you could say I was a girl. I was unique.

I used to wear loafers, and a woman came in and said—this was the time that Capezio shoes came on the market, with the long point and the stiletto heels—and she said, "Oh, your outfit is fabulous, but those shoes don't do anything for you." She said, "Try my shoes on." And lo and behold, they fit. She had an eight and a half foot and I put them on, and oh, they were beautiful. I stood and I pranced around. Prancing around in heeled shoes was not difficult for me to do, so I wore them all evening at the Cat. I sang my songs and carried on, and everybody just roared because I was wearing high-heeled shoes. When it came time to go I said, "Well, here's your shoes, thank you very much," and she said, "No, no, no, those are a gift for you, to remember me." I said, "I can't take them," and she said, "Well, I'll take your shoes. I need a pair of shoes to loaf around in." She took my loafers and I got her high-heel shoes, and from that moment on I wore only high-heeled shoes. I worked forty-odd years in heeled shoes. Then red heeled shoes. I worked for another gentleman part time—I always kept some kind of a job with Social Security taken out—and his wife gave me a pair of red heels. Since then I've always had red heels. I think this is about the third or fourth pair of heels, and I won't give them up. They look raggedy, but they fit so good.

That's how I began at the Black Cat, I began singing. I also used to cocktail wait, but soon there was no more cocktail waiting. I was the entertainer, and I, whether or not I knew it at the time or whether or not anyone else realized it, I changed the character of the Black Cat. I became the Black Cat.

The Black Cat was a bohemian bar where women smoked in public, where people believed in free love, where there were artists wanting to talk about their artwork, where you could sit in the bar and play chess and cribbage, where you would go and have one glass of wine, where you would go and recite poetry. It was a bohemian bar. "Gay" was never used. It was not a gay bar as we today know gay bars. And I changed that because I found out something. You must remember that I'd been arrested. I did not get chosen for Finocchio's. Instead, I began my career at the Black Cat. The tour buses would come by the Black Cat, and the drivers would say, "You want to see a good show, go there and see this. He does four shows a night." Just like Finocchio's but I was the star. I got up, told my stories, sang my songs, and it was fantastic. The people would come back, and we would have two to three hundred people at a show. But I noticed something: people were living double lives. Women, not so much, because women could get away with dressing with short hair—Coco Chanel styles were in. You could wear the tweed suits and it was alright, you just had a very business look. And girls could rent together. Men could not do this. Women could get away with a little bit more because they weren't as far out there.

Then I started to preach that gay is good. I ran for public office to prove that if you were gay you had a right to do such a thing. I led parades, screaming. I helped fight for different rights at the Black Cat. I helped feed the people. But they would arrest you if you wore women's clothes. I wore makeup, my eyebrows were plucked, I wore heeled shoes, but I wore men's clothes in the daytime, like to go to the bank. Going to the bank was like a three-ring circus. I went side-saddle on a motorcycle, up to the front door, at high noon in the financial district. People would line up to see me, and I'd arrive with my money in a shopping bag. I had a driver, and I would laugh at everybody, saying "You've given me all of this on the weekend, and I'm making my deposit!" Like Liberace used to say, "I laugh all the way to the bank." And that was it.

I've been a very unique person. The chief of police in those days would send their messages to me at the Black Cat to warn everybody to stay out of the parks, to stay out of certain toilets, to curb their ways because the heat was on. And I organized the first gay nonprofit corporation in the state of California. That was called the League for Civil Education. That later became SIR [the Society for Individual Rights]. I was an early member of the Tavern Guild. That's how I helped.

When the Cat closed in '63, that was the end of the gay community's communication center. When the Cat closed, there was no centralized place, and all of a sudden thirty-two ad hoc committees started up saying that they represented the gay community. "Well," I thought, "Mary, you don't represent the right type." So after I was crowned queen of the Tavern Guild Ball, which was a thank-you by the guild, I crowned myself Empress. And that is how the Empress began. I reestablished myself as the leader of the community—with much discussion, with much fight, but I won. Today I am the grandma of the community. No one ever denies me that right. It's twenty-seven years now since we started to have Emperors and Empresses—since 1965. I saw what was coming and we changed our direction. Instead of just dress-up and party time, we had to do something constructive. We, the Empresses, the court system, are now the largest fundraising organization in the gay community in San Francisco.

1 | TRANSGENDER AND GAY MALE CULTURES FROM THE 1890S THROUGH THE 1960S

> While most of San Francisco's reputable citizens publicly bemoaned the inequities of the Barbary Coast and performed lip-service to the many campaigns designed to eliminate its more objectionable features, secretly they were, for the most part, enormously proud of their city's reputation as the Paris of America and the wickedest town on the continent.
>
> *Herbert Asbury,* Barbary Coast, *1933*

In 1906, just after the great earthquake and fire destroyed much of San Francisco, the Seattle Saloon and Dance Hall opened in the city's Barbary Coast district. The Seattle Saloon employed twenty "dance girls" who, according to Barbary Coast chronicler Herbert Asbury, were paid up to twenty dollars a week to entertain male customers. "They wore thin blouses cut very low, skirts cut very high, and black silk stockings held in place by fancy garters."[1] This popular dive, at 574 Pacific Street, was the largest dance hall in the rebuilt Barbary Coast, and it exemplified the kind of sex traffic for which San Francisco had grown famous. However, in 1908 the Seattle Saloon closed, and a city employee reopened the place and called it the Dash. Here, female impersonators entertained customers, and homosexual sex could be purchased in booths for a dollar. "Inside is a small stage, on which a low variety of performance is given," the *San Francisco Call* reported. "Flanking the stage on either side of the big room are curtained boxes, in which are ensconced degenerate female impersonators. The 'Dash' is the home of unspeakable vices."[2] The Dash would have escaped notice if not for the fact that it was owned by a clerk in municipal judge Carroll Cook's court. Instead, the Dash came to be known as San Francisco's "most notorious and disreputable" establishment. The Dash's link to municipal government heightened a fear of urban decay and judicial graft, particularly since Judge Cook was part of San Francisco's infamous and corrupt political machine.[3] Cook's association with the Dash gave law-and-order dailies ammunition to use against his reelection: "The employment of Barbary Coast dive keepers as officers of his court and as associate campaign managers is one phase of the judicial 'record' on which Carroll Cook 'stands,' but it is a phase which he has seen fit not to discuss with the voters whom he asks to retain him in the office he has degraded and disgraced."[4] In a pattern that would recur through the next half-century, queer clubs and taverns existed at the intersection of vice and reform. Places like the Dash depended on the city's appetite for sexually transgressive entertainments, but they often grew famous through the city's sporadic efforts to curb its own excesses.

The emergence of publicly visible transgender and gay male cultures in San Francisco's North Beach district is thus rooted in the sexualized entertainments of the Barbary Coast. The Barbary Coast ran along Pacific Street from the waterfront to Kearny, in what is today San Francisco's North Beach district. Here, the rough-and-tumble saloons of the Gold Rush developed into dance halls, honky-tonks, and bawdy houses that provided a space for men to gamble, dance, and satisfy their sexual desires. Moreover, in the decades following California's Gold Rush, from the 1860s through the turn of the century, San Francisco was wide open. Police had little incentive to stem the traffic in liquor, gambling, and prostitution that earned the city its reputation for vice. "Vice and depravity ruled this limbo between the Paris Montmartre and the New York Bowery—but life, laughter and gayety, too, and that was what drew slummers to it from all parts of the world," wrote Anna Sommer in a 1934 retrospective of the Barbary Coast.[5] While sex and vice found a comfortable home in the Barbary Coast, the homosocial environment of saloons and dance halls served a number of other important functions. They functioned as social centers, leisure-time institutions, and transmitters of working-class and immigrant values. For working men who rented rooms in boarding houses, bars and taverns were a second home, a place to eat, drink, and enjoy the company of other men.[6] In fact, by the end of the nineteenth century, drinking establishments overwhelmed the city. In 1890, there was one saloon for every ninety-six residents, the highest proportion in the United States—double that of New York or Chicago.[7]

As early gay cultures developed inside San Francisco's many bars and taverns, they were bolstered by the disproportionate number of men in the city. Through the second half of the nineteenth century, the economic boom from gold and silver mining attracted a stream of single men to the California foothills and the Sierra Nevada, and the vast migration of miners, speculators, and merchants through San Francisco created a city of bachelors.[8] This, compounded by the fact that San Francisco functioned as a port city—its economy trafficked through the Golden Gate—meant that San Francisco sustained large transient populations that were less likely to conform to social rules and regulations.[9] San Francisco's architecture and city planning, its streets lined with boardinghouses and one-room flats, reflected a bachelor existence and lodging-house mentality.[10] In fact, the Montgomery Block Building, an immense North Beach rooming house (which, upon completion in 1853, was the largest building west of the Mississippi), would figure importantly in San Francisco's post–World War II bohemian revival for many of the same reasons it was built: to provide housing for the city's migrant, tourist, and pleasure-seeking populations.[11] All this meant that a permissive quality of life evolved around bachelor entertainments, and the Barbary Coast, "that section of San Francisco where the unattached men were concentrated," filled with licentious distractions, enhancing San Francisco's reputation as "the gayest, lightest-hearted, most pleasure-loving city on the Western continent."[12]

Barbary Coast entertainments catered to single men who had money to spend, and same-sex prostitution and gender-transgressive entertainments existed alongside other Barbary Coast attractions. According to historian Stephen Longstreet, in 1890, "a small huddle of homosexuals . . . worked out of a certain Turkish bath," and by the turn of the century, female impersonators were not unknown to the San Francisco stage.[13] Most establishments hired prostitutes or sex workers to sell liquor, dances, and, more generally, separate men from their money. While the smallest grog-houses or deadfalls hired only a handful of "entertainers," larger dance halls or concert saloons employed up to fifty women and, sometimes, a handful of men to work the patrons. These workers, called "pretty waiter girls," earned a weekly wage of fifteen to twenty-five dollars, a commission on the liquor and dances they sold, and often half the proceeds of their own prostitution.[14] The Barbary Coast also housed a number of upscale brothels where madams, who enjoyed relatively high status in San Francisco's social circles, ran the business end of things, and employees earned up to two hundred dollars a week.[15] In fact, prostitution was so central to Barbary Coast amusements that when anti-prostitution legislation shut down Barbary Coast brothels in 1917, the Barbary Coast collapsed.

The rise and fall of the Barbary Coast foretold the story of post-Prohibition entertainments and the emergence of queer public space in that the tension between vice and regulation advertised San Francisco's nighttime entertainments even while it worked to curb and control them. For instance, after the earthquake and fire of 1906 burned San Francisco's Barbary Coast to the ground, it resurfaced—newer and bigger—at the same time that a renewed sense of civic pride pressured police to quell violence on the waterfront and clean up the city's vice districts. As a result, the Barbary Coast became something of a tourist strip, a slummer's paradise, with cleaned-up entertainments and variety shows designed to shock rather than repulse. Through the early 1900s, the Barbary Coast gained a wider appeal as a place where large dance halls drew tremendous crowds. It was here that the most popular dances of this era—the turkey trot, the bunny hug, the chicken glide, and the pony prance—originated. And proprietors, "in direct violation of the ancient code of the Barbary Coast," did their best to protect slumming tourists from theft and harassment.[16] Therefore, at places like the Dash, a tradition of female impersonation developed alongside and within a culture of sex tourism and prostitution. As a result, the female impersonators who entertained at the Dash served as a link between homosocial Gold Rush entertainments and the homosexual clubs that would dot Broadway in the post-Prohibition era.

Because female impersonation links San Francisco's post-Prohibition queer clubs, cultures, and communities to its Barbary Coast beginnings, this chapter begins with a look at the roots of female impersonation in the burlesque traditions of the American stage. It continues by charting the role of female impersonators in San Francisco's vice and entertainment districts. It also traces the impact that early-twentieth-century reform movements had on the development of gay and transgender cultures and communities. Because of the city's strong opposition to anti-prostitution and temperance movements, queer cultures often developed under the protection of local resistance movements that saw queer entertainments as part of San Francisco's unique personality. In fact, policing and vice control were often obscured by the establishment of extralegal lines of authority, and tourist venues like the Dash were able to survive in San Francisco when they would have been quickly shut down in other cities. In this way, queer cultures sometimes profited from the city's tradition of civic graft. Graft, in the form of favors or payoffs, enabled gay nightclub owners to find protection and, later, manipulate public outrage so to secure their own interests. As a result, the gender-transgressive entertainments that existed at the turn of the century developed into an extensive network of gay and lesbian nightclubs after Prohibition was repealed in 1933. Like the saloons that energized the Barbary Coast, gay nightclubs became the social center for queer San Francisco.

A SHORT HISTORY OF FEMALE IMPERSONATION

The theatrical tradition of female impersonation begins in the United States with mid-nineteenth-century minstrel shows, where troupes of white men entertained each other by mimicking African American song and dance.[17] As minstrel troupes became more popular, female characters developed, and white men in "blackface" often performed highly stereotypical female roles.[18] As David Roediger notes, minstrel shows functioned to consolidate a white working-class culture at a time when African American and immigrant workers challenged the organization of industrial labor. Minstrel shows parodied African American culture to all-white audiences, but they also worked to resolve tensions between "native" whites and more recent immigrants. For instance, even though minstrel comedies often poked fun at Irish and German immigrants, they provided a forum for the association of white workers.[19] As minstrel shows developed, a variety of female impersonator roles evolved, and many performers gained notoriety by "playing the wench."[20] Blackface allowed white men to experiment with race, ethnicity, gender—and sexuality. In fact, the homoerotic quality of early female impersonation is an important aspect of antebellum race relations.[21] Did the fantasy white men attached to Black men through minstrel shows stimulate or resolve pre–Civil War anxieties? How did white men play out their desire to be (or to have) Black men through blackface and female impersonation? Through highly coded comedy and performance, minstrel shows addressed (and potentially resolved) anxieties about race, ethnicity, class, gender, and sexuality in antebellum America. In doing so, the minstrel tradition secured a role for female impersonators in American popular theater.

Female Impersonation on the Vaudeville Stage

As minstrelsy gave way to vaudeville, the comedic and misogynistic "wench" evolved into the more serious and artful character of the "prima donna."[22] By the turn of the century, vaudeville shows featured female impersonators as a regular part of their performance, and the variety show, which vaudeville popularized, became a mainstay in public entertainment through the Prohibition era.[23] Vaudeville shows featured a succession of acts such as animal tricks, acrobats, slapstick comedy, magicians, song and dance troupes, dramatic readings, opera singers, ethnic parodies, blackface performance, and female impersonators.[24] Vaudeville's variety show format reached the height of its popularity at a transitional moment in American history. As industrialization, urbanization, and immigration changed the pace and tone of American culture, popular amusements expanded to nourish a growing consumer economy. Between 1870 and 1920, urban populations grew 500 percent—to over fifty-four million people—and in cities like San Francisco, popular theaters sprang up almost overnight. In 1870, San Francisco had only two playhouses and an opera house, but by 1912, the city's population filled five playhouses, eleven vaudeville theaters, and sixty-nine nickelodeons and movie houses with a weekly attendance of over half a million.[25] Meanwhile, the movement of white Americans from rural farms to urban factories, the vast in-migration of non-English-speaking Europeans, Asians, and Mexicans, and the Great Migration of African Americans to northern cities expanded the base of vaudeville's clientele. Vaudeville's variety show format reached across race and class and drew from a host of popular amusements such as musical comedy, minstrelsy, circus acts, dime museums, and popular theater to provide entertainment to a fast-growing and heterogeneous urban culture.

Big-house vaudeville sought to broaden and democratize the historically masculine and working-class appeal of popular theater. It juxtaposed high and low acts against comedy routines that lampooned white working-class concerns such as ethnic assimilation, women's suffrage, and temperance. It also balanced "female" entertainments such as opera and Shakespeare against the traditionally masculine features of slapstick comedy, minstrelsy, and trained animal acts.[26] While house managers segregated audiences by race and often prohibited the entrance of prostitutes, vaudeville's booking agents worked to provide "something for everybody"—particularly white women, who agents anticipated would lend an air of respectability to the popular stage.[27] White women quickly became voracious consumers of the vaudeville stage—by 1912, women and children made up almost half of San Francisco's vaudeville audiences.[28] However, as new segments of society became consumers of popular culture, audiences often responded unpredictably, enjoying crossover acts not initially meant for them. White women, for example, sometimes responded more immediately and energetically to rowdy "masculine" acts (such as boxing) than booking agents anticipated. As historian Alison Kibler notes, "Vaudeville theaters were sites in which patrons could test new freedoms and cross social boundaries."[29]

Female impersonators dazzled and delighted variety show audiences through the turn of the century, and impersonators—both male and female—were often the most celebrated acts, particularly on the small-time vaudeville circuit.[30] As with minstrels, many vaudeville performers made their start through female impersonation. As historian Sharon Ullman notes, "From the top to the bottom of the bill—from comedy to drama, from blackface to formal gowns—individuals breaking into vaudeville used female impersonation to pave their way."[31] By the 1910s, stars like Julian Eltinge claimed top billing and high pay. Eltinge was, by far, the most successful female impersonator in vaudeville—and beyond. He made his start in 1904 in New York's Bijou Theater, playing a "lovely lady" in the musical comedy *Mr. Wix of Wickham,* and moved up the vaudeville circuit through the 1910s, performing for two years (1908–1909) with Cohan & Harris Minstrels. In vaudeville, he took top billing with impersonations of a Gibson Girl, a "dainty young miss in a pink party dress," Salome and her dance of the seven veils, and for his grand finale, a little girl.[32] In 1910, Eltinge landed a role in a full-length Broadway musical, *The Fascinating Widow,* followed by impersonator roles in a host of musical comedies such as *The Crinoline Girl* (1914) and *Cousin Lucy* (1915).[33] In 1912, at the pinnacle of Eltinge's career, his producer, Al Woods, opened the Julian Eltinge Theater on Forty-second Street in New York City, showcasing Eltinge as a skilled illusionist—a man who, like a magician, could masterfully defy the natural world with props and accoutrements.[34]

On the west coast, Bothwell Browne challenged Eltinge's reputation as a top female impersonator as he toured the vaudeville circuit with flashy and seductive impersonations. Born in 1877 in Copenhagen, Browne grew up in San Francisco, and by the early 1900s he had become a darling of San Francisco's vaudeville stage.[35] By day, he ran a dance studio called the Bothwell Browne School of Dancing and Stage Culture at 1881 Fillmore Street, and by night he staged elaborate impersonations at theaters such as the Grand Opera House.[36] In 1904, at the Central Theater (on Market Street near Eighth), Browne staged a "Champagne Ballet" and "Persian Scarf Dance" in a performance called "Around the World in Eighty Days." In 1905, the Chutes Theater advertised Bothwell Browne's troupe, the Gaiety Girls, in a performance called "Mikado, on the Half Shell."[37] In 1908, Browne toured with United Vaudeville, performing a series of impersonations that included a Gibson Girl, a plantation girl, a suffragette, a showgirl, and a fencing maid (a girl with a sword). His trademark soon became the sensual and erotic quality he brought to his performances. For instance, in 1910 Browne developed a "Serpent of the Nile" act in which he played Cleopatra and performed a live snake dance, playfully mocking the sexual innuendo of his gender-bending performance. A Los Angeles review described Browne as "fondling the reptile, then holding it from her in horrible fascination of fear, determined upon death, yet putting it away from her, [she] finally crushes the venomed head to her bosom and expires in ecstatic agony."[38] By 1919, Browne was at the height of his career. He played the role of a femme fatale in a Hollywood-produced silent film, *Yankee Doodle in Britain* (produced by Mack Sennett), and booked appearances at the Palace Theater and R. F. Keith's Colonial Theater in New York City.[39]

The Commercialization of Drag

Female impersonators staged glamorous song and dance routines with multiple dress changes that resembled contemporary fashion shows.[40] Indeed, the culture of consumption that encircled early-twentieth-century femininity became an important part of the female impersonator's act—clothing, cosmetics, shoes, and corsets became integral to the impersonator's image.[41] Female fans delighted in the charade that female impersonators provided, often taking advice from stars. Eltinge's *Magazine and Beauty Hints,* published in 1913, for example, fed a beauty culture that was fast shifting from the matronly Victorian woman to the curvy Gibson Girl and the slender and boyish flapper. In his magazine, Eltinge provided beauty tips and lessons on femininity. He described his own labored transformations and posed for advertisements for corsets, cosmetics, and a bust developer.[42] As theater historian Laurence Senelick notes, female impersonators like Eltinge straddled gender styles. His "gender intermediacy qualified him to serve as a middleman between traditional standards of curried comeliness and the newer ideal of 'masculinized' femininity."[43] Female impersonators thus played liminal characters, and male reviewers were drawn into the fantasy that impersonators inspired. A *Variety* review noted that "any man would rave over the genuine reproduction of Eltinge's impersonation. His 'Brinkley Girl' is a dream; his 'Bathing Girl' a gasp."[44] A Bothwell Browne performance puzzled another reviewer: "It was difficult to realize that the slender, lithe, and sinuous figure with its serpentine grace and wild abandon of dance was a man."[45] Audience members, both male and female, seemed fascinated by the idea that femininity could be so convincingly constructed by a man.

The commercialization of femininity through the first few decades of the twentieth century went hand in hand with the emergence of popular entertainments in that, as historian Kathy Peiss argues, "cheap amusements" drew urban men and women more frequently into mixed or heterosocial environments.[46] The increasing popularity of heterosocial entertainments and the sexualization of popular culture enabled new modes of desire to emerge; indeed, urban and industrial life seemed to radically transform the rituals of heterosexual courtship.[47] Meanwhile, a shift from Victorian notions of sex and gender to modern understandings of gender and sexuality raised powerful new narratives of homosexual pathology and disease. Scientific and psychoanalytic literature asserted the dangers of gender transgression and homosexuality, linking them to Darwinian notions of social contamination and biological degeneracy.[48] Female impersonators and their fans were often caught in the swirl of controversy (and desire) that sex- and gender-transgressive behaviors stimulated. Female impersonators, subject to intense public scrutiny, walked a fine line between respectable and deviant behaviors, but fans had more room to play with their desires. Because audience reception remained unpredictable, booking agents often had a difficult time determining which acts would appeal to which audiences. According to popular magazine reviews, men and women (presumably heterosexual) seemed to respond to female impersonators in a number of different ways—not the least of which was sexual. Women, for example, who found themselves attracted to the glamour and allure of female impersonators (wanting to be the performer) might also feel sexual attraction, and men who appreciated the charade of gender might confuse their heterosexual gaze with homosexual desire (wanting to have the performer).[49] Through the 1920s, as the possibility of desire between performer and audience increasingly raised the specter of sexual deviancy, booking agents nervously asked impersonators to tone down their shows. Popular performers like Eltinge skirted accusations of sexual deviancy by asserting offstage masculinity. Eltinge showed off his muscles, boxed with journalists, and fought stagehands.[50] Browne similarly—though less successfully—constructed a "respectable public persona" despite his homoerotic allure.[51]

The Queer Culture of Female Impersonation

Even though many female impersonators successfully denied their connection to homosexual communities, queer cultural styles and female impersonation existed in tandem and often in dialogue with one another. As theater historian Laurence Senelick argues, female impersonation had its roots not simply in minstrelsy and vaudeville, but a "thriving transvestite demi-monde impinging on the norms of popular entertainment."[52] In port cities like San Francisco, a queer and transgender demimonde existed on the edge of mainstream entertainments—in the old Barbary Coast and, later, the Tenderloin, where prostitutes mingled with queers. Here, female impersonators transported the language and gestures of a nascent queer culture to the popular stage. In the 1860s and 1870s, San Francisco's all-male concert saloons featured male sopranos and minstrel "wenches" who made good money entertaining miners alongside "peroxide blondes" and male impersonators.[53] And as the queer and transgender performers who perfected early female impersonator stage roles became commercially viable, (presumably) heterosexual performers, like Francis Leon and Julian Eltinge, moved into the genre.[54] Meanwhile, unabashedly queer "fairy impersonators" continued to ply their trade in skid row drag shows and frontier town honky-tonks.[55] The notoriously effeminate Bert Savoy, for example, started out as a dancer in a Boston dime museum and moved to New York's Bowery, where he performed as a female impersonator. He then made his way through the Dakotas, Montana, and Alaska, performing in mining town wine-rooms under the name Maude.[56] Like Bothwell Browne, Savoy represented unbridled sexuality, but Savoy's saucy and promiscuous characters infused the female impersonator act with what Senelick calls "the patois of the homosexual culture."[57] As Savoy gained popularity and worked his way up the ranks of vaudeville performers, his campy skits and lisping argot ("You don't know the half of it," "I'm *glad* you ast me," and "You slay me") slipped into the language of popular culture. According to Senelick, Savoy become one of the most quoted comedians of the time.[58]

The success of female impersonators depended not only on glamorous costumes, comedic repartee, and theatrical skill but also on the ability to stay within the pale of acceptable behavior. Bert Savoy seemed to be the exception. He moved quickly from honky-tonk to vaudeville and performed in major revues such as the 1918 Ziegfeld Follies in New York City. Along with his partner, Jay Brennan, Savoy mocked his own life on stage, playing an outlandish female impersonator who sought a life in the queer demimonde.[59] Through the height of his career, he never denied his history as a cross-dresser, his homoerotic allure, or his friendships with homosexuals. In fact, he used the allusion of homosexuality to bolster his act. Historian Thomas Bolze argues that flamboyant personalities like Savoy could never have succeeded in vaudeville without "straight" impersonators like Eltinge to set the stage, but Savoy provided a comedic response to the complex desires of a changing and increasingly heterosexual society. As Savoy emphasized the overlap between sex and gender, he poked fun at the sexual ambiguity of female impersonators. Savoy became the fop—a non-threatening representation of the newly outcast sexual deviant. Eltinge, on the other hand, reassuringly divorced gender from sexuality. His offstage masculinity and presumed heterosexuality reassured audiences that cross-gender performance did not imply sexual deviancy. Both performers, in different ways, enabled audiences to negotiate the boundaries of a changing sexual landscape.

In the 1920s, with the increased slippage between transgender behavior and sexual deviancy (and the stigmatization of same-sex sexuality), female impersonators came under heightened scrutiny from audiences, booking agents, reviewers, and each other. Impersonators like Julian Eltinge distanced themselves from drag queens and fairies in order to protect the viability of their careers. Historians, too, have been quick to differentiate female impersonators from drag queens and fairies, citing the formal theatrical quality of female impersonation and the informal subcultural quality of drag.[60] But, as Senelick reminds us, "that deviant behavior which invited prosecution on the street received considerable acclaim on the stage."[61] Popular theater, as a result, continued to provide queers access to a public culture of homosexuality and gender transgression well into the twentieth century. In Prohibition-era San Francisco, the line between female impersonators and drag queens became, perhaps, even less clear than it did in other cities. In an unpublished memoir, "The Golden Age of Queens," Lou Rand remembers that drag queens, who often took stage names, moved easily between the vaudeville circuit, burlesque theaters, and the "gay life" of the streets. In the 1920s, Rand notes, "there were more and more 'impersonators' in vaudeville (and out), all trying to take over Julian Eltinge's throne."[62] San Francisco's frontier town ethic enabled greater interaction between performer and audience, and there was a fluid exchange of culture and personality between the street and the stage. Or, as historian Marybeth Hamilton puts it, "drawn from the ranks of the gay underworld, the underworld impersonator used the stage to flaunt an illicit off-stage sexual self."[63]

Drag queens vied for female impersonator roles on the stage, but many also took straight roles, performing as leggy women in risqué burlesque and girlie shows. C. J. Bulliet, in his 1928 study of female impersonation, notes that "Eltinge's revival of the art of female impersonation and his sensational success, of course, started a whole swarm of men flocking to the stage in women's attire."[64] Using the language of sexologist Havelock Ellis, Bulliet takes a condescending tone in reference to the "superabundance" of female impersonators. He comments that unlike the Greek, Roman, or Shakespearean men who took female roles in classical theater, early-twentieth-century impersonators were motivated by gender inversion and/or transvestism. "The stage is full of chorus men, with all the symptoms of homosexuality worn on their sleeve," Bulliet observes. "The comedians of the musical revues can hardly escape wearing a red necktie in some skit or other, with the broadest hints of its acquired significance, and they and the vaudeville comedians are continually invading more and more the regions of the pathologically effeminate."[65]

Performing as chorus girls or comedians, queer and transgendered "men" passed as women to perform in burlesque and vaudeville theater, but they also passed in real life, citing their performer status as a justification for cross-dressing. "Ruby," for instance, was discovered by police to be a man after a Greenwich Village cafe raid. When questioned by police, Ruby cited her occupation as a chorus girl in an uptown musical comedy.[66] In another instance, a "pretty girl" arrested in San Francisco turned out to be John Reed Erskine, a "female impersonator of stage and screen."[67] Similarly, Lou Rand took the name Sonia Pavlijev and performed as a chorus girl in San Francisco productions of *The Desert Song, Good News,* and *Varsity Drag.*[68] She also bandied the name Bubbles on the street, occupying with her friends the north side of Market Street between Powell and Golden Gate: "'Market Street' was the focal point of all the action; remember, up until 1932, there were no bars, open as such: you 'met' on the street. Every foot of it, from the Anchor Bar at the Embarcadero corner, to the Crystal Palace market, could tell a story, all interesting. . . . And Gawd! Was Market St. gay! Local belles all had to make the scene each evening; the 'promenade' was marvelous to behold."[69] The live theatrical performance of female impersonators enabled a queer public culture to evolve both on and off the stage, and in cities like San Francisco the slippage between stage and street was difficult to contain.

Whether drag queens imitated female impersonators on the streets or female impersonators transported queer style and subjectivity to the stage, female impersonators signified public respectability for drag queens. Gay men, as a result, followed the careers of their favorite impersonators, attending their shows and, at times, waiting outside the stage door to welcome them to town.[70] Also, because theater life often spilled out onto the streets, late at night queens and theatergoers could blend in with the painted faces of vaudeville and burlesque performers. According to Rand's memoir, a coffee shop in Los Angeles near three vaudeville theaters became an important late-night drag scene after the owners posted a sign advising customers not to be alarmed by "sitting with people in full theatrical make-up."[71] In San Francisco, the presence of vaudeville and female impersonators in the city's entertainment district functioned to expand queer public space, and homosexuality took on a theatrical quality. As Rand notes, "In pre-War days, there was always a sort of 'theatrical' connotation to off-beat sex; the 'boys' often referred to themselves as 'mattress-actresses' [and] there was an illusive mystique about practiced homosexuality."[72] Similarly, in New York, historian George Chauncey documents that gay men "regularly sought to emphasize the theatricality of everyday interactions and to use their style to turn the Life [a New York cafeteria] and other such locales into the equivalent of a stage."[73] The theater of gender, as it evolved in urban areas through the first decades of the twentieth century, fed the development of newly queer cultural styles and sexualities.

The late nineteenth and early twentieth centuries afforded a brief window of experimentation for queer and transgender performers. Through the first two decades of the twentieth century, vaudeville impersonators functioned like magicians: they amazed audiences with skilled illusion that seemed to defy the natural world. As a result, liminal characters like Bothwell Browne and Bert Savoy were able to play up the homoerotic or homosexual quality of female impersonation without much censorship. They were performers, non-threatening in both their physical separation from the audience and the fantasy that men might become women for the sole purpose of entertainment. The incubation of queer culture in and around the theater through this period, however, brought a sensational aspect to female impersonation, and in the 1930s, with Progressive Era reforms in place and the onset of the Great Depression, female impersonation lost its place on the legitimate stage. Morality crusades, coupled with the increased stigmatization of queer and gender-transgressive behaviors, associated female impersonation with sexual deviancy. The fear that female impersonators might not be virile performers but rather sexual deviants whose "illusion" reflected everyday life fueled a campaign to rid the popular stage of any explicit reference to homosexuality.[74] Between 1935 and 1937, female impersonation was banned in large cities like Chicago, Milwaukee, New York, Philadelphia, Detroit, New Orleans, Baltimore, and Los Angeles.[75] With bans in place and the decreased popularity of transgender characters, female impersonators began to disappear from the popular stage. However, with the reorganization of liquor-based entertainment in the post-Prohibition era, queer public space in San Francisco shifted, like prostitution, to new urban zones.

THE REFORM MOVEMENTS: ANTI-PROSTITUTION, PROHIBITION, AND REPEAL

The theatrical world of female impersonation that overlapped with a network of drag queens, fairies, and homosexuals in the city's urban center also had an association with prostitution. In the early twentieth century, the link between performance and prostitution was difficult to shake. In fact, female actresses who took to the vaudeville stage in the later years of their career often feared that their reputations would sink. As historian Alison Kibler notes, "Both [actresses and prostitutes] were objects of desire whose company was purchased through commercial exchange."[76] Gender transgression, with its association to sexual deviancy, tied female impersonators even more closely to prostitutes. In fact, the fairy impersonators who performed in underworld dives and Tenderloin saloons often patterned their impersonations on the prostitutes who worked the crowds where they performed.[77] As a result, female impersonation, drag shows, and campy street theater contributed to the development of an urban sex trade that existed in and around San Francisco's entertainment district. Through the first few decades of the twentieth century, however, anti-prostitution and anti-alcohol reforms had a profound impact on the queer and sex-tourist cultures that encircled urban amusements.

At the national level, Progressive Era politics registered changes in labor laws, immigration policy, alcohol control, and suffrage rights. Progressive Era reform, particularly efforts where women played a large role, sought to clean up the city, infuse public culture with virtue, and reinvest civic leaders with the responsibility of public welfare. In the words of political scientist Paula Baker, the Progressive Era brought the "domestication of politics," the adoption of white middle-class women's social welfare issues by mainstream political parties.[78] In San Francisco, white women's participation in social and political activism was strong; they organized to outlaw prostitution, provide aid to the poor, protect child laborers, limit men's access to alcohol, and gain suffrage rights.[79] Despite women's political participation and influence, anti-prostitution and anti-alcohol crusades were not widely popular in San Francisco. City officials, police officers, and business leaders overwhelmingly opposed anti-prostitution and anti-alcohol ordinances. Nevertheless, by 1920 national reform movements had successfully reached the Golden State. In 1913, the California state legislature passed a Red-Light Abatement Act outlawing prostitution, and in 1919 the state ratified the Eighteenth Amendment to the U.S. Constitution prohibiting alcohol.

Both campaigns, successful at the national level, had a significant impact on the organization of San Francisco's queer communities, particularly in the use of public space. Morality and public decency crusades transformed the city's prostitution and entertainment districts. They also functioned to curtail the stage presence of female impersonators who provided public access to a nascent queer culture. Female impersonators were linked, like prostitutes, to sexual deviancy and thus the degradation of public morality. With the Red-Light Abatement Act, prostitution zones shifted from centrally located brothels to the streets and small taverns near the Tenderloin—a district that would become known for same-sex prostitution. Temperance movements had a different impact. Anti-alcohol efforts, staunchly resisted in San Francisco, functioned to reorganize and, ironically, strengthen the city's liquor industry. By the time of repeal, liquor interests controlled the city. By the mid-1930s, a combination of several factors—the collapse of large-scale public entertainments, the increased stigmatization of homosexuality, the shift in prostitution from the brothel to the street, and the reorganization of the city's liquor industry—functioned to establish for queer and transgender San Franciscans a new and somewhat more favorable public space: the nightclub.

The Social Geography of Prostitution

In the nineteenth century, San Francisco's red-light district overlapped with its gaming and entertainment districts. With Chinatown and the Barbary Coast at the heart of San Francisco's vice industry, brothels encircled this area, and prostitutes occupied the district that bordered Broadway, the waterfront, Commercial Street, and Powell. In this district, brothels often burned a red light from dusk till dawn and placed a red shade in one front window during the day.[80] Well-financed madams ran elite parlor houses, but cheaper brothels were by far the more popular type of prostitution house. Both parlor houses and brothels consisted of a brothel keeper (usually a mistress or former prostitute), a male backer, a house, and a handful of prostitutes.[81] Early on, upscale prostitutes provided the city with its own version of a social aristocracy. During the Gold Rush, prostitutes were welcome in "polite society"—they socialized at masquerade balls, and in theaters men remained standing until the painted ladies were seated.[82] Later, with the organization of prostitution into an exploitative and highly profitable enterprise, the status of the common prostitute was degraded as large "crib yards" (also known as "cowyards") became popular in the city's red-light district.[83] Crib yards also sprang up in Chinatown, where hundreds of women worked without profit in crowded and unsanitary houses, and many occupied rooms (or cribs) as small as five by seven feet.[84] By the turn of the century, the theater district also supported a large population of dance-hall prostitutes and streetwalkers, many of whom found jobs in saloons selling sex or working as percentage girls. Others entertained as dancers or strippers in small burlesque theaters.[85] Prior to the criminalization of prostitution, however, brothel workers were much more common than streetwalkers or percentage girls.[86]

In the early twentieth century, legal and economic changes shifted San Francisco's prostitution zones. As the business and shopping districts expanded westward (business interests were unwilling to cross Market Street and venture into the ghettoized South of Market district), they cut into the southern part of the city's original red-light district. By 1915, Maiden Lane, the long-standing home of the city's most decadent parlor houses, had become the core of the women's apparel district, and, according to Neil Shumsky and Larry Springer's study of San Francisco's prostitution zones, "as the shopping districts moved in, prostitutes moved out."[87] Meanwhile, morality crusaders and activists (such as Father Terence Caraher, who ran the parish adjacent to the red-light district) successfully limited prostitutes' use of urban space. Anti-prostitution activists lobbied city hall to reduce the size of the city's red-light district, and by the time of abatement, legally run brothels had been squeezed into a two-block area near the old Barbary Coast. The criminalization of prostitution in San Francisco thus came in stages. City officials pushed zones of prostitution further and further away from the city's business and retail districts, while state legislators capitulated to a national anti-prostitution campaign. In the post-abatement period, as prostitutes struggled to survive, they dispersed throughout the city. Many prostitutes remained close to the city's historic vice and entertainment districts, occupying bars and taverns rather than brothels, but many others moved south and west of the business district, into Union Square and the Tenderloin.[88]

The pressure to control prostitution in San Francisco stemmed from reform activists rather than elected officials or police. Through the nineteenth and early twentieth centuries, the city's urban economy benefited from the existence of prostitutes on the street and in brothels. Prostitutes enlivened the entertainment district and sustained a lucrative sex-based economy that included pimps, madams, merchants, landlords, organized crime, and the local police.[89] The "progressive" impulse to control and, later, criminalize prostitution grew as the numbers of Anglo-American migrants increased, bringing a Protestant-based reform agenda to the city. Westering migrants also helped balance San Francisco's sex ratio, which, as a result of the mining industry, had overwhelmingly favored men. By the turn of the century, the number of women in San Francisco almost equaled that of men, and elite white women became increasingly important to city politics. Upper-class and educated women formed the nucleus of social reform movements that targeted the criminalization of prostitution. Calling themselves "social purity" and "moral reform" activists, elite white women often stressed their superiority over prostitutes. Some activists pursued the criminalization of prostitution in order to distance themselves from the "social evil," while others engaged in rigorous rescue efforts, attempting to save the prostitute from her plight. As the movement progressed, reformers successfully linked prostitution to concerns about public health and the spread of venereal disease. They linked prostitution to public morality and the corruption of women and girls, to urban decay and the seemingly dehumanizing quality of city life.[90]

On the west coast, anti-immigration and anti-miscegenation activism also played a role in anti-prostitution efforts in that reformers often blamed Chinese immigrants for the growth of prostitution in San Francisco. In 1879, as state representatives worked to ratify the California constitution, most delegates agreed to limit Chinese immigration, and John C. Stedman, a San Francisco representative, introduced an amendment to the constitution prohibiting "the intermarriage of white persons with Chinese, negroes, mulattoes, or persons of mixed blood, descended from a Chinaman or negro." Legal scholar Megumi Dick Osumi argues that anti-immigration and anti-miscegenation legislation was derived, in part, from the belief among white lawmakers that the Chinese were sexually promiscuous and perverse. Anti-miscegenation policies became law in California in 1880, and in 1882, with the federal Chinese Exclusion Act, Chinese immigration was all but suspended.[91] Anti-Chinese policies had an impact on anti-prostitution efforts and on the lives of Chinese prostitutes. From the mid–nineteenth century, when the number of Chinese immigrants reached the thousands, Chinese brothels endured a much higher level of police scrutiny and harassment. Chinese prostitutes and their clientele were routinely arrested for legal infractions of which European and Anglo-American prostitutes were rarely accused.[92]

Still, in San Francisco, where the availability of drugs, gambling, and prostitution sustained its reputation as a wide-open town, a legally organized sex trade was tolerated much longer than in eastern and midwestern cities. In fact, San Franciscans often elected officials who promised to protect the city's penchant for vice, and officials regularly teamed up with vice interests to fight moral reform.[93] In 1909, labor candidate P. H. McCarthy successfully ran for mayor on the platform that anti-vice interests were bad for business—he vowed to make San Francisco "the Paris of America."[94] Between 1909 and 1911, McCarthy's administration worked alongside vice interests—district landlords, brothel owners, bail bondsmen, and licensing agents—to secure the continued legalization of prostitution at a time when most cities and states were working to ban it altogether. In 1911, San Francisco began a system of controlled prostitution whereby prostitutes were restricted to a single district near the old Barbary Coast. Under this ordinance, prostitutes inhabiting the red-light district were required to register at a city-run health clinic, where they were checked periodically by a medical examiner. City officials benefited economically from the municipal control of prostitution in the same way officials had long benefited from vice—through payoffs and graft. For instance, Mayor McCarthy allegedly received a share of profits from city-run "cribs" as well as payoffs from upscale restaurants that maintained illegal brothels.[95]

The city's investment in prostitution was not confined to vice, however. Longstanding business interests also resisted the criminalization of prostitution. In April 1913, when California's legislature passed the Red-Light Abatement Act, San Francisco's Real Estate Board, the Northern California Hotel Association, and the San Francisco Restaurant Men's Association teamed up to challenge the act through a popular referendum.[96] The referendum gained double the number of signatures needed, and abatement was suspended until November 1914, when a referendum election was held. Despite the interference of San Francisco's vice and business interests, red light abatement became law in California in 1915. Under this law, houses of prostitution were deemed a public nuisance, and any citizen could bring suit against the owner for damages. Still, San Francisco continued to allow some prostitution as late as 1917. On January 30, 1917, for example, the city's police commissioners passed an ordinance calling for the closure of the city's "parlor houses."[97] Criminologist Brenda Pillors asserts that brothels continued to exist quasi-legally in San Francisco until World War I, when military officials targeted prostitutes as a threat to public health.[98] While east coast civic leaders often colluded with moral reformers, San Francisco's civic and business leaders fought the closing of its prostitution district and, later, the criminalization of prostitution because they were aware of the money to be gained through the city's nascent tourist economy.[99]

The criminalization of prostitution and the closing of the Barbary Coast did not rid the city of prostitutes; rather, it shifted the social geography that prostitutes occupied.[100] In the post-abatement period many prostitutes remained close to the city's entertainment district, but others moved beyond the expanding central business district, into the Tenderloin. In 1917, for instance, violations of California's Red-Light Abatement Act occurred most frequently near Chinatown and the old Barbary Coast, but the district southwest of Union Square and north of Market Street also registered a high frequency of arrests.[101] Brothel houses had long occupied the old Tenderloin, a district of lavish Victorians and gilded parlor houses, but the district was destroyed by the 1906 earthquake and fire. In 1910, under pressure from businessmen, the city identified a new uptown Tenderloin district on Golden Gate from Fillmore to Van Ness. In the post-abatement period, the areas in and around this district became the foundation for a new, less organized, and less reputable prostitution zone.[102]

San Francisco's Tenderloin overlaps with the district drag queens and female impersonators occupied. Homosexuals and male prostitutes often trafficked the stretch of Market Street from the waterfront, where sailors disembarked, to the Tenderloin, where male prostitutes turned tricks. For instance, Lou Rand's memoirs reveal that drag queens sold sex at the Unique Theater on Market Street, at hotels on the outskirts of Chinatown (that rented by the hour), in Union Square, and by picking up tricks on the street: "Recall a mad 'girl' called Anne Pennington, who would stop anything male, on the pave, and purr: 'Would you like a fancy boy, tonight?!'"[103] The police that worked the north side of Market Street into the Tenderloin often looked the other way or took payoffs from drag queens and prostitutes who became too overt in their solicitations: "When groups of clattering queens, on Market St., grew a little too shrill, a big, handsome, burly (Irish!) policeman would look at them sternly and might remark, pleasantly enough, 'Come now, bhoys [*sic*], . . . let's move it up and down.' Often he'd make somewhat suggestive, but always humorous, gestures with his club, . . . er, baton."[104] As the Barbary Coast began to market itself as a tourist district and red light abatement pushed prostitutes into new urban zones, the area from the north side of Market Street into the Tenderloin became a public space where gay male and transgender prostitutes lived, mingled, and paraded Market Street to sell sex to passersby.

San Francisco's Resistance to Temperance

Just as San Franciscans opposed the illegalization of prostitution, the city was a stronghold against the prohibition of alcohol. San Francisco's pro-liquor interests were so concentrated that during Prohibition the city gained the reputation as the "wettest in the west."[105] By 1926, for example, bootlegging operations in San Francisco had established a way around the Eighteenth Amendment, and according to historian Gilman Ostrander, "anyone willing to pay bootlegger prices could buy imported liquor of all descriptions."[106] The city flagrantly defied both the federal Volstead Act, which enforced Prohibition, and the state of California's Harris and Wright Acts.[107] So intense was the city's commitment to drinking that San Francisco's Board of Supervisors passed a resolution in 1926 opposing the use of city police to enforce "on any basis" the prohibition of alcohol. To drive their point home, the Board of Supervisors sent a copy of the 1926 resolution to the San Francisco chief of police, the federal Prohibition administrators, and the State Senate.[108] San Francisco's resistance to temperance, its dedication to maintaining a wide-open town, contributed greatly to the form and function of its early-twentieth-century public entertainments. Indeed, the reorganization of power in San Francisco and the consolidation of the liquor industry after repeal determined the path that queer social movements would take. The policing of alcohol consumption, as it established itself in the early twentieth century, became the single most important aspect of San Francisco's queer public life.

As with moral reform, anti-alcohol efforts began in California in the 1880s with the migration of Anglo-Americans from the east coast and midwest regions of the United States to Los Angeles County. In 1880, Southern California contained only 7 percent of California's population, but by 1890 this part of the state's population had expanded to almost 20 percent. Migrants to Los Angeles, mostly Protestant, brought a long history of temperance activism with them, and as they settled, California's temperance movement strengthened. San Francisco, in contrast, remained largely foreign-born through the early twentieth century. Irish, German, Mexican, Chinese, Japanese, and Italian immigrants to San Francisco saw no need for the anti-alcohol politics that swept through the midwestern states in the mid– to late nineteenth century. In 1910, almost 70 percent of San Franciscans were foreign born or the children of foreign born, and the city remained mostly Catholic. These figures reveal fundamental differences in the attitudes and politics of Northern and Southern California, differences that would play themselves out in San Francisco's resistance to anti-alcohol activism.[109]

In the early twentieth century, San Francisco's resistance to temperance was a formidable force against the prohibition of alcohol.[110] From the time of the Gold Rush, a lack of government regulation had encouraged the liquor industry to shape its own policy, and drinking had become important to San Francisco's business interests. In Gunther Barth's meditation on "instant cities," he argues that drinking was an accepted part of the accelerated pace of urban development, and temperance campaigns had little effect. "Drinking simply was big business in cities where many people drank heavily."[111] And people drank heavily in San Francisco. In 1866 there were thirty-one saloons for every place of worship.[112] In addition to drinking in saloons, San Franciscans drank in brothels, groceries, honky-tonks, and hotels. Free lunches and treating, strategies bar owners used to draw patrons to their bars, encouraged drinking, and a convivial culture of inebriation became part of San Francisco's civic life.[113] Business interests, as a result, were not sympathetic to temperance advocates. In the early 1870s, when the Women's Christian Temperance Union teamed up with the national Prohibition Party to attempt to control San Francisco's liquor industry, grocers who sold liquor and ran small bars in back rooms organized alongside wholesale liquor dealers to oppose restricted sales ordinances. By 1894, prohibition ordinances had taken effect in every part of the state except San Francisco. In his study of the prohibition movement in California, Gilman Ostrander notes that San Francisco remained an exception: "Nowhere in the state were there fewer regulations governing the saloons."[114]

In San Francisco, there was little resistance to liquor interests, and public drinking remained a protected aspect of city life. An 1892 article in *The Pacific* complained that "this city is ruled by the saloons, no matter whether [the] Republican or Democratic Party is in power."[115] As Southern California–based temperance movements organized to control California's liquor interests, San Francisco's liquor industry organized a strong response. In 1881, when a Sunday closing law was enacted, the liquor-based League of Freedom organized a campaign of civil disobedience, advising the city's saloons to stay open on Sundays. The League posted bail for cooperating saloons, and all two thousand arrestees demanded a jury trial, resulting in only five convictions and an extremely congested courtroom. The liquor industry had flexed its muscles, and the law was repealed.[116] Moreover, the nucleus of the state's anti-temperance effort, the California Protective Association, listed an impressive number of high-ranking San Franciscans on its ledger. In 1894, nine of twelve city supervisors were on the saloon ticket, and fifteen of its eighteen state assemblymen were "wet." And in 1911, at the height of anti-liquor organizing, "Sunny Jim" Rolph, San Francisco's popular mayor, ran for reelection as a "thoroughly wet candidate."[117]

California's 1911 election also brought women's suffrage to the state, and quickly thereafter California passed a "local option" law, whereby municipalities could determine their own liquor laws. Many Southern California cities and counties passed temperance laws, but San Francisco held out against the rising tide of prohibition. With state and federal temperance legislation looming, San Francisco's business associations banded together. In 1916, the Importers and Wholesale Liquor

Merchants Association, the San Francisco Brewers Protective Association, the San Francisco Hotel Men's Association, the Bottlers' Protective Association, and the Knights of the Royal Arch (an anti-prohibition coalition) joined forces as the Allied Interests of San Francisco. To fund their campaign, they asked for contributions of one month's rent from all landlords and property owners in the city, certain that pro-liquor politics would benefit business and property owners. As a result, San Francisco's business interests won out against statewide temperance legislation in both 1914 and 1916. "The 1916 campaign demonstrated that San Francisco's wet vote was sufficient to keep the state wet," Ostrander notes.[118] Nevertheless, in 1917, the national Prohibition Party's amendment passed Congress and was submitted to the states. By 1920, the Eighteenth Amendment had become law.

During Prohibition (1920–1933), San Francisco openly defied both federal and state efforts to enforce the prohibition of alcohol. The city's long shoreline made the federal Volstead Act and the California Harris and Wright Acts difficult to enforce, but the greatest handicap to enforcement was the lack of public support. San Francisco was notoriously wet during Prohibition. Liquor was imported by ship from Mexico and Canada and unloaded on small craft in ocean waters just outside federal jurisdiction.[119] Inside city limits, the production and distribution of wine and liquor continued unhindered. In San Francisco's Italian district, wine presses dried peacefully in the streets while fermenting vats of wine sat in garages and basements. Gin and brandy were produced locally in industrial plants—quart-size jugs were bottled, labeled, and distributed, all within the city limits.[120] According to Ostrander, by 1929, "One could buy liquor in unlimited quantities in the city in open bars and cafes particularly in the cheaper sections of town."[121] Moreover, the collusion of the local police and the Board of Supervisors against Prohibition contributed wholeheartedly to the consolidation of San Francisco's pro-liquor forces. In 1921, the Board of Supervisors publicly reprimanded two police captains for enforcing Prohibition laws while on duty.

By the late 1920s, repeal efforts were the most popular brand of city politics and one of the few venues where business cooperated with labor.[122] To rally public support around the repeal of Prohibition, state politicians developed a "Committee of One Hundred" that included sixty-eight members from San Francisco. Of the sixty-eight, twenty-nine were labor leaders and almost all of the rest were San Francisco businessmen and lawyers.[123] Also opposing Prohibition were David Starr Jordon, president of Stanford University, and Matthew I. Sullivan, former chief justice of the state supreme court. Jordon and Sullivan teamed up to draft legislation calling for a repeal of California's Wright Act. In 1929, the California Bar Association voted overwhelmingly for repeal, citing economic arguments; in 1930, California elected San Francisco's "wet" mayor, James Rolph, as governor; and in 1932, the Wright Act was repudiated in California by a two-to-one majority. Finally, in 1933 the Eighteenth Amendment was repealed at the California polls by a three-to-one margin.

With the repeal of Prohibition in 1933, California voters granted the complete control of liquor distribution and sales to the State Board of Equalization, the state's tax agency. Placing liquor in a tax board gave the liquor industry an advantage, as it fostered the development of a taxable liquor trade. In other states, municipalities retained a local-control option, but not in California. There, the 1933 Liquor Control Act and the 1935 Alcoholic Beverage Control Act prohibited local liquor control, and this weakened the Board of Equalization's ability to enforce its own law. The liquor industry, well organized from its Prohibition-era experiences, soon exploited the state's weaknesses. Small-time investors and entrepreneurs scurried to carve out a niche in the newly legalized liquor market. As a result, the 1930s saw the mushrooming of smaller entertainment venues like nightclubs. Nightclubs were not only less expensive to open and run than larger venues, but they circumvented a post-Prohibition liquor regulation that restricted the sale of hard liquor to hotels, clubs, and restaurants. By staging cheap entertainment, nightclubs capitalized on the patrons once held by saloons, and their small size encouraged a specialized clientele. No longer did public entertainment need to appeal to the large and diverse audiences of the vaudeville circuit. Nightclubs became the terrain of the owner-entrepreneur, and in the words of Robert Sylvester, nightclub owners "made their own society, made their own rules, [and] meted out their own disciplinary measures."[124] The intimate nature of nightclubs also made the surveillance of activities inside the bar difficult, and performers from the dying vaudeville stage—like female impersonators—were sought out to draw a specialized clientele into the nightclub.[125] In this way, female impersonators found a new venue, and the queer subculture that encircled the popular world of vaudeville performance moved to the more intimate sphere of nightclub entertainment.

Nightclubs, Graft, and the Emergence of Gay Entertainment

San Francisco's post-Prohibition nightlife emerged as flamboyantly gender-transgressive, and through the 1930s publicly visible queer cultures flourished in the city's tourist districts. Homosexual and transgender populations socialized alongside adventurous heterosexuals and voyeuristic tourists in popular nightclubs such as Mona's and Finocchio's. The 1940s brought the emergence of bars that catered specifically to a queer clientele. These bars were adjacent to Broadway, the central artery of San Francisco's vice and tourist district. In contrast, New York City saw the separation of gay life from the city's heterosocial and bohemian nightlife in the post-Prohibition era. There, the transfer of authority over the sale and consumption of liquor from local and Progressive Era agencies to the newly formed State Liquor Authority resulted in the criminalization and increased marginalization of gay social spaces. The New York State Liquor Authority, as historian George Chauncey argues, exercised a pervasive presence through the employment of plainclothes undercover agents who, in the immediate post-Prohibition era, revoked the liquor licenses of establishments catering to a gender-transgressive or homosexual clientele.[126] San Francisco's queer cultures remained important to its Broadway nighttime amusements, however, because through the post-Prohibition era the city's tourist industry expanded and leaned heavily on its reputation for sexual license to bolster its revenues.[127]

Until 1954, California was one of ten states to control the post-Prohibition distribution of liquor licenses through a fiscal agency, the State Board of Equalization, rather than a specially appointed state liquor agency. "Liquor control as a state function, as far as these states are concerned, amounts to liquor tax collection," a 1936 publication reported.[128] In order to eliminate graft and the generation of untaxed revenues, the State Board of Equalization centralized the state's post-Prohibition alcohol policies. The board would not cooperate with city police, nor would it administer liquor licenses on a local level.[129] San Francisco police could arrest individuals for disorderly conduct; they could arrest bars owners for operating a "disorderly house" or a "house of ill repute"; they could arrest bartenders for serving alcohol to minors, but San Francisco police had little control over a bar's function. Perhaps overzealous in protecting liquor traffic from police payoffs and more concerned with tax revenue than the control of vice, California's State

Board of Equalization was less effective than other state agencies in regulating queer public space.[130] As a result, in the 1930s a number of nightclubs sprang up in San Francisco's North Beach and Tenderloin districts that mixed a queer and tourist clientele.[131]

In addition to the absence of liquor control, two other factors contributed to the growth of queer public space in post-Prohibition and depression-era San Francisco. The 1934 longshoreman's strike and the city's 1935 Atherton Report curbed the influence of crime syndicates in the city and thus the extralegal control of queer entertainments. Organized crime has a long history in San Francisco—from the presence of Chinese tongs that controlled opium, gambling, and prostitution in and around San Francisco's Chinatown to the bail bondsmen who paid off and controlled a range of city employees. By the time of Prohibition, the coupling of vice and graft had become a natural part of city life. J. W. Ehrlich, a criminal lawyer in San Francisco's stormy 1930s, complained that "San Francisco had convinced itself that vice was a necessary evil. There were many, as a matter of fact, who weren't nearly as convinced that it was an evil as that it was necessary."[132] In New York, on the other hand, organized crime syndicates that established control over liquor traffic during Prohibition became "the only entities powerful enough to offer bars systemic protection," and crime syndicates "took over the gay bar business."[133] Why did crime syndicates lose ground in San Francisco in the 1930s rather than, as the pattern in east coast cities reveals, consolidate their control?

The Great Depression brought San Francisco's economy to the brink of collapse, and organized labor, which had long been in the pocket of organized crime, was radically disrupted. As historian Michael Kazin explains, through the turn of the century, organized labor used city politics to consolidate a powerful labor party in San Francisco.[134] Labor candidate McCarthy's 1909 mayoral election capped labor's political consolidation, and by 1910, San Francisco had become a union town. Through the first two decades of the twentieth century, a closed-shop (union workers only) practice prevailed in construction, transportation, manufacturing, and (non-Chinese) service industries.[135] Labor's rise to power depended on cooperation with extralegal influences, however, and crime kingpins such as bail bondsman Peter P. McDonough held organized labor in their hands. McDonough financed labor's success through the early twentieth century by providing bail without charge to striking workers, and he contributed heavily to labor leaders' campaigns for public office. He paid the bail of union streetcar workers during the strike of 1907–1908, for example, and according to historian Merritt Barnes, "organized labor did not fail to show its gratitude when McDonough himself was in trouble."[136] But McDonough was rarely in trouble. His only conviction resulted from a 1923 bootlegging charge by federal (Volstead Act) agents. A petition for clemency is evidence of the impressive range of McDonough's influence; it was signed by a list of politicians that included a former governor, the mayor, three congressmen, the police commissioner, twelve judges, the city district attorney, the city tax collector, and the vice president of the Bank of Italy (soon to be the Bank of America).

In the 1920s, however, Progressive Era politics nurtured popular reformers such as "Sunny" Jim Rolph, who took control of city politics from American Federation of Labor (AFL) candidates. While Rolph was no stranger to organized crime, he drove a wedge in the relationship between crime and labor. Rolph's administration refused to intervene while employers and bankers financed an offensive against labor in the turbulent post–World War I years, and San Francisco reverted to an open-shop town.[137] By 1934, just a year after the repeal of Prohibition and at the height of depression-era politics, radical labor organizations such as the International Workers of the World (IWW) and the Congress of Industrial Organizations (CIO) increased union membership in San Francisco and sparked a longshoremen's strike. Two months later and on the heels of "bloody Thursday"—the day (July 3) on which fighting broke out between striking workers, scabs, and the police, and two men were killed—the waterfront strike developed into a general strike that shut down the city for three days.[138] The 1934 strikes strengthened the role of labor unions in the city, but they ended the cooperation of McDonough-dominated organized crime and AFL-dominated organized labor. Increasingly large numbers of IWW and CIO affiliates replaced AFL workers who had relied on the benefits of crime-labor cooperation.[139] Vice interests, as a result, scurried to build new sources of political influence, and queer bars and taverns opened without the "protection" of old-school crime bosses like Peter P. McDonough.

The Atherton Report also contributed to the demise of organized crime's control over vice. When former FBI agent Edwin N. Atherton published his 1935 report on San Francisco's vice economy (at the behest of the Internal Revenue Service), he revealed that vice and graft revenue in San Francisco reached as high as five million dollars a year—with graft payoffs at almost one million dollars a year. With the backing of anti-vice activist and news mogul William Randolph Hearst, Atherton's report made headline news, and city officials were pressed into action. Despite San Francisco's tolerance for organized crime, the fantastic sums shocked citizens who were struggling to make ends meet at the height of the Great Depression. With the publication of the Atherton Report, public opinion rallied against civic graft, and the prosecution of crime bosses like McDonough began in earnest. As a result, organized crime was temporarily weakened.[140] With post-Prohibition alcohol control limited to a state-run tax agency and the disabling of organized crime through both the reorganization of labor and the Atherton Report, bars and taverns that sprang up in the post-Prohibition 1930s did so without the kind of control evidenced in east coast cities, where crime syndicates and alcohol control agencies played "good cop / bad cop" with queer bars and taverns.

THE CONSTRUCTION OF A BAR-BASED GAY COMMUNITY

Finocchio's: Sex and Race Tourism

In post-Prohibition San Francisco, queer nightclubs functioned as part of an urban economy of visible and highly trafficked sex tourism. While the legalization of alcohol promised the revival of the city's vice districts, San Francisco entrepreneurs sought new ways to capture liquor revenue and, later, tourist dollars. Finocchio's, the North Beach nightclub that featured female impersonators, exemplified this trend. Italian immigrant Joseph Finocchio opened Finocchio's on Stockton Street as a speakeasy during Prohibition.[141] One night, an impromptu performance by a female impersonator sparked Joseph Finocchio's interest. As journalist Jesse Hamlin notes, "A well-oiled customer got up and sang in [a] dazzling style that sounded exactly like Sophie Tucker. The crowd ate it up, and Finocchio saw his future."[142] Female impersonators "were a sensation," Joe Finocchio recalls. "*Everyone* came to see the show. And to drink."[143] Initially the show featured a female impersonator paired with an "exotic" dancer—a "hula dancer" or a "young Chinese dancer." In this way, Finocchio's combined gender-transgressive and racialized entertainments, establishing a pattern that would continue through the postwar years. With the repeal of Prohibition in 1933, however, Finocchio's expanded its floor show and hired a larger group of female impersonators, pushing the limits of propriety—even in San Francisco. In 1936 the place was raided. Police arrested five female impersonators, including the young Walter Hart and Carroll Davis, both of whom in later years would become famous in gay clubs for their campy drag performances.[144] The police also arrested the owners for employing entertainers on a percentage basis—an activity where waitresses received a percentage of the drinks they sold. Often, to encourage sales, the price of drinks included sexual favors. Female impersonators thus generated revenue for the club in the waning style of Barbary Coast bawdy houses in that male customers were willing to purchase the attention of female impersonators for the inflated price of a couple of drinks. In the tradition of San Francisco establishments like the Dash, Finocchio's blended queer entertainments with a culture of sex trade and prostitution.

Nightclubs like Finocchio's were not gay bars in the sense that they sustained an overtly gay or homosexual-identified clientele, but because they profited from men willing to buy drinks for and sex from female impersonators, they helped establish a public culture for homosexuals in San Francisco. This phenomenon, the public emergence of queer and transgender clubs, can be measured in part by the civic outcry it generated. Police regulation can, at times, be read as a product of the increased visibility of the city's queer entertainments rather than proof of the weakness, invisibility, or oppression of queer communities. In 1937, for example, Police Chief Quinn "declared war" on female impersonators and announced that "lewd entertainers must be stopped!" Following the raid on Finocchio's, he revoked the dance permit at the 201 Club at Jefferson and Taylor Streets, noting that they, too, employed female impersonators on a percentage basis and that employees often mingled with guests, soliciting drinks.[145] The policing of bars like Finocchio's and the 201 Club illustrates the city's nervous response to the public display of transgender entertainments. Shows featuring female impersonators were allowed to exist as an emblem of the city's sophistication—its desire to sustain a tourist culture—but periodic purges occurred that drew bar owners into negotiations with the police. For example, after the 1936 raid, Finocchio's moved from Stockton Street to a much larger venue on Broadway. With more space, Finocchio hired a larger troupe of female impersonators, purchased spectacular costumes, and according to the nightclub's playbill, advertised "public entertainment that was so unusual and spectacular, . . . it would set the entire country talking."[146] The use of female impersonators was risky, but Finocchio's legitimized its entertainment as a tourist attraction. "I had to fight a little bit of trouble," Joseph Finocchio remembered, "but then they [the police] told me if you run the place straight everything would be fine. They don't want the entertainment to mingle with the customers. [So] I promised to run it like a regular theater."[147] Finocchio's was not raided again. In fact, it became central to the development of San Francisco's North Beach tourist district.

Through the mid-1930s, San Franciscans witnessed the completion of three breathtaking architectural feats: the construction of the Golden Gate Bridge, the construction of the San Francisco–Oakland Bay Bridge, and the building of Treasure Island, a landfill space that rose from the bay to house San Francisco's 1939 World's Fair. Billed as the Golden Gate Exposition, San Francisco's World's Fair promised to bring unprecedented numbers of tourists to the west coast, and as the opening day neared, city leaders became savvy to the benefits of San Francisco's local tourist trade. As historian David Nasaw notes, expositions and fairs marketed the city to faraway tourists through hotel and railroad magazines, and "visitors to the city were fed a steady diet of urban adventure stories before they even reached the metropolis."[148] In San Francisco, hotel magazines like *San Francisco Life* and *San Francisco Hotel Greeters Guide* called the city the "Paris of America" and cautioned police against restrictive ordinances: "Blue laws are foreign to the lightheartedness of San Francisco, a city that has always been able to distinguish between liberty and license. Away with them—let us be gay while the mood is on us."[149] Calling itself the "Pageant of the Pacific," the Golden Gate Exposition created a carnival-like atmosphere that complemented San Francisco's tourist entertainments. The exposition featured grand architecture, musical parades, an abundance of flowers, talent shows, live music, an aquacade, games of chance, technological exhibits, educational pavilions, and breathtaking views of the city. The fair also featured racial, ethnic, and sexual entertainments such as rickshaw races, Jewish days, and a burlesque-inspired "nude ranch," where women wore little more than gun belts and bandannas.[150]

The fair marketed both the nostalgic lure of "the west" and California's cultural (and anticipated economic) hegemony in the Pacific Rim. Nightclubs like Finocchio's that featured quirky, exotic, and racialized entertainments tapped into the fair's tourist appeal. As part of the exoticization that characterized San Francisco's growing tourist economy, Finocchio's capitalized on the sexualization of both gender transgression and racial difference. Tourist magazines directed out-of-town visitors to Finocchio's, billing it as "America's Most Unusual Night Club," and the show's lineup always included Asian and Latino female impersonators.[151] Li-Kar, for example, performed an "authentic and elaborate Geisha dance," and Billy Herrero impersonated Hedy Lamarr's appearance in the Hollywood film *Algiers.*[152] In 1940, Finocchio's developed a number called "Down Argentine Way," which featured South American rhythms and dancing.[153] Later, the show featured a wider range of racialized entertainments: "Juan Jose is a flamenco expert, clacking with castanets. Rene de Carlo is a lithe hula dancer in green skirt and bra. Bobby de Castro, billed as the 'Cuban King Kong,' performs a strip comedy complete with gorilla costume."[154] The combination of racialized and sexualized entertainments was not unique to San Francisco. The Jewel Box Revue, an impersonator show that toured the United States for over thirty years, featured a multiracial troupe and "exotic" themes such as "Arabian Nights," "Cleopatra," "Helen of Troy," "Madam Butterfly," "Mata Hari," and "Lady Godiva." The Jewel Box got its start in 1936 in Miami, under the leadership of mixed-race performer Stormé DeLarverié. With DeLarverié in male drag, performing alongside a troupe of female impersonators, the show advertised itself as "twenty-five men and a girl" and challenged the audience to figure out who was the "real" girl.[155] In the tradition of vaudeville-style entertainment, the Jewel Box featured a variety show format, but like Finocchio's it capitalized on a combination of racialized and sexualized entertainments.

In the postwar era, even when the Jewel Box Revue was in town, Finocchio's filled to capacity with four different shows, six nights a week, attracting locals, tourists, and such celebrities as Bob Hope, Frank Sinatra, Bette Davis, and Tallulah Bankhead. Finocchio's lured audiences with the titillating appeal of sexual deviancy and display.[156] A 1948 edition of the San Francisco "underground" guide book "Where to Sin in San Francisco" plugged Finocchio's to locals with a leading "Is it true what they say about Finocchio's?"

> Yes, it is. Even if the girls were women, the shows would be provocative. But the artists in the costly gowns are not women. Without saying what they are, twinkling Marjorie Finocchio does declare, "They're the only stable ones in the country." Tall, beautiful, stable Freddie Renault, the $200-a-week MC, has been here fourteen years. . . . Cute, Oriental Li Kar, double stable after ten years, is both a dancer and the club's costume designer. . . . Stablest of all is Walter Hart, $275-a-week specialist in murky songs.[157]

With impersonators safely on stage and patrons in the audience, Finocchio's clientele could anticipate a pleasurably voyeuristic experience. An instructive review observed, "Guys and their gals in the know sit at least three tables from ringside and let themselves be sucked in by insidious illusion."[158] With a post-exposition increase in tourist trade,

Finocchio's entertainment was based in voyeuristic exposé, distancing entertainers from customers, discouraging sexual traffic, and (over time) denying its homosexual appeal. The distance between patron and performers closed off Finocchio's entertainers from the queer clientele who frequented the place, and by the 1970s, Finocchio's was "strictly for tourists," according to Bob Damron's gay bar guide.[159] Still, as transgender and racialized entertainments became part of San Francisco's tourist industry, they established a liminal public space for gay bars to emerge. Clubs like Finocchio's legitimized queer entertainments, and bars featuring female impersonators became a standard in gay male culture.

The Black Cat: Drag Performance and the Gay Bar

The Black Cat Cafe grew out of a Prohibition-era tradition that combined sex trade with queer entertainment, and it exemplifies the shift from a tourist-based queer culture to a bar-based community developed by and for gay men. The Black Cat opened in 1906 at Eddy and Mason, just after the great earthquake and fire leveled much of the old Barbary Coast. Charles Ridley took over management in 1911, and like Joseph Finocchio, he sought to transform the bar into "the most popular place in Bohemia." In 1913, he staged a program of events "startling for originality and uniqueness," where waiters were "costumed in carnival dress" and entertainers promised "to outshine anything ever before attempted . . . in San Francisco."[160] The bar became famous for its unconventionality, attracting union organizers, local artists, vaudeville performers, and, later, Hollywood entertainers. In 1917, the Black Cat came under the scrutiny of city supervisors, who claimed the bar was loyal to labor and hired only union workers.[161] California writers William Saroyan and John Steinbeck frequented the Black Cat, and entertainers Tallulah Bankhead and Bette Davis stopped in while performing in town.[162] Between 1915 and 1919, when anti-prostitution forces grew strong, the Black Cat came under scrutiny for hiring "disreputable" women.[163] In 1921, after police commissioners witnessed women who, according to a *San Francisco Chronicle* writer, "mingled with the guests, singing to them, sometimes eating and drinking at their tables, and usually dancing with them," the Black Cat lost its dance permit and temporarily closed.[164] It reopened after the repeal of Prohibition at 710 Montgomery Street, and Ridley again managed the place.

In the 1940s, Sol Stoumen purchased the Black Cat, and its patronage shifted. Ever popular with local bohemians and waterfront workers, the Black Cat became a fashionable spot for homosexuals and, increasingly, tourists seeking a taste of San Francisco's wild side. One entertainment guide announced, "Rebels have been flaunting convention at the Black Cat for over twenty years. During the war, many a Montgomery Street Bohemian went forth to work or fight, but they're back now. Any night you can watch genuine artists, intellectuals and andsoforths boisterously protesting, or being loudly indifferent to such common social practices as sobriety and amiable conversation."[165] With high numbers of military personnel stationed in San Francisco in the postwar years, however, the Black Cat again came under police scrutiny. In 1949 the bar was raided as part of a police crackdown against night spots "featuring lascivious entertainment and catering to lewd persons." Police arrested ten people, held seven for vagrancy, and prosecuted three.[166] By 1951, the Black Cat also found itself on the Armed Forces Disciplinary Control Board's list of establishments that were "off limits and out of bounds." This required that armed forces personnel stay out of the Black Cat, whether in uniform or civilian clothing. It also required that the cafe post a sign advertising its off-limits status.[167] Still, the Black Cat's popularity soared. In fact, the management stepped up its commitment to providing a radically bohemian environment by hiring the young José Sarria as a nightly entertainer.

Sarria began his career entertaining at the Black Cat serendipitously. When he got out of the service, Sarria returned to his hometown, San Francisco, and enrolled in a teaching certificate program at a local college. At night, he toured Broadway, frequenting popular North Beach clubs such as the hungry i and the Purple Onion. At the Black Cat, he met his great love, Jimmy Moore, who worked as a waiter.[168] About this time, San Francisco police arrested Sarria in the Oak Room, the men's bar at the St. Francis Hotel, for sexual solicitation. This spot was notorious through the 1950s as an upscale pick-up place for gay men. With a "sex crime" offense on his record, his teaching career was ruined, and Sarria considered the theater. He had a good voice, but little experience. With encouragement from Michelle, a drag queen who would later become the darling of San Francisco's "SIR-lebrity circuit," Sarria entered a drag contest at Pearl's, an Oakland gay bar, and won second place. This entitled him to a two-week engagement at the Beige Room, which led him, indirectly, to a career entertaining at the Black Cat. Sarria started at the Black Cat waiting tables, but he soon began singing and dressing in drag.[169] At first, his performances were spontaneous, then they became part of the bar's nightly entertainment.

Sarria's performances galvanized the gay community and transformed the Black Cat. Through the 1950s, the Black Cat became a gay bar, a social and cultural center for San Francisco's queer communities. Sarria started with a regular nightclub act, singing popular songs and telling clever stories. In the early 1950s, he performed three shows a night, at 9:00, 10:30, and 11:30, accompanied by Hazel, the pianist. In between shows, he played host, greeting people at the door and chatting with customers. According to Sarria, his shows attracted a large number of ostensibly straight tourists, but Sarria addressed everyone, without discrimination, as if they were gay. "I told everybody that once you came in here your reputation was lost."[170] He bantered with the crowd, lavishing attention on beautiful men and mocking the discomfort of naive out-of-towners. Because business was slow on Sundays, Sarria performed at brunch, where he staged campy interpretations of popular operas. He dressed outrageously, played all the parts, and often interrupted arias with witty repartee, political commentary, or his own interpretations of the opera's characters. As his shows grew popular, they attracted upwards of three hundred people a show, and the bar became, as sociologist Sherri Cavan describes, a "home territory" for gay regulars.[171]

Cavan's early 1960s study of the Black Cat illustrates, from a sociological perspective, how gay patrons carved out a public niche at the Black Cat and protected this space for themselves. Through the manipulation of newcomers to the bar, gay regulars defended their space from being overrun by tourists and outsiders. In particular, Cavan describes four classes of patrons: homosexual regulars, non-homosexual regulars ("friends"), homosexual tourists ("possible trade"), and non-homosexual tourists ("outsiders"). Gay waiters and regulars, whom Cavan identifies as the indigenous group, protected their space through defense behaviors that included a quick assessment of the newcomer's status (e.g., friend, possible trade, or outsider) upon arrival at the bar, loud and forceful interaction with anyone perceived to be an outsider, and an overt performance that included the outsider in an exchange of presumed homosexuality. Heterosexual couples, for example, would run a gauntlet of comments implying that the man was a frequent habitué of the Black Cat. Waiters would call out, "I didn't know I was merely another woman" or "Why haven't you ever told me you were married?" or "My God—a bisexual!" This performance, Cavan argues, signaled to outsiders their status, and most tourists accepted their lot with blushing embarrassment, good humor, or a quick retreat. As gay regulars engaged with tourists, regulars stripped tourists of their anonymity, positioning the tourist as an object of attention—a participant rather than a voyeur. Gay patrons of the Black Cat thus betrayed the straight outsider's expectation that he or she would be inconspicuous, a watcher or a judge, and in doing so, they protected their own fledgling culture.[172]

Sarria's performances perfected a defensive style of interaction, and, as a result, he was able to transform the culture of the Black Cat into something that boosted inchoate feelings of community and connectedness. In essence, the kind of humor Sarria and the Black Cat's coterie of handsome young waiters performed displaced the feelings of humiliation that were often attached to homosexuality. In the thick of the McCarthy era, inside the Black Cat it was no longer shameful to be gay or to seek out gay entertainment. By enforcing a culture that assumed everyone in the bar was gay—and gayness was not simply the norm but a preferred way of being—the bar sacrificed quiet anonymity for a surge of cultural pride—a pride in being different. "Now you see, I'd been arrested. I did not get chosen for Finocchio's. Instead, I began my career at the Black Cat," Sarria explains, "and I noticed something: that people were living double lives."[173] Through his performances, Sarria worked the crowd; he teased the audience and brought it to the point of good-humored receptivity. Then he took a more serious tone and began to address the Black Cat's regular customers as part of a community, a "gay community."

Sarria's performances, indeed, the culture of the Black Cat encouraged gay people to accept their homosexuality. Sarria insisted that living a double life (or staying in the closet) left gay people vulnerable to the police, and he championed the slogan "United we stand, divided they arrest us one by one." At the end of each performance, he had the audience stand and sing a parody of "God Save the Queen." He remembers, "I sang the song as a kind of anthem, to get them realizing that we had to work together, that we were responsible for our lives. We could change the laws if we weren't always hiding."[174] In 1961, almost as if to assert the notion of queer citizenship, Sarria staged a run for city supervisor from his pulpit at the Black Cat. Built on a campaign that insisted "Gay Is Good!" he raised the consciousness of the gay community. Moreover, through the performance of a "real" political campaign, he raised the possibility of gay voter solidarity. Sarria's defensive humor thus evolved from a protection of the Black Cat as a gay home territory into a much more serious prospect: the development of a unified and resistant bar-based gay and transgender community.

Sarria's campaign enabled him to link San Francisco's gay and transgender communities to an explicitly politicized social movement, but it also functioned to link queer social movements to San Francisco's largely disenfranchised communities of color. If Sarria had won a seat on the city's Board of Supervisors in 1961, he not only would have been the first self-identified gay man to serve on the board, but he also would have been the first Latino. Indeed, his seemingly anomalous voice for gay political mobilization can not be detached from larger social movements to end racial oppression and gain civil rights. As a Latino (Columbian/Nicaraguan) man, a drag queen, and a performer, Sarria's leadership anticipated one direction that a politicized queer social movement might (but ultimately did not) go—toward a true coalition between disenfranchised groups. At the same time, his performances reflected a new mode of cultural visibility in which queers of color could literally move between the theatrical stage and the political arena. Sarria's performativity, particularly his defensive humor and gender-transgressive style, highlights the way the marketing of queer bodies through San Francisco's history of sex and race tourism could under certain circumstances shift into new and counterdiscursive modes of social, cultural, and political visibility. In the early 1960s, Sarria's stage presence shifted toward political mobilization, but his capacity to engineer this shift reflects a legacy of queer entertainers who pushed themselves away from the objectifying gaze of the tourist or voyeur to creatively assert a critique of normative same-race heterosexuality.

The Black Cat was a perfect place for Sarria to affect this transformation. It had long welcomed a variety of sexual transgressions—same-sex, cross-race, for hire—but it had also been a location where progressive thinkers and political radicals gathered. Over time, and under Sarria's influence, the culture of the Black Cat became part of the emergence of the gay bar as a visible and defensible institution in San Francisco. Through the 1940 and 1950s, many gay bars opened, sometimes run by non-gay entrepreneurs, but, increasingly, lesbians and gay men opened and managed their own bars. The development of the gay bar as a public institution enabled the legitimization and solidification of San Francisco's queer community because, as sociologists argue, public institutions legitimize and normalize deviancy.[175] Or, as Donald Webster Cory notes in his 1951 classic, *The Homosexual in America,* gay bars elicit a kind of respectability among gay people: "From the gay street to the gay bar may be but a few steps, or several miles, but an aura of respectability is to be found at the latter that is lacking at the former. One need not hide one's head as an acquaintance walks by; one does not deny encounters, but on the contrary makes appointments, utilizes the meeting-place for social convenience."[176]

In San Francisco, the emergence of the gay bar as a public institution had a number of important effects. First, it enabled the city's queer and transgender populations to sustain a publicly visible urban space. This enabled greater numbers of people, particularly those who were new in town, to connect with a community or collective. Gay bars also legitimized a space where it was not shameful or an insult to assume others were gay. This facilitated the development of a shared public culture, a new language and lexicon of sexual meanings.[177] Gay bars, particularly neighborhood bars like the Black Cat, the Beige Room, Mona's, and the Paper Doll, also functioned as community centers where gay, lesbian, and transgendered people could make friends, find lovers, get information, or plan activities. As a result, San Francisco's queer bar-based community was able to pool its resources, strengthen its ties, and ultimately, develop a foundation for its own brand of political mobilization.[178]

In San Francisco, the gay bar developed out of a unique combination of factors, including a history of intersecting sexual cultures and a tension between turn-of-the-century vice, graft, and urban reform. The cultures of prostitution and female impersonation collided on the vaudeville stage and in theater districts where painted ladies were sometimes difficult to distinguish from actresses, performers, and female impersonators. As a queer culture developed in and around the public space of theaters and brothels, social and political changes stimulated the development of a more intimate space, the nightclub. Moral reform movements shifted the zones of prostitution in San Francisco and created a community of sexual outlaws that often overlapped with San Francisco's burgeoning queer communities. Meanwhile, temperance movements upset the balance of power in San Francisco and, curiously, pushed queer clubs into the somewhat protected space of urban tourism. As a result, after the repeal of Prohibition in 1933, a number of queer nightclubs appeared on Broadway, at the center of San Francisco's vice and tourist districts. Out of these tourist venues emerged gender-transgressive gay bars, where a defensive style of social interaction both protected bar-goers from hostile outsiders and encouraged the development of a new culture of resistance. By the mid-century, community leaders like José Sarria, who combined transgender activism with a politic of civic responsibility, used the gay bar to shape a nascent gay movement. Sarria insisted not only that "gay is good" but that gay and lesbian San Franciscans ought to assert their civil rights. Thus, out of the vice-filled barrooms of the Barbary Coast, the gay bar evolved into a kind of politicized community center—a site for the development of new political ideas and responsibilities.

ORAL HISTORY

Reba Hudson

You've got to remember that dating back to its Gold Rush days San Francisco has always been known for its tolerance. That's what drew all these people here—its liberalism and its acceptance of everything. And San Francisco was never a religious town. It's always been wild and woolly. As a matter of fact, it's been more shut down since George Christopher became mayor in the 1950s. That and the two wars sort of closed it down, but it used to be wide open. When we came here we used to go to jazz clubs after 2:00 and drink liquor out of coffee cups. Relations between blacks and whites were excellent. They were glad to have us out in the Fillmore, out at the jazz clubs. We were treated like queens, and I don't mean in that sense [laughs]. I mean it was a whole different world then.

Things changed during World War II when so many people from different parts of the country came here and brought their prejudices with them. Then, of course, the Civil Rights Movement had two different forces at work: those who wanted civil rights and those who were committed to not giving them. It created a lot of open hostility than never existed before. Then there was Christopher. He was our first Greek mayor, and he was a very moral man. A great churchgoer. After-hours joints started to get closed down, and the harassment of gays increased under him.

The only time that I was ever personally hassled was in the early 1950s. With the exception of the Paper Doll, almost all the gay bars were down on Broadway. Finocchio's was down there, and Mona's 440 was down there. Other gay bars opened, but they were mainly run by straight people because if a gay person was openly gay, they could not get a liquor license. So straight people ran them and hired gay people. There was about five or six gay bars down there, and you could go out for the evening and just go from one to the

Reba Hudson, interviewed by Nan Alamilla Boyd, tape recording, San Francisco, 29 May 1992 and 10 July 1992, Wide Open Town History Project, GLBT Historical Society. These interviews have been edited by the author.

other. I remember that four of us were out one day, and we were dressed, I mean *dressed,* in suits and heels. We'd been somewhere dressy, and we were sitting in what was Mona's Candlelight. I think Mona had had it briefly, but then a young Chinese woman named Mary Lee was the actual owner. We were just sitting in there at a table having a drink, and the police told the four of us just to get up and get out of there. I said, "What for, what have we done?" They said, "Don't talk to us." Then they lined us up out there in front of the building. We've all got long hair—Helen's a student, Eve's a student, Mary's going to med school at Stanford, and me, I'm unemployed. So they say, "What do you mean you don't have a job?" They told us that if they ever caught us around that kind of place again they were going to run us in. They threatened us and intimidated us, and I told them to go to hell. I hadn't done anything.

They were plainclothesmen that were out to hassle gay bar owners, and we just happened to be in there. They'd conduct little raids, right? And now we know that the bar owners that were running gay bars that weren't bothered were paying off the cops. We fell into the vice squad category, right along with the whores and the pimps and other vice squad victims. But that's the only time that I was ever actually personally harassed. Others got harassed more often, like the dykes that dressed up in men's clothing. But they always wore women's underpants, because if you wore one article of feminine apparel—the same thing was true of drag queens—they couldn't book you for impersonating a person of the opposite sex. I think that was the way they phrased it. Seems incredible now.

There was a lot of that, though. The police intimidated and threatened people, tried to discourage them from going to gay bars, and that's how they got even with the owners for not paying off. The same thing happened in New York. I think most of the gay bars back there worked for the Mafia. But not here. There was no Mafia, but people still paid off the cops. Mona never paid off. Finocchio's either. But see, Mona ran an out-and-out entertainment place.

This is the story Mona told me. Mona lived in the old "Monkey Block." Are you familiar with that? It was an old building on Montgomery that was full of studios and artists' lofts, and painters and writers lived there. As a matter of fact, Mona told me that they called themselves the "mad bohemians." Prohibition wasn't lifted until, what, '32, '33? When that was lifted, Mona decided that she'd like to open a bar. She had all these friends she was living with in the Monkey Block—it's famous in North Beach history but was torn down about twenty years ago as part of some high-rise. The Iron Pot was down there, the Black Cat was not too far, and Mona just was going to open a place for her friends. Just a bohemian joint, a little beer and wine place to have a drink and talk and discuss ideas and do what bohemians do, right? Drink and carry on and have intellectual conversations. The bar was already there—it had operated as a bar prior to Prohibition. I think she said she opened it on a hundred dollars or something like that, just enough to buy the beer and wine because everything was there. And that bar became the Purple Onion. It's down, you know where it is. I can remember when it was mostly folk singers, and the Smothers Brothers came out of there. A lot of other people too.

When Mona opened Mona's 440 it was probably about her fourth place. She had a lot of little bars around the neighborhood there. She said that she even had one that she ran out of a flat over a grocery store that ran after hours. But she was never interested in running a gay place, and how she came to do this, she said, was because of the tolerance in North Beach. There were a lot of parents who found out their daughters were gay and told them to never darken their doors again. Kay Scott was one of the first. She was one of the male impersonators that worked in Mona's as long as it ran. She sang—terrible voice—but did clever parodies. I can remember one really awful one that she did to the tune of "The Isle of Capri." "On an isle of debris that I found her," that kind of awful parody. Mona just sort of took them in, because everybody was very tolerant of everybody else's lifestyle. The next thing you know she gave them whatever job there was, and then she found out that some of them could sing. So they started to sing, and it evolved into something that she never intended. Later, she was forced to take in a partner because she had tuberculosis and was confined to her bed for a year. That's when it turned commercial. It became a tourist spot. A woman's Finocchio's is what it was. I don't think they ever had tour buses coming in and that kind of thing, but that's what it became. I think they even paraphrased Finocchio's and called Mona's "The Place Where Girls Will Be Boys."

Besides the bars we had dinner parties at home, lots of parties at home. We did a lot of socializing because we were all right here within blocks of each other, right? There was about fifteen of us that hung out together. There were little cliques. Then there were what are referred to now as the working-class dykes, the ones that had tattoos and rolled up their sleeves and went with hookers, usually. They acted just like men. Those were what we referred to as dykes. That was sort of a pejorative word, really, but they were very masculine. Anybody could spot them—they got into a lot of trouble. They hung around at the bars down on Broadway.

There was a Filipino bar called Blanco's down in Filipino Town where dykes hung out because most of them went with hookers, and that's where the hookers were. Kay Blanco's father owned Blanco's, and Kay was gay. She tended bar there when she got old enough. She was half Filipino and half Caucasian, and she drew a lot of the, well, it wasn't necessarily a gay bar but a lot of gay people hung around there because Kay condoned it. She owned the bar after her father died. The Filipinos were so ostracized from the rest of the world that they were all kind of drawn to each other, because they were all outsiders. And a lot of them, the so-called dykes, were hookers. It was funny that the more masculine ones would be the hookers, and they also went with hookers of a more feminine type. They hung around that section of town.

A lot of them also hung out at the 299, which was Tommy's first joint. The 299 was right where you hit the freeway off Broadway—it was at Broadway and Front. The dykes hung out at Tommy's because Tommy was a dyke. She dressed in a tie, kept her hair short, and went with hookers. Call girls, mainly. She was a cut above them in the sense that she also ran the parking lot across the street. She ran around with gangsters and drove a Cadillac convertible.

Later, Tommy had Tommy's Place, which was on the top level at Broadway and Columbus, and she had the 12 Adler, which was down below. It's called Specs now. It's in that little alleyway right across from City Lights Books and just a couple doors down from the Tosca Cafe, the old operatic cafe. Tommy's and the 12 Adler were one and the same thing. You could walk upstairs to Tommy's from downstairs. I mean they were both owned by Jeanne Sullivan and Tommy Vasu. Tommy's Place had a restaurant and a back room and a piano player up on the top level, so it was sort of like whichever suited you, noise or conversation or food or not.

Tommy's Place and the 12 Adler operated from '52 to '54, but in '54 they were closed by the vice squad. As a matter of fact, two of her bartenders were arrested. They were accused of serving minors, and the girls *were* minors but they had forged IDs. It sort of escalated, and the PTA got involved. Then the police planted some drugs in the ladies' room, some heroin and the works or something like that, and then they pretended to find it. Grace and Joyce tended bar down on the lower level, at the 12 Adler, which was the more popular of the two. The arrests were splashed all over the front pages, and Gracie went to trial long before Joyce did. Joyce didn't do any time. Everybody figured, due to everything that was happening there at the time, that someone had planted the heroin. We didn't know anyone who used heroin, and Grace, certainly, and Joyce, well, they were real nice. But it just didn't make any sense for somebody to tape this stuff to a pipe beneath the sink because they certainly weren't shooting up in there. It just would never have been wise. It wouldn't even have been possible to do it, so everybody figured it was a police plant. People might have been smoking a little grass, but besides the World War II Benzedrine that came in from the pilots, there weren't even that many drugs around.

Tommy lost her license because of the arrests. As an owner anything that goes on on the premises you're supposed to be aware of, but the person who actually serves the minor is the one who does the time. Right now it's usually a fine, but back then the ABC [Alcoholic Beverage Control Board] worked very closely with the cops. The cops were very much involved in this. Oh yeah. There was a period here where they really did hassle gay bars. A lot of us knew that Tommy would have paid off—she was a real piece of work—but the two bartenders, they were the victims of this whole thing. Gracie went to trial right at the height of the publicity, that's really why she was convicted. Joyce didn't go to trial until about three or four months later, and she got off with, I don't know, probation or something. Gracie was just a scapegoat because she went to trial when the anti-gay stuff was at its most hysterical peak.

2 | LESBIAN SPACE, LESBIAN TERRITORY

San Francisco's North Beach District, 1933–1954

> The waitress was very worldly wise and cynical, and we were just a bunch of fresh-faced kids. We're wearing Levi's and cowboy boots, you know, dressed nicely and crisp and starched and everything. She said to us . . . "You kids don't belong here. You should go to Mona's 440." "What's that like?" And she said, "You'll love it, just take my word for it!" So the next night we went to Mona's 440. Boy, you should have seen our faces. Here's all these women in tuxes, right? And they're entertaining and singing and working as waitresses. We continued to go there often. They made us very very welcome.
>
> *Reba Hudson*

Mona's was San Francisco's first lesbian nightclub. It opened on Union Street in 1934, just after the repeal of Prohibition, but moved in 1936 to Columbus Avenue. Originally intending it as a hangout for writers and artists, Mona Sargent and her then-husband, Jimmie Sargent, covered the floors at 140 Columbus with sawdust to give the place a bohemian atmosphere.[1] Nightclub-style entertainment soon grew out of impromptu performances, and Sargent hired the most popular singers as waitresses. Over time, singing waitresses developed a floor show where women dressed as men and sang parodies of popular songs.[2] The bar's popularity brought it to the attention of local writers—and the police. Through 1936, *San Francisco Life* listed Mona's in its "Guide to Cocktailing, Dancing, and Dining" as a "bohemian" club, a code word for sexual unconventionality, and the magazine ran suggestive advertisements of individual performers.[3] In 1938, as part of a routine check on Mona's tavern, San Francisco Police Sergeant Glen Hughes reported that he couldn't tell "which were the men and which were the women."

He arrested Mona and charged her with keeping a disorderly house.[4] Still, as Sargent remembers, "The girls came in!"—but the performances remained relatively informal until 1939, when Mona's moved to 440 Broadway.[5] At this location, Sargent hired male impersonators from Los Angeles and New York City, and she paid to advertise their performances in tourist magazines. *San Francisco Life* ran quarter-page advertisements of Mona's through the World War II years, and "underground" tourist guides like *Where to Sin in San Francisco* directed tourists "in the mood mauve" to Mona's, noting that "the little girl waitresses look like boys. The little-girls-who-sing-sweet-song look like boys. And many of the little girl customers look like boys."[6] Located at the center of San Francisco's entertainment district, Mona's 440 opened up lesbian entertainment and brought it into the public eye.[7]

The incorporation of lesbian and transgender entertainments into San Francisco's tourist economy opened up a space in which lesbian culture could grow. According to Reba Hudson, Mona's was a big place: "It was a real long room with a stage at the end of it, typical nightclub kind of thing. You entered at the front and the bar was over at your left, hat-check room at the end of the bar. Then a big arch and you entered what they called the show room in nightclubs in those days. There was a line of booths down one wall, then tables in where you could utilize space around the stage. And the stage was right in the center."[8] The popularity of Mona's enabled other lesbian nightclubs to open, and through the 1940s, lesbian bars populated San Francisco's North Beach district. There was the Paper Doll, the Artist's Club, the Beaded Bag, Mona's Candlelight, Blanco's, the Chi-Chi Club, the Beige Room, and Tommy's 299. Through the 1950s, even more lesbian nightspots opened, many of them lesbian owned and operated. There was Tommy's Place, 12 Adler Place, Ann's 440, Miss Smith's Tea Room, the Tin Angel, the Copper Lantern, the Anxious Asp, the Front, and Our Club. All of these clubs opened on or near Broadway, at the heart of San Francisco's tourist district, and while they were not all open at the same time, between 1949 and 1959 there were always at least four and up to seven bars or nightclubs that lesbians frequented within a few blocks of each other. Many lesbians rented rooms on nearby Telegraph Hill, and as a result, North Beach became San Francisco's first lesbian neighborhood.

The evolution of lesbian bars follows the pattern of gay bars in that lesbian bars developed at the conjunction of San Francisco's tourist and vice interests. The proliferation of lesbian bars in San Francisco's North Beach district follows a somewhat different trajectory than that of gay bars, however. Gay bars found their roots in the same-sex prostitution houses of the turn-of-the-century Barbary Coast, but there is little evidence of the existence of lesbian bars or public spaces in San Francisco prior to the repeal of Prohibition.[9] Still, the histories of gay and lesbian bars have much in common. Both gay and lesbian bars evolved in a culture tightly bound to sex trade and prostitution, and both were influenced by moral reform movements. Also, both gay and lesbian bars emerged in relation to sexualized and racialized entertainments, and both became visible on or near Broadway, the central artery of San Francisco's touristed vice district. As a result, both gay bars and lesbian bars emerged at the intersection of overlapping entertainment cultures. And while it is important to distinguish between gay and lesbian public spaces, most bars were shared by both gay men and lesbians, though some, like Mona's, had a higher proportion of lesbians than gay men, and many, like the Beige Room, had a preponderance of gay men. Through the 1930s and 1940s, San Francisco's queer public culture could be characterized as one that both gay men and lesbians shared, rather than one that made finite distinctions between the sexes of its clientele.

What is unique about San Francisco, however, is the evolution of a lesbian territory or district at midcentury. In the 1950s, a distinct culture emerged in a handful of bars and taverns that catered specifically to lesbians. This finding contradicts earlier studies of San Francisco that characterize lesbians as either invisible or unterritorial.[10] Manuel Castell's landmark study of San Francisco's urban social movements, for example, asserts that lesbians do not concentrate geographically and "do not acquire a geographical basis for their political organization."[11] Deborah Wolf's ethnographic study of San Francisco's lesbian-feminist communities echoes these concerns. She argues that although lesbians in the 1970s occupied contiguous geographic districts (Bernal Heights and the Mission District), their community—and incipient political power—reflected ideological rather than geographical boundaries.[12] These arguments raise two concerns, both of which are increasingly contested: lesbian uses of public space, and the relationship between territoriality and politics. How are lesbians visible in public culture? How has lesbian visibility and/or territoriality translated into a demand for civil rights? What are the terms upon which we understand the meaningful use of public space?[13]

While the bars and taverns catering to lesbians that emerged in San Francisco's North Beach district in the 1930s and 1940s occupied a specific geographic area—they were clustered around Broadway and Montgomery—their presence did not, in the end, invest lesbians with political power in traditional ways. The lesbians who became publicly visible in bars and taverns did not elect a representative to city council, nor did they knowingly shape public policy. But they did take up public space. They did acquire a geographic basis for the development of new social identities. Moreover, the visible presence of lesbians in the public sphere altered the relationship between the state—the policing agencies that regulated public life—and lesbian society.[14] Lesbian visibility forged a new relationship between homosexuals and the state in that although lesbians had long been visible to the state as social deviants, they were treated as anomalous individuals; they were assumed to be detached from an identifiable culture or community. Public visibility in bars, taverns, and nightclubs engaged lesbians in a relationship with the state as a collective, a social group. Lesbian visibility thus became a form of cultural politics and collective resistance in midcentury San Francisco.

Cultural politics were particularly important in the post–World War II years because as the United States celebrated its wartime successes, social and political activism waned. Despite a strong postwar economy and the solidification of U.S. international power, the economic and political advances the United States had gained through its participation in the war seemed fragile, and postwar American culture expressed layers of anxiety.[15] Fears of economic depression and political weakness stimulated an assertive foreign policy (e.g., the Marshall Plan and Truman Doctrine), while domestic ideology and Senator Joseph McCarthy's quest to rid the country of "subversives" drove most progressive political organizations underground.[16] As a result, the postwar years saw a decrease in organized social or political activism, and cultural politics—the politics of everyday life—became an important venue for resisting dominant social structures. For example, in an effort to stop wildcat strikes and control international markets, Congress passed the Taft-Hartley Act in 1947, the same year that the House Un-American Activities Committee began to "ferret out" communists from federal government agencies.[17] Through a number of provisions, the Taft-Hartley Act deeply curtailed the power and autonomy of labor unions in the United States.[18] As a result, George Lipsitz notes, "Feelings and aspirations denied political and institutional expression surfaced within the politics of everyday life, on the shop floor, in the community, and in the home."[19] Political expression embedded in film, music, and art, as well as daily interaction—at work, in bars, taverns, or churches—temporarily replaced formal organizations as the site of political resistance.[20]

Cultural resistance extended beyond labor relations and anti-communism, however, as the meanings of gender and sexuality became contested sites for the expression of domestic policy. McCarthy's quest to rid the country of communism soon developed into a drive against any form of "internal decay," and symbolic gestures replaced the actual containment of communist organizations and ideologies.[21] Popular culture absorbed domestic political ideology, and the nuclear family ideal of patriarchal leadership and female sexual monogamy worked to insure the reproduction of moral ("democratic") and loyal (wage-earning) citizens. As a result, femininity and homosexuality became potent symbols for weakness and vulnerability, and "domestic containment," as an evolving set of social and cultural ideologies, perceived sexual desire—particularly homosexual desire—as a dangerous chasm filled with destabilizing possibilities.[22] "Don't go about the house half-dressed," J. Edgar Hoover warned U.S. teenagers in a full-page magazine advertisement. "This may seem harmless, but it's an invitation to 'Peeping Toms'—who may later become something more dangerous."[23] Cold war domestic ideology (and its focus on nuclear preparedness) dictated complete social control, and sexual transgression became tantamount to treason. Homosexuality, prostitution, drugs, and juvenile delinquency bled tautologically into each other as both the cause and effect of America's failure to defeat the Russians. Lesbian and gay cultures and their publicly visible social worlds flew in the face of postwar gender and sexual constructions: they seemed dangerous and subversive—resistant to dominant political ideologies.

This chapter traces the history of several overlapping communities whose members lived out the meaning of same-sex sexuality in lesbian bars and queer public spaces. It illustrates how lesbian bars evolved within San Francisco's tourist districts and how the queer entertainers who worked at these bars forged a public space in which lesbians could gather. In doing so, this chapter explores the relationships between sex tourism, race tourism, and the kinds of voyeuristic entertainments that allowed queer venues to exist in San Francisco's North Beach district. Because geographies of sex tourism overlap with sex trade and sex work, this chapter also documents the social relationships between lesbians and prostitutes. As with gay men, San Francisco's publicly visible lesbians often occupied the same bars, taverns, and nightclubs as prostitutes, and as a result, they were often harassed and prosecuted by the police in similar ways. Finally, in order to illustrate the politics of lesbian visibility in midcentury San Francisco, and the slippage between homosexuality, prostitution, drugs, and juvenile delinquency, this chapter looks closely at one lesbian bar, Tommy's Place, which found itself in the public eye and, in 1954, the subject of a U.S. Senate subcommittee hearing.

LESBIAN ENTERTAINERS, TOURIST CULTURES, AND THE COMMODIFICATION OF LESBIAN BARS

In the 1930s, lesbian bars and nightclubs became an important aspect of San Francisco's tourist entertainments. In a 1979 column entitled "Mr. San Francisco," San Francisco's daily columnist Herb Caen nostalgically remembers cruising North Beach in the 1930s: "An evening of gaiety included visits to Finocchio's, 'where boys will be girls,' as he [Mr. San Francisco] was fond of saying, and to Mona's, a smoky Columbus Ave. basement jammed with mannish women. In retrospect, it was all quite unself-conscious. The evening might end at the Black Cat, where Whitney Warren, a true blue socialite, would be looking bemusedly at John Horton Cooper, a dandified young pianist who wore a big 'Stanford' belt buckle and an expensive riding habit, with boots and riding crop. John never went to Stanford nor had he ever been astride a horse. He simply liked the cut of the clothes."[24] On Broadway, nightclubs featuring queer entertainment stood alongside Italian eateries, coffee shops, pool halls, sandwich shops, and jazz clubs—and a mix of people gathered in each. In nearby Chinatown, Chinese restaurants and nightclubs attracted white patrons eager to sample the flavors of the east.

Tourist magazines advertised the variety of entertainments San Francisco's nightlife provided, and tour buses rolled through North Beach and Chinatown, promising tourists a trip through the exotic side of San Francisco. As a result, tourists became an important part of the queer cultures that emerged in San Francisco's North Beach district. Similarly, some of the entertainers that performed at places like Mona's became local celebrities. Patrons speculated about their lives, journalists followed their activities, and tourists had them pose for nightclub photos. Babe Scott, for example, was a native San Franciscan who gained some notice in 1933 when she swam from Alcatraz Island to San Francisco.[25] Several years later, a gossip columnist noted that, "Scott . . . is now working part-time in Mona Sargent's North Beach night spot, '440 Broadway.'"[26] In 1941, another columnist quipped that Mona's "has a girl manager, Babe Scott, who plays baseball like a veteran in her spare time."[27] Babe Scott was one of a handful of entertainers who performed at Mona's, and because of Mona's popularity—its centrality to San Francisco's tourist economy—Scott's activities were noticed by the local press.

When Babe Scott took over the management of Mona's 440 in 1941, she brought female entertainers from New York and Los Angeles—stars such as Tina Rubio, Kay Scott, and Beverly Shaw who, according to a tourist magazine, sang songs that "your mother didn't teach you."[28] Tina Rubio, who was called "the dynamic Latin star" in tourist magazines, performed ethnic entertainments that combined sexual innuendo with references to Spanish, Mexican, and Pacific Island cultures. According to one review, Rubio sang in "Tahitian, Spanish, English, and Double Entendre." She performed at Mona's 440 from August 1941 through May 1942.[29] Kay Scott, one of the most popular performers, started out at the original Mona's in 1936 and performed at Mona's 440 until 1946. She dressed, as all of Mona's entertainers did, in a tuxedo and sang parodies of popular songs.[30] The memoirs of Pat Bond, a patron of Mona's in the late 1940s, recount some of Kay Scott's tunes:

> There goes my gal, she's changed her name to Mike,
> There goes my gal, she's turned into a dyke.
> She cut her hair,
> She's wearing shirts and ties,
> She used to make men stare,
> Now she gives the girls the eyes,
> I just can't figure out how it all began,
> There goes my gal, a lesbian.[31]

Here the term "dyke" flags female masculinity, and like the female impersonators of the vaudeville stage, Scott's lyrics underscored the socially constructed nature of gender and sexuality—almost as if to say that with a haircut, shirt, and tie anyone could become a dyke. In this way Scott plays on and reverses commonly held assumptions about the fixed nature of gender and sexuality. Because she "can't figure out how it all began," Scott upsets the security of sex and gender normativity and raises the possibility of new transgendered and queer subjectivities.

In another tune, the lyrics more directly address a queer point of view, asserting both the sexuality of lesbian subjectivity and the centrality of North Beach (Telegraph Hill) to lesbian community development:

When it's early in the morning and I stagger up the hill,
To test out my Simmons while everything is still,
I make frantic love to a cute little Jill,
Who is shacking up with me on Telegraph Hill.
Tiddle da, tiddly do da for peace and good will,
We're all on the make up on Telegraph Hill.[32]

Other lyrics more directly addressed a tourist's point of view, seeking to welcome and reassure rather than assert a queer sensibility:

At Mona's Club on old Broadway,
you'll hear some people pass and say,
"If you go in there, you'll be surprised,
the boys are girlies in disguise."
Never falter, never fear
we're here to give the patrons cheer.
You'll never fall and you'll never flub
If you come to Mona's Club.[33]

While parodic and suggestive lyrics often addressed tourists, they "queered" Mona's tavern, providing a public display of lesbian life and allowing a certain amount of identification between lesbian patrons and entertainers. "She's one reason why visitors and natives are seen frequently on Broadway," one review noted in a photo advertisement of Kay Scott's performances at the 440.[34] Tourists wanted to experience unfamiliar sexual worlds as much as lesbians wanted their lives reflected back at them.[35]

Another favorite performer, Beverly Shaw, sang torch songs at Mona's from its inception through the mid-1940s, when she moved across the street to the Chi-Chi Club.[36] "Somebody knew [Shaw] in Los Angeles and brought her up [to San Francisco]," Mona Sargent recalls, "and I said, 'Beverly's got class!' She had style and everything!"[37] During the war, Shaw drove a cab by day and at night worked at Mona's, where she quickly became a headlining entertainer.[38] She "had a real penchant for young attractive new faces in town," one patron remembered, noting that she always had more than a few girlfriends at a time.[39] Another patron remembered Shaw's raw sexuality: "Talk about basic sex appeal! Wow, wow, wow!"[40] Shaw spent her entire life in the entertainment business, performing at lesbian bars and perfecting a sultry style: "On the show songs, I would drape the microphone over my shoulder and look right into the audience. I always chose a few women in the audience and sang directly to them. It gave a personal feeling to the show which is so important."[41] In the 1950s, Shaw returned to Los Angeles, where she recorded a popular album, *Songs Tailored to Your Taste,* and for fourteen years ran a lesbian bar, the Club Laurel, at Laurel Canyon and Ventura Boulevard.[42]

Perhaps the most important entertainer to appear at Mona's was African American performer Gladys Bentley. Advertised as "America's Great Sepia Piano Artist" and the "Brown Bomber of Sophisticated Songs," Bentley headlined at Mona's during the war years, promising to provide "the same type of gay entertainment that has made the 440 Club famous."[43] At Mona's, Bentley "packed her 250 pound frame into a tuxedo, flirted with women in her audience, and dedicated songs to her lesbian lover."[44]

Following a vibrant career in Harlem during the 1920s and 1930s, where she performed at clubs such as the Clam House, Rockland Palace, and the Ubangi Club, in 1937 Bentley moved to Los Angeles to seek new opportunities.[45] There she performed at Joaquin's El Rancho on Vine Street until the local authorities prohibited her from wearing trousers during her act.[46] At the onset of World War II, she began performing at gay-identified nightclubs, and she landed in San Francisco in July 1942.[47] Bentley was certainly the biggest name to play at Mona's. "Bentley was quite famous," one of Mona's regulars recalls; "She was a great big Black woman who accompanied herself on the piano [and] wore a top hat and a tux."[48] And the mainstream press adored her: "If you're looking for quiet, soothing music that will lull you to sleep, put a record on your phonograph and spend the evening at home . . . but if you want to hear singing that will make the blood pound in your pulse, listen to the brown bomber of sophisticated song at Mona's Club 440. Her name is Gladys Bentley and she's as gifted with the piano keys as with her vocal cords."[49] Bentley's ability to "make the 440 Club famous" depended on her high-spirited cross-gender performance, but she also fit in on Broadway, where voyeuristic sex- and race-tourism grew popular in the post-Prohibition era.[50]

Sex tourism and the spectacle of gender transgression remained central to Mona's popularity. In fact, sex tourism—an entertainment culture built on the promise of sex and/or sexualized amusements—underscored the emergence of publicly visible queer subcultures in San Francisco's North Beach district. For instance, San Francisco's long-lasting female impersonator club, Finocchio's, was a speakeasy during Prohibition, and entertainers often sold dances to men for the price of a couple of drinks. A culture of prostitution grew inside the club. While this was not true of Finocchio's, many speakeasies even had rooms that rented by the hour. With the criminalization of prostitution and the closure of legitimate brothels, sex workers often found their livelihood in clubs that sold sex on the side. As a tourist economy developed in San Francisco, however, an underground sex trade blossomed around the city's extralegal bars and taverns. With the repeal of Prohibition in 1933, places like Finocchio's worked to both legitimize their business and retain the tourist appeal of sexualized entertainment. Mona's functioned in a similar way. Cross-dressed entertainers allowed Mona's to maintain a lawful yet titillating atmosphere, and Mona's, like Finocchio's, became popular with local artists, queers, and a steady tourist clientele. In fact, in the post-Prohibition years, when Finocchio's advertised itself as the place "Where Boys Will Be Girls," Mona's marketed itself as the place "Where Girls Will Be Boys." Advertisements opened Finocchio's and Mona's to queer society, but they also brought in tourists eager to experience the world of sex and gender transgression.

On the late-nineteenth-century vaudeville stage, male impersonators were never as popular as female impersonators, and the theatrical tradition of male impersonation is much less developed. Theater historian Laurence Senelick attributes this disparity to the infringement on patriarchal right that male impersonation suggested.[51] Still, through the 1930s and 1940s, as gender norms tightened and heterosexuality became ever more compulsory, tourists in San Francisco sought out entertainments that played out their fantasies of the topsy-turvy world where women looked and acted like men. "That's what people would come to see," Mona Sargent remembers, noting the fascination tourists had with her waitresses. "They'd say, 'That's not really a girl.' I'd say, 'Yes it is.'"[52] Kay Scott, one of Mona's regular performers, was slight and boyish-looking—a liminal and intriguing presence. The success of Mona's rested on this intrigue, and Mona Sargent encouraged tourists to interact with her transgender entertainers. In fact, she exploited their liminal status. "Go talk to Kay," she prodded a customer one night:

> I'd say, "No, I'll tell you what . . . take her in the back room, and if you can prove to me [that Scott's a boy] I'll give her five dollars." I'd hand her a twenty-dollar bill or something like that. They'd say, "That's alright," but I'd say, "You better know what you're talking about." So I'd say, "Kay, come here. . . . He doesn't think you're a girl. We're going in the back room." We went in the back room, [and] Kay took down her pants and says, "I'm a girl." So he hands her twenty bucks and says, "I didn't mean any harm. I just had to know."[53]

Kay Scott's body and bodies like hers thus became part of a tourist economy that supported the emergence of publicly visible lesbian cultures. Bodily difference and a social fascination with sex- and gender-transgression sustained San Francisco's North Beach entertainment district through the war years. Mona's, Finocchio's, the Condor Club, the Forbidden City, and other popular nightclubs marketed voyeuristic or interactive experiences where tourists could experiment with new social realities or sexual fantasies.[54]

At the same time that transgender and gay entertainment became part of San Francisco's tourist economies, race tourism and a fascination with the culturally exotic began to generate its own tourist trade.[55] Chinatown, in particular, underwent a radical public transformation in the early twentieth century. From the passage in 1882 of the Chinese Exclusion Act until its repeal in 1946, Chinatown functioned as a ghetto prison, a racially segregated area that also served as a refuge from the violence of California's anti-Chinese policies and practices. Sequestered within a few square blocks of San Francisco, bordered by Broadway, Stockton, California, and Kearny Streets, Chinatown was a city unto itself.[56] To outsiders, it was best known for its prostitution houses, gambling operations, and opium dens—and the anti-vice raids that netted high-volume arrests.[57] By the turn of the century, however, sightseers began to enter Chinatown for "a firsthand glimpse at Oriental depravity."[58] At the same time, Chinese merchants began to capitalize on the increasingly steady flow of tourists into their neighborhood. Restaurants and bars featuring American inventions like "chop-suey" became more common, and the Chinese Chamber of Commerce worked to insure the safety of visitors. As art historian Anthony Lee observes, "A whole subculture of abjection was constructed in order to naturalize the increasing commodification of an ethnic neighborhood and culture."[59] By 1939, real-estate developers had transformed Chinatown's central avenue into a block-long entertainment district, lavishly decorated with pagoda-style towers that safely marked the district's entrance and exit: "When fireworks herald the coming of the Chinese new year . . . the casual visitor to Cameron Alley will find neither the barred windows nor the triple-thick doors which gave so much trouble to the vice squads of an earlier generation, but instead, a Chinatown lifted bodily out of the past, replete with the color and glamour of old days, but sans the forbidding aspects. . . . Visitors will be cordially welcomed by the management, which is reminding everybody that the 'open door' policy will be in effect."[60]

By the late 1930s, when sex-tourist clubs drew the attention of San Francisco's nascent tourist industry, Chinese-style entertainment drew tourists to stylish cocktail lounges like the Jade Palace, Li Po's, and Charlie Low's Forbidden City. Li Po's, on Grant Street, marketed itself as an informal but exotic cocktail lounge: "Love, passion, and nighttime . . . what a combination! You find all three any evening you stroll into the jovial and informal Chinatown cocktail lounge, the Li Po. You twine your fingers around a 'Shanghai Love,' and presently you are tasting passion fruit and other delectable ingredients that go into this drink sensation. Peter Wong keeps you in a mirthful mood with his extraordinary Chinese versions of Irish songs."[61] Forbidden City, however, was a spectacular supper club with a "sensational all-star Chinese floor show" featuring vaudeville-style dancers, singers, and a "modern Chinese orchestra."[62] Like Li-Po's, Forbidden City combined western entertainments with what it called "authentic" and "Oriental" culture. The place boasted a "lavishly beautiful lobby, which is ornate with idols in niches, ancient Chinese urns, and rich, silken hangings. Incense burning in Oriental braziers adds to the exotic atmosphere. In the dining room, which is glorified by novel indirect lighting effects, are ancient embroidered tapestries brought from China."[63] But Forbidden City also lured tourists with the promise of sexualized entertainments: "The all-new show is titled 'Orient 66' and features a bevy of Oriental cookies, Kaouri—exotic dancing star from Japan, and the sensational act of Karnak and the 'Girl on the Sword.'"[64] Popular with locals, tourists, and, later, military personnel, the Forbidden City's combination of sex and race tourism attracted a significant queer clientele. In fact, San Francisco native Merle Woo remembers that lesbians of color often frequented Forbidden City in the 1950s.[65]

The marketing of Chinatown to white tourists signaled the beginning of a new era of racial exploitation, one in which cultural difference became a valuable, even protected commodity to the city. This is best exemplified by the construction of San Francisco's extravagant Golden Gate International Exposition.[66] Architects worked for two years (1936–1938) to build pavilions modeled on what they called a Pacific Basin theme, an amalgam of Mayan, Incan, Malaysian, and Cambodian cultural references. Anticipating, perhaps, California's dominance of Pacific Rim economies in the late twentieth century, the exposition featured images and attractions meant to introduce Pacific Island and Latin American cultures to California and the West. As one review of the exposition noted, "Around the central fountain the designers had placed more than a dozen thick-limbed, pouty-lipped statues—Indian women hunkering over stone metates, Tehuantepec boys riding alligators, Inca girls playing flutes, Polynesians strumming ukuleles and other characteristic denizens of the Pacific Basin. Chunky, sleek and imperturbable, these statues epitomized the style of the Exposition."[67]

World's fairs like the Golden Gate International Exposition were popular in the United States through the early twentieth century, and many large American cities hosted them—not simply to attract tourists (and revenue), but to showcase the city's natural resources and summertime entertainments. San Francisco's 1939 fair celebrated the completion of its architectural marvel, the Golden Gate Bridge, but it followed in the tradition of earlier fairs in that it projected a panoply of sexualized and racialized imagery. Sally Rand's "Nude Ranch," for instance, featured a score of women who pitched horseshoes and swung lariats in G-strings while tourists peeked at them through glass panels. The fair also featured ethnic festivals, racialized entertainments, and an architectural style that foregrounded cultural difference. San Francisco's Golden Gate International Exposition fed the city's growing tourist economy not simply because it attracted tourists from afar, but because it stimulated a market for sex and race tourism within the city. As a result, neighborhoods with distinct racial or cultural qualities, like Chinatown and North Beach, became revenue-netting attractions for the city. In fact, in 1936 Pardee Lowe quipped that Chinatown had become "the chief jewel in San Francisco's starry diadem of tourist attractions."[68]

Sex tourism was therefore a primary factor in the emergence of San Francisco's publicly visible queer communities, and race tourism was its constant companion. Sex and race tourism functioned as two sides of the same coin, often working to enhance and bolster the other's appeal. Racialized entertainers like the dancing girls at Charlie Low's Forbidden City projected a highly sexualized style, and transgender entertainers at places like Finocchio's and Mona's often staged racialized performances. At Mona's, the performers were often either gender-transgressive or non-white women who performed for mostly white audiences. But while clever parodies or sultry melodies sustained the careers of white entertainers like Kay Scott or Beverly Shaw, the "Latin star," Tina Rubio, made her mark with "Hawaiian war chants" and "warbles in Tahitian and Spanish as well as in U.S.A."[69] Rose O'Neal, a mixed-race dancer who performed with Gladys Bentley at Mona's through 1942, sparked interest as her liminal features—"a blonde 'colored' gal, if you please"—drew the attention of tourist reviews.[70] And while there's no doubt that tourists came to see Gladys Bentley's musical talents, her dark skin, mannish attire, brazen sexuality, and massive body accentuated her appeal. She provided a spectacle of racial, gender, sexual, and bodily difference. "Gladys Bentley's wrestling matches with the piano are as exciting to watch as to hear when the 440 Club's famous sepia pianist lets herself go on the keyboard. And when she sings . . . no wonder they call her 'the brown bomber of sophisticated song.'"[71]

The reception and social function of sex and race tourism is difficult to untangle. The anthropology of tourism suggests that sexual and racial or ethnic entertainments function as hegemonic texts for white or western tourists who seek meaning and bring authenticity to their own lives through experiencing cultural practices beyond their own life sphere.[72] Sex and race tourism, as a result, can solidify social and sexual boundaries rather than break them down. In the case of Mona's, while sexually and racially exotic entertainments provided tourists with new experiences, the spectacle of difference might reassure audiences of the normalcy or naturalness of whiteness and/or heterosexuality.[73] At the same time, through double entendre and the coded display of queer culture, lesbian and transgender entertainers modeled queer representations for the bar's queer clientele.[74] Performances at Mona's that mixed racial, gender, and sexual transgression depended on a complex layering of social needs and identifications—they stabilized some social boundaries while they destabilized others.

Sex and race tourism generated a great deal of revenue for the city. A 1940 report by an organization called Californians Inc. noted that in 1939 tourists spent over $15 million in the Bay Area, an increase of 123 percent over 1938. The increase in tourism was attributed to the 1939 Golden Gate International Exposition, and Californians Inc. lobbied business leaders to fund a campaign to draw even more tourism to the San Francisco Bay Area. "The record infusion of tourist money into this part of the state was reflected in a higher level of business here . . . than obtained elsewhere in the country," John F. Forbes, president of Californians Inc., reported.[75]

With business interests cognizant of the benefits of a healthy tourist economy, San Francisco's tourist industry wrapped a layer of protection around clubs like Mona's that obviously catered to a tourist clientele. While tourism altered the function of queer culture and community, the success of early tourist clubs identified a market for queer entertainments and encouraged other queer clubs to open. By the late 1940s, several new lesbian and gay nightspots clustered just off Broadway's tourist strip. Tom Arbulich's Paper Doll, for example, quickly became a favorite spot. "That's where we all met and grew up," Charlotte Coleman remembers: "They had these big booths and you'd get there, there'd be two in a booth. And then all of a sudden they'd push people in and push people in with you. So after you went there every Friday night, you got to know everybody because everybody had to sit with each other. There wasn't any other seats. The men would sit at the bar, but the women sat in the booths. It was a wonderful way to meet people."[76]

Located just off Broadway, at Union and Grant, the Paper Doll was run by Arbulich from 1949 to 1956, when he sold it to Dante Benedetti, and it felt intimate and private to its lesbian and gay clientele.[77] Like the Black Cat, the Paper Doll became a "home-territory" bar—a bar where locals from the neighborhood gathered.[78] Not coincidentally, Mona Sargent helped Arbulich open the club—she "sort of turned it on as a gay bar," and both gay men and lesbians frequented the place.[79] After a while it became a supper club, where inexpensive meals were served and a dress code (for men) was strictly enforced: "slacks and a jacket, shirt and tie."[80] Still, the Paper Doll did not escape the notice of San Francisco's tourist reviews:

> If you are one of those old-fashioned sinners who thinks "gay" means "merry," you may disabuse yourself by spending an evening at The Paper Doll. This is a rendezvous of the Gay People. You'll see gay women who walk and talk like men and gay men who walk and talk like girls and often you'll find it hard to tell whether a gay man is a man or a gay woman is a woman because sometimes a gay woman cuts her hair like a man's and puts on men's clothes and looks more like a gay man than a gay woman and a gay man sometimes lets his hair grow and plucks his brows and puts on fawn slacks and looks more like a gay woman than a gay man and maybe they are both so anyway but it is very confusing what with gay boys calling each other bitches and gay girls calling each other joes.[81]

Even though the Paper Doll was located a few blocks off Broadway's main tourist strip and did not offer live entertainment, the spectacle of queer culture made it a popular, albeit offbeat, tourist spot.

Through the midcentury, as San Francisco's tourist economy began to embrace queer and transgender entertainments, many of the women who had participated in lesbian bar culture as waitresses and entertainers began to open their own bars and restaurants. In 1952, for example, Tommy Vasu opened Tommy's Place at 529 Broadway, and downstairs, connected by a stairwell, she ran another lesbian bar at 12 Adler Place.

Also in 1952, Ann Dee and Norma Clayton opened Ann's 440, replacing Mona's nightclub at 440 Broadway. Popular with lesbians and, later, the tourist trade, Clayton managed the bar while Dee brought in entertainers like Charles Pierce, Ray Bourbon, and, later, Johnny Mathis and Lennie Bruce.[82] In 1954, Connie Smith, who had previously waitressed at the Artist's Club (a divey straight-owned lesbian hangout in the late 1940s) began running Miss Smith's Tea Room, which she managed until 1960.[83] Located on Grant Avenue, it was called "dark and dreary" by the Daughters of Bilitis convention guide, but most visitors remembered it as a fun beer joint, a bohemian place, with sawdust on the floor.[84] In 1955, Lisa and Mike, two lesbian waitresses from Mona's and the Paper Doll, opened the Copper Lantern, just down the street from Miss Smith's Tea Room. The Copper Lantern was a supper club, a restaurant with a small stage, and in the mid-1960s go-go dancers performed there.[85] In 1958, Arlene Arbuckle's Anxious Asp opened on Green Street. Here, one customer remembers that the restrooms were "papered with [pages from] the Kinsey Report," and others remember it as "a true pillar of North Beach bohemia . . . with a mixed bag of patrons."[86] And in 1958, with the retirement monies she received from the IRS after being fired for having homosexual associations, Charlotte Coleman opened the Front.[87] However, the first known lesbian-run establishments in San Francisco were bars, like Tommy's 299, that served lesbians, prostitutes, and their clientele.

LESBIANS AND PROSTITUTES

Lesbians and prostitutes share a common place in American society. Through the post–World War II era, both were configured as outsiders or fallen women because they did not adhere to society's prescriptions for appropriate female gender roles or sexuality. For instance, neither lesbians nor prostitutes confined their sexuality to monogamous heterosexual marriage, and both occupied public space in ways that marked their difference. The ideological connection between lesbians and prostitutes has a much longer history, however, a history grounded in scientific notions of sexual difference. Sexologists at the turn of the twentieth century searched, classified, and codified the bodies of lesbians and prostitutes, looking for physical clues to their sexual difference.[88] Later, eugenicists, social scientists, and journalists traced the moral disintegration of society to what they understood to be the evident physical degeneration of lesbian and prostitute bodies.[89] Other texts linked lesbians to prostitutes through metaphors of infection and disease. Richard von Krafft-Ebing, the turn-of-the-century German psychiatrist, advised that one common source of "acquired" lesbianism was prostitutes who, "disgusted with the intercourse with perverse and impotent men . . . seek compensation in the sympathetic embrace of persons of their own sex."[90] In this view, prostitutes functioned to pollute society, drawing "sympathetic" women to them with their overt sexual nature. The mid-century work of popular journalist Jess Stern tells this story from a different angle. Stern's exposé of U.S. postwar lesbian life describes many lesbians' tragic fall into prostitution, as if lesbianism were a slippery slope, a path toward greater and greater socio-sexual transgression.[91] Through a history of pseudo- and social-science literature, lesbian prostitutes have also become a familiar icon in popular culture. Lesbian prostitutes riddle postwar pulp novels, film noir, and hippie-era "swing" literature, which depicted combinations of sexual perversions in order to increase sales. One "true" sex story of the day confides that for most prostitutes "johns don't mean a thing" and "most of the girls . . . take their kicks from other girls."[92] Recurring images of lesbian degeneracy and sexual excess cemented an association between lesbians and prostitutes in both pseudo-scientific literature and popular culture.

In the postwar years, female sexuality came under heightened scrutiny, and the idea of lesbianism as a social problem—something that could be addressed and contained—grew in the popular imagination. As Elaine Tyler May explains, the postwar threat of nuclear annihilation sparked the development of national policies that influenced new social and sexual standards. National security, at least on the domestic front, seemed to depend on the solidification of masculine authority and the stability of heterosexual families.[93] The regulation and control of fe male sexuality thus became an important aspect of "social containment" in cold war America, and lesbians and prostitutes suffered new levels of stigma and social control. As historian Donna Penn notes, "The very essence of the lesbian, like the prostitute, was an expression of uncontained female sexuality."[94] The stigma of lesbianism as a kind of sexuality out of control grew in popular culture, and postwar lesbian and feminist organizations strove to unhinge the historical connections between lesbianism, prostitution, and sexual deviance. As a result, the history of lesbians and prostitutes and the relationships between them are difficult to untangle. In the 1970s, as historians and activists worked to dissolve the image of lesbians as promiscuous, oversexed, conquering, or sexually aggressive, the historical relationships between lesbians and prostitutes were denied. As a result, despite a wealth of evidence and images, the social history of the relationships between lesbians and prostitutes remains for the most part undocumented.[95]

In San Francisco's North Beach district, prostitutes and lesbians shared a common turf. Through the nineteenth century, prostitutes occupied public space, sustained tourist economies, and resisted police harassment in ways that lesbians would later follow. Indeed, San Francisco's history of prostitution foreshadows the ways lesbians in the city began to use and fight for public space. Prostitutes, for example, were San Francisco's first female entrepreneurs, and prostitution remained central to San Francisco's economic development from the Gold Rush through the turn of the century. One historian notes that San Francisco's sex trade "began in the same entrepreneurial spirit" as San Francisco's Gold Rush.[96] Working to make a quick profit in a gender-imbalanced society, women sold their bodies as sexual capital as soon as Gold Rush migrants had money to spend. The earliest migrant gold diggers were Chileans and Peruvians, who, because of their proximity, reached California's gold first. As a result, the original "prostitutes' colony" in San Francisco emerged on the slopes of Telegraph Hill, in Chiletown, where Chilean, Peruvian, and Mexican migrants settled.[97] Later, Anglo-American, Chinese, and European women entered the sex trade, working in different districts, and with their profits many women moved from selling sex to managing brothels or "bawdy houses."[98] "Madams" or female brothel-keepers who ran their businesses profitably often brought in more cash than their gold-digging patrons.[99] The wealth of capital that prostitution generated, however, quickly spread beyond prostitutes and madams to landlords, police racketeers, traders, and tavern owners. Historian Lucie Cheng Hirata argues that the "free-capital" years—in which prostitutes netted the bulk of the profit from their labor—were short, and with time, prostitutes, particularly Chinese prostitutes, became more vulnerable to sex-trade exploitations.[100]

Through the late nineteenth century, anti-prostitution law in California overlapped with the state's anti-immigration policies. In 1882, partly as an effort to control Chinese prostitution, California lobbyists successfully convinced the U.S. Congress to pass the Chinese Exclusion Act prohibiting Chinese migration into the United States. By 1910, Japanese immigration had also been curtailed, and in that same year, in an effort to halt "white slavery" and curb prostitution, Congress passed the Mann Act, prohibiting the transportation of women across state borders for "immoral" purposes. Ostensibly created to protect white women's sexual virtue, the Mann Act was also a response to the shifting racial and ethnic composition of many American cities in the early twentieth century.[101] Anti–"white slavery" and anti-prostitution legislation became important political tools in a rapidly changing society where non-white populations and women gained economic footing and social autonomy through the new socioeconomic conditions brought on by industrialization. Indeed, when the Red Light Abatement Act was passed in California in 1913, its policies addressed much more than the social problem of organized prostitution; they also addressed the issues of racial mobility, miscegenation, and female sexual autonomy.[102]

With red light abatement laws on the books, prostitution did not end in San Francisco; instead, it began to function illegally. As brothels closed, prostitutes gathered in bars, taverns, or nightclubs, securing patrons through informal means. Sex work shifted from being something conducted at publicly visible business sites to being a clandestine activity with secret, ever-changing networks of information and protection. As a result, prostitutes began to function as an outlaw society, and local police engineered a number of ordinances to restrict their movements and their use of public space.[103] Prostitutes were most commonly arrested under California Penal Codes 647(b), for "prostitution," and 650½, for "outraging public decency," but a number of local measures specifically restricted their use of bars and taverns.[104] For example, in the early 1940s and again in the mid-1950s, San Francisco police initiated a "war on vice," targeting prostitutes and B-girls—or "percentage girls"—who encouraged patrons to buy drinks and, later, received a percentage of the sales they generated. After 1954, the local police teamed up with the Alcoholic Beverage Control Board, which controlled liquor licenses, to pressure taverns to stop serving prostitutes.[105] San Francisco police also initiated a series of local ordinances directed at restricting women's use of bars and taverns. At different times, police instituted curfews and prohibited the sale of alcohol to women standing or sitting at a bar. They also prohibited female employees from pouring or serving alcohol unless they owned a percentage of the bar, and they prohibited female employees from accepting drinks from patrons.[106] While anti-prostitution sentiment was used to justify these ordinances, they restricted women's access to the alcohol and public space that taverns provided. In doing so, the ordinances affected all women who used bars, whether they were looking for relaxation, entertainment, or sexual liaisons. Because the criminalization of prostitution restricted women's use of public space, the harassment and policing of prostitutes can be seen as a method for the more general regulation and control of female economic autonomy and sexual agency.

As anti-prostitution legislation affected women's use of public space, it shaped and influenced the emergence of publicly visible lesbian cultures. Prostitutes adjusted to criminalization in the 1920s by forming subcultural networks for safety and protection. At the same time, lesbians moved from relative secrecy and isolation to greater public visibility in San Francisco's entertainment district. Thus, the social history of lesbians and prostitutes met at a crucial juncture in San Francisco's post-Prohibition North Beach. Through the 1930s, lesbians were beginning to claim territorial "ownership" of a few bars like Mona's, and lesbians, no doubt, learned from prostitutes how to use these spaces effectively. Like prostitutes, lesbians used bars and taverns to make sexual contacts, form associations, and protect themselves from the police. For both prostitutes and lesbians, the key to public safety was loyal bar management, and both sets relied on "straight" bartenders and bar owners to protect them from troublemakers and police.[107] Bar owners who profited from the sex trade discouraged hostile patrons from entering the bar. They spotted potential undercover cops, signaling prostitutes with coded messages. Bartenders also worked with sex workers by screening clients, providing information, or negotiating contact between prostitutes and their clientele.[108] Similarly, lesbian bars remained relatively safe only if the management protected lesbian clientele from hostile outsiders and police. Bar owners and "hostesses" screened patrons at the door; they signaled queer patrons when police entered the bar (by flashing the lights or abruptly changing the music); and they discouraged potentially hostile patrons by watering down their drinks, overcharging them, or ignoring their presence at the bar.[109]

Lesbians also took advantage of tourist district protections in ways long established by prostitutes. Prostitution, as one theorist argues, remained central to San Francisco's tourist industry because "the reputation of this city as an adult vacation spot rests on its adult entertainments."[110] It was to the city's economic advantage to allow a certain amount of prostitution to remain visible in tourist districts like North Beach. From the formation of its original Gold Rush colony to the popularity of Carol Doda's Condor Club in the late 1960s, North Beach, particularly Broadway, remained San Francisco's central sex district. Therefore, when lesbians began to congregate in bars on Broadway's tourist strip, they did so in a territory already marked by a long history of sex trade. Lesbians negotiated North Beach, its tourist industry protections as well as its periodic police crackdowns, in collusion with prostitutes. In fact, San Francisco's first lesbian-owned bar, Tommy's 299, was a site that both lesbians and prostitutes occupied.

Tommy Vasu ran Tommy's 299 from 1948 to 1952. Located at 299 Broadway, just around the corner from Gordon's Restaurant, the 299 had a hotel upstairs, the Firenze, and a bar downstairs.[111] Lesbians frequented the bar, as did the prostitutes who worked out of the hotel upstairs.[112] Vasu herself became something of a mythical character—"She dressed in a tie, kept her hair short and went with hookers," one narrator recalls. She also owned a parking lot on Broadway near Columbus, "ran around with gangsters, and drove a Cadillac convertible."[113] Herb Caen remembers her as "the short-haired, long-tempered girl named Tommy who runs the best parking lot on B'way in North Beach—a gentleman among ladies."[114] Tommy's 299 became a site on Broadway where the connection between lesbians and prostitutes materialized. In June 1949, when the bar was raided by San Francisco's sex detail, eight women were arrested on vagrancy charges.[115] At Tommy's 299, lesbians and prostitutes forged a public space and shared an outlaw culture.[116]

Blanco's, another club that operated through the late 1940s and early 1950s, also found itself home to a number of lesbian sex workers. Blanco's was located on Kearny near Columbus and Jackson, in what was San Francisco's Manilatown. Manilatown was a three-square-block bachelor community of up to 10,000 Filipino laborers who lived in residential hotels and frequented the many bars and restaurants of the neighborhood.[117] Kay Blanco, the owner's daughter, tended bar at Blanco's, and, according to an oral history with Reba Hudson, "a lot of gay people hung around there because Kay condoned it."[118] A rougher set of dykes or "mannish lesbians" patronized Blanco's "because most of them went with hookers, and that's where the hookers were."[119] But many of the dykes were also selling sex. As Reba Hudson remembers, "the ones that we regarded as dykes that were very masculine and had tattoos and dressed in men's clothing, habitually were . . . hookers."[120] Because the 1934 Tydings-McDuffie Act restricted Filipino immigration into the United States, Filipino communities in California remained at their pre-1934 gender imbalance of fourteen men to every woman. This sex ratio imbalance within the Filipino community encouraged prostitution (as was the case with mid-nineteenth-century Chinese prostitution), and a number of white women and men worked alongside Asian women and men as prostitutes in San Francisco's Manilatown through the 1940s and 1950s.[121]

The existence of lesbian cross-sex and cross-race prostitution at Blanco's highlights the ways in which queer sexual practice both reflects and complicates sexism and racism in the larger society. Throughout California's history, public officials alternately condoned and condemned Asian prostitution as either a necessary part of maintaining a cheap male immigrant labor pool—wives were discouraged from immigrating because the development of families would foster more permanent Asian communities—or evidence of Asian unassimilability, which rationalized restricted Asian immigration.[122] As prostitution served to negotiate an economically driven state agenda that manipulated systems of race and gender around immigration policy, it was also the site where hierarchies of power and the relationships between class, race, and gender played themselves out on a local level. In the United States, cross-race prostitution generally ran in one direction, especially during wartime, when an abundance of white servicemen flocked to local prostitutes within communities of color.[123] So for Asian and white lesbians, particularly "mannish" or masculine lesbians, to sell sex to men at mixed-race queer bars like Blanco's, the meanings of both race and gender demanded renegotiation. Cross-race sex challenged California's anti-miscegenation laws, and lesbian involvement in a cross-gender sex trade challenged emerging notions of lesbian sexuality. Complex interactions like these evidence a dynamic interplay between race, sex, and gender at the local level that, like sex tourism and race tourism, functioned to both reiterate and challenge racial and sexual boundaries.

In a world with few options for women to pursue economically independent lives, the life choices lesbians and prostitutes made for themselves—to live outside the law in order to maintain a semblance of sexual and, perhaps, economic autonomy—often bound them to a highly structured and regulated subcultural society. But prostitutes did not simply teach lesbians how to negotiate public space and protect themselves from police harassment; many prostitutes had lesbian lovers, and many lesbians worked in the sex trade. In her path-breaking article on the historical connection between lesbians and prostitutes, Joan Nestle traces a history of sexual relationships between lesbians and prostitutes. She concludes that prostitutes, "the first policed community of outlaw women," often found their most intimate connections with other women.[124] San Francisco's history reveals that it was not uncommon for lesbians to work in the sex trade. Marilyn Braiger, in an oral history interview, remembered a fem prostitute who used her income to support a butch lover: "I knew a couple, two women, who lived together, but one, the hooker, was supporting the other one. They had a very definite role-playing kind of situation. The one she was supporting was definitely the butch, and she [the hooker] was definitely the fem although she was bringing in all the money." [125] Charlotte Coleman, who at one point shared a flat with a prostitute, remembers that prostitutes sometimes took lesbians for lovers on their day off. "I guess you'd have to say they were bisexual. On their days off they preferred a lesbian, that kind of stuff." [126] In another oral history interview, Cheryl Gonzales also remembered meeting lesbians who worked in the sex trade: "I met a woman that was a prostitute. She had women that pimped for her. I met all kinds of women." [127] Others, like Rikki Streicher and her close friend "Nicki," worked for a brief time in the mid-1940s as "pimps" for their fem lovers who sold sex to the sailors and stevedores who frequented Broadway's queer bars, and Reba Hudson remembered that bar owner Tommy Vasu managed the sex work of a number of her girlfriends while running Tommy's 299.[128] Lesbian entrepreneurs like Vasu were able to open bars and taverns from the capital they garnered in the sex trade. Like the cross-dressing entertainers who worked at Mona's and later opened their own nightclubs, policed women like Vasu manipulated the laws and cultural practices that restricted their behavior to build economic resources and expand the public space available to lesbians in San Francisco.

The social relations prostitutes and lesbians shared often extended to their legal status. In times of political repression—such as the McCarthy era, when law-and-order candidates struck a chord with voters—lesbian bars came under heightened scrutiny. As they did, their patrons were harassed, policed, and prosecuted on the same terms as prostitutes. The raid on Kelly's, also known as the Alamo Club, illustrates this dynamic. Kelly's opened in the early 1950s on Fulton Street, and by the mid-1950s it had become a lesbian hangout. On Friday, 21 September 1956, the police raided Kelly's, and thirty-four women were arrested on charges of "frequenting a house of ill repute," an anti-prostitution ordinance to which all but four women pleaded guilty.[129] It is curious that the women arrested, most of whom were probably not working as prostitutes at the time, pleaded guilty to charges related to prostitution. Del Martin, vice president of San Francisco's lesbian civil rights organization, the Daughters of Bilitis, explained their motivation in a 1956 editorial on Kelly's. She argued that because lesbians too often saw themselves as sexual outlaws, they did not think to challenge the prostitution charges brought against them. "There is a marked reaction of fear and retrenchment among the Lesbian population of San Francisco after the recent raid [at] Kelly's," she observed. In a subsequent oral history interview, Martin reiterated the fact that the police liberally applied anti-prostitution charges to the lesbians arrested at Kelly's. "When they [lesbians] were caught up in a raid, they would plead guilty. Well, what were they pleading guilty to?[130] In other words, whether or not it was legal to be homosexual in San Francisco (a topic addressed in the next chapter), the officers who arrived at Kelly's confused lesbians with prostitutes and used a history of anti-prostitution law to regulate and control lesbian space.

THE RAID ON TOMMY'S PLACE

In the 1950s, lesbian society evolved in the context of cold war ideologies that asserted the stability of rigidly defined gender roles and the containment of female sexuality to heterosexual marriage.[131] The uncontained or aggressive sexuality projected on lesbian bodies rendered lesbians a threat to the stability of heterosexual families, in that because (most) lesbians were not safely ensconced in families and producing children, their sexual transgression implied the breakdown of the family unit and the corruption of minors. The 1954 raid on Tommy's Place, a lesbian bar in San Francisco's North Beach district, illustrates this dynamic and highlights the vulnerabilities of San Francisco's lesbian communities in the postwar era. Not only were publicly visible lesbian communities based in the bars—and thus associated with alcohol and drug abuse—but as lesbian culture crystallized around cross-gender performance and entertainment, the very foundation of this culture seemed to threaten the delicate social fabric constructed by McCarthy-era politics.

After Tommy's bar at 299 Broadway closed down, Tommy Vasu and Jeanne Sullivan opened Tommy's Place at 529 Broadway, just down the street. At Tommy's Place, Vasu and her coterie of lesbian bartenders, waitresses, and performers continued to attract a mixed crowd of artists, queers, prostitutes, and local bohemians. Around the corner and downstairs was 12 Adler Place, another popular lesbian hangout and, as one bar guide exclaims, "one of the bastions of bohemianism."[132] Tommy's Place and 12 Adler Place were in many ways the same nightclub; they shared a single liquor license and the same building, and they were connected inside by a split-level mezzanine. "You could sit up there on the mezzanine and kind of watch people down below or across the way," one patron remembers.[133] The fact that one could enter the bar at different addresses and access interior space voyeuristically gave an air of mystery and excitement to the place. Inside the bar, different groups inhabited different spaces, and "most of the women" congregated downstairs.[134] At Tommy's Place, tables for two lined both walls, a bar seating fifteen or so patrons crowded the far corner, and framed photos and large posters of women decorated the walls. The club at 12 Adler Place was a smaller and darker space; it was the place where butch and fem lesbians interacted, or, as one woman remembers, while most of the women dressed in slacks and wore their hair short, "I learned to tell which were fems and which were butch."[135] From 1952 to 1954, Tommy's Place and 12 Adler Place opened up a large and centrally located venue for the emergence of lesbian and transgender cultures. In 1954, however, at the height of McCarthy-era policing, these bars became the focus of a citywide scandal and an ensuing U.S. Senate subcommittee investigation that ultimately shut the place down and put two of Tommy's bartenders on trial.

As in other large cities in the United States during the McCarthy era, civic leaders made sporadic attempts, especially during election time, to rid San Francisco of vice, and the policing of sex and sexuality became an important part of the San Francisco Police Department's mission. Between 1951 and 1957, SFPD annual reports distinguish between rape, prostitution, and sex offenses. "Sex offenses" was a new category and a catchall phrase for nonviolent sex-related crimes. It included contributing to the delinquency of a minor, indecent exposure, obscene literature, lewd and indecent acts, and sex perversion. In San Francisco, the annual number of persons charged with sex offenses did not significantly increase through the 1950s, but there was a jump in 1954, the year Tommy's Place was raided.[136] Because of national trends and a rhetoric connecting homosexuality to violent crimes, sex offenses related to homosexuality became a predominant concern for city officials.

While local police units beefed up their departments, parents were encouraged to take special measures to curtail the danger "perverts" posed to their children. And in 1957, in an open letter from the director of the FBI, J. Edgar Hoover encouraged U.S. teenagers to follow a series of friendly, fatherly tips. His advice responded to "the sex-crime headlines in the newspapers today" that "worry everyone with any decency." In a full-page bulletin instructing readers to "clip out these rules and save," ten tips advise teenagers to notify parents about any pornographic pictures or literature being passed around their communities, because "obscene reading matter is a favorite habit of the degenerate"; to stay away from lovers' lanes because "experience shows that 'Lovers' Lanes' are favorite haunts of sex criminals"; and to remain within calling distance at picnics because "sex criminals are easily attracted to any group of young people." [137] In this way Hoover strategically refocused the concerns of an anxious generation away from nuclear annihilation and toward the perception that violent sex crimes (i.e., rape) were connected to homosexuality, prostitution, and the corruption of minors.[138]

As part of this phenomenon, in June 1954 the *Examiner,* one of San Francisco's daily newspapers, published a series of threatening articles that claimed "a marked influx recently of homosexuals" into San Francisco. Using metaphors of infection and disease, one article stressed that homosexuals "prey upon the unfortunate weaknesses of others. They prey upon teen-agers." [139] A follow-up editorial demanded that police move in to clean up San Francisco's "unwholesome" condition: "The condition is marked by the increase of homosexuals in the parks, public gathering places and certain taverns in the city. It is a bad situation. It is a situation that has resulted in extortion and blackmail. Even worse, these deviates multiply by recruiting teen-agers." [140]

Michael Gaffey, San Francisco's chief of police, announced that he would start a drive to "clean the homosexuals from the streets, the public rooms and the parks where their actions have become intolerably offensive." [141] Teaming up with the district attorney's office and lauded by the grand jury, Gaffey continued to pressure homosexual nightspots, claiming "the drive . . . will be gradually enlarged to include all known spots where the homosexuals congregate." [142] In July of 1954, the Armed Forces Disciplinary Control Board (AFDCB) joined forces with the SFPD and moved against five San Francisco taverns "suspected of being frequented by sex deviates": the Crystal Bowl, Lena's Burger Basket, the 1228 Club, Kip's, and the Rocket Club. These Tenderloin district clubs, frequented by prostitutes and homosexuals, were ordered "off limits" to military service personnel unless conditions improved. The *Examiner* applauded the SFPD and the AFDCB's efforts, noting that both organizations relied on uniformed and undercover police surveillance as well as periodic raids.[143] Thus, when Tommy's Place was raided on 8 September 1954, it was part of a much larger police agenda. Because the arrests involved a handful of underage girls, the event escalated into a multifaceted investigation into juvenile delinquency that fleshed out the ostensible connection between organized "sex deviates" and the corruption of minors.[144]

"Repercussions were swift yesterday following the smashing of a narcotics and sex 'thrill' ring which had enmeshed teen-age girls here," begins an *Examiner* report on the raid at Tommy's Place.[145] A front page article reiterated "the growing, unwholesome sexual deviate problem in San Francisco," while an editorial in the same edition charged Police Chief Gaffey with conducting a lackadaisical and ineffectual campaign against homosexuals.[146] The coverage linked the corruption of minors to drug abuse and homosexuality, charging that "teen-age girls were being recruited" by homosexuals, and "sex deviates have used drugs, including barbiturates and benzedrine, to make youngsters in the 14–15 age group more pliable."[147] Civic response to such inflammatory reports was swift: local chapters of the PTA (Parent-Teacher Association) demanded police protection; Police Chief Gaffey directed the vice squad to "move in on sexual deviates"; the State Board of Equalization filed charges to revoke the liquor license for Tommy's Place; the district attorney considered abatement proceedings to immediately close the bar; the San Francisco County Grand Jury initiated an investigation "into the sexual deviate problem"; and a United States Senate subcommittee investigating juvenile delinquency took up the case.[148]

The case involved a dozen high school girls who "donned mannish clothes and frequented pool halls."[149] After a couple of concerned parents reported their daughter's behavior to San Francisco's juvenile bureau, a five-month investigation led police to the home of Mr. Jesse Joseph Winston on Telegraph Hill and, one week later, to Tommy's Place. The young women had reported that they frequented Tommy's, where they bought each other drinks, purchased Benzedrine tablets, and "met older women who were sex deviates." There they also met Winston who allegedly invited them to his plush Kearny Street apartment for after-hours entertainment. Here, according to policeman Russell Woods, Winston taught the girls to smoke marijuana, encouraged them to peddle Benzedrine, and schooled them in "sexual rebellion."[150] Tommy's Place thus served as a conduit that, according to journalistic accounts, fed innocent girls from good families into a "vice academy" run by Winston: "The bar, police said, has long served as a happy hunting ground for a group of adult debauchees, who recruited school girls into their academy of dope addiction and sexual perversion. 'At least a dozen' teen-age girls have been ensnared, according to Inspector L. G.

Etherington and taken from the bar to other places in the Latin Quarter for a full education in abominable practices."[151]

Front page news coverage with banner headlines such as "SCHOOLGIRLS' VICE, DOPE REVEALED IN S.F. BAR RAID" and "S.F. TEEN-AGE GIRLS TELL OF 'VICE ACADEMY'" pulled readers into a "white slavery" story that read like copy from early-twentieth-century scandal sheets. Front page photos of Winston, an African American man, accompanied lurid details that suggested the kidnapping and sexual exploitation of innocent white girls.[152] As the case deepened and journalists gained information about Tommy's, however, their stories moved away from the exploitation of racial anxieties to a fascination with the infectious nature of female homosexuality. As Officer Woods explains:

> The girls admitted frequenting a "gay" bar—one catering to sexual deviates. Some of the girls recruited others from among their school classmates. It started as a lark. Then some of the girls began wearing mannish clothing. They called themselves "Butches." Others, becoming sexual deviates, were the female counterparts and called themselves "Femmes." We found that the activity was centering in Tommy's Place. There were other "gay" bars in the vicinity, but they declined to cater to minors, preferring older women and tourists.[153]

The *Examiner*'s reports maintained that a "drug ring" was supplied through Fillmore Street taverns in the city's African American neighborhood, "which had long been under police surveillance as a hangout for narcotics peddlers and addicts," but civic response increasingly focused on Tommy's Place and maintained that "sex deviates" were the source of juvenile delinquency.

When police arrested Winston in his home on 1 September 1954, they found firearms and three marijuana cigarettes, two of them marked with lipstick. Winston was charged with contributing to the delinquency of a minor and giving narcotics to minors. When police raided Tommy's Place and 12 Adler Place, a week later, they found a hypodermic needle, an eyedropper, and a spoon hidden under the wash basin in the women's restroom. Two of the bar's owners, Grace Miller and Joyce Van de Veer, were arrested. Miller and Van de Veer worked as bartenders downstairs at 12 Adler Place, the part of the bar more popular with butch and fem lesbians. Later, they were charged with contributing to the delinquency of a minor. Another owner, Jeanne Sullivan, was not arrested, though her name and address were printed in newspaper accounts of the raid and ensuing trials.[154] Interestingly, because Tommy Vasu had been convicted of an earlier offense, her name was not listed on the bar's liquor license, and she was not arrested by police or cited in newspaper accounts, though many oral history accounts maintain her centrality to the bar.[155]

Reba Hudson, a longtime North Beach resident, remembers the raid on Tommy's Place with a roll of her eyes. "They were framed as part of this harassment of gay bars," she claims. "Two of her [Tommy's] bartenders were arrested. . . . One of them is a good friend of mine. She . . . did six months. They were accused of serving minors, and the girls *were* minors but they had forged IDs. It sort of escalated, and the PTA got involved. Then the police planted some drugs in the ladies' room, some heroin and the works or something like that, and then they pretended to find it. . . . The *Examiner* just ran with it. At that time it was a real sensational tabloid."[156] John Kiely, police captain and, in 1954, head of the SFPD Juvenile Bureau, agreed that the press coverage of the raid on Tommy's Place exaggerated the connections between drug abuse, homosexuality, and juvenile delinquency. "The press gives the public what they want to read," he commented, "but I think they have exploited it in this area beyond the actual danger that it is."[157]

The public trial of Tommy's Place sparked a citywide panic and intensified a police crackdown against homosexuals.[158] It also contributed to the reorganization of California's alcohol control administration. In response to the raid on Tommy's Place, George R. Reilly, chairman of the State Board of Equalization, California's tax and alcohol control board, asserted that liquor could be better regulated if state taxes and liquor licensing did not occupy the same agency. In order to quell public fears, he encouraged voters to approve California Proposition 3, a measure on the November ballot that would split the agency's responsibilities and allow an independent alcohol control board to better police the city's bars and taverns.[159]

Just after the raid on Tommy's Place, San Francisco played host to two investigations into juvenile delinquency, a San Francisco County Grand Jury investigation and a U.S. Senate subcommittee hearing. Both investigations, like J. Edgar Hoover's warnings, tied juvenile delinquency to "sex perversion." On 11 September 1954, Dr. Charles Ertola, foreman of the San Francisco County Grand Jury, called for an examination of the city's "sexual deviate problem," to much public attention and acclaim.[160] Later that month, however, the city's top juvenile authorities asserted at grand jury hearings that the city's juvenile delinquency problems were primarily a product of alcohol abuse rather than narcotics. Furthermore, the city's superintendent of schools testified that "the problem of sex perversion in the city's schools is not acute."[161] Juvenile authorities unaffiliated with the police or the alcohol control board did not agree with the grand jury's assertion that juvenile delinquency was a product of narcotic use or connected to the city's homosexual communities. A few weeks later, however, during the U.S. Senate subcommittee's prehearing, a spokesperson argued that in San Francisco "sex deviates" were "a big factor in juvenile delinquency and drug addiction."[162] The U.S. Senate subcommittee visited San Francisco on 4–5 October 1954, and the hearings were broadcast over local television. Through the proceedings, Senate prosecutors continued to tie sexual deviance to prostitution, drug use, and juvenile delinquency, despite San Francisco Grand Jury findings to the contrary. The questioning of Officer Wood, a San Francisco police investigator, by Mr. Bobo, a Senate aide, and the committee chairman reveals this dynamic:

Mr. Bobo: There are certain taverns that are drops for contraband narcotics brought into the country?

Officer Wood: In the cases last year we found two. . . .

Mr. Bobo: Was there any connection between prostitution and narcotics?

Officer Wood: Very definitely.

Mr. Bobo: Through the furnishing of narcotics, and so forth, they led these 15- to 18-year-old girls into prostitution?

Officer Wood: Yes, sir.

Mr. Bobo: Would you say that that is a very wide-spread condition, Mr. Wood?

Officer Wood: No . . . this year I just ran across one case.

Mr. Bobo: Were you on this raid of the so-called Tommy's Place?

Officer Wood: Yes, sir.

Mr. Bobo: How old were the girls involved in that particular case?

Officer Wood: That case is mixed up with the narcotic peddler we arrested.

The Chairman: Where is that, Mr. [Wood]?

Officer Wood: Broadway and Columbus.

The Chairman: Here in the city?

Officer Wood: Yes, sir.

Mr. Bobo: Were there narcotics found in this bar?

Officer Wood: No. We went in there with the idea of arresting two of the bartenders, female bartenders, whose names appeared on the license. While we searched the place, 2 officers found

2 complete narcotic outfits under the wash basin which included a tourniquet, dropper, needles. There was a white residue in the spoon. It was analyzed and it contained heroin.

The Chairman: How do you account for the fact that the place is still operating?

Officer Wood: That is the usual procedure.

The Chairman: Is that because of the procedure that was described here this morning by one of the witnesses?

Officer Wood: I did not hear that, sir. Usually they are out on appeal and it takes sometimes a year.

The Chairman: How long has this place been opened since this discovery was made?

Officer Wood: It has been about a month.

Mr. Bobo: Is it still run and operated by the same people operating it at the time of the raid?

Officer Wood: Yes, the two women are out on bail. I imagine they are still working there. . . .

Mr. Bobo: This was one of the many deviate bars in San Francisco?

Officer Wood: Yes, sir; there are.

Mr. Bobo: There are quite a few of those here?

Officer Wood: I don't know what you would call quite a few, but there are several that cater to the so-called gay people.

Mr. Bobo: Would it be 20?

Officer Wood: To my knowledge the places we checked for juveniles, about 8 or 9 that my partner and I usually checked on weekends.

Mr. Bobo: Do you find juveniles in these places?

Officer Wood: No; that is surprising. The girls fix themselves up, they may be juveniles, but they would fool anyone, but we know most of them from past experiences, and we do find those girls there once in a while, but they appear to be much older.

Mr. Bobo: Do you find minors other than juveniles, 18 to 21?

Officer Wood: Very seldom.[163]

Through 1954, the Senate Subcommittee on Juvenile Delinquency held hearings in Boston, Philadelphia, New York City, Denver, El Paso, Los Angeles, San Diego, and San Francisco, and the raid on Tommy's Place occurred just before the Senate hearings were to take place in San Francisco. The raid on Tommy's Place framed a relationship between homosexuality, drug use, prostitution, and juvenile delinquency that fit the senators' expectations. Despite consistent denial from local authorities, Senate hearings worked to scapegoat homosexuals; by doing so, they condoned and encouraged the continued harassment and persecution of lesbians and gay men in San Francisco.

While news coverage in the *Examiner* worked to sensationalize the raid on Tommy's Place, a fledgling homophile newsletter voiced the bar owners' concerns. Homophile coverage maintained that both Tommy's Place and 12 Adler Place ran drug-free establishments that were off-limits to teenagers. "The owners deny these charges," the Mattachine *Newsletter* reported in a short article. "They have forced strict identification rules and have not tolerated the presence of any suspected or known drug addicts."[164] The Mattachine Society became implicated in the case a couple of weeks later, when the Senate subcommittee connected "the organization of sexual deviates" to the raid on Tommy's Place. According to the *Examiner,* the San Francisco branch of the Mattachine Society was "one of the largest memberships in a nationwide organization of sexual deviates suspected of being a big factor in juvenile delinquency and drug addiction."[165] These allegations didn't pan out, however. Harold G. Robinson, chief criminal investigator for California's Attorney General, Edmund G. Brown, conceded that his office had been aware of the Mattachine Society for some time but had not connected it to juvenile delinquency or drug addiction. The district attorney maintained a similar line, stating that "I've seen a copy of the magazine it puts out. It was very arty, and there was nothing lewd in it."[166] Indeed, after the storm had passed, both the Senate subcommittee hearings and the San Francisco County Grand Jury found that although narcotics and liquor played a role in the city's juvenile delinquency problem, it was not connected with the Mattachine Society or attempts by "sex deviates" to organize into groups.[167]

Unfortunately, unlike the Mattachine Society, Jesse Winston and the women who ran Tommy's Place were more vulnerable to media hype and social recrimination. Jeanne Sullivan, Grace Miller, and Joyce Van de Veer, along with Winston, were unable to defend themselves from the kinds of lurid associations produced by McCarthy-era politics, and Tommy's Place and the 12 Adler were shut down. More importantly, a handful of young women found themselves publicly humiliated at hearings where they were encouraged to testify against the women who had welcomed them into a bar that supported their sexually unconventional and gender-transgressive behavior. For instance, a journalist for the *Chronicle* who covered the Tommy's Place hearings noted that at least one woman, an eighteen-year-old "brunette," was a "reluctant witness" who testified against the owners of Tommy's Place in order to avoid "going on trial herself as an adult."[168] Finally, two people, Grace Miller and Jesse Winston, served time in jail. Miller was convicted of serving alcohol to a minor and served six months in the county jail. Winston was convicted on three counts of furnishing marijuana to a minor and one count of possession of marijuana and was sentenced to a term of one to twenty years at San Quentin.[169] These prosecutions functioned to placate an anxious society eager to connect juvenile delinquency to drugs and homosexuality.

This chapter documents the emergence of a lesbian neighborhood or district in post-Prohibition San Francisco. It illustrates that lesbians did concentrate geographically, and through a culture of tourist entertainments, lesbians asserted a public presence in San Francisco's North Beach district. However, a close look at the nightclubs that supported the emergence of lesbian entertainments reveals, first, that lesbian visibility was often linked to the sexual entertainment cultures of male impersonation and prostitution and, second, that sexualized entertainments and sex tourism often overlapped with racialized entertainments and race tourism. As a result, lesbian public visibility was often tied to the exploitations of sex work and a voyeuristic tourist economy that commodified lesbian bodies and sustained, at times, the hegemony of both whiteness and heterosexuality. Still, the lesbian culture that emerged in bars and nightclubs through the midcentury in San Francisco is evidence of a resistance to postwar sex and gender normativity. Lesbians resisted postwar consumption by not buying into domesticity and sexual containment, and through the emergence of lesbian-owned bars such as Tommy's Place, lesbians manipulated their commodification to gain capital—both cultural and economic—that enabled the establishment of queer institutions beyond the exploitations of San Francisco's tourist cultures. The establishment of lesbian institutions (bars and restaurants) opened up the possibility of new life choices—choices made on the basis of a rejection of cold war domesticity and compulsory heterosexuality. As a result, lesbians who inhabited San Francisco's historic North Beach district negotiated a public presence that asserted a collective identity and thus a new engagement with the state. As the next chapter will reveal, the heightened group consciousness that gay men and lesbians secured in bars and taverns through the 1930s and 1940s enabled them to resist more forcefully the repressive policing and prosecutions of the 1950s.

ORAL HISTORY

Joe Baron

I arrived in San Francisco on August 1, 1954. Officially I was from Daytona Beach, Florida, but I had also lived in Gainesville and Miami. At that point, I had completed my military obligation, but I didn't want to go back to Florida. Most people from Florida either went to New York, Chicago, or Atlanta, but none of those alternatives were appealing to me. A friend of mine who was getting out of the service at the same time said, "I'm going to San Francisco, why don't you come with me?" So I went.

Later, I moved in with a bunch of guys who lived in a large house on Twin Peaks. We weren't all close friends, but we enjoyed each other's company. We went out to dinner together, and we went to the bars. For the "fuzzy sweater set," there were two bars. One of them was called Gordon's, and it was on the corner of Sansome and Broadway. It was a restaurant as well as a bar, and it was dressy, which meant that you wore a tie. Actually, there were very few bars where you didn't wear a tie. You were judged by the other people in the bar by the way you dressed, and if you didn't come, you know, appropriately dressed, you were more or less ignored. So, that was Gordon's. And then, up near what is now the Stockton-Sutter Garage, there was a very elegant bar known as Dolan's. It had a grand piano and chandeliers. At Dolan's, wearing a suit or a dressy sport coat with a tie was de rigueur. There was also a great big lofty second-floor place on Sutter Street called the Rendezvous. It was full of collegiate types and, again, people in ties. Ties there were optional, but if you came in wearing a T-shirt or a sports shirt or a sweater, it established you as a different, you know, a different group.

As I remember, there was a lot of very stylized, formal behavior where people introduced people to people. They did it in this very elaborate way, and if you didn't do it correctly people looked at you strangely. It was like the

Joe Baron (pseud.), interviewed by Nan Alamilla Boyd, tape recording, San Francisco, 21 July 1991 and 4 August 1991, Wide Open Town History Project, GLBT Historical Society. These interviews have been edited by the author.

queen's tea party. For instance, if you had a suspicion that somebody that you were thrown into proximity with was gay, you would start this whole ritualistic, coded kind of communication. If they picked up on it, you knew they were gay, and pretty soon you had this little secret society kind of conversation going. I had a friend who had a whole series of what he considered visual indexes of a gay person. For instance, if they wore a pinky ring; if they wore penny loafers—especially with a penny in them; if they drove convertibles with the top down. I mean, it was just absolutely absurd.

Once, though, I was arrested. It was either late '55 or early '56. I had met this guy in San Francisco from Los Angeles, and we clicked, so to speak, so I found myself driving to Los Angeles practically every weekend. This had been going on for several months. I was down there one weekend, and we went out for some drinks with some girls he knew. Gay girls. The scene was in this notorious place called the Red Raven, which I believe still exists. We were sitting at a table in the back of the room, and it was quite late. As a matter of fact, it was so late that they were saying last call. So I said, "Would anybody like a last drink?" I think one or two people allowed as how they would, so I went off to the bar to get the last drinks. It was very, very crowded. It was a Saturday night, and people were about three deep at the bar. I got the bartender's attention, called him over, and gave him my order. He mixed the drinks, and then he sort of handed them out to me. I say sort of because I couldn't get any closer to the bar than at least two bodies. So I lean forward, you know, to accept the drinks, and as I did so somebody groped me. It was dark and murky and crowded, and when I looked down, I saw the person who had done this with a shit-eating grin on his face. I said, irritated, "Do you mind?" At which point this other face appeared out of the gloom holding an LAPD badge, saying, "I saw that. You're under arrest." I said, "What in hell for?" And with that another badge and face appeared, saying, "Yes, and I saw it too." Without further ado, they said, "Now let's not make a fuss out of this, just come with us. Out." And I said, "Well I'm with friends, I can't just disappear. They'll be concerned. And one friend just happens to have my car." That didn't impress them in the least. They just led me out of this bar, into an unmarked cruiser, and off we went to the Hollywood substation.

They arrested me for, well, I don't know whether they arrested me for what I was charged with or whether they arrested me for something else. I was ultimately charged with "lewd vagrancy," which was the catchall thing in those days. Maybe it still is today. The Red Raven, I believe, was in Hollywood. So the police collect all these people and take them to the nearest substation. Then around dawn a truck comes and makes the rounds at all the substations to pick up all these wretches and take them to what used to be called Lincoln

Heights. There was a big county jail at Lincoln Heights. I don't know whether it's there anymore or not. I think it's been turned into a baseball stadium or something [laughs]. And so the big thing, the big thing—I'm trying to say something suspenseful—is that at one point somebody comes to the cell and says, "Do you want a bail bondsman?" The cliff-hanger was that if you didn't get action with a bondsman and a release before they transported you to Lincoln Heights, then there was no possibility of it. That's the way it supposedly went. So I said, "Yes I do."

They got me this real fun little gal who interviewed me to see if I was a good bonding risk or not. I said, "I'm from San Francisco," she said, "Well, that's not so good." I said, "I'm employed. I can pay the bonding fees." She said, "Well, we like to see something more tangible." I said, "I have a practically brand new car. I'll be very happy to sign it over as a security deposit, if you will." She said, "That's a possibility." Anyway, she sprang me. She also gave me the name of an attorney. The big fear was if you get convicted of, well, sexual misconduct, you become classified as a sexual deviant. You have to sign a deviant register, which is kept in the big book in Sacramento. The big book in the sky. And whenever there's any kind of a sex crime, anything that has sexual overtones to it, they go out and round up all the suspects on file. So that was just about the worst thing that could happen to you anytime. This is why it was important to keep your record clean and spend however much money it took to keep yourself off that register. Anyway, she got this attorney for me, Heller of Taylor, Sherman & Heller. They specialized in this kind of matter.

They were tough birds; they really were. Even the secretary in the office was a tough old bird. When I came into the office to see Heller, she said, "What happened, you get busted in the park?" And here I was so innocent. I felt so violated, you know. So he interviewed me and said, "Well, this is a pretty clear open and shut case. We do these things by the hundreds. We'll plead innocent, and we'll"—I forget what all he said, the legal jargon he used. He said, "The whole thing is to approach the right people." You know, in other words, cop a plea. They're just interested in getting a conviction of some sort, clearing their books, and being able to point to yet one more, you know, great service they have done to protect the public. So the plea that he dug up and which they bought was this old statute that's been on the books since the early Gold Rush days. Which said, in effect, that if you made unseemly noise and ran a horse race at night in the city limits, this was punishable by thus and such. So that's what I pled guilty to.

About six months later [back in San Francisco], I had a friend who was pretty wild. His m.o. was to go out and entice sailors to come up to his apartment. It was an obsession with him. We were out one night, carrying on, drinking and so on, and he spotted a sailor on the street who was ostensibly hitchhiking, which meant he was looking to be picked up. So we stopped and we picked him up. He allowed as how he was going up to the base in Vallejo. Mare Island was a big base in those days. Along the way my friend jumped in the back seat with the sailor, and they did a number. That didn't satisfy my friend, it just sort of spurred him on. It stimulated him. Oh, it was nuts because I was driving and the two of them were in the back seat, and this got me all sort of jittery. I was taking slugs out of a whiskey bottle as I was driving, you know, really smart stuff. This went on and on, and finally we dropped the sailor off. I think we took him to Vallejo and then we headed back to San Francisco. I dropped my friend off at his apartment, which was down in the Tenderloin. He had a good job with an insurance company, but he lived in this tacky part of town because lots of sailors frequented the Tenderloin for one reason or another, and it was very easy to pick them up. So he, not satiated by this experience, found two more sailors walking on Turk Street and invited them up to his apartment. And, um, you know, he allowed as to what he wanted to do with them and they very courteously but firmly declined. Said no. I don't know why they came with him in the first place, but who knows. Of course sailors—having been one—don't like to do compromising things in the presence of friends so that there's a witness to anything. They can keep it very cool. So I think this is why they refused. They didn't get nasty about it, you know, they just said, "Thanks a lot, but no thanks, and we're leaving now." So they went out, back on the street. My friend, again, now he's not only turned on but he's frustrated, so he's really wild. He goes out on the street in search of more quarry. He comes round the corner and there are the two sailors talking to a policeman. They're reporting that an evil man who's only about this tall picked them up and took them to his apartment and suggested lewd and lascivious activities, and they say, "As a matter of fact, there he is!" So the cop busted him.

I had long since gone home. It was late for me, but about 4:30 my phone rings and this very official voice says, "Are you Joseph Baron?" I say, "Yes I am." He identifies himself as the bail bondsman and says, "Do you know this person?" I said, "Yes," and he says he's been arrested and is in SFPD, in the jail down there, and, um, "Will you come down and post bail for him?" So I drag myself out of bed.

He was charged with "grand vag," grand vagrancy. Grand vagrancy implies a sex crime. It's more than just, you know, loitering around without money in your pocket. So we bailed him out. At that time I shared a house with some other people, and one of the people I shared a house with was an attorney. He knew this attorney whose name is Ken Zwerin. You know the name? Anyway he specialized, as he put it, in "gay law." My housemate had been to a cocktail party and had talked to him. Of course being an attorney himself, he was naturally interested in all of this, so he recommended this guy and we called him up that very morning. He came down to the police station and talked to my friend and said, "I'll take care of it. It ain't cheap, but I'll take care of it."

Then there were the raids. There was a particular one that is quite famous. This was in the spring of 1956. That's as close as I can get to the date. I had driven down to Monterey for some reason and was on my way back. It had become nighttime. Well, we had heard that there was an oceanfront roadhouse down in Pacifica, I believe it was Sharp Park, that was hot, you know, a neat place to go. So I thought I'd give the place a look-see. It was this great big barn-like place called Hazel's. It was sort of like that place in Dallas, Tilly's, only gay, you know. There was a great cross-section of the gay world in there. I mean there were girls dancing with girls, sailors dancing with sailors, just everybody. There was the western crowd and the fuzzy sweater crowd and the whole trip. So I thought, wow, this is really terrific. But I noticed, also, that there were a whole bunch of these heavy looking honchos leaning up against the wall. And I thought well that's funny, they don't look like they belong here. Well, it turns out that they didn't. What happened was that they were spotters, and about a week after I visited the place, the sheriff of San Mateo County borrowed some personnel carriers from the Army and with his trusty band of jolly men went and busted the whole place.

Everyone must have noticed the spotters. They had to have because I don't consider myself that observant. All these spotters, it turns out, were deputies. What they did was they formed a double line on the dance floor, and everybody had to march down that line. They were identified by these spotters as people that had been there before. That was very clever on the part of the police, because they eliminated a lot of people whose attorneys would present the defense of "Well I just stumbled in, I was just looking for a place to buy a Coke," or "I didn't know anything about the place." They were all habitues as far as the sheriff was concerned. I had a number of friends who fell on that one, including one who was extremely closeted. He never went out. He never went to gay bars. He practically was never seen on the street until the one night when he goes out and that happens to him. And at that time it was conventional to publish the names and addresses of anybody that was arrested, naturally, for the purpose of getting them fired.

Raids were talked about constantly. There was a time in early 1957 where the vibes were so bad that even the most devoted barflies did not go out. Just simply did not go out. It was like the big purge at the University of Florida, which you may have heard about. It was in '54 or '55. I had already left, but I would say that that whole thing was fostered by the McCarthy climate. No question about it. And I think that the whole repressive climate in San Francisco in the mid-50s was an extension of that whole movement. The other thing that I think really fostered a repressive quality in San Francisco was George Christopher. He was mayor from 1956 to 1964, and he was an extremely—trying to think of the right word—sanctimonious, goody-goody-two-shoes-type person. His platform was that he was going to clean up San Francisco. According to Christopher, San Francisco was just a snake pit of vice and perverted sex, and the downtown merchants were complaining because so much of their business depended on convention trade. People from the conventions were being harassed and approached and all that kind of stuff. So, old George, you know, he engaged in this huge crusade, and he was very successful. I mean he just shut the whole city down. Everything. So much so that the downtown merchants started complaining just the opposite. They complained that he had cleaned the city up to such an extent that nobody would come here any more because it was no fun. Conventioneers wanted to go some other place. This, coupled with Ahern, who was chief of police under Christopher. He was very much like, I don't know if you've heard of Chief Parker down in Los Angeles? I mean, they were devils! But then there was a sudden alleviation of all this repression at the end of Christopher's administration—and also Ahern died—so that you have in the early 1960s this tremendous liberalization of everything and the whole flower power movement and all of that. I think the gay culture started to grow in this very, you know, in this very benign and fertile environment.

3 | POLICING QUEERS IN THE 1940S AND 1950S

Harassment, Prosecution, and the Legal Defense of Gay Bars

> [T]here must be sustained action by the police and the district attorney to stop the influx of homosexuals. Too many taverns cater to them openly. Only police action can drive them out of the city. It is to be hoped that the courts here will finally recognize this problem for what it is and before the situation so deteriorates that San Francisco finds itself as the complete haven for undesirables. The courts heretofore have failed to support the arresting and prosecuting authorities. Without the support of the courts, the police and the district attorney cannot attack the problem effectively.
>
> San Francisco Examiner, *1954*

"Why does the Bay City have such an overlarge percentage of these queer people?" a federal agent asks in Lou Rand's 1964 detective novel *Rough Trade*.[1] "They seem to be actually encouraged here. Why, they even have their own clubs and bars. I may be old fashioned, but I just don't get this local tolerance." Rand's novel, set in San Francisco in the early 1950s, wraps a murder mystery around the agent's pressing question. Why did local police seem to allow gay bars and clubs to exist? Was there some degree of tolerance for gay life in San Francisco? To answer these questions, Rand introduces private investigator Francis Morley, a "gay detective" who efficiently guides the reader through San Francisco's queer underworld. Before too long, however, the gay detective is drawn into an intriguing collaboration with police. With three murders to solve and a federal agent on his tail, San Francisco's captain of detectives, John Starr, realizes that the local police are ill prepared to investigate San Francisco's gay world. Vice, he notes, "used to consist of three things: gambling, dope, and 'hoors.' . . . Now, since the war, we've got this new thing in Bay City. Everyone calls them 'gay.' We have gay bars, gay parks, gay clubs, theaters and hotels."[2] Protected by a seemingly undecipherable lexicon, San Francisco's circuit of queer bars, baths, and after-hours clubs remains inaccessible to local police. As a result, Starr invites Morley, the "gay detective," to join the case. In order to solve the murders, however, Morley becomes a kind of double agent. Pretending to be a straight man acting gay, Morley investigates the crimes only to discover the corrupt influence of Starr's inner circle.

Set in the McCarthy era, Rand's novel introduces a number of important themes to the study of policing queers in San Francisco's wartime and postwar era. First, it describes the collaboration of local, state, and federal policing agencies. With the influx of military personnel during World War II and the postwar transfer of liquor authority from California's State Board of Equalization to the Alcoholic Beverage Control Board (ABC), new policing agencies took hold of San Francisco. Both the military police and the ABC brought new strategies, techniques, and targets to the suppression of gay and transgender nightspots. Next, Rand's novel introduces the undercover cop as an important figure in San Francisco's gay subculture. In *Rough Trade,* the gay detective poses as a fairy (an effeminate man) and passes into San Francisco's gay "underworld." While this aspect of the novel is humorous, the existence of undercover agents in San Francisco's gay bars profoundly changed the quality of life in gay public spaces. Undercover agents threatened the safety of bars and taverns—no one knew who was watching whom—and fear intensified the policing of patrons by management, turning hosts and hostesses into guardians of appropriate speech and behavior. Finally, Rand's novel addresses the post-Prohibition breakdown of organized crime in San Francisco. "Y'see, this town used to be wide open," an aging vice detective laments. "It was the talk of the world, being a seaport and all. Things were pretty much under control, and everyone was making a little money. Then these people that always want to clean up everything lost out on prohibition, so they decided to run all the 'hoors' out of town. Finally, we had to close up all those quiet, friendly, well-regulated houses."[3] With the post-Prohibition reorganization of crime and the postwar reorganization of policing, local police struggled to find a place in the new order of things. Ironically, they often did so in collaboration with gay bars and bar owners.

This chapter tells the story of policing in San Francisco through the midcentury. It describes the impact of World War II on the city and the emergence of new policing agencies. With much of World War II focused on the Pacific theater, San Francisco became both a port of embarkation and a strategic stronghold. Soldiers and sailors traveling to war zones in the Pacific—Guam, the Philippines, the Midway and Solomon Islands—often moved through San Francisco on the way to their destinations. Over a million servicemen and women traveled through the region on their way to war, and military personnel sometimes spent their last nights of freedom in the city, carousing around town with new friends and lovers. Meanwhile, with the bombing of Pearl Harbor, the defense of San Francisco became even more crucial to national security. Military bases at Fort Mason and the Presidio filled to capacity, and the number of military personnel stationed in San Francisco grew to almost 60,000. Historian Charles Wollenberg notes that during World War II San Francisco became a "quasi-military base," and as the city absorbed large numbers of military personnel, it adopted new social practices.[4] Locals braced themselves for attack by plotting evacuation routes and enduring lengthy blackouts, and volunteer defense units counting almost 80,000 patrolled beaches and searched the sky for planes.[5] Wartime brought a heightened degree of cooperation between local civilians and military personnel, but it also brought new levels of policing and social control.

In San Francisco, three agencies shared the onus of policing queers: the San Francisco Police Department, the California Board of Equalization (the state's liquor control agency), and the U.S. Military Police, and the degree to which policing agencies coordinated their efforts corresponded to the degree to which gay bars and taverns were policed. However, because the ability of local, state, and federal agencies to coordinate their efforts rose and fell, the severity of policing waxed and waned through the 1940s and 1950s. For instance, between 1942 and 1951 queers in San Francisco noticed a phase of intensified policing. During these years, gay bars were increasingly harassed, and many bars were shut down by the coordinated efforts of local, state, and federal agents. Between 1951 and 1955, however, queer bars and taverns experienced a period of reestablishment as a result of legal challenges to the police harassment of gay bars. During these years, policing agencies were unable to coordinate their efforts, and new bars opened—many of them gay owned and/or operated. Queer San Franciscans used these years to consolidate a culture of resistance within the bars and taverns that they frequented. In 1955, however, two events disrupted the growth of queer bar culture, and new forms of policing developed. The California legislature transferred the authority of liquor control to the ABC, and the citizens of San Francisco elected a law-and-order mayor, George Christopher. These events, and the legal battles that occurred simultaneously, changed the legal status of homosexuals and transformed the form and function of policing. After 1955, homosexual status was increasingly conflated with conduct, so actions previously understood to be innocent (such as, in the case of men, effeminate behavior) now signaled illegal behavior (such as sexual solicitation). During this period, policing agencies also increasingly relied on the testimony of undercover agents to substantiate their cases against gay bars. As a result, bar owners and patrons developed new modes of social resistance that led the way to more effective resistance strategies, such as structural defenses, internal policing, and a vibrant communication network. Interestingly, the resistance strategies that developed in bars and taverns through the 1950s leaned toward group or collective rights—the right to public assembly—rather than individual civil rights. This chapter reveals the extent to which queer bar owners and patrons shared a group identity, and it challenges the standard view that the homophile movement led the way in developing formal political resistance strategies.

WORLD WAR II

Much has been written on the impact of World War II on California and the west, and historians disagree on the extent to which war radically transformed western cities like San Francisco.[6] But clearly, the war sparked a production boom that lifted California—and much of the United States—out of a decade-long economic depression. Billions of dollars pulsed through the state as burgeoning military bases and industrial plants picked up the frantic pace of wartime production.[7] In 1942, for example, Roosevelt's production goals included 60,000 airplanes, 45,000 tanks, 20,000 antiaircraft guns, and 8 million tons of merchant shipping. To accomplish these goals, automobile factories were converted to tank and truck production, metal manufacturers churned out the raw material for ammunitions, and aircraft production greatly accelerated its pace. In the San Francisco Bay Area, shipyards sprang up in Richmond, Alameda, Oakland, and San Francisco, and war jobs lured tens of thousands of migrants to the city.[8]

With civilians pouring into the city, San Francisco's population jumped to new heights. By 1945, the city's population had risen to a high of 825,000, and demographic changes had a dramatic effect on city life—they shifted populations and transformed neighborhoods. For instance, Henry Kaiser's shipyards recruited workers from the southern states of Louisiana, Texas, Oklahoma, and Arkansas, but they also recruited workers from Nicaragua and El Salvador who settled in the city's South of Market district.[9] President Roosevelt's 1941 Executive Order 8802, which prohibited racial discrimination in war industries, opened up jobs to new worker populations, and southern Blacks migrated west in unprecedented numbers. More than one million African Americans left the south during the war, and almost 85 percent headed west for jobs in war industries like shipbuilding.[10] Between 1940 and 1950, the city's African American population jumped 600 percent, from 4,846 to 43,460, and while wartime migrants settled all over the city, African Americans faced intensified degrees of housing discrimination. Only a small percentage of San Francisco's landlords would rent to non-whites during the war, and African Americans either moved into newly built war housing that segregated them into de facto "war-worker ghettoes" like Hunter's Point, or they took houses in the Western Addition and Fillmore districts that had been vacated by Japanese families forcibly displaced by wartime internment.[11]

World War II transformed San Francisco, at least for the duration, in that it sparked new industries, created jobs, stimulated migrations, and transformed neighborhoods, but the increased military presence had a profound impact on city policy and policing. A military presence in San Francisco was nothing new—from the time of Spanish colonization, San Francisco had functioned as a strategic port and military stronghold—but the heightened military presence during World War II forced a new set of priorities on the city. It disrupted local politics and superimposed a national and military-oriented agenda on the city.[12] The heightened military presence also returned San Francisco to the unbalanced sex ratio of its mining-camp years. With thousands of furloughed sailors and soldiers traversing the city, there were far more men than women in the city's entertainment districts. Nightlife, as a result, took on a new aura, and entertaining the troops became an important vector of San Francisco's underworld entertainments. Servicemen and women often expected sex for entertainment, and San Francisco's sex tourist culture was eager to provide. Soldiers and sailors cruised Broadway in the city's North Beach district or Market Street to the Tenderloin. In doing so, they occupied the city in new ways.[13] Historian John D'Emilio even argues that World War II "marks the beginning of the nation's, and San Francisco's, modern gay history."[14]

To accommodate both the vast influx of military personnel and the quick pace of shore leave, gay and lesbian bars clustered in areas close to the center of town. Queer life, as a result, became much more accessible to both locals and military personnel looking for a good time.[15] Gay officers and enlisted men cruised upscale hotel bars like the Oak Room at the St. Francis or the Top of the Mark at the Mark Hopkins in San Francisco's Union Square. But they also frequented "rough bars" in the Tenderloin and on the waterfront, like the Silver Rail and the Old Crow, where enlisted men mingled with locals and "rough trade" (masculine-looking men willing to have sex with gay men, sometimes for a price).[16] The increased popularity of gay bars in the city center during wartime hastened the development of both a gay sensibility and an urban infrastructure. World War II historian Allan Bérubé observes that military life displaced young men and women who, in cities like San Francisco, often learned to think of themselves as gay. They "located gay nightspots, met each other, formed relationship, used a new language, followed new codes of behavior, and carved out places for themselves in the world as gay men and lesbians."[17] The intimacy and loneliness of war, coupled with the excitement of travel and the danger of combat, brought gay culture and community to a new level. And in cities like San Francisco, where the anonymity and conviviality of gay and lesbian bars quickened the process of self- and group identification, gay and lesbian GIs developed a "gay point of view," Bérubé argues. "By uprooting an entire generation, the war helped to channel urban gay life into a particular path of growth—away from stable private networks and toward public commercial establishments serving the needs of a displaced, transient, and younger clientele."[18] But as a new generation of lesbians and gay men learned the language and pleasures of queer life, they also learned how to manage its dangers.

The military's presence in San Francisco brought new modes of policing, and as soon as the United States entered World War II, port cities became the territory of federal agents acting on behalf of the armed forces. In 1941, for example, the U.S. Congress passed the May Act, which authorized the military to survey recreational areas near military bases and shut down places that catered to prostitutes and vice.[19] The Army and Navy also required that servicemen on leave stay in uniform so as to be easily detected. While the military often relied on cues from local police, they quickly established their own policing agencies. The Army's Military Police, or MPs, and the Navy's Shore Patrol, or SPs, controlled the leave activities of military personnel. They could arrest a GI for being out of uniform, visiting off-limits establishments, or participating in a wide range of "disorderly" activities.[20] But the presence of military police on the streets and in bars also had an impact on the lives of locals in that MPs established a threatening presence inside bars and taverns. They also communicated with local police and state liquor agents, instigating raids or other kinds of harassment that might have otherwise been avoided. Gay bar owners, as a result, determined new ways to manage both larger crowds and increased policing. They sometimes cooperated, sometimes cajoled, and often manipulated policing agencies, and in the postwar years, as these strategies increasingly failed, bar owners began to fight the harassment they experienced through the courts.

While tourism remained central to the existence of San Francisco's queer and transgender nightlife, during wartime the gay bar became increasingly vulnerable to state surveillance and regulation. In order to serve a homosexual clientele, bar owners as well as patrons fought ongoing battles with city police, state liquor control agencies, and military police. These battles remain hidden from history except when newspaper reports recorded large-scale police raids or bar owners brought lengthy and expensive cases to court. San Francisco's history of bar raids, shutdowns, and court cases documents its transformation in the 1940s and 1950s from a wide-open town where sexual subcultures flourished to a city frequently hostile to its emergent gay and lesbian communities.

THE FIRST PHASE OF POLICING, 1942–1951

The persecution of gay and lesbian bars and the control of queer public space began in earnest in the 1940s as Army and Navy officers began to coordinate their efforts to control military personnel in the city of San Francisco.[21] In 1942, the first summer after the United States entered World War II, military officials initiated anti-vice crackdowns in many United States cities, particularly port towns, in an effort to regulate the vast influx of military personnel.[22] In July of that year, Army Commander Major General Walter K. Wilson declared three San Francisco bars "off limits" to Army personnel—the Silver Dollar, the Pirate's Cave, and the Silver Rail—and the Navy's top brass immediately followed suit, declaring the same bars "out of bounds" for all Navy, Coast Guard, and Marine Corps personnel.[23] At least one of these bars, the Silver Rail, was a popular Tenderloin nightspot where "nelly queens" and the "cuff-link set" mixed with servicemen during the war years.[24] Later that year, the

State Board of Equalization (SBE) joined the military's crackdown on gay bars and shut down two Tenderloin nightspots, the Brass Rail and the Old Adobe. The Brass Rail was a "rough trade" hotel bar at Fourth and Mission, and the Old Adobe, at Eddy and Jones, featured an African American drag show.[25] Later that year, the SBE issued a warning to more than fifty San Francisco bars and taverns, including the Silver Rail and the Old Crow, stating that they must "conform strictly to the State liquor laws or their licenses would be revoked." Citing problems like the presence of "percentage girls" and venereal diseases traced to specific taverns, SBE enforcement officer Don Marshall emphasized a concern for the health and safety of military personnel. Women employees were not to drink with members of the armed forces, and the sale of alcohol to obviously intoxicated men in uniform would mean the immediate revocation of the bar's liquor license. "If the Board [of Equalization] does not crack down on you," he warned bar owners, "the Army and Navy will."[26]

By 1944, the Army and Navy had consolidated their efforts into a single agency, the Joint Army-Navy Disciplinary Control Board (later renamed the Armed Forces Disciplinary Control Board), and this agency created new methods to "protect" servicemen and women from delinquency, disease, or disorder. One strategy was to work more directly with municipal police and state liquor agents. They used city arrest records to identify "problem spots," and they circulated memos to San Francisco's chief of police, the city's district attorney, the state Department of Health, and the SBE's District Liquor Control Administrator. In wartime meetings, the Joint Army-Navy Disciplinary Control Board expressed concern about bars that sold drinks to obviously intoxicated service personnel and allowed prostitutes to remain on the premises, but through the years they became increasingly concerned with bars that maintained a "disorderly establishment," a phrase that often signified queer or "deviate" activity.[27] To regulate the leave time of military personnel, the Army-Navy Board worked with the state's liquor administrators. They asked liquor administrators to enact a wartime emergency measure requiring bars off-limits to military personnel to post visible signs declaring their status.[28] In San Francisco, these efforts resulted in the identification and demarcation of almost one hundred bars and nightclubs, many of which served a queer clientele.[29] Placing bars off-limits to servicemen, posting signs, and stationing military police outside the door intimidated patrons, particularly military personnel, but these actions posed little threat to the livelihood of the bar—sometimes they even functioned to advertise the bar as a queer nightspot. The liquor board, however, often followed up on military concerns by investigating and possibly suspending the licenses of gay bars. In 1942, several gay bars were targeted by state liquor authorities, and citations were issued to Finocchio's, the Black Cat, and the Top of the Mark. In May of 1943, local police joined the Army-Navy and liquor board's harassment of gay bars by raiding a number of places popular with queers and military personnel, including the Silver Dollar, the Black Cat, and the Rickshaw, a gay bar in Chinatown where, during the raid, a couple of lesbians were beaten up.[30]

By 1945, the local police, the military police, and the liquor board had developed a system to regulate and control queer public space. If district beat cops noticed that a bar had a specifically queer clientele, the Armed Forces Disciplinary Control Board would follow up with its own investigation. The Disciplinary Control Board's practice was to send warning letters to "trouble spots," instructing them to "clean up conditions."[31] Bars and taverns that would not stop serving homosexuals became off-limits to military personnel, their names and addresses were listed in city and military newspapers, off-limits signs were posted, and military police made rounds so as to arrest military personnel who entered the offending bars and taverns. If the bar continued to serve gay and lesbian clientele and/or allow queer entertainments, the SBE would cite, suspend or revoke the license of the bar, and city police would, under certain circumstances, raid the bar to scare off its regular clientele.

With the end of World War II, the SBE's "emergency" cooperation with the Armed Forces Disciplinary Control Board ceased, but the policing of "resorts for sex deviates" and "havens for homosexuals" did not stop. In a history of gay and lesbian GIs during World War II, Allan Bérubé notes that the end of war intensified the prosecution of gays and lesbians in the U.S. military in that demobilization ushered in a period of "witch hunts" and dishonorable discharges.[32] The war had been a profoundly mixed experience for gay and lesbian GIs. While many were harassed, persecuted, thrown into "queer stockades," and discharged without benefits, the war had a positive effect on the whole in that it "weakened the barriers that had kept gay people trapped and hidden at the margins of society."[33] Early in the war, lax draft and recruitment policies allowed thousands of gay men and lesbians to serve. They lived on sex-segregated bases, found others, formed cliques, explored cities, and created a culture of their own within the context of military service.[34] With the end of war and the decreased need for raw numbers of soldiers and sailors, gay and lesbian personnel were forced out of the military.[35] In August 1949, the Defense Department Personnel Policy Board recommended standard procedures regarding homosexuals: "Homosexual personnel, irrespective of sex, should not be permitted to serve in any branch of the Armed Forces in any capacity, and prompt separation of known homosexuals from the Armed Forces is mandatory."[36] This recommendation, adopted in October 1949, clarified for the first time a consistent policy for all branches of the armed forces, and its impact was immediate.[37] Not only did it increase the dismissal of gay and lesbian GIs but it ushered in a period of heightened intolerance.[38] In the 1950s, the military began a vehement campaign to educate enlistees about the dangers of homosexuality. "The military began to teach millions of young men and women to accept a uniform image of homosexuals, to fear them and report them, and to police their own feelings, friendships, and environment for signs of homosexual attractions," notes Bérubé. In a shift from wartime procedure, where gay and lesbian GIs were often tolerated (or channeled into "queer jobs"), Bérubé smartly observes that in the cold war era, military officials institutionalized an overt campaign to indoctrinate recruits with what we would today call homophobia: "the irrational fear of homosexuality and of homosexual people."[39]

Military policy was part of a larger federal campaign against homosexuals. In 1950 the U.S. Senate Committee on Expenditure in Executive Departments investigated the employment of homosexuals in the civil service through a subcommittee chaired by North Carolina Senator Clyde Hoey. As part of a growing concern with communism, the government became fearful of communist sympathizers employed by the U.S. government who might be in the position to reveal military and/or domestic secrets to so-called enemies of the state. Because homosexuals were often characterized as immoral, secretive, and untrustworthy—a counter-discourse opposing these characterizations had yet to be developed—homosexuals fell under special consideration by legislative committees such as Hoey's Subcommittee on Investigations and HUAC, the House Un-American Activities Committee.[40] Hoey's subcommittee reported that "those who engage in overt acts of perversion lack the emotional stability of normal persons . . . [and] [t]he social stigma attached to sex perversion is so great that many perverts go to great lengths to conceal their perverted tendencies . . . [from] gangs of blackmailers."[41] The subcommittee thus recommended that government agencies take a more active role in identifying and separating homosexual employees. It also recommended that agencies terminate homosexual employees rather than allow them to resign, fearing that without termination homosexuals might find employment in other government agencies and return to their potentially subversive activities. "One homosexual can pollute an entire office," the report warned.[42] As a result, the rate of dismissal of homosexuals from civil service increased dramatically after 1950, and in April 1953, Dwight Eisenhower issued Executive Order 10450 banning "sexual perverts" from government employment.[43] Between 1953 and 1955, over 800 federal workers lost their jobs as a result of anti-homosexual policies crafted by federal policy makers.[44]

The culture of homophobia generated by military officials in the cold war had a measurable impact on the policing of San Francisco in that by 1951, all of the bars and taverns off-limits to military personnel were places "patronized by persons considered to be homosexuals."[45] During the war years, homosexuality was discussed, but its dangers were far outweighed by the debilitating effects of intoxication and disease. In the postwar years, Army and Navy officials continued to worry about military access to prostitutes and venereal disease, but they punished the presence of homosexuals to a much greater degree. Cold war paranoia demanded preparedness, and urban entertainments, particularly those in port cities and military towns, fell under the watchful eye of military police. In San Francisco, the Armed Forces Disciplinary Control Board (AFDCB) convened monthly meetings throughout the 1950s to discuss policy, evaluate procedures, and hear testimony on the status of the city's many bars and taverns. To cast as wide a net as possible, the AFDCB invited the participation of a range of policing agencies. A meeting on May 23, 1951, for instance, was attended by members of the Army, Navy, and Coast Guard, as well as the venereal disease investigators from the California Department of Public Health, sex crimes investigators from the SFPD, and field representatives from the SBE's liquor control agency.

The May 1951 meeting considered evidence from twenty-one San Francisco establishments, including the Club Alabam, the Silver Dollar, the 585 Club, and the Echo Club—all Tenderloin nightspots that featured queer patrons and/or entertainers. Proceedings note that the Club Alabam, at 1820 Post Street, was visited over twenty times by military police, who witnessed a number of prostitutes but also "certain homosexual elements." The bar was placed "off limits and out of bounds" to military personnel for ninety days. At the 585 Club on Post Street, it was noted that although the place was patronized by homosexuals, the owner asked persons in uniform to leave during the evening hours. Military police who checked the place admitted that few men in uniform frequented the club. Still, the place was placed off-limits with the rationale that "this establishment caters to persons who are considered to be persons of abnormal character and whose conduct is questionable."[46] In reference to the Echo Club, however, owner Douglas Felter, a veteran of the U.S. Navy, came before the Board to request that restrictions be lifted. The meeting's minutes noted that "he succeeded in removing homosexuals from his place of business and will not condone their presence during business hours." A military police agent concurred that there had been a change in clientele since Mr. Felter had taken over the bar, and the board lifted restrictions against it.[47] By the end of the meeting, a list of bars off-limits to military personnel was drawn up, and all but one of the bars on it were gay bars. The list included the Beige Room, the Black Cat, the Chi-Chi Club, the Club Alabam, Jim Dolan's Supper Club, Finocchio's, the 585 Club, George's Bar, Mona's Candlelight, the Paper Doll, and Tommy's 299. Of those listed, the vast majority were located either in San Francisco's North Beach district or the Tenderloin.

Interestingly, the bars and taverns listed as off-limits to military personnel included all three lesbian bars in San Francisco at the time—Mona's, the Chi-Chi Club, and Tommy's 299. The heightened scrutiny of lesbian public space in the 1950s reflects a pattern evidenced in U.S. culture more generally—and in military policy. As several historians have noted, the cold war brought the heightened policing of gender roles and, thus, the increased stigmatization of sexualized and/or masculine women.[48] Women on the home front who had taken civilian war jobs were pressured to give them up as men returned home from military service, and women in the military who retained their jobs in the postwar period faced an increasingly hostile workplace.[49] Women were not subject to the draft, so of the 200,000 women to participate in military service during World War II, all were volunteers. The military branches that included women's divisions—Army WACS, Navy WAVES, and Coast Guard SPARS—had screened volunteers for "sexual deviancy," but the screening process was fairly lax until the war's end. With demobilization, women's participation seemed less crucial to the armed forces, and lesbianism—or simply the suspicion of lesbianism—became an easy justification for dismissal. Also, because the military used masculinity as a signifier of lesbianism, women in the military who performed "men's jobs" were particularly vulnerable.[50] In the Navy, for example, there was a much higher incidence of detection of homosexual activity among women than men in the postwar years, even though there were many more men than women, and women's sexual activities were, according to a Navy report, more difficult to detect.[51] Women in the military, like women who retained their war jobs, were misunderstood by mainstream society. Their desire to continue to work after the war seemed unwomanly, unpatriotic, and socially deviant, and women in the military, particularly masculine women and lesbians, were often harassed and/or discharged from service.

Thousands of gay and lesbian GIs were dishonorably dismissed—up to two thousand a year during the 1950s—and they returned home from a popular war without the status of service or self-esteem they may have once had.[52] Women and men who received undesirable or "blue" discharges for homosexuality (printed on blue paper) were stripped of their uniform and sent home to explain their situation over and over to friends and family. Undesirably discharged personnel were also denied a host of GI benefits that helped other veterans readjust to civilian life—benefits such as career counseling, college loans, home loans, and business loans.[53] Because GIs often traveled through San Francisco on their way to or from war, many who remembered its beauty, charm, and sophistication returned to the city after the war to make a new home. Those who had experienced San Francisco's gay nightlife and were later dismissed for homosexuality had even more reason to return to the city. Gay life had expanded during the war years. New bars had opened, the community had grown, and networks had developed in response to the multiplication of queer cultures and communities. As a result, gay and lesbian veterans often sought refuge in large-sized port cities like San Francisco, where they could participate in a gay world but still live relatively anonymously.[54]

Gay and lesbian veterans may have also chosen to live in San Francisco because in the postwar years the city seemed relatively tolerant—particularly compared to cities like Miami, where an all-out "war on perverts" resulted in an exodus of queers. In Florida, the harassment of homosexuals followed a pattern in which politicians jockeyed for public favor by scapegoating weak and vulnerable constituencies. In Miami, much like in San Francisco, local media worried that the city was becoming a favorite gathering spot for homosexuals. Unlike in San Francisco, however, this characterization became a powerful rallying point for Miami politicians. In 1954, Florida's governor instructed the state's attorney general to investigate the situation in Miami, and shortly thereafter Miami's mayor accused the city's police chief of coddling homosexuals by allowing them to assemble in public places. The mayor threatened to fire the police chief if he did not shut down the city's gay bars, and through 1954 gay and lesbian bars (and beaches) were continuously raided, many of them closing out of fear and a lack of patronage. More dramatically, Florida's state legislature initiated a well-funded campaign in the 1950s against gay and lesbian public school teachers, on the grounds that homosexual teachers recruited students into a homosexual "lifestyle." Through the late 1950s, a legislative committee investigated hundreds of teachers, terminating the contracts and revoking the teaching certificates of university instructors and public school teachers accused of homosexuality.[55] Homosexual purges in Miami followed a national pattern where, without strong voices of opposition, the harassment and containment of lesbian and gay public spaces continued unabated.

In San Francisco, a different pattern emerged. In the postwar years, gay and lesbian bar owners began to challenge police harassment through the municipal and state courts. The most important example of this trend involved the Black Cat, a downtown bar on Montgomery Street. The case began in 1949, when the Board of Equalization indefinitely suspended the liquor license of the Black Cat on the grounds that it was "a hangout for persons of homosexual tendencies." San Francisco's daily *Chronicle* put it this way: "All was not so gay, gay, gay as usual yesterday at the free thinking Black Cat Restaurant at 710 Montgomery Street. Agents of the State Board of Equalization arrived on an errand: to take away the bohemianesque joint's liquor license from Bartender Sol M. Stoumen."[56] The management of the Black Cat responded by challenging the Board's decision, and in an appeal to the State Board of Equalization, Sol Stoumen rejected the state's allegation that the bar was a "hangout for homosexuals."[57] In rebuttal, police testified that they had been investigating the bar for over a year, and the bar not only served "persons of known homosexual tendencies" but was a meeting place for homosexuals. On this basis, Stoumen lost his liquor license.

Facing the loss of a prosperous business, Stoumen hired an attorney, Morris Lowenthal, who shifted the focus of the plaintiff's case from one of denial to a justification of homosexual civil rights. Using unique sources for evidence, including the recently published Kinsey Report, Lowenthal argued in two separate appeals, one to the San Francisco Superior Court and another to the First District Court of Appeals, that homosexuals had the right to assemble in bars and restaurants. Both the Superior Court and the Court of Appeals disagreed with Lowenthal's argument and upheld the Board of Equalization's decision. In fact, Superior Court Judge Robert L. McWilliams' decision vehemently denied the right to assembly to lesbians and gay men. He claimed:

> It would be a sorry commentary on the law as well as on the morals of the community to find that persons holding liquor licenses could permit their premises to be used month after month as meeting places for persons of known homosexual tendencies. . . . An occasional fortuitous meeting of such persons at restaurants for the innocent purpose mentioned is one thing. But for a proprietor of a restaurant knowingly to permit his premises to be regularly used "as a meeting place" by persons of the type mentioned with all of the potentialities for evil and immorality drawing out of such meetings is, in my opinion, conduct of an entirely different nature.[58]

Serving alcohol to queers was one thing, but the public assembly of homosexuals on a regular basis was clearly a frightening prospect to lawmakers like Robert L. McWilliams.

The question of public assembly thus became fundamental to the Black Cat's case against the state, and in late 1950 the California Supreme Court agreed to hear the case. Later, in 1951, it overruled the Board of Equalization's decision and ordered the Black Cat's liquor license restored. The supreme court's decision, *Stoumen v. Reilly,* cited an Oklahoma case where prostitutes were classified as human beings entitled to basic human rights such as food, clothing, and shelter. The courts reasoned that "it is not a crime to give them [prostitutes] lodging unless it is done for immoral purposes."[59] Arguing that there was no evidence of "illegal or immoral conduct on the premises" of the Black Cat, the California Supreme Court extended the logic of the Oklahoma case to *Stoumen.*[60] In other words, the California Supreme Court affirmed that homosexuals were, indeed, human beings, and the public assembly of homosexuals was not in itself illegal. The court's decision asserted that "even habitual or regular meetings may be for purely social and harmless purposes, such as the consumption of food and drink, and it is to be presumed that a person is innocent of crime or wrong and that the law has been obeyed."[61] *Stoumen v. Reilly* was an important victory in the struggle for lesbian and gay civil rights in that it legalized the public assembly of homosexuals in California. However, as legal theorist Arthur Leonard observes, the stipulation that unlawful acts must be committed on the premises for policing agencies to act against a bar generated a whole new set of policing strategies.[62] This stipulation also problematically differentiated between homosexuality as a state of being (status) and homosexuality as an illegal act (conduct)—a distinction that potentially identified any behavior construed as lesbian or gay to be automatically immoral and illegal.[63]

After *Stoumen v. Reilly* the State Board of Equalization stopped targeting homosexual bars, and the military once again became the primary policing agency. Through the early 1950s, the Armed Forces Disciplinary Control Board set a number of bars and taverns off-limits to military personnel, but it had neither the liquor board's authority to force bars to post "off limits" signs nor the power to suspend liquor licenses. The SFPD also seemed wary in the wake of *Stoumen*. In a 1951 hearing on the 585 Club, a gay bar on Post Street, SFPD investigators testified that while they had checked identification cards of men entering the bar and warned patrons not to leave with homosexuals, they could do nothing further "unless a crime is committed."[64] As a result, in the period between 1951 and 1955, gay and lesbian bars proliferated, particularly in San Francisco's North Beach district. Tommy's Place and the 12 Adler opened; Miss Smith's Tea Room and the Tin Angel opened; the Beige Room moved to Broadway during this period; and three supper clubs, the Paper Doll, Dolan's, and Gordon's, sustained a big following. Gay and lesbian nightclubs solidified their patronage, and the community grew strong despite the momentum of McCarthy-era politics and a postwar culture of conformity.

THE PERIOD OF REESTABLISHMENT, 1951–1955

With a break from rigorous policing, the period between 1951 and 1955 allowed an urban culture of queer conviviality and sexual transgression to consolidate in the city's Tenderloin and North Beach districts. During this period, gay bars in the city became more visible, and they began to use public space in new ways. This was also the period in which the Beat generation began to show a public face in San Francisco, bringing a new level of unconventionality to the city. Many scholars have noted the homoerotics of Beat culture, and some have argued that the Beat poets who took up residence in San Francisco's North Beach district contributed significantly to the development of queer culture and politics.[65] However, while the territory Beats occupied often overlapped with nascent queer communities, the cultures that developed around them were distinct. Beats often projected disdain for "the Faggot" or the feminine, while San Francisco's queer communities remained imbued with male-to-female gender expressions and a campy culture of drag performance.[66] Homosexuality existed as part of Beat iconography only when same-sex representations renounced popular myths of emotional dependence and gender transgression. Much of Jack Kerouac's and Allan Ginsberg's writings, for example, embraced the power of men together and laced homoerotic representations with riotous masculinity.[67] Beat writers asserted a reinterpretation of male sexuality that ran counter to the homophobia of cold war America, but their celebration of masculinity remained too narrow and distinct from the more flamboyant and effeminate homosexualities ruminating in San Francisco's sexual underworld for it to have contributed to a broad-based refiguring of queer culture or community.[68]

Still, as John D'Emilio argues, Beat culture legitimized some homosexual life choices. The publication of Ginsberg's *Howl* and its subsequent censorship trials cemented a connection between Beat cultural iconography and homosexual practice.[69] And as Beats found themselves increasingly in the public eye they often brought homosexuality with them. *Howl* celebrates male homosexuality as painfully joyous, remembering those "who let themselves be fucked in the ass by saintly motorcyclists, and screamed with joy," and those "who copulated ecstatic and insatiate with a bottle of beer a sweetheart a package of cigarettes a candle and fell off the bed."[70] *Howl* projects the exuberant goodness of uncensored sexuality, and the connection between homosexuality and San Francisco's Beat poets pressed itself into the popular imagination despite the sometimes glaring differences between Beat and queer cultures. A journalist reporting on Beat culture in San Francisco, for example, visited the Paper Doll. Looking for "Beatniks" but unable to find any, he wryly noted, "you could stay for hours without realizing that this is the hard core of a Beat Generation group that practices its own peculiar protest against the conforming American ideal of home and family: Homosexuality."[71] To some, homosexuality in and of itself flagged a Beat sensibility, but many queer San Franciscans saw Beat culture as something quite separate from their lives.

"The Beats were not somebody or some group that was too influential on me," Marilyn Braiger comments. She frequently participated in San Francisco's North Beach cafe scene, attending Beat-era poetry readings at the Cellar and Vesuvio's, "but in terms of gay life, I didn't think of them as gay." She continues, "I knew Ginsberg was gay and some of the others, but it didn't have any influence or bearing on my life. The way he was gay was probably a very different way from the way I was gay."[72] George Mendenhall, a gay activist, acknowledged the impact of Beat culture on San Francisco's North Beach community, but he didn't participate in it. "Occasionally I used to go out there [North Beach] on a bus, and I guess I used to enjoy watching all that like I was a tourist in my own city, but I never got into it or took part."[73] Gerald Belchick reasoned that "Beat culture permitted one to be kooky."[74] Through their writings, Beats publicized the possibility of homosexuality, and through their lifestyle they made other kinds of "kooky" people, like homosexuals, more tolerable to the mainstream. Still, the two communities remained distinct. The gender-transgressive quality of queer culture looked very different from the mystic and masculine culture of the Beat poets.

In San Francisco in the early 1950s, queer life took shape alongside Beat culture but also inside what were increasingly called "gay bars"—even lesbians called the bars they frequented "gay bars."[75] And while a mix of people (gays, lesbians, drag queens, transgenders, bisexuals, tourists, prostitutes, Beats, and bohemians) continued to frequent these places, gay bars took on an insider quality in the 1950s. Prior to World War II, there were many bars, such as the Oak Room or Finocchio's, that functioned as homosexual pick-up spots or provided transgender entertainments, but as Burt Gerrits remembers, "In those days there were very few places that were purely gay."

> There were a lot of these kind of like mixtures like the Top of the Mark. Whereas now a place like the Pendulum—do you suppose a straight person would go in there? Even if they knew about it, they probably wouldn't go in there. So I think there was just a gay undercurrent in a lot of these other places. Very respectable bars. The Oak Room at the St. Francis was the same way. It was a men-only bar. It was right along Powell Street, on that side. It was well known as a gay man's meeting place.[76]

In the 1930s and 1940s, "mixed" bars and cafes were popular with lesbians and gay men, but the "gay bar" that emerged in the postwar period was an altogether different species. Guy Strait (his given name), an activist in 1960s San Francisco, argued that gay bars could be distinguished from homosexual hangouts in several ways. First, queer patrons had the freedom of self-disclosure in a gay bar, and an insider culture developed. Second, as lesbians and gay men began to express their own culture in gay bars, a queer language developed to describe the nuances of same-sex desire. Words such as "butch," "trade," "ki-ki," "top," and "bottom" emerged to express the complex relationships between sex, gender, and sexuality. Finally, gay bars always provided a self-policing management.[77]

Because San Francisco's gay bars never fell under the full control of organized crime, bar owners typically remained petty entrepreneurs. They invested their own money into the bar, managed the business themselves, and frequently tended bar.[78] From this vantage, bar owners watched the behavior of their clientele, both to exert control over the bar's character and to protect patrons from entrapment and arrest. Because gay bar owners, bartenders, and patrons frequently shared the intimacy of insider status, bar owners often looked out for the welfare of their clientele.[79] "They [bartenders] were allies in the sense that they wouldn't let anyone hurt you or try to make you," Pat Bond remembers. "A man trying to make a lesbian would be thrown out."[80] But many bar owners were straight, and their motives could be self-serving. A raid on a gay bar or a series of arrests might ruin a bar's reputation, and in the pre-*Stoumen* era, a single arrest could easily lead to the suspension or revocation of an owner's liquor license.[81] Bar owners, as a result, often found themselves in the unfriendly position of exerting more control over their patrons than they might expect from the police. "You weren't allowed to touch in [bars]. You couldn't even put your hands on someone's shoulder. . . . One of my friends one night was in there with a sister of hers she hadn't seen in three or four years, and they embraced and they threw them both out."[82] Another patron, Joe Baron, remembers being ejected from the Paper Doll for suggestive language. "I was in there one night sort of being a smartass as always . . . and it was getting late [and] somebody said, 'What are we going to do now?' and I said 'Why don't we go have an orgy?' and the owner heard me and threw me out."[83] Bar owners, fearful of losing clientele, or worse, their liquor license, took a defensive position against police. They watched the door, censored suggestive language, and warned gay patrons against dancing and/or overt sexual behavior.

Gay bar owners also used spatial defenses to create an environment safe from the intrusion of outsiders. These defenses made the bar a physically uncomfortable place to enter, and once inside the bar they made it easy for bartenders to see newcomers. Spatial defenses included utilizing a back rather than a front entrance to the building, covering windows and darkening the bar so patrons could see newcomers quicker than they could be seen, locating the dance floor in a back room, away from the entrance, and hiring a door-person or "hostess" to watch and regulate the entrance.[84] Pat Healey, a Women's Army Corps recruit, remembers being stopped at the door of the Beige Room while home on leave in the early 1950s: "The ostensible check was 'Are you over age?' I guess if they thought you weren't gay, they turned you away on the pretense of not being old enough. . . . You had to know somebody. And I was busy trying to explain to them that you can't do that to me, I'm Pat, I'm well known in San Francisco."[85] Defensive strategies, common in most gay and lesbian bars, put newcomers—and police—in the vulnerable position of being watched by the management as they entered the bar. Defense mechanisms may seem, from contemporary standards, evidence of the marginalization of gay bars, but they functioned to insure the greatest degree of privacy for the bar's queer clientele. In fact, self-policing and spatial defenses became instrumental to the development of gay bars in San Francisco. As the management and staff worked to protect queer public space from invasion by police or hostile outsiders, they secured a niche for an evolving queer culture and community.[86]

In the period between 1951 and 1955, with the *Stoumen* case still fresh in the minds of lawmakers and police, bar owners relaxed a bit as the overt harassment of bars subsided. *Stoumen* established that serving alcohol to "known homosexuals" was not in itself unlawful even though homosexuality itself continued to be illegal (through sodomy laws). For a few years after *Stoumen,* the legal standing of lesbians and gay men seemed ambiguous in that the complex relationship between status and conduct had yet to flesh itself out.[87] For the time being, behaviors such as gender-ambiguous dress, flirtatious language, or same-sex dancing did not necessarily invoke "unlawful acts" like sodomy or sexual solicitation, and patrons of gay bars could still flirt with each other or dance together without implicating the bar as a hazard to the community. Many bar owners took advantage of the more liberal climate and expanded their service to gay patrons. The 585 Club in the Tenderloin, for example, continued to serve homosexuals despite warnings from the AFDCB. The owner even declined to attend a May 1951 hearing, and city police investigators who were present stated that unless patrons broke the law there was nothing they could do to control or limit the bar's homosexual clientele. Pearl's, in Oakland, also faced the board in 1951. As recorded in the minutes, the owner stated that "he could see no reason for eliminating homosexuals from patronage as long as they did not annoy the other customers." The owner then thumbed his nose at the board, commenting that instead of limiting the presence of homosexuals he "would rather not have service personnel."[88] By

1954, a number of gay bars retained a semi-permanent place on the AFDCB's off-limits list. Colonel Jarrel, board chairman, commented that "apparently they are not interested in trying to get the bans lifted."[89]

In the period between 1951 and 1955, the AFDCB struggled to exert pressure on gay bars in the San Francisco Bay Area, but without the SFPD and the SBE's liquor control agency to back it up, the military had little influence. The AFDCB continued to hold monthly hearings in an effort to identify gay bars and taverns, but there was no way to control these spaces or limit their growth. In 1951, C. V. Cadwell, Chairman of the Armed Forces Disciplinary Control Board, petitioned the State Board of Equalization to reinstate the wartime emergency measure that required State of California liquor control agents to post signs in bars and taverns that were off-limits to military personnel.[90] Cadwell gathered the support of high-ranking public health officials, citing increased cases of venereal disease as well as the high number of military personnel passing through San Francisco on their way to Korea. In early 1952, the SBE's liquor control agency acquiesced and Don Marshall, San Francisco Liquor Control Administrator, posted "off limits and out of bounds" signs in the Beige Room, the Black Cat Café, the 299 Club, Finocchio's, the Fang Club (formerly the 585 Club), George's Place, Jim Dolan's Supper Club, Mona's Candlelight Club, the Paper Doll Club, and the 65 Club (connected to the Silver Rail).[91] Clearly, the primary concern of the armed forces was to control not venereal disease but queer public space, and they pressured the State Board of Equalization to follow suit.

In a 1954 memo, however, the SBE questioned AFDCB tactics. The SBE had cooperated with the armed forces through the war and often followed their lead in policing unruly bars and taverns. In the postwar period, however, the SBE came under pressure from state legislators, who argued that the SBE, as a tax agency, was unable to effectively control the state's liquor traffic.[92] Indeed, the SBE paid much more attention to liquor-based tax revenue than policing. The text of the board's 1953 annual report discussed liquor revenue at length, explaining in detail a slight decrease in sales, but it dedicated only one short paragraph to policing.[93] Under pressure from state legislators, however, liquor control agents began to assert their authority. "Of the 15 premises now posted," a letter from the SBE's District Liquor Control Administrator to the AFDCB began, "12 have been so declared for the reason that they are reported to be resorts for homosexuals, and not because of incidents or allegations pertaining to other offenses." Following the language of *Stoumen,* the SBE's liquor control agency cautioned the AFDCB against relying too heavily on the simple presence of homosexuals as a reason for disciplinary action: "It is generally found that the reasons for Out of Bounds orders do not constitute grounds for disciplinary action under the ABC Act, and the military order is given upon opinion rather than on evidence," SBE agent Don Marshall quipped, and he observed that three (non-gay) bars whose liquor licenses had been revoked by the SBE had recently had their off-limits orders rescinded by the AFDCB. He curtly concluded that "it is evident that the methods of determining a cause of action employed by the military differs greatly from those of civilian agencies, and the results achieved by the different methods do not always coincide."[94]

As legal theorist William Eskridge argues, the success of postwar anti-homosexual movements in the U.S. required "a sustained level of institutional cooperation,"[95] and for a number of reasons this kind of cooperation was not available to military agencies in the period between 1951 and 1955. Frustrated by a lack of support, AFDCB members quizzed San Francisco police and liquor control agents about what action they might take against "establishments reported to be hang-outs for homos [*sic*] and other such obvious undesirable characters." The minutes of a 1955 meeting between the AFDCB, the SFPD, and the newly formed Alcoholic Beverage Control Board (ABC) clarify the policies of these agencies:

> Both Inspector Murphy, SFPD, and Mr. Falvey, ABC, advised that a case [*Stoumen v. Reilly*] in which a former Board of Equalization license had been revoked because of the congregating of homos [*sic*] on the premises had been appealed up through the California Supreme Court where the revocation was reversed on the grounds that the mere congregating of such persons was not sufficient, that there must be overt acts by these people in such a manner as to constitute an unlawful act. Therefore, since this decision, it has not been the policy of either the Police Department or the Board of Equalization (now the ABC) to institute proceedings against such establishments where only such congregation of undesirable persons was taking place.[96]

As far as the SFPD and the ABC were concerned, the public assembly of lesbians and gay men in bars and taverns was legal and, thus, unpunishable. Only the armed forces seemed oblivious to California state law, but their power at this time was minimal. They could not shut a bar down, and they could only police the presence of military personnel in bars considered deleterious by the board. As a result, the early 1950s brought the revitalization of gay life in the city. Cliques formed and communities multiplied as bars like the Beige Room established a booming business and a steady clientele.

The Beige Room opened in 1949 on Powell Street but moved to a more centrally located Broadway address in 1951. Like the Black Cat, the Beige Room was a nightclub that featured female impersonators and served a queer clientele. "It was very popular with gay people," Burt Gerrits, an old-time San Franciscan, remembers. "It wasn't so much a tourist trap or so imposing as Finocchio's."[97] T. C. Jones, Lynne Carter, Ray Saunders, and Kenneth Marlowe performed at the Beige Room, and José Sarria got his start working there. The club had an insider's appeal—many of the performers were openly gay—and headlining performers like Lynne Carter often socialized with bar patrons after the show.[98] As with vaudeville, female impersonators at the Beige Room both legitimized queer culture and set the standard for flamboyant drag performance. But unlike vaudeville, the Beige Room encouraged interaction between customers and entertainers. The bar featured dancing on Sunday afternoons, and during late-night performances entertainers often walked through the audience, teasing and joking with customers. "I remember one of those performers was perhaps a little bit annoyed by a straight woman who had such a terrible spell of laughing, she thought everything was so terribly funny. And this the entertainer put her hands on her hips and said, 'You know, you look like a *real* woman!'"[99]

Because of the level of interaction inside the bar, the culture and community of the Beige Room often spilled into after-hours clubs and parties. In fact, it was at private parties that a queer culture of high drag evolved. The private journal of Henry Diekow—who called herself the Baroness Von Dieckoff and referred to queens (like herself) with female pronouns—reveals a circle of gay socialites who moved regularly from the Beige Room to private parties and nightclubs. Written in the style of a weekly gossip column, Diekow's journal chronicles the comings and goings of the "mink and coronet set," a clique of well-dressed queers and queens who frequented the Beige Room but also staged parties and informal drag contests in their homes. Consider Diekow's June 1951 journal entry:

> On Wednesday last Mr. Al Burgess entertained some 300 guests at a private party, held in his Powell street supper club [the Beige Room]. This is an annual affair. Refreshments and entertainment were provided for the enjoyment of all. AN ARRAY OF STARS topped by such names as WALTER HART, Mr. Glenn De Mar, LYNN Carter, Gilda, Mr. Ray Saunders and Jackie Gordon gave their talents for the occasion. Society was there EN MASSE. ALL

> THE TOP names were present. After the entertainment began the parade of the "QUEENS OF SAN FRANCISCO". Prizes were awarded to the ladies who wore the most striking gowns. MRS. JACKLINE SUMMERS walked off with the FIRST prize without the slightest bit of trouble. She was BY FAR the smartest gowned person in the room. Her gown was of ice blue satin, extremely décolletage, from each hip fell cascades of loose panels which were lined with Black satin, in her hair she wore Gardenias perched high, which reminded one of the hair-do's of the great ladies of the first Empire, her ensemble was completed by diamond necklace and long pendant earrings. Among the other smartly gowned women were Mrs. Charles Lynn, Dinner gown of flesh taffeta overlaid with hundred year old black lace. Mrs. Patricia Russell, Wine Velvet and diamond jewels. Mrs. Ray Saunders, white muslin de-soie, pearls, Mrs. Chase Holiday, Black Moiré and Pearls, Baroness Von Die-Ckoff, Black Lace, Pearl jewels, Countess Evine Blanchard, Pink satin, Mrs. Charles Howard, Pink Chinese Tribute Silk. Mr. Burgess really went to town for LABELLE SOCIETY.[100]

Titled "Bag-a-Drag by the Bay," Diekow's journal refers to Herb Caen's daily column "Baghdad-by-the-Bay," which chronicled the activities of San Francisco personalities, characters, and events.[101] Diekow's journal does more than satirize San Francisco's high society, however. It documents the interplay between the public and private socializing that sustained queer and transgender communities in the cold war era.

Gays and lesbians socialized regularly at the Beige Room in the early 1950s, but they also met at popular restaurants such as the Paper Doll, Gordon's, and Dolan's Supper Club. Gay men met informally in parks and public baths, and they found each other in favorite pick-up spots like Union Square and Buena Vista Park.[102] Gays and lesbians hosted special-occasion parties, met at the opera, shared birthdays, and attended spring picnics at Stinson Beach in Marin County. In the winter of 1951, the Baroness Von Dieckoff hosted a weekly salon: "The beautifully appointed drawingroom is always filled with the crème of the intellectual cliché. Music, Art and sparkling conversation soon fill the house."[103] And, of course, there was Halloween. Through the 1950s, Halloween was the most important party of the year, and in 1954 the party was held at the Beige Room. "THE ANNUAL BEIGE BALL LURES FASHIONABLES," Diekow's 29 October 1952 journal entry begins. It describes in lush detail the night's festivities, noting, "Many hundreds of both the social and café society worlds would attend these lavish affairs. Mixing coronets and the gentry with the greatest of ease. It has not been a rarity to have seen as many as 2,000 of the mink and coronet sets gathered together in one club at the same time."[104] The end-of-October event included not simply a drag ball and a "parade of queens" but the selection of the best dressed participant. Anticipating the annual coronations that would become central to the organization of San Francisco's drag circuit—the Tavern Guild's Beaux Arts Ball and the development of José Sarria's court system—the Beige Room was the place where San Francisco's drag culture flourished.

Like the Beige Room, the Paper Doll attracted a gay and lesbian following. More of a supper club than a drag bar, the Paper Doll changed hands in 1956, when Dante Benedetti, an Italian restaurateur, purchased the bar from Tom Arbulich. "Every night there'd be at least one hundred people," Benedetti recalls, "and by the time they took my license from me that was a really popular restaurant . . . serving steaks and roast beef all for $1.65 a dinner. It brought in all kind of people. The place was packed all the time."[105] Not only was the Paper Doll important to gay and lesbian socializing, it functioned as a springboard for gay and lesbian entrepreneurs. William Bowman and Gordon Jones, who ran the Paper Doll's restaurant concession, later opened Gordon's, a popular gay bar and restaurant on Sansome Street, and Tom Redmon, who worked the Paper Doll with Jones, later ran the concession at Dolan's Supper Club on Stockton and Sutter.[106]

It was during this period that the operation of gay bars shifted somewhat to the hands of lesbian and gay entrepreneurs. Women were particularly active in opening queer bars and cafes in the North Beach district. In fact, the period between 1951 and 1955 seems to have been something of a heyday in San Francisco's lesbian bar scene because, as one interviewee noted, "When women opened bars, women followed."[107] Following the success of Mona's 440, which ran from 1939 to 1948 at 440 Broadway, Mona Sargent moved her business across the street to 473 Broadway and called it Mona's Candlelight. Co-owned by lesbian entrepreneur Wilma Swarts, the place featured a piano bar. Lesbian entertainer Kay Caroll sang at the Candlelight, and she later opened the Vieux Carré, a dance bar in Guerneville, near the Russian River.[108] In 1949, the Marefos brothers, a couple of ex–football players, opened the Chi-Chi Club at 467 Broadway, right next door to Mona's Candlelight, and while Mona's attracted mostly women, the Chi-Chi Club was mixed. It featured nightclub-style entertainment, bringing in artists such as Beverly Shaw, T. C. Jones, Ray Bourbon, Carroll Davis, Dwight Fiske, and a young Johnny Mathis.[109] However, because of its proximity to Mona's and its often queer entertainment, many women remember the Chi-Chi Club as a lesbian bar.

As discussed in the previous chapter, in 1948 Tommy Vasu opened the 299 at the corner of Broadway and Sansome, and in 1952 she opened Tommy's Place and 12 Adler Place at Broadway and Columbus. At Tommy's Place, she put Jeanne Sullivan on the liquor license, and at 12 Adler Place, Grace Miller and Joyce Van De Veer were listed as owners, and that meant they could also tend bar. San Francisco's anti-prostitution regulations prohibited women from tending bar unless they owned a percentage of the bar. Because of the women bartenders, Tommy's Place and the 12 Adler filled with lesbians. Bar owner Charlotte Coleman recalls that "when Tommy's moved up to Broadway . . . that was a good bar for many years . . . that was a great hangout."[110]

The success of places like the Beige Room, the Paper Doll, the Chi-Chi Club, Mona's Candlelight, and Tommy's bars encouraged a larger group of women to open their own North Beach bars and cafes. As described earlier, Ann's 440 replaced Mona's 440 in 1952, and it lasted for over ten years. In 1954, Connie Smith opened Miss Smith's Tea Room. It soon came under investigation by federal narcotics agents but somehow managed to stay open through the 1950s.[111] Also in 1954, Peggy Tolk-Watkins, in partnership with San Francisco's favorite brothel-keeper Sally Stanford, opened the Tin Angel down on the waterfront. Journalist Herb Caen noted that "the décor is wackily off-beat in this waterfront spa, but the music is two-beat, and the practitioners are almost always first-rate. The most off-beat character in the place will undoubtedly turn out to be the owner, Miss Peggy Tolk-Watkins, who doesn't know much about Dixieland but has a knack for creating a carnival atmosphere."[112] And in 1955 Lisa and Mike, lesbian waitresses from the Paper Doll, opened the Copper Lantern on Grant Street. The Copper Lantern survived the crackdown of the mid-1950s (although it was temporarily closed), and it went on to be one of the first places in North Beach that featured go-go dancers in the 1960s.[113] All of these bars were beer and wine joints, and while they often featured nightclub-style entertainment, they retained an informal atmosphere in which women could hang out, drink, smoke, and generally get to know each other.

THE CRACKDOWN

Through the 1940s, the weight of policing queers in San Francisco rested on a tripod of agencies: the SFPD, the SBE's liquor control agency, and the Armed Forces Disciplinary Control Board (AFDCB). After

Stoumen v. Reilly, the SFPD and SBE left policing to the AFDCB, a federal agency with little power to influence the lives of civilians, and queer life enjoyed a period of relative growth and reestablishment. In early 1955, however, California's legislature created a new agency, the Alcoholic Beverage Control Board (ABC), and later that year San Franciscans elected a new mayor, George Christopher. Both events transformed the organization of policing in San Francisco, and both responded at least indirectly to civic concerns about liquor-related crime and homosexuality. The ABC steered liquor control away from issues of revenue and taxation and focused wholeheartedly on fighting vice and graft. Christopher's election reflected a similar agenda. In 1955, he campaigned against George Reilly, the former head of the State Board of Equalization's liquor control agency, insisting that Reilly had been unable to control liquor-related vice and thus would be unfit to run the city. After the election, Christopher quickly reorganized the SFPD, naming a relative outsider (and a purported anti-graft crusader), Frank Ahern, as chief of police. With these changes to the form and function of policing, the three agencies that had been integral to a wartime anti-homosexual campaign began once again to work together.

The seeds of change were planted in 1954 when William Randolph Hearst's daily, the *San Francisco Examiner,* called upon then mayor Robinson to clean up the city. In an editorial that probably sounded familiar to anyone living in a large American city during the McCarthy era, the *Examiner* lamented the city's "unwholesome" condition and decried the "increase of homosexuals in the parks, public gathering places and certain taverns in the city." But in language only appropriate to a post-*Stoumen* California, Hearst's jeremiad leveled its strongest criticism at the courts:

> [T]here must be sustained action by the police and the district attorney to stop the influx of homosexuals. Too many taverns cater to them openly. Only police action can drive them out of the city. It is to be hoped that the courts here will finally recognize this problem for what it is and before the situation so deteriorates that San Francisco finds itself as the complete haven for undesirables. The courts heretofore have failed to support the arresting and prosecuting authorities. Without the support of the courts, the police and the district attorney cannot attack the problem effectively.[114]

Through the last week of June 1954, San Francisco police initiated a "drive on sex deviates" in which plainclothes officers from the city's sex crimes detail joined a special force of uniformed men to prowl the city looking for homosexuals.[115] On the night of 26 June, for instance, police patrolled the city's bars, parks, baths, and beaches and arrested thirteen men, including "a business executive, a college professor, a salesman, married men with children, and men picked up in Union Square, the favorite after dark rendezvous of homosexual prostitutes."[116] Two days later, the Armed Forces Disciplinary Control Board joined the fray with investigations of five Tenderloin bars: the Crystal Bowl, Lena's Burger Basket, the 1228 Club, Kip's Bar, and the Rocket Club.[117] Police Chief Michael Gaffey justified the raids as a remedy for a purported influx of homosexuals, and he worked alongside the military to control queer public space. But without the cooperation of the courts' prosecuting agents or the liquor control board, there was little more either agency could do.

The SFPD tried other strategies to shut down the city's gay bars. In August 1954 Gaffey lodged a protest against the State Board of Equalization's lame-duck liquor control agency, complaining that their "hands off policy" toward homosexual bars and taverns created a "police problem" in the city.[118] Gaffey protested the Board's issuance of a liquor license to the 181 Club on Eddy Street. Two of the license holders, Norma Clayton and Angela De Spirito, had operated Mona's 440 on Broadway, and the third, Edwin T. Atkins, performed as Lynne Carter at the Beige Room and the 440.[119] Police guessed that the three would use the 181 Club as a gay bar, and despite Gaffey's protest, that's exactly what they did. The 181 Club opened in 1954 and ran for years at 181 Eddy, featuring live entertainment, drag shows, dancing, and in the early 1970s, nude go-go boys.[120] In September 1954, however, the SFPD took a more successful stab at shutting down the city's gay bars. Just before the U.S. Senate Subcommittee on Juvenile Delinquency came to San Francisco, city police raided the 12 Adler and found underage girls. As discussed in chapter 2, a quick search revealed heroin taped behind a wash basin, and police arrested the two female bartenders.[121] Later, journalists linked the 12 Adler to a circuit of drugs, prostitution, and juvenile delinquency in the Fillmore district, the city's African American neighborhood. According to an *Examiner* editorial, it was a "harrowing situation" that involved "the corruption of young girls by . . . deviates," and the bar was quickly shut down. Still, the local press was unimpressed, asking, "Will this drive fizzle out, too? Does Chief Gaffey really mean to take effective measures? Will he get results?"[122]

Results came when liquor control in California transferred hands. In January 1955, the Alcoholic Beverage Control Board came to life, and with Russell Munro at its head, the agency boasted of "integrity," "honesty," and a uniformity of policy that was a "significant improvement from the previous . . . administration of the Board of Equalization."[123] These characteristics notwithstanding, the ABC was tough on crime and much less friendly toward queers. ABC agents carried firearms, and liquor investigations were much more serious—and sinister—than they had been under the State Board of Equalization.[124] Also, while the SBE had at times seemed wary of working with local police and/or the armed forces, the ABC stepped up a commitment to cooperative policing. ABC records reveal numerous meetings between ABC administrators, Bay Area police, and military leaders, as well as polite letters of introduction to city mayors and other elected officials.[125]

In late May 1955, just months after its establishment, the ABC "declared war on homosexual bars in San Francisco."[126] Frank Fullenwider, San Francisco area administrator, argued that the ABC need not be bound by the Black Cat case (*Stoumen v. Reilly*) if it could acquire evidence of unlawful acts within a bar. To do so, the ABC began to use undercover agents who dressed and acted gay in order to pass unnoticed in queer bars and taverns (though many agents didn't find the "acting" too difficult). A subsequent press release clarified the ABC's new policy and justified accusations against five Bay Area bars:

> The Accusations . . . include allegations of the occurrence on the premises in plain view of the proprietors, their bartenders or employees, and of members of the public, of various lewd and lascivious acts of a homosexual nature. . . . It is the position of the Department of Alcoholic Beverage Control that licensees cannot permit or participate in such acts on premises to which the general public, as a matter of law, has access. . . . It is felt that the present cases can be distinguished from that of STOUMEN V. REILLY (The Black Cat case) in which the Supreme Court refused to concur in a revocation by the State Board of Equalization, in that in that case there was simply a showing of a patronage by homosexuals and not a showing of acts of the nature involved in these cases.[127]

This policy reflected the bold nature of the ABC. Rather than submit to California law, the agency hired a team of lawyers to wrap a new interpretation around the 1951 Black Cat case. *Stoumen* had protected the public assembly of homosexuals as long as patrons were orderly, and in the period between 1951 and 1955 it was legal for homosexuals to gather in bars as long as illegal acts were not performed. Gay bars became subject to investigation, however, as ABC lawyers expanded the definition of illegal acts. To do this, they collapsed the difference between homosexual status (a state of being) and conduct (behavior) and suggested that any behavior that signified homosexual status could be construed as an illegal act. Simple acts such as random touching, mannish attire (in the case of lesbians), limp wrists, high-pitched voices, and/or tight clothing (in the case of gay men) became evidence of a bar's dubious character. More serious behaviors such as same-sex dancing, kissing, caressing, and hand-holding could be interpreted as a violation of state or municipal laws regulating public decency.[128] Most serious was same-sex sexual solicitation, a felony in California, and it was often the proposition of an undercover agent by a patron that held up most firmly in court.[129]

To make matters worse, the California State Legislature also worked to supplant *Stoumen*. Under the direction of Assemblyman Casper Weinberger (later President Ronald Reagan's secretary of defense), the 1955 legislature unanimously passed an amendment to the California Business and Professions Code that allowed the state's liquor authority to investigate any bar functioning as a "resort for sexual perverts." The full text of the code, numbered 24200(e), provided for the revocation of a bar owner's liquor license under the following conditions:

> Where the portion of the premises of the licensee upon which the activities permitted by the license are conducted are a resort for illegal possessors or users of narcotics, prostitutes, pimps, panderers, or sexual perverts. In addition to any other legally competent evidence, the character of the premises may be proved by the general reputation of the premises in the community as a resort of illegal possessors or users of narcotics, prostitutes, pimps, panderers, or sexual perverts.[130]

With the erosion of *Stoumen* and with ABC policy bolstered by state law, gay bars once again became vulnerable to intensified policing. In 1955, the Armed Forces Disciplinary Control Board, the SFPD, and the ABC coordinated an aggressive campaign to shut down and control the city's gay bars.

Soon after the ABC stepped up its commitment to policing gay bars, the police department launched an attack on queer public space. In a six-page directive to district captains, acting chief George Healy outlined a "blueprint of action" to keep "gathering places of homosexuals under constant pressure."[131] The "blueprint" targeted specific parks, baths, beaches, squares, streets, parking lots, bars, and taverns, and it ordered beat cops and plainclothes investigators from the sex crimes detail to work together. They alternated visits to places where queers congregated because "homosexuals do not like the presence of the police and will not frequent places visited by the police." Beat cops and investigators were also commanded to question young people and make arrests when possible. "Obvious homosexuals" were singled out. "The directive ordered that obvious homosexuals, or the effeminate type, are to be stopped on the streets and questioned. Arrests should be made 'if warranted.'" Chief Healy further encouraged police to park a radio car or patrol wagon "in front of a homosexual hangout a few minutes before closing time" so as to frighten customers and discourage future patronage of the bar. Finally, beat cops were instructed to forward the name, address, place of employment, and physical description of people questioned and/or arrested to sex crimes investigators, so they could flesh out a list of "known homosexuals" in the city.[132]

While beat cops and police investigators worked together to patrol the queer use of city streets, parks, and beaches, SFPD and ABC agents worked together inside bars to both entrap individuals and gather evidence of illicit behaviors. Undercover agents or decoys would flirt, buy drinks, and engage in sexual repartee with patrons.[133] On assignment, ABC agents typically carried firearms, small flasks (to sample alcoholic beverages), and notebooks (to record observations), but in gay bars, agents kept themselves free of accoutrements that might give away their status.[134] Instead, agents traveled in packs, two or three at a time, and watched each other interact with patrons so they could corroborate the evidence of their experiences.[135] In late 1959, for example, on a Saturday night just after Thanksgiving, three agents visited the Handlebar, a gay bar on California Street. Leo Orrin had opened the Handlebar in 1956, and in 1957 an accusation was filed against the bar by ABC agents who called the place a disorderly house under California Business and Professions Code 24200(e), citing the presence of homosexuals. The bar's license was revoked in 1958, and an appeal was set to be heard in early 1960. The visit by undercover agents was thus timed to occur just a month before the appeal hearing, so agents' memories would be fresh and details could easily be used as evidence against the bar.

On the night of 28 November, ABC agents Jay D. Caldis, Alexander A. Ralli, and Ronald M. Lockyer entered the Handlebar, circulated, bought drinks, and positioned themselves in different areas of the bar. Agent Caldis remembers seeing about seventy or eighty patrons, all male, when he entered the bar. He wandered around for about fifteen minutes, bought a drink, and noticed Agent Ralli talking with a patron, so he took a seat across the bar and watched them for a while. Later, a patron approached agent Caldis, asking him for a cigarette and a light.

"As I held the light for him to light his cigarette, he took hold of my hands and held on to them and squeezed them, and he looked at me, and he told me how he liked my face and thought I had a very beautiful face," Agent Caldis later testified. Agent Caldis then engaged the patron in conversation, and, later, the patron asked Caldis to go home with him:

> He asked me if I had ever been in love with another male, of which I said, "No." And he looked at me and he said, "I sure like your face." He said, "I don't love you," he says, "but I could learn to love you." And during this conversation, he says, "Would you like to come up to my place and make love tonight?" and I asked him, "What do you mean?" and he says, and he kind of hem and hawed, and he never said anything, and he—so I decided I would leave, and I says, "I will be going now," and he says, "No, don't leave me." So, I kept talking to him, and he started to rub his hands over my arms and my legs and my buttocks, and he bent over and kissed me on the cheek and on the neck. And he said finally, "I want you to love me, and I want to love you at my place tonight." [136]

Across the bar, Agent Ralli watched Caldis and the patron: "I observed him [the patron] lean forward and kiss the agent on the cheek and the ear." Later Ralli observed them standing face to face and "very very close" for about ten minutes, during which time "on many occasions their bodies were touching." [137] When Ralli saw the two men rise and walk out of the bar, he quickly followed, and in the words of Agent Caldis "immediately outside the front door of the premises, we placed [the patron] under arrest." [138]

ABC agents thus worked together to snare gay men, promising a sexual liaison and then entrapping and arresting them once they left the bar. But that was not all. ABC agents also worked to procure enough evidence against the bar to warrant a revocation of its license under the newly applied ABC law. In the lower courts, cases against gay bars did not rely as heavily on the testimony of police decoys, but under appeal, undercover agents had to present and defend their stories. Leo Orrin's attorney Clifford J. Krueger, for example, won his appeal to the ABC partly on the basis of inconsistent evidence, and the case proceeded to the San Francisco Superior Court.[139] Through each of these hearings, the testimony of Agents Caldis and Ralli functioned as the backbone of the state's argument against the bar, and defense attorneys protested the viability of their stories. Was Agent Caldis telling the truth about his experience inside the Handlebar? Did the patron really make the first move? Was sexually suggestive speech indicative of lewd behavior? Did swishing movements, high-pitched voices, or limp wrists, as Agent Ralli observed, signify a disorderly establishment? Or did these behaviors simply signal the presence of homosexuals, as defense attorney Krueger asserted? Could Agent Ralli really see what was going on between Agent Caldis and the patron or was the bar too crowded for his testimony to hold any weight? And most important, where were the bartenders? Did they try to stop or control the behaviors of the men in the bar? What responsibility did a bar owner have for the actions of patrons?[140]

It was only through a series of ABC hearings and intermediate appellate court cases that the answers to these questions worked themselves out. *Nickola v. Munro,* for instance, relied on California Business and Professions Code 24200(e) to revoke the liquor license of a bar called Hazel's, and in doing so it eroded *Stoumen*'s ability to protect the assembly of homosexuals inside bars and taverns. Code 24200(e) allowed ABC agents to move against a bar that catered to "sex perverts" even though no serious crimes such as sodomy or oral copulation were being committed.[141] And as attorneys debated the definition of "sex pervert," case testimony registered a litany of lesser crimes that could be used to establish the bar's disorderly character. Court testimony from *Nickola* registered the presence of men dancing with men and women dancing with women. "Many of the men had their arms wrapped around each other's waists, or shoulders, or buttocks. Many men were observed kissing or fondling or biting each other, or holding hands, and other men were seen sitting on the laps of their male companions and kissing and fondling each other."[142] Also, because ABC agents only needed to produce evidence of the presence of "perverts" in order to shut down the bar under Code 24200(e), gender-transgressive speech and gestures became important observations in the eyes of the court. Agents testified that "female patrons were dressed in mannish attire," and "men were seen powdering their faces, talking in effeminate voices, and generally acting like over-affectionate females."[143] But even as *Nickola* empowered the ABC to broaden its definition of "illicit behavior" and defy *Stoumen,* it inserted a new language about the responsibilities of bar owners into the public record. *Nickola* insisted that in order for the ABC to revoke the liquor license of a gay bar owner, the owner "must have actual knowledge that his premises are being used for such purposes."[144] This gave bar owners new defenses in protesting cases against them. In fact, this was the most effective defense Krueger used in the Handlebar's initial hearing.

Nickola was also an important case in California's legal history in that it revealed the heightened coordination of ABC agents, police, prosecuting attorneys, and the courts. *Nickola* followed an uncommonly large raid on Hazel's, a popular gay bar just south of San Francisco. Hazel Nickola opened Hazel's in 1939, and she ran the place herself, tending bar and overseeing the premises at night. On 19 February 1956, after watching the bar for several months, Sheriff Whitmore of San Mateo County led a raid on Hazel's.[145] Although the sheriff's staff could have easily handled the raid, they called in extra deputies, ABC agents, military police, and the California Highway Patrol—a total of thirty-five people—to help with the arrests. "Prior to the entry of uniformed officers," the next day's news reported, "five undercover agents—including Harry Kunst, San Francisco District enforcement supervisor for the liquor control unit—mingled with 'Hazel's' predominantly male clientele."[146] Shortly after midnight, police and other law enforcement officers rounded up the almost 300 patrons and picked out 90 regulars who undercover agents insisted they recognized from previous visits. Those arrested included seventy-seven men, ten women, and three minors, all of whom were booked on vagrancy charges.[147] Police also arrested Hazel Nickola for "operating a dance without a permit" and three bartenders for "serving drinks to a minor."[148] Calling the action "headline hunting" and illegal, the American Civil Liberties Union (ACLU) took up the case, arguing that it denied due process to those arrested and ignored the statutory requirement of a speedy trial. More importantly, ACLU lawyers challenged the constitutionality of vagrancy law. "Vagrancy," the appeal brief read, "is a crime of condition, of status; one in which character is involved."[149] Civil rights protections thus gave lawyers some ground to stand on, and the individuals arrested at Hazel's were difficult to prosecute en masse. A separate ABC hearing, however, was much more efficient than the civil cases that preceded it. The ABC trial resulted in a quickly issued state order to revoke Hazel's liquor license.[150]

As the case against Hazel's wound its way through the California appeals process, it whittled down the homosexual right to assembly and bolstered the state's ability to permanently shut down gay bars and taverns. Meanwhile, with the election of Mayor George Christopher, the city of San Francisco became an increasingly hostile environment for queers. On 8 November 1955, when Christopher was elected mayor, he had already served ten years on the city's Board of Supervisors. A Greek immigrant, the new mayor had grown up in the city's South of Market district, where he learned firsthand how crime functioned in the city. He knew that police captains and beat cops guarded their territory with a vigilance that was often connected to cash payoffs, and he knew that San Francisco's lucrative tourist economy depended on vice interests protected by the SFPD. Moreover, he knew that the citizens of San Francisco were more likely to support free-wheeling and commercialized vice over puritanical interests that held to the letter of the law. "There were many upright citizens who had no objection to 'houses' and a bit of gambling," former Chief of Police Michael Riordan explained. "It was all right if San Francisco was 'a *little* crooked.'"[151] Still, Christopher campaigned on a pro-business and anti-vice platform, and the election was a landslide. He defeated challenger George Reilly almost two votes to one. Perhaps Christopher simply seemed the better of the two candidates to vice interests, but if they were surprised to find him elected, they were even more surprised to find him making good on anti-vice campaign promises.[152]

Christopher's war on vice began almost as soon as he was elected, and his first order of business was to reorganize the city's police department.[153] After a scandal that involved a Treasury Department raid on a big midcity booking agency, the new mayor asked for Police Chief Healy's resignation. He warned that if outside agents knew more about crime than the chief of police did, he had no business running the department.[154] The new chief was to be appointed by Christopher's squeaky-clean trio of new police commissioners, and after much deliberation and allegedly no input from the mayor, they put forward Frank Ahern, a square-jawed man with a reputation for stern dealings with vice and crime.[155] Ahern sought to break down the department's well-entrenched alliances, and to do this he transferred all captains and lieutenants out of their districts. Later, he moved over half of the department's sergeants, transferring lax officers to quiet residential neighborhoods and moving those he considered trustworthy to the city center.[156] Breaking alliances meant disrupting a circuit of payoffs that had long sustained vice in the city, and the city responded with a resounding "No!" Letters poured into the mayor's office, and the dailies printed the protests of taxpaying citizens—law abiding or not. Christopher recalls, "It got to the point where you'd have thought *they* were the crusaders and *I* was the bad guy."[157]

Police payoffs had greased the wheels of vice in San Francisco from the 1920s, when speakeasies flagrantly ignored federal law and cops protected the local right to defy Prohibition. In the 1930s, crime bosses like bail bondsman Pete McDonough shifted their business from the protection of individuals after arrest (securing bail through a judge's quickly issued order of release) to the protection of individuals before arrest. "Immunity from arrest" could be secured through intricate networks of payoffs, and Pete McDonough and his brother made it their business to get to know everyone in the path of their particular brand of justice. From their post at the Corner, a family-owned saloon near the Hall of Justice, the McDonough brothers mixed with lawmakers of all stripes—from beat cops to the district attorney and the mayor—and they took payments from anyone in need of protection. Tenderloin prostitutes contributed 10 percent of their income to the McDonough brothers, and bookies siphoned off revenue to pay for protection. "No one can conduct a prostitution or gambling enterprise in San Francisco without approval direct or indirect of the McDonough Brothers," a popular journalist noted.[158] And payoffs were no secret. San Franciscans seemed smugly satisfied that crime in the city was a home industry, presided over by locals rather than outside agents or organized crime.[159]

In a 1943 bid for San Francisco district attorney, Edmund G. (Pat) Brown concluded, "There is no organized crime in San Francisco; the crime is all organized by the police department."[160] San Francisco was indeed a town where local police took the lead in protecting the city's vice interests, and despite Brown's victory at the polls, police payoffs continued well into the next decade. Police graft made headlines in 1952, for example, when the State Crime Commission raided the Beach Chalet on San Francisco's Ocean Beach. Fronted as a nightclub, the Beach Chalet had long functioned as a gambling den, but city police refused to move against the bar. When state agents raided the place they found expense sheets that recorded "juice" (payoffs) to police for up to $250.[161] It seemed that with the right connections, an illegal business could continue almost indefinitely. "Abortion queen" Inez Brown Burns, for example, ran a clinic in San Francisco for over thirty years, and she regularly paid off police and politicians. Between 1920 and 1955, Burns performed over twenty abortions a day, and at $50 an abortion, she grossed up to $50,000 a month. Burns always kept some cash available for payoffs; in fact, she once offered Frank Ahern, who was then a rackets investigator, a bribe of $250,000 to forget her arrest.[162] His refusal guaranteed his reputation as a straight dealer, and later it netted him a top position in Christopher's administration.[163]

Christopher and Ahern's partnership transformed the city. Bookies moved to South San Francisco, gambling houses moved across the bay, and prostitutes shut down shop for a while. Gay bars suffered a similar fate. Already under the gun from ABC agents, the reorganization of the

SFPD tightened the screws on the city's gay bars. Long-standing gay bars like the Black Cat and Paper Doll that had, no doubt, secured protections from beat cops and/or district captains, found themselves under investigation by a coterie of law enforcement agents, including SFPD and ABC investigators. The Paper Doll, for example, had run smoothly from the time of its opening in 1949, but when Dante Benedetti purchased the place from Tom Arbulich in 1956, he noticed discrepancies in revenues that indicated payoffs had probably been a part of Arbulich's monthly expenses.[164] Benedetti did not pay off the police, and he naively considered the Paper Doll to be a reputable business. "I never had any idea whatsoever that there was anything wrong with operating a gay bar," he noted in an oral history.[165] His family ran the New Pisa, a popular Italian restaurant in North Beach, and Dante, the oldest son, had purchased the Paper Doll as a side interest. His timing was bad, however, because the mid-1950s brought a change in city policing as well as state law, and in August 1956, the ABC filed accusations against four gay bars, including the Paper Doll.[166] Based on the testimony of undercover agents who had allegedly been solicited by men inside the bar, an ABC hearing in May 1957 concluded that the Paper Doll functioned as a "resort of sex perverts." Benedetti lost his liquor license and appealed his case twice before shutting the place down in early 1961.[167]

The case against the Paper Doll was part of a much larger police offensive in which the armed forces, SFPD, and ABC investigators worked to put gay bars out of business. In November 1957, Frank Fullenwider, San Francisco area administrator for the ABC, discussed his strategy with journalists. The state's First District Court of Appeals had just upheld a liquor license revocation against Pearl's in Oakland, and Fullenwider felt vindicated. The case against Pearl's (*Kershaw v. Munro*) was the first to be tested in a California high court after the 1951 *Stoumen* decision, and a victory for the ABC affirmed the agency's legal strategy of ignoring *Stoumen*'s distinction between status and behavior, as well as its tactic of using undercover agents to procure evidence against gay bars. Fullenwider noted that the *Kershaw* decision would set a precedent for the dozen other "sex deviate" cases currently moving through the system. At the time, there were revocation hearings pending for four gay clubs: the 57 Club, the Uptown Club, the Handlebar, and the On the Hill. There were also appeals pending for six gay taverns in the San Francisco area—the Black Cat, the Paper Doll, Ethel's, the Spur Club, the Crossroads, and the Frontier Village—and two popular gay bars just outside of San Francisco, Hazel's in Sharp Park (Pacifica) and the Albatross at Muir Beach in Marin County.[168]

Because of its notoriety, the case against the Black Cat offers the best picture of how these cases proceeded. After *Stoumen v. Reilly,* the Black Cat continued to be a "hangout for homosexuals" through the turbulent 1950s. In fact, it was during this period that entertainer José Sarria began to encourage queers to think of themselves as part of a larger gay community. As a part of his performances, he warned gay men to avoid entrapment and, if arrested, to assert their rights. Later, he used his platform at the Black Cat to stage an unsuccessful bid for a seat on the San Francisco Board of Supervisors. In 1956, however, SFPD and ABC agents delivered a blow to the bar that would become fatal. Based on evidence procured by undercover agents, the ABC ordered a hearing, and in a pattern established in previous hearings, ABC witnesses testified that patrons had solicited them to engage in "lewd acts." On the basis of this evidence, the hearing board reasoned that the bar catered to "sexual perverts," and it ordered the revocation of Sol Stoumen's liquor license. However, defending attorney Morris Lowenthal argued that undercover agents "induced patrons to solicit them" and were thus acting in bad faith, entrapping patrons and using these occasions as evidence against the bar. Lowenthal further argued that the California Business and Professions Code 24200(e) was unconstitutional in light of the California Supreme Court's 1951 *Stoumen* decision. With these objections in mind, the case proceeded to the ABC Appeals Court.[169]

In the appeal case, Lowenthal attacked the ABC's application of California Business and Professions Code 24200(e) to the city's gay bars on the grounds that homosexuals could not be proven to be "sexual perverts." In a strategy similar to the one he used in *Stoumen v. Reilly,* Lowenthal used the Kinsey Report as evidence, reasoning that "modern researchers on sex have shown that a large number of persons have homosexual relations at one time or another."[170] Moreover, he argued that because homosexuals can not be distinguished by their mannerisms or physical features, a bartender should not be held accountable for serving drinks to homosexuals. The state's deputy attorney general disagreed: "It is our contention anyone can tell a homosexual," he retorted, and noted that gay bars "constitute a danger . . . to morals and health. If it constitutes a danger to the public, a bar owner's license will be taken away from him to protect the greater public interest."[171] Despite the tremendous case assembled by Lowenthal, the testimony of undercover agents sealed the case, and Stoumen lost his appeal to the ABC, the California Superior Court, and the First District Court of Appeals. The California Supreme Court refused to hear the case, and on 30 October 1963, the bar finally shut down.[172]

The 1940s and 1950s presented a curious combination of opportunities and hazards for queers in San Francisco. Wartime migrations stimulated the city's economy, and gay life blossomed around the city center despite the warnings of military police. In the postwar period, the "gay bar" emerged as the center of community life, and through the next few decades it became an important institution in the development of San Francisco's queer history. The gay bar was a public space where lesbians and gay men were able to meet others like themselves, and a culture developed inside bars that transformed a random or fleeting cohort of individuals into a collective. The bar was the space where queers learned to resist police harassment and to demand the right to public assembly. Those who participated in queer bar life experienced the thrill of camaraderie that singing, dancing, and socializing brought, but when the thrill quickened to fear, lesbians and gay men connived to come up with new ways to resist. Structural defenses, networking, and legal debate became the backbone of queer community resistance in the 1950s. And although bar raids continued through these years, it was not until the mid-1950s that a combination of local, state, and federal agencies determined an airtight strategy to shut down gay bars and taverns.

Just as World War II brought military policing to San Francisco, the McCarthy era brought cold war concerns and paranoia. Juvenile delinquency, narcotics, and alcohol control consumed lawmakers, and San Francisco police were pushed to control vice more vigorously than ever before. Well established practices like police payoffs and civic graft became suspect as straight-talking lawyers like Edmund G. Brown and law-and-order officials like George Christopher came into power. In the mid-1950s, the extralegal protection of bars and taverns fell into disarray, and undercover agents serendipitously collected evidence against gay bars. By the end of the 1950s, most gay bars had faced ABC hearings, and only a few survived the charges brought against them. Interestingly, just as the state sealed its case against gay bars, new institutions rose up to defend queer civil rights and demand justice. In the mid-1950s two homophile organizations, the Mattachine Society and the Daughters of Bilitis, began a civil rights campaign on behalf of homosexuals in San Francisco. These organizations functioned differently than bars—their priorities ran in a completely different direction—but their contribution to queer life in the city was profound. Homophile activism built upon and complemented the groundswell created by queer bar culture in San Francisco.

ORAL HISTORY

Del Martin and Phyllis Lyon

D.M.: In the 1940s and 1950s there were bars out in North Beach: Mona's, the Chi-Chi Club—

P.L.: —the Paper Doll.

D.M.: But it wasn't like we had a community. It was like there were places to go for entertainment and there was a certain ambiance, but there was not the sense of community that we have developed since.

N.B.: What is a community? How would you define that?

P.L.: Well, I vary from talking about a gay or lesbian community to saying that I don't know if we have one. And if we have one, we've got ten. There are many different communities. We've got a sense of community now, but I don't think the idea of a community ever occurred to any of us in the '40s and '50s.

D.M.: When Phyllis and I got together—

P.L.: —1953—

D.M.: —we went to North Beach. We didn't know any other lesbians, but we'd heard about these places, so we went to them. In North Beach there were people who knew each other and little cliques and so on—

P.L.: —at least that's what it appeared to us—

D.M.: —and we did not know how to mix with them. We felt like tourists.

P.L.: We were too shy to go over and say, "Hi! We just moved here from Seattle. What's going on?" There were cliques. If you went into a restaurant now and you saw a big table full of people and they were having, you know, dinner together or something, you'd figure it's somebody's birthday or somebody's having a party. These are

Del Martin and Phyllis Lyon, interviewed by Nan Alamilla Boyd, tape recording, San Francisco, 2 December 1992, Wide Open Town History Project, GLBT Historical Society. This interview has been edited by the author.

all people who know each other and you don't, or can't, or wouldn't or whatever, go over and interrupt that.

D.M.: I didn't see that as a community. I see a community as much broader than just a small group of people that know each other. My sense of community is much broader.

P.L.: Well, I guess what I was saying was about Scott's Pit. Are you familiar with Scott's Pit? When Kate Ullman took that bar over [in the early 1970s], it became a focal point for the community. Or a certain part of the community.

D.M.: But she called us up one time and asked us to come speak at the bar—

P.L.: —to the bar scene.

D.M.: And we said, "Are you crazy?"

P.L.: "You want us to speak at a bar?"

D.M.: But she talked us into it. She brought NOW [the National Organization of Women] into it, she brought different groups to come and talk about women's issues, and she got people to read poetry. It was packed! Who ever thought there would be a packed bar for a poetry reading? So that, the buildup she had been working towards and the sense of community she brought to it all, let that happen.

N.B.: Yes. Pat Bond has a thing that she wrote and, I guess, performed called "The Only Gay Bar in Town" or something. I don't know if you ever saw it or if she ever performed it. She talks about the bar as a site of community in the '50s—

D.M.: Well, she's a very different type of lesbian. Of course, I'm just talking about when we were new to the bars. She would be right there, you know, leading the group—

P.L.: Yeah, there was nothing shy about Ms. Bond. What I was going to say was that feeling for us of bars being a place of community or at least a place where you had friends—people knew you, you knew them, you felt really at ease with them—came probably in the '60s for us.

D.M.: Well, when we got to know more people it helped.

P.L.: Yeah, right.

D.M.: Remember, we didn't know any lesbians. So there we were. But we did meet a lesbian through a couple of gay men that lived around the corner from us (incidentally, we were on Castro Street), and she called up one time and said would we be interested in a lesbian club that they were going to form. A social club. And we jumped at the chance. Here was our chance to meet other lesbians. That's how Daughters of Bilitis came into existence, as a very secret lesbian social club.

N.B.: Do you remember who that person was?

D.M.: Yes, we know who she was. Her name was Noni.

N.B.: Does she not want to be known?

P.L.: Well, believe it or not, we've lost track of everybody who was involved in the early days of DOB, so we don't know.

D.M.: When Daughters of Bilitis started, there were eight of us. There were four blue-collar workers and four, you know, white-collar workers.

P.L.: It simply—

D.M.: And the thing was that it split when we decided that we wanted to see more happen than just social, you know, parties and so on. The split was on the part of the blue-collar workers because they wanted to really stay under cover. They did not want to get involved in anything more, it was just like a—

P.L.: —ceremony and stuff.

D.M.: —ceremonial.

P.L.: Investitures. Ceremonies. A lodge kind of thing.

D.M.: A sorority thing or something. And the Filipino woman whose idea was it, the club, she just wanted to have parties and dance. You couldn't dance in the bars then.

N.B.: Do you know who she was?

P.L.: Well, her name was Rose, Noni's friend.

N.B.: Could you get in touch with her if you needed to?

D.M.: No, I don't think so. We've lost track of them.

N.B.: You don't know if she's still alive or not?

D.M.: Don't know.

P.L.: We heard from her, God, ten years ago or something—

D.M.: It was twenty years ago.

P.L.: Twenty years ago, when the book [*Lesbian/Woman*] came out. And that's the last time. I mean, she was strictly in the closet and was going to stay there. I don't think that she would talk to you. I doubt it. You know in our age group most people were in the closet, and there's a lot of them, even though they're a lot older and retired and everything else, that remain in the closet. That was their life.

N.B.: It might be interesting just to ask her, you know—

D.M.: Well, I don't know how to get in touch with her. The thing about our training in the '50s is you don't blow anybody's cover. That's really ingrained in us. We had to live through that time when you didn't acknowledge somebody's presence unless they gave you the cue that it was okay because they had other people with them.

N.B.: Do you remember what the cue was?

P.L.: Well, they'd speak to you. In other words, if you saw a lesbian across the street with some people you didn't know, you weren't going to say, "Hi Sally!" or anything unless she saw you and said, "Hi Phyllis. I'd like you to meet blah blah" or something. It was just a very scary time. People were deeply in the closet.

P.L.: So you didn't ask. Somebody didn't come to DOB and you said, "Oh hi! Now where do you work? And what's your last name? Give me your address and phone number and da da da." You were very careful—

P.L.: I've forgotten how we heard of Mattachine. Was that how we got started—

D.M.: No, we—

P.L.: How did we hear about them? One Institute. But I wonder how we heard about One? That must have been earlier.

D.M.: I don't remember how we met Mattachine.

P.L.: But we did, and then we ended up using a corner of their office as our office.

N.B.: Do you think that you were really influenced by what Mattachine was doing?

D.M.: Well, I'm sure there was some influence. We did go to their public discussion meetings.

P.L.: The main difference was that we were aware we were an organization for lesbians. Not only for all women, but primarily for lesbians. Whereas Mattachine was an organization that was interested in the homosexual condition and stuff like that.

N.B.: So you feel like DOB was much more—

P.L.: Open. If you will—[laughter]

D.M.: Well, for example, we had out first national convention in 1960 at the Wickham Hotel, on the top—

P.L.: —floor—

D.M.: —floor. And Phyllis was doing the PR, and she was saying this was the first, you know, lesbian—

P.L.: National lesbian convention, which it was.

D.M.: And Hal [Call] called—

P.L.: Mattachine.

D.M.: —he said that there was a distinction, you know, that their organization had always said they were interested in homosexuality but they were not called a gay organization or anything—

P.L.: Oh, Hal said he didn't know if any of the Mattachine members could come because of this outrageous stance that we had taken.

D.M.: So the chapter president of DOB at the time wrote him a letter and said that if the members of Mattachine, who were 99 percent men, dressed properly and conducted themselves—

P.L.: —with decorum—

D.M.: —with decorum, that they surely wouldn't be taken for lesbians.

P.L.: We still had the largest gathering of lesbians that had been held in the country, to our knowledge anyhow, at that time, without hardly anybody from Mattachine.

D.M.: Well, the whole thing was that everybody was scared spitless, so we had to deal with all their fears. When we had public discussion meetings we had lawyers and psychiatrists and different professional people who came and talked and tried to get over the message that lesbians were okay—

P.L.: They weren't sick—

D.M.: A lot of them, when they were caught up in a raid, they would plead guilty. Well, what were they pleading guilty to? They were pleading guilty to being homosexual, which was not against the law. It was not what the police were accusing them of. Our best lesson was once, after we got an attorney for some women who got caught up in a bar raid, the attorney said just plead not guilty. Later, when they were questioning the officer about what these women did, he didn't have any notion at all. He just dragged them all out. So the cases got dismissed. A lot of it was just fear and not knowing what the law really was. What a lot of them would do was just plead guilty to some silly thing—disturbing the peace or something—and pay a fine and get out of it. But we learned how to get them free altogether. We learned a lot about the law, and we found the more liberal therapists—those that would support us. And we did need validation. We did need to build self-esteem. So did those women who were scared spitless. We weren't exactly real brave, but we sort of got into the role of leadership and, I guess, in the process of having to do it you get over your own fears and then you help others get over theirs. But people say, "Well, why weren't you out there picketing and doing all this in the '50s?" Well, hell, you can't have a movement until you've got yourself—

P.L.: —and some people to move!

D.M.: People need to have a sense of self-worth to fight for. What we were trying to do at that time is survive. What we were trying to do is build a sense of community, among those of us who could, that gave us self-esteem and gave us a sense of our own individual power—and then our power as a group. I don't care what you call it, but that's what we were trying to do. When we had what we called Gab-and-Java, which were discussions and so on, they were really consciousness-raising groups, but we didn't have that language. You have to build a sense of community within your group before you can do anything else.

P.L.: I think a lot of to-do came out about the clothing restrictions. We had a rule at some point that said that nobody should wear men's clothing. That came about because we had some members who were wearing men's clothing and looking very butch. That upset some of the others who were sure that if they were seen next to the butches they might be targeted as the same, so we passed this rule and everyone was happy and nothing ever happened again. I mean, people wore men's clothing anyway and nobody said anything about it. Nobody was ever called on the carpet because of it or anything else, and that was it.

D.M.: It was just to appease the group at the time. But I recall once when we went to a brunch, and I had gotten this new suit that had a pants and a vest and a jacket—

P.L.: God—that was great.

D.M.: And I just loved it.

P.L.: Striped and it had a skirt and jacket and vest and pants.

D.M.: The whole works. And later we heard that there'd been all this to-do about what Del was wearing—

P.L. and D.M.: Men's clothes!

P.L.: The other part about clothing is that lesbians ought to be able to wear and be comfortable in any kind of clothing, from an evening gown to whatever—

D.M.: Whatever the occasion called for.

P.L.: The whole thing was to keep from being excluded because you wouldn't or didn't feel comfortable in or couldn't wear the kinds of clothes that at that time were called for. But, for the most part, nobody wore pants to work.

D.M.: No. Heavens no.

P.L.: Nobody I knew. Well if you saw anybody, I mean, I was working temporary when we first got together, so that must have been '53 or something, and there was a woman with very short hair and a Pendleton jacket. I had determined that Pendleton jackets meant lesbian. That was it. And she wore pants.

D.M.: Well, she was working at a cafeteria.

P.L.: I thought, "I bet she's a lesbian," so I would have these weird conversations with her where I would say, "Did you have a *date* last night?" But nothing ever happened. Nothing ever happened. To this day I do not know.

D.M.: Yeah, but we got into pants as often as possible. It was okay in the gay bars.

P.L.: It wasn't always okay, though.

D.M.: Oh, no. The men wanted the—

P.L.: —lesbians to dress up.

D.M.: Talk about gender! They wanted women in their bars to wear skirts.

P.L.: Gay men's bars. We didn't go to a lot of them because of that.

D.M.: I remember Charlotte Coleman and her bars. She opened, what was the one on Haight Street, the Golden—

P.L.: —the Golden Cask.

D.M.: When she first opened, lesbians were required to dress in skirts until the guys got used to them. When she opened the Mint, it was the same thing. Because where you made the money is on the gay men. Lesbians don't go to bars as often.

N.B.: Did you go to the Paper Doll?

D.M.: Yeah, we went to the Paper Doll.

N.B.: Did you have to dress in skirts for the Paper Doll?

D.M.: No.

P.L.: Because up in North Beach, early on, lesbians were part of the floor show, in a sense. They wanted you to look at the queer, not—

D.M.: I remember Mona's, when they had a charge to get in, and lesbians could get in for free because they were part of the floor show. And they had a nightclub with—

P.L.: —male impersonators.

D.M.: Male impersonators. This time it was the woman impersonating a man.

D.M.: Later, there was Ann's 440 and the place across the street was Mona's Candlelight. Mona's Candlelight I particularly remember as, well, the way we described it going into a bar and not knowing anybody. I remember that was a bar that we felt very uncomfortable in.

P.L.: Yeah. Because we felt so out of it.

D.M.: We *were* out of it.

N.B.: What about the impact of the Civil Rights Movement on the homophile movement?

D.M.: It certainly had an influence on getting us out in the streets, and we got out in the streets long before Stonewall. We did by the mid-60s. In fact, in 1966 we had our first national demonstration around the armed services issue, which is rather prominent now. And we demonstrated out in front of the Federal Building.

N.B.: Here in San Francisco?

D.M.: Yeah. And in Los Angeles, they had a—

P.L.: Caravan, or something.

D.M.: Cars, you know, driving around with their banners and so on. Then there was something going on in New York, Washington, DC, and someplace in the midwest. The thing is, though, while DOB was represented in a lot of these things, it was mostly Phyllis and me. I think back east there was, you know, Barbara Giddings and some of the others, but there were just a few of us who were really involved. But the DOB name was used as a sponsor, along with the others. I remember that with the founding of the Council on Religion and the Homosexual, which happened in '64, some of the DOB people said to us, "You can't get all involved in that. What about DOB?"

P.L.: But we stayed with DOB for a while.

D.M.: Yeah, we did.

P.L.: We also figured that there was no rule that said you had to stay with an organization just because you had been involved in starting it. If it wasn't strong enough to stand by its own without you then there was something wrong.

D.M.: It was about '68 when I dropped out—

P.L.: And I took a little longer.

D.M.: Yeah, you took a little longer. But part of our interest in DOB when we started was dealing with the fact that we were considered to be illegal, immoral, and sick. So one of the things we got involved in was acting as guinea pigs for researchers on lesbians because we just said, "We're not sick!"

P.L.: No!

D.M.: And they said, "You are too." So we figured we had to do something that could influence their thinking, and where they came from—

D.M.: We were not so well known in the '50s. But then, in 1960, when we had our first national convention, the police arrived as we were about to sit down for a luncheon. It was the homosexual detail of the vice squad that showed up.

P.L.: Who knew nothing whatsoever.

D.M.: And their biggest question was, "Do you advocate wearing the clothes of the opposite sex?" That was their big concern. At that point, though, everybody was dressed up. It was our first public event.

P.L.: There wasn't a woman in pants in the place.

D.M.: So I said, "Look around you. Does it look like it?" We always heard the story that you had to wear at least three items of clothing of your own sex, and it does seem that the police were concerned about cross-dressing, that that was a big thing. I guess that was the way that could identify us, you know. And that's how we could identify ourselves. Probably the reason for dressing butch was to let you know, "Here I am! I want to meet some of you." We didn't have many ways of finding each other. It was very difficult. So they pegged onto that because that was all the cops could figure out about us.

N.B.: Because lesbians weren't arrested for—

P.L.: Well, we weren't arrested for public sex because basically we didn't do public sex.

N.B.: And when lesbians were arrested in bars, it was for vagrancy?

P.L.: Well, it depended. Sometimes it was visiting a house of ill repute. Or it was disturbing the peace. Or it was, like with Mary's First and Last Chance, this butch said to an undercover woman cop, "You're a cute little butch," or something like that. Big deal. I mean, big horrendous deal. They were just mostly doing that to harass.

N.B.: What was your relationship like with the bar community beyond when you first initially were in Ann's 440 and didn't feel comfortable there? My assumption is that the kind of women who went to DOB functions weren't necessarily the kind of women who went to bars, or was there cross—

P.L.: Oh, there was cross-fertilization.

D.M.: Well Charlotte Coleman had a bar called the—

P.L.: —the Front.

D.M.: The Front. In the '50s. And we got acquainted—

P.L.: It was beer and wine—

D.M.: Yeah, we got acquainted with her, and during the 1960 convention she closed down one night so we could have a party at her place.

P.L.: And in those days you had to go to the ABC and get permission to close down for a private party.

D.M.: And so I guess—

P.L.: Rikki [Streicher] has determined that we are anti-bar, but we are not. Except for now because their music is so loud, you can't stand it. But we used to go to bars all the time.

D.M.: Yeah, but we followed Charlotte more than we did Rikki.

P.L.: That's true. Charlotte did a lot of things to help DOB. If we were having a party and we needed liquor, or she'd help us get food, or whatever. She was helpful in those ways.

P.L.: She gave money.

D.M.: She gave money and when she opened the Golden Cask, we followed her along there. We followed her to the Mint. She was our bar person.

P.L.: We tried to get her to start a women's bar and restaurant, and she said if we'd paid for it she'd do it. It would never make it—I'm sure she was right.

D.M.: I remember once having a brunch down at the Front. We had invited some of our heterosexual friends and they—

P.L.: —women—

D.M.: Women. And they were hugging and kissing and Charlotte's having a fit. We said, "They're straight," but she said, "The ABC wouldn't know that."

N.B.: Why do you think Rikki thinks you are anti-bar?

D.M.: Because there were some references, certainly in the *Ladder* and so on, that DOB was started as an alternative to gay bars.

P.L.: Which was true!

D.M.: Because bars got raided, you know. There were a lot of raids.

P.L.: And people would look at you and stare at you like you were a freak, you know, that kind of stuff.

D.M.: And so there was that, you know, privatization that came along.

N.B.: So you see DOB as a privatization?

D.M.: Well, at that point it was an alternative to gay bars. Getting away from the cops coming in to the bars and being able to dance, which was in the privacy of your own home. Then later Rikki was saying we were anti-bars, but we were the ones who got attorneys to get the lesbians off and tell them what their rights were. Not to run in there and plead guilty right away.

N.B.: Were there women in DOB who had been arrested and needed legal services? Or what was your—

P.L.: Well, maybe at Kelly's. Yeah, they called us and said, "Ah! Help!" This one woman said, "I want to be a teacher!" So we said, "Well, we better find an attorney."

D.M.: And then what was that bar out on Irving Street?

P.L.: Finn Alley. Now that was hilarious. This one member of DOB used to go out there, and we'd go out there and so on and so forth. Anyhow, they had go-go girls on the bar. That was a wild place, right on Irving Street. And we kept saying, "You know, this place is going to get raided any day now." I remember talking to the school teacher in the middle of this bar. The place is just packed with lesbians, right, and we're standing in the passageway next to the bar and she said, "Oh. I couldn't possibly join DOB. Somebody might find out I was a lesbian." And I said, "Well, what do you think they think now."

D.M.: I remember that some of our members would go to bars and they wouldn't tell anybody they belonged to DOB.

P.L.: Because there were also these strange stories that we were all pinko-commies, for one thing.

D.M.: Yeah.

P.L.: And another one was that you had to be in a couple. And then there was the one that we had orgies. When did we have an orgy? So there was a lot of that. Some of the members were ashamed or afraid or insecure about being a member.

D.M.: They thought they might be ridiculed for belonging to DOB, I think.

N.B.: Because DOB wasn't cool or hip?

P.L.: Depends on whose story you'd heard, I guess.

N.B.: Is that what you're implying, or am I misunderstanding?

P.L.: Yeah, I think that was part of it. They were afraid that people would think there was something wrong if they belonged to DOB. If you were a real dyke you just went to the bars, maybe. Who needed this old club thing.

4 | "A QUEER LADDER OF SOCIAL MOBILITY"

San Francisco's Homophile Movements, 1953–1960

> Since variants desire to be accepted by society, it behooves them to assume community responsibility. . . . For only as they make positive contributions to the general welfare can they expect acceptance and full assimilation into the communities in which they live.
>
> *Mattachine Society, 1956*

In her 1993 video *Last Call at Maud's,* director Paris Poirier captures the energy and nostalgia of a quirky cast of characters who gathered to celebrate—and mourn—the closing of Maud's, a popular lesbian bar. Maud's opened in 1966 at 937 Cole Street, near San Francisco's Haight-Ashbury neighborhood, and for almost twenty-five years it functioned as a lesbian bar, clubhouse, and community center. How did Maud's survive the often hostile and turbulent atmosphere of the city's gay bar scene? To answer this question, Poirier solicits commentary by Del Martin and Phyllis Lyon, the charter members and charismatic leaders of the Daughters of Bilitis (DOB), a lesbian civil rights organization. From its inception in 1955, the Daughters of Bilitis worked to improve lesbian visibility—to crack the "conspiracy of silence" that trapped lesbians in damaging stereotypes. As part of this project, DOB encouraged lesbians to gather outside of bars. They sought to broaden the social spaces lesbians might use to meet others like themselves. In many ways, the movement away from bar life was central to the organization's purpose, particularly in the early years. Why, then, does Poirier's video ground the popularity and exuberance of a bar-based lesbian community in the activism of 1950s homophile movements?

Despite their desire to build a social world for lesbians outside of bars, the women of the Daughters of Bilitis often depended on bar life—the central artery of queer life—for their activities. They met many of their friends in bars, sometimes held social events there, and concerned themselves with the legalities of bar-related socializing. In fact, midway through the video Phyllis Lyon quibbles with her longtime lover and comrade, Del Martin, and concedes that she and Martin were quite familiar with bars. "We went to a lot of bars in those days. I mean we really did!" Lyon exclaims. Poirier's video works to connect DOB to the vibrancy—and sexuality—of bars like Maud's. To strengthen this point, Poirier jumps from Lyon's disclosure to the testimony of a secondary character, Kay Wiley, who was a DOB neophyte in the early 1960s. Just out of the closet and eager to find a girlfriend, Wiley sought the advice of Martin and Lyon. Where, she wondered, might she find more women like herself? Surprisingly, Martin and Lyon directed Wiley to a gay bar rather than one of the many social gatherings organized by DOB. "They told me, they said, Kay, the only way you can meet women is to go to a gay bar." On this advice, Wiley made a beeline for Romeo's, a "very small, dirty, sleazy bar on Haight Street," where she met her first female lover.[1]

As part of the project of historical recuperation, Poirier positions homophile activism as the necessary precursor to the success of lesbian bars like Maud's. In doing so, she complicates the image of homophile activists, imbuing them with heightened qualities of sexuality and conviviality. But while Poirier's narrative works to recuperate homophile activism, it does a disservice to the bar owners and bargoers who also fought, through the 1950s and early 1960s, to secure public space for queers in San Francisco. As the previous chapter has shown, bar owners, bartenders, and patrons fought long and difficult battles with the police and state liquor authorities to secure the right to public association. Homophile activism ran in a different direction. Homophile activists worked to integrate themselves into mainstream institutions, seeking acceptance and understanding from outsiders. Underlying this assimilative program was a firm commitment to individual civil rights based on the right to privacy rather than the right to public association. Bar-based and homophile activism overlapped, sometimes sympathetically, but the two groups' different ideologies, strategies, and tactics often led to painful disagreements. And because the records of formal organizations like DOB remain much more accessible to historians than the exploits of bargoing lesbians and gay men, the contributions of bar-based communities have often been overshadowed by the contributions of homophile activism. Such is the case with *Last Call at Maud's*. Poirier's video smoothes over the differences—and at times animosity—between homophile activists like Martin and Lyon and bar owners like Rikki Streicher (who ran Maud's for over twenty years), configuring them instead as part of a happy family of historical actors.

Only briefly does Poirier hint at the tension between bar-based and homophile sensibilities. Early in the video, Rikki Streicher tells a story to the camera-person—a story she also tells in an oral history interview—of a moment, long past, when Martin and Lyon urged her to join DOB. "They kept saying, 'Rikki, you should really join this,' and I said 'Why?' and they said, 'Because these are your people.'"[2] Poirier feeds this dialogue over a still photo of a young and contemptuous-looking Streicher, but before the viewer can take in Streicher's meaning, the narrative turns to Martin and Lyon's lengthy description of the birth of the Daughters of Bilitis. Streicher's defiance and her refusal to see that Martin and Lyon are "her people" are lost in the much larger story of homophile activism. Streicher's oral history testimony offers a different account of this dynamic: "I remember Phyllis and Del marching up . . . and Del said . . . 'Why don't you join this organization, Rikki? You know there's no reason for you not to—' and I said, 'because we have nothing in common.' And she said, 'What do you mean we have nothing in common?' I said, 'I have nothing in common with those women. You know I'm over here . . . my whole attitude and approach to life is different from theirs. I'm not beating the same drum.'"[3] Despite their knowledge of and familiarity with bars, Streicher argues that the women who participated in the Daughters of Bilitis were not interested in bar life. They were not interested in taking risks to secure the kind of public space that 1940s and 1950s bars like Mona's and the Paper Doll provided for women. "They weren't improving themselves. They were simply finding fortification with each other," Streicher opines.[4]

Streicher's commentary, which floats just under the surface of Poirier's narrative, provides a potent response to and critical account of the role that homophile organizations played in San Francisco's postwar queer social worlds. Homophile activism overlapped and, at times, intersected with the activities of bar owners and patrons. They shared the public space of bars and often found their mutual interests empowering. But homophile organizations in San Francisco engaged in an assimilationist project of social uplift—they used the language of integration and, at times, expressed disdain for the queer and gender-transgressive qualities of bar-based communities. As a result, bar owners like Rikki Streicher often saw homophile activists as outsiders and interlopers. In Streicher's mind, the Daughters of Bilitis were not "her people" because they did not face the same kind of dangers—and pleasures—that characterized the queer social world of bars and taverns. While homophile activists like Martin and Lyon recognized the powerful pull of bar-based socializing, they worked to project new images of lesbians and gay men onto the screen of public opinion. In doing so, they at times turned their backs on the queer culture of bars and taverns for the wider arena of mainstream political action.[5]

THE CONTEXT OF HOMOPHILE ACTIVISM

Three important gay and lesbian civil rights organizations emerged in the United States during the 1950s: the Mattachine Society, ONE, Inc., and the Daughters of Bilitis. While ONE was located in Los Angeles, by 1955 both the Mattachine Society and the Daughters of Bilitis called San Francisco their home.[6] Both the Mattachine Society and DOB relied on the volunteer labor of a small coterie of friends and like-minded activists. Both had monthly meetings open to the public, and both worked toward the integration of homosexuals into mainstream society.[7] The Mattachine Society and DOB were not the first homosexual emancipation organizations in the United States.[8] They were, however, the first to develop a national identity and help shape the formation of organizational chapters in other large cities. Both were able to bridge the gap of geographical separation that had previously isolated queer communities across the United States. In other words, through the 1950s and early 1960s these remarkable organizations were able to introduce the necessary fiction of national community into the lesbian and gay world. Through press releases, monthly publications, and the effective use of social and scientific experts to speak on their behalf, homophile organizations projected themselves as the voice and public representation of homosexuals in the United States.

Through the first half of the twentieth century, however, San Francisco's queer communities inhabited a contradictory space on the cusp of private and public social worlds. Pockets of lesbian and gay life flourished in San Francisco's North Beach neighborhood, where a culture of sex and race tourism fed the popularity of bars such as Mona's and the Black Cat. Lesbians and gay men also gathered in private homes for parties and meetings, and a host of public spaces like parks and beaches served as meeting places for social events as well as sexual encounters. The territory lesbians and gay men occupied bordered the public/private world of social articulation in that while many homosexual activities took place in the public sphere, they did so most often as a hidden society—outside the perusal of dominant society. No lesbian or gay newspapers or journals existed in San Francisco prior to the mid-1950s, and while pulp novels and popular science books addressing homosexual subjects were available nationwide, most of these were marketed to heterosexual (male) audiences. They relied on formulaic endings that reinforced stereotypical images of homosexuals and homosexuality.[9] As a result, prior to the formation of homophile organizations, a queer-generated discourse about the meaning of homosexual subjectivity most often took place within the sanctions of homosexual subcultures. Beyond a legal discourse about homosexual crime, a scientific discourse about homosexual illness, and a religious discourse about homosexual immorality, there were few ways for homosexuals to talk publicly about their relationship to the state.[10]

Jürgen Habermas defines the public sphere as "a sphere mediating between state and society," and as state institutions worked to regulate and discipline San Francisco's public culture, they helped shape the formation of a queer public sphere.[11] For instance, the San Francisco Police Department disrupted queer spaces like bars, beaches, and parks, sometimes to the point of shutting them down entirely. The state also intervened in the regulation of homosexuality by hiring scientists, especially psychiatrists, who worked to cure homosexuals of their presumed sickness, sometimes to the extent of forced hospitalization and imprisonment. In California, for example, male "sexual psychopaths" (those twice arrested for public sex) were sometimes committed to Atascadero State Hospital, a maximum security hospital just north of Santa Barbara. Once there, doctors were legally permitted to indefinitely hold any patient "whose mental condition we believe would make him dangerous to be released."[12] In fact, accused homosexuals could be committed to Atascadero without arrest or trial for a ninety-day observation period, during which time hormonal and/or shock treatments might be imposed on the patient.[13] The state also intervened in homosexual lives through the U.S. Department of Defense and the U.S. State Department, both of which not only enforced a policy that projected an image of homosexuality as threatening to foreign and domestic security (conflating communism with homosexuality) but actively investigated and discharged homosexuals from their jobs.[14] The use of public space by homosexuals, even in work-related environments, rendered homosexuals vulnerable to repressive state practices. As lesbians and gay men began to take up more public space, however, a range of resistance practices emerged within their communities. The public sphere and the public opinion it engendered enabled the formation of a discursive space in which homosexuals could resist and contest the ideas vigilantly regulated by the dominant society.[15]

The tensions between the meaning of private and public lives—shaped, on the one hand, by interactions experienced in the "privacy" of homes and those, on the other hand, generated in public spaces—fueled the development of both resistant and acquiescent social groups.[16] A 1956 study by Maurice Leznoff and William Westley of male homosexuals in a large Canadian city discusses a similar dynamic.[17] Leznoff and Westley's report reveals that secret or covert homosexuals often occupied a higher socioeconomic position than overt homosexuals, who relied on "low status" jobs where their sexuality did not need to be contained or hidden. For this reason, they argue, a certain amount of social distance and hostility existed between the two classes. Secret homosexuals did not want to be publicly associated with overt homosexuals, and overt homosexuals disdained the hypocrisy of secrecy. Nevertheless, because secret and overt homosexuals continued to interact sexually (in parks, bathhouses, and bars), secret homosexuals remained vulnerable to and somewhat dependent on the visibility of overt homosexuals. This dynamic required secret and overt homosexuals to interact "on the basis of antagonistic cooperation," which became the keystone of a shared culture and community.

The double dialectic in gay and lesbian history between public/private and overt/covert provides a language for talking about the emergence of a queer public sphere. It also illuminates the ways that homosexual visibility may have been negotiated outside of explicitly political organizations. In other words, what was seemingly unique about the homophile movement—that it was able to insert what it considered positive representations of homosexuality into mainstream culture—was in fact a subjective and contested strategy for affecting social change. Prior to the organization of homophile movements, a multiplicity of queer cultures had developed intricate symbols and codes as a means of communication and self-protection. Symbolic language and an iconography of performance and self-representation often shifted queer meanings from the intimacy of private relationships into public society, enabling homosexuals to enter the public sphere as recognizably homosexual—

even if only to other homosexuals. A private homosexual language could be used in homosexualized public spaces (such as gay bars and parks) to identify and engage other homosexuals. Queer semiotics thus framed the emergence of publicly visible lesbian and gay communities in San Francisco.

Like the covert homosexuals of Leznoff and Westley's study, homophile organizations were, at least initially, dependent on bar-based queer communities to mobilize a political constituency. But as they began to function as national organizations whose publications reached a wide audience, they worked to articulate an explicitly public discourse about homosexuality that responded directly to mainstream concerns. Rejecting the symbolic language and iconography of queer subcultures, homophile activists rallied to combat negative or stereotypical images and worked to negotiate limited social and legal entitlements for lesbians and gay men. Addressing themselves to professional journals and the mainstream press, they functioned as overt and publicly visible reform movements. As a result, homophile organizations developed a language about homosexuality that positioned self-identified lesbians and gay men within a mainstream discourse about homosexual subjectivity. Although this assimilationist strategy was radically daring at a time when homosexuals rarely spoke publicly as homosexuals, a homophile-generated language about homosexual subjectivity created both a tension and a climate of "antagonistic cooperation" between homophile and bar-based activists. Different strategies of resistance enriched the meaning of same-sex sexuality and enlivened the public sphere, but as homophile movements grew more discursively competent, their influence threatened to eclipse the nascent culture of San Francisco's queer bars and taverns.

The Early Mattachine Society

The Mattachine Society was founded in Los Angeles by five men. The original members were intellectuals and political activists—three had experience with the Communist Party. Harry Hay, who provided the impetus for the formation of what was to become the Mattachine Society, was probably the member most acutely aware of the relationship between cultural expression and political mobilization. He had taken an interest in drama while attending Stanford University. Hay had also been active in the Communist Party between 1938 and 1950, and under its influence he participated in People's Songs, a group for leftist songwriters and musicians in Los Angeles. In fact, Hay was teaching a course on "The Historical Development of Folk Music" at Los Angeles' People's Education Center when he founded the Mattachine Society in 1950.[18]

The original members of the Mattachine Society argued that the majority of homosexuals remained unaware of the fact that they constituted a social minority because they were unable to develop and reflect a language and culture that admitted their existence. Early members expressed a cultural authority that referenced homosexuals as the focus of activity and organizing, rather than using the assimilative appeal to heterosexuals that the society later followed in San Francisco. As historian John D'Emilio notes, this analysis reflected "the Marxist distinction between a class 'in itself' and a class 'for itself.'"[19] To early Mattachine members, homosexual subcultures composed a class in themselves, and knowledge about cultural difference was the key to transforming homosexuals into a class able to articulate its own needs and fight on its own behalf. Political mobilization, then, depended on fostering the idea of the existence of a distinct homosexual minority out of which autonomous and resistant homosexual communities would emerge.

As D'Emilio documents in *Sexual Politics, Sexual Communities,* in the spring of 1953, with the increased popularity of the Mattachine Society, the diffusion of leadership and ideas, and the simultaneous intensification of anti-communism in the United States, allegations emerged from rank-and-file members that Mattachine's leadership was communist-informed. With this, the original leaders agreed to open up and democratize the organization. At the first of several "constitutional conventions," however, Mattachine's ideological foundation took a beating. Leaders from Mattachine guilds attending the April 1953 convention lobbied not only for anti-communist loyalty oaths but for an organization less structured around notions of difference and better designed to help homosexuals fit into an intolerant society.[20]

Instrumental in engineering the ideological rift that fractured the Mattachine Society and eventually landed the national leadership in San Francisco was Harold (Hal) Call. In February 1953, Call attended his first Mattachine Society meeting in Berkeley, and soon thereafter he began organizing a local group in San Francisco. His participation in Mattachine–San Francisco grew contentious because even as his power increased on a local level, he became ever more aware of its limits. The core of the Los Angeles leadership was secret and thus out of reach. In the spring of 1953, when Chuck Rowland, a charter member of Mattachine–Los Angeles, and others suggested the democratization of the highly structured, secretive, and increasingly unmanageable organization, Hal Call organized his supporters. As D'Emilio documents, at the April 1953 convention, Call helped propose a constitution that reflected anti-communist and assimilationist ideologies.[21] Although the delegates to the convention defeated many of Call and his cohorts' proposals, three of the Mattachine Society's original five members, Hay, Rowland, and Hull, resigned from the organization.[22] After the May and November 1953 meetings, Mattachine's national leadership began to shift to San Francisco, where Call, in 1955, began publishing the *Mattachine Review,* a monthly magazine that quickly became the mouthpiece of the organization.[23]

In 1954, Call purchased a used eleven by seventeen offset press, and he later established a small company, PanGraphic Press, which allowed him and various business partners to control the publication of homophile materials and, thus, mold an image of the Mattachine Society in their own reflection. Even though it remained financially separate from the Mattachine Society, PanGraphic functioned as an integral part of San Francisco's homophile movement.[24] PanGraphic produced the *Mattachine Review,* other Mattachine publications, and early issues of the Daughters of Bilitis' *Ladder.* All revenue from the *Review* was returned to PanGraphic, and this allowed Call to work almost full time at the arduous task of publishing. His influence was immense. Not only did Call write many of the *Review*'s articles and columns—he used multiple bylines to mask his influence—but his position as writer, editor, and publisher gave him unilateral control over the magazine's content.[25] As Call remembers (referring to himself in the third person): "[in] every issue of the Mattachine Review . . . a lot of it was written by, most of it was composed on the typewriter by, and it was printed on an offset press by, and folded, and stitched, and trimmed out on a paper cutter by Harold Call."[26]

Call and his colleagues used the *Mattachine Review* to shift the ideological grounds of the early Mattachine Society. Because participation in Bay Area chapters was much lower than magazine sales and subscriptions, the *Review* increasingly functioned as the primary vehicle for Mattachine influence. For instance, while participation in a single chapter often remained as low as five members, by 1956 single issues of the *Review* were mailed to over five hundred subscribers, and readers could purchase copies at over one hundred bookstores and newsstands.[27] Featuring articles by sympathetic outsiders, medical professionals, social scientists, and homophile activists, the *Review* created a new image of homosexuality and made it available for public consumption. "In the *Mattachine Review* we knew we were going to have to ride on the shirttails of other respectable professional people to make an inroad into the prejudiced areas of the mainstream of society," Call later reminisced. Through their outreach to lawyers, doctors, professors, scientists, social workers, and clergymen, Mattachine leaders drew public attention to homophile issues. "We got serious attention on our problem [and] the problems of the homosexual adult were treated as something that needed attention."[28]

By 1956 San Francisco's Mattachine Society was a completely different organization from the one initially imagined in Los Angeles. Absent from its agenda was the original emphasis on homosexual culture and its sociopolitical potential. Hal Call's Mattachine also chafed under the original organization's secret leadership. Central to the newly structured Mattachine's ideological base was a commitment to publicly accessible leadership and democratic structure. Indeed, as the Mattachine Society developed a constituency in San Francisco, it debunked the value of homosexual culture and promoted the idea of homo-hetero sameness. San Francisco's Mattachine was committed to working as a mediator between the private world homosexuals "withdrew into" and a public world that could only imagine illegal and immoral homosexual subjects.[29] Homophile mediation, however, was not intended to engender a level of homosexual class-consciousness "in and for itself," but rather to stimulate and regulate a homosexual desire for integration into mainstream society.[30]

The Early Years of the Daughters of Bilitis

The Daughters of Bilitis was a San Francisco–based organization for the "female sex variant."[31] Founded in September 1955 by eight lesbians, four "blue-collar" women and four "white-collar" women, DOB is the first known lesbian emancipation organization in the United States.[32] Although Del Martin and Phyllis Lyon are frequently identified as the founders of this organization, DOB's initial inspiration came from a woman named Rose, a working-class Filipina who wanted to organize a social club for lesbians. Since dancing wasn't allowed in San Francisco's lesbian and gay bars and raids were frequent, Rose was particularly interested in providing a social space where women could dance together, privately, outside the public eye. Rose contacted a woman called Noni who shared her interest in organizing a social club for lesbians. It was through Noni that Del Martin and Phyllis Lyon became involved in the group. They eagerly joined because they, too, wanted more social contact with other lesbians, having found lesbian bars inaccessible and alienating.[33]

At their first meeting, on 21 September 1955, the eight original members (four couples) batted around different names for their club. They rejected the Musketeers, the Amazons, and the Chameleons in favor of the more obscure and conservative-sounding Daughters of Bilitis, a reference to a Pierre Louÿs poem, *The Songs of Bilitis,* written as a tribute to Sappho.[34] In the spirit of a sorority, the group agreed that the club should have colors (sapphire blue and gold) and a club pin in the shape of a triangle. At the second meeting, the group elected officers and established guidelines for membership. Protective of the size and quality of the group, they agreed that new members must be sponsored by charter members; they must also be over twenty-one years old, "Gay," "a girl," and "of good moral character." Early members regulated the size and quality of the group in an effort to protect their privacy and shield themselves from trouble with the police. They did not want to be accused of contributing to the delinquency of underage girls, for example. At the same time, they tried to create and protect a space for women only. Charter members decided that male guests would not be allowed to attend social events unless specifically invited.[35] After several months, as new members began to show their faces at social meetings and the initial guidelines became cumbersome, the president, Del Martin, requested a special meeting open only to the eight original members. The group re-evaluated the purpose of the club, instituted new membership rules, considered penalties for lackluster participation, and initiated a dress code for its members. Scared that the presence of butch or masculine-looking women would frighten others away, they stated simply that "if slacks are worn they must be women's slacks."[36]

By February 1956, the Daughters of Bilitis had fallen into a cycle of two meetings per month, alternating between business meetings and discussion groups. Attendance varied between six and twelve members, and the group began to reach beyond itself. It encouraged members to write their legislators and began to talk about incorporating as a nonprofit organization. The original eight members, however, soon split over the group's changing function. The four working-class women wanted to maintain an entirely secret social club. As the middle-class women, including Martin and Lyon, steered the group away from strictly social functions and toward greater interaction in the public sphere, four of the original eight members dropped out of the group. Meanwhile, Martin and Lyon came in contact with ONE, Inc., a Los Angeles–based homophile organization, and through it, with San Francisco's Mattachine Society.[37] In the fall of 1956, under the influence of these two organizations, the Daughters of Bilitis initiated public discussion meetings focused on lesbian issues and encouraged a new cohort of "female sex variants" to join their organization. By the end of 1956, DOB's foundation had completely shifted from that of a private or secret social organization to one, like the Mattachine Society's, less reliant on the promotion of queer culture and more invested in entering the public sphere.

In November 1956, DOB began publishing a monthly newsletter, *The Ladder,* which they distributed continuously and nationally until 1972. Except for the short-lived and limited publication of Lisa Ben's *Vice Versa,* DOB's *Ladder* was the first widely distributed lesbian magazine.[38] *The Ladder* quickly became DOB's mouthpiece and, literally, its ladder to public visibility and social mobility.[39] In fact, in order to make connections with San Francisco's female professionals, DOB mailed a copy of its second issue to all the women lawyers in the San Francisco phone book, many of whom then angrily demanded to be removed from DOB's mailing list. However, one woman, Juliet Lowenthal, became a friend of DOB through this mailing. She would later figure prominently in the organization when she and her husband, at the behest of DOB, prepared an *amicus curiae* brief on behalf of Mary's First and Last Chance bar.[40]

On the inside cover of each edition of the *Ladder* ran the organization's statement of purpose. It claimed that the Daughters of Bilitis' foremost purpose was promoting "the integration of the homosexual into society." DOB proposed to help lesbians adjust to society "in all its social, civic and economic implications" by educating female variants on the psychological, physiological, and sociological meanings of homosexuality. Indeed, one of the first goals the group identified was the establishment of a library, and the first book purchased was a medical and psychological dictionary.[41] DOB also aimed to educate the public through discussion groups and the distribution of educational literature, in an effort to help break down "erroneous taboos and prejudices." DOB encouraged members to cooperate with scientists in their research on the variant and to investigate the penal code in order to provide "an equitable handling of cases involving this minority group."[42] In fact, in early 1956, DOB's leadership made it compulsory that dues-paying members regularly write their legislators.[43] The Daughters of Bilitis saw the infusion of information about the variant into mainstream society as a step toward gaining a more positive relationship with the state on both practical and ideological levels, and with San Francisco as its place of publication, the *Ladder* positioned the Daughters of Bilitis at the center of lesbian activism.

HOMOPHILE ACTIVISM, 1953–1960

Through discussion groups, workshops, seminars, annual conventions, and the publication of newsletters and magazines, both the Mattachine Society and the Daughters of Bilitis pushed new visions of homosexual subjectivity into the public sphere. As a result, these organizations engaged directly in a state-regulated dialogue about homosexuality. The Mattachine Society, for instance, hosted speakers from a variety of public and mental health institutions. An official from the U.S. Public Health Service spoke to the San Francisco chapter of the Mattachine Society about venereal disease in late 1953; a former patient and inmate of the Norwalk, California, hospital for sex offenders addressed the group in 1954; a San Francisco psychotherapist spoke at a 1955 discussion group meeting; and a psychiatrist, Blanche M. Baker, visited the offices of the Mattachine Society in 1957 along with a group of professional caregivers and social scientists.[44] The Mattachine Society saw speaker presentations as an opportunity for members to appreciate the insights of professionals, but it also functioned as a method of educating outsiders to the existence of a homophile constituency. After a 1957 meeting between the Mattachine staff and a coterie of professionals, for example, Mattachine officers gave the group a tour of the organization's office and answered questions. As a Mattachine newsletter reported, "Many members of the group announced after the discussion that they had no idea of the extent and importance of education, research and social service in the homophile field, nor did they realize the extent of homosexualism in modern cultures."[45]

Homophile organizations also fought censorship and worked to keep their publications available. In 1955, the *Mattachine Review* could be purchased through the mail, but it could also be found at City Lights Books on Columbus Avenue, the Golden Gate News Agency on Third Street, the Pine & Jones Market just north of the Tenderloin, and at the R & W Cigar Company on Market Street.[46] The *Review* could also be purchased in Berkeley at the Campus Smoke Shop, the Phoenix Book

Shop, and at the U.C. Corner. It could be found in Hollywood at the Universal News Agency and in Los Angeles at the Belmont Newsstand and the Smith News Agency. Outside of California, the *Review* could be found in New York City at the Village Theater Center on Christopher Street; in Buffalo, New York, at the Little Book Bar; in Cleveland, Ohio, at Kay Books; and in the Virgin Islands at Tram Combs Books. While DOB mailed copies of *The Ladder* to each of its members, in 1957 five copies were offered for sale at Village Theater Center Books in San Francisco at a price of fifty cents per copy.[47] Despite their relatively low level of distribution, homophile magazines received increased scrutiny by censors. In 1954, the Los Angeles Postmaster refused to distribute ONE, Inc.'s magazine because of its references to homosexuality.[48] In 1958, a U.S. Supreme Court ruling overturned the postmaster's ban, but censorship problems continued to plague the distribution of homophile publications. In 1959 two Bay Area organizations, San Francisco's Smut Vigilantes and San Mateo County's Citizens for Decent Literature, worked to have "obscene literature" removed from local newsstands. The Smut Vigilantes organized public meetings, and the Citizens for Decent Literature prepared lists of obscene books and magazines. While these organizations were not directly targeting gay publications, they threatened the future of gay and lesbian publishing. In response, the Mattachine Society organized a Publications Day Forum entitled "Should Americans Read about Sex?"[49] They printed articles like Curtis Dewees' "On the Suppression of Homosexual Literature"; ran editorials blasting the conservative Citizens for Decent Literature; and supported the activities of San Francisco's Freedom-to-Read Citizens' Committee.[50] DOB joined the fray with lively discussions about the form and function of censorship in midcentury America.[51]

In addition to fighting censorship, homophile activists organized against police harassment and entrapment. In fact, the early Los Angeles–based Mattachine Society had made entrapment one of its most important causes. Its members organized the Citizens' Committee to Outlaw Entrapment and sought to expose an "unconstitutional police conspiracy which, under the cloak of protecting public morals, threatens not only all Minorities but civil rights and privileges generally."[52] Using strong language, the committee advocated an end to the witch hunts against homosexuals, a stronger use of Fifth Amendment rights, and a reexamination of the rights of citizenship. Before long, the committee had its first test case. It supplied funds and support to fight the entrapment and arrest of one of its members, Dale Jennings. While walking home, Jennings was followed by a member of the Los Angeles Vice Squad, who subjected him to sexual advances and later arrested him for lewd vagrancy. Jennings did not resist arrest or admit any guilt; he did not plea-bargain or sign documents. Instead, Jennings demanded to hear the charges against him, and he refused to speak without the presence of a lawyer. At a subsequent trial, Jennings' lawyer based his defense on the fact that while Jennings was a homosexual, his conduct was not lewd or dissolute. The jury returned a vote of acquittal, and the city dismissed the case upon appeal. Jennings' victory bolstered the early Mattachine Society's belief that standing up to police intimidation could result in an end to police entrapment. The Jennings case invigorated the Mattachine Society; it threw the weight of guilt on police entrapment rather than homosexual behavior.[53]

The radical nature of early Mattachine activism was not reflected in the activities of the organization after its leadership moved to San Francisco. Still, the post-1953 Mattachine Society continued to fight against entrapment. The organization published materials encouraging members to know and assert their rights at the time of arrest. It printed up wallet-sized cards entitled "What to do in case of arrest." But the San Francisco–based Mattachine Society maintained a respect for the law and its enforcement. "The public has a right and duty to provide self-protection," a *Mattachine Review* article conceded. "We earnestly support law enforcement aimed at preventing sexual indecencies in public."[54] The revision of laws and statutes continued to be an important part of its mission, but Mattachine's legal director advised that individuals turn to their legislators to protest discriminatory regulations. "We do not advocate sexual license . . . [but] it is believed that sexual activity between two willing and consenting adults should not be a legal matter governed by public law but rather a matter of individual personal morals." To encourage greater participation in the democratic process, a Mattachine newsletter printed the names and districts of state legislators, reminding readers, "Change can only be accomplished in the proper way and manner and by the proper people."[55]

The shift in organizational strategy from a criticism of the police to a willingness to work within a repressive system mirrors the difference between bar-based and post-1953 homophile organizing. While bar owners and patrons asserted their First Amendment right to association (based on the right to free speech and assembly) and worked to protect queer public space through legal challenges to police harassment and alcohol control measures, homophile activists asserted their right to privacy and worked to protect individual freedoms. The ideological movement away from public association and toward privacy hastened the creation of the legal closet. In his important article "Privacy Jurisprudence and the Apartheid of the Closet, 1946–1961," William N. Eskridge, Jr., outlines a postwar government campaign against homosexuals and details the case law behind homosexual repression and resistance. In the postwar years, as greater numbers of homosexuals transgressed the border between private and public life, homophobic lawmakers sought to contain what they perceived to be a homosexual menace. They punished publicly visible homosexuals with an ever increasing number of laws, prohibitions, strategies, and tactics. The apartheid of the closet, as Eskridge describes it, occurred as homosexuals became psychically and morally segregated by a legal system that differentiated between the quasi-legal closeted homosexual and the outlaw. "So long as they confined their expressions and actions to a mutually protective closet, homosexuals were promised a regime of 'separate but equal' toleration from the liberals and legal protection from witch hunters."[56] Homosexuals who refused to comply with a closeting regime suffered at the hands of police, but they were free to openly criticize repressive state practices. This was the strategy of many bar owners and patrons. Homophile activists, on the other hand, positioned themselves as quasi-legal homosexuals.

This does not mean that homophile activists were "in the closet" or invisible to lawmakers or each other. To the contrary, the Mattachine Society and the Daughters of Bilitis based many of their activities on increasing the public visibility of lesbians and gay men.[57] As a result, homophile activists felt the pointed edge of state prohibitions. They were followed by the FBI, and they were subjected to public censorship.[58] But the visibility they sought was conditional. Homophile organizations encouraged members to be visible only as they complied with the law and embraced the limited entitlements of loyal citizenship—they eschewed overt or outlaw characters such as cross-dressers and sex offenders. Through the 1950s, as prohibitions against homosexuality grew, a double standard or apartheid between quasi-legal and outlaw homosexuals took shape. It was as if a line had been drawn between those homosexuals who contained their sexuality to the privacy of homes (and masked gender-inappropriate behaviors) and those who brought their sexuality (and gender) out in public. The former, quasi-legal homosexuals, could enjoy the possibilities of citizenship, while the latter, outlaws, carried the full weight of the law. For example, in 1947, the State of California initiated statewide registration for sex offenders, and individuals convicted of sex-related crimes (including lewd vagrancy) were stripped of many of their civil rights.[59] Sex offenders could not teach in public school, hold government jobs, or legitimately run for public office. They had to report their movements to police and withstand the increased pressure of state surveillance.[60] Sex crimes spanned a gamut of activities from violent and non-consensual sex to consensual sex and public lewdness, but the law often did not differentiate between the perpetrators of violent crimes like rape and the participants of consensual acts like same-sex kissing and dancing. Both suffered fines, potential jail sentences, and police registration. Often, the mere suspicion of homosexuality (gender-transgressive gestures, clothing, and verbal inflections) could lead to a sex-related conviction. As more and more homosexuals suffered the penalties of an increasingly repressive regime, it drove a wedge between overt and covert homosexuals. The idea that homosexuals might lead upstanding lives from the position of the closeting apparatus of privacy rights sharpened homophile ideology and constrained homophile activism to strictly legal behavior.

Historian Martin Meeker argues that behind the Mattachine Society's mask of respectability lay a number of activities that belied its ideologically conservative front. Central to his argument is evidence that between 1954 and 1961 the Mattachine Society functioned as a social service agency that met the needs of thousands of "sex variants" who sought the aid of the organization. He documents how the Mattachine Society provided lay counseling, employment and housing referrals, advice on veterans' affairs, and referrals to sympathetic lawyers and psychologists.[61] Still, during this period homophile activists sought to improve conditions for homosexuals by participating legitimately in the realm of mainstream political action. To accomplish this goal, they distanced themselves from the extralegal behavior of bar-based homosexuals and aligned themselves with social and scientific experts who espoused degrees of tolerance for homosexuals while they decried state intervention in socially defined personal freedoms.

The reliance on tolerant outsiders and a liberal philosophy of live and let live provided a new venue for homophile activism, but it lent a conservative air to homophile political work. "Homophile leaders of the 1950s emphasized their legal privacy rights and de-emphasized their legal equity rights," Eskridge argues. They believed that if they demonstrated their similarities with law-abiding heterosexuals, they might secure a place for themselves at the table of civil rights protections. As a result, homophile leadership left little room for the assertion of equity rights based on the equal protection clause of the Fourteenth Amendment. Equity rights protected groups or classes of people from arbitrary state discrimination. Just as race-based classifications provided the foundation for successful equity claims like the U.S. Supreme Court's 1954 *Brown v. Board of Education* decision, homophile organizations might have made a radical claim for group-based anti-discrimination protections. But because homophile organizations privileged hetero-homo sameness over group identification, equity rights seemed far-fetched and out of reach. Moreover, the civil rights negotiated by homophile activists were based on the lawful participation of homosexuals in an already corrupt political system, and homophile activists restrained themselves from direct criticism of the state. They favored assimilationist approaches to achieving lesbian and gay civil rights over more radical ideas and approaches.[62]

The discursive limits of assimilationist or integrationist strategies demanded that the Mattachine Society and DOB meet public society on its own terms, and the transgressive quality of homosexual sex (and culture) became oblique. Both the Mattachine Society and DOB downplayed the sex in homosexual subjectivity, and while DOB and the Mattachine Society eagerly enlisted the aid of experts and professionals like scientists and lawyers to fortify their claim to civic entitlements, they relied heavily on the leadership of ministers who promoted a love-based discourse of human empowerment. Ministers regularly spoke at DOB and Mattachine functions, and while this shifted the discursive limits of public resistance from juridical narratives to that of Christian epistemology, Christian ideas of morality created a new set of ideological problems. Del Martin and Phyllis Lyon remember an Episcopal minister's address at the first national DOB convention in San Francisco. "His speech was anything but comforting to gays," they reminisce. "He said that we would be accepted in the church, as all sinners are. But once there, we would be expected to change."[63] Early volumes of the *Mattachine Review* similarly trace a lengthy and contentious discourse about the relationships between homosexuality, morality, and religion. Luther Allen, a regular writer for the *Review,* noted that "if the homosexual genuinely loves his God and his neighbor . . . it is possible for him to posses integrity and self-respect even though his own way of life may violate the mores where his sexuality is concerned."[64] Only an asexual love could transcend both Christian notions of moral fortitude and postwar sexual ideologies.[65]

Differences between the Mattachine Society and the Daughters of Bilitis

Despite striking similarities, the Mattachine Society and the Daughters of Bilitis differed significantly in their approaches to guiding homosexuals through a process of social integration. Mattachine's eleven-part "Aims and Principles" employs the language of public integration and assimilation much more forcefully than DOB's four-part statement. Mattachine's January 1956 statement lists "education of the general public" as its first aim and "education of variants" second. The Daughters of Bilitis' statement, published in *The Ladder*'s first issue, inverts these principles, prioritizing the variant's education over the public's. While DOB sought to aid the education and integration of lesbians through discussion groups and the maintenance of a library, Mattachine's goals compelled members further into the public sphere, insisting that variants "assume community responsibilities" by participating in "civic and welfare organizations, religious activities, and citizenship responsibilities." Mattachine pushed homophile activists toward "full assimilation into the communities in which [variants] live," while DOB seemed protective of lesbian-only space.[66]

Despite the oblique language of sexual variation, DOB understood itself, from the very beginning, as an association of lesbians (or "Gay girls," as members called themselves early on).[67] In their publications, they capitalized the word "lesbian," using a proper noun to assert a prideful group identification. Del Martin and Phyllis Lyon also saw the Daughters of Bilitis as "more open about the sexuality aspect" of the organization than the Mattachine Society. They discussed sex and sexuality at monthly meetings and included information about sexuality in their organizational questionnaires. "The main difference was we were aware we were an organization . . . primarily for lesbians," Phyllis Lyons recalls in an oral history interview.[68] Mattachine, on the other hand, did not promote itself as a homosexual organization but, rather, as an organization open to anyone interested in the condition of the homosexual. In fact, in preparation for the Daughters of Bilitis' first national convention in 1960, DOB leaders advertised the event as a "national lesbian conference," and, Martin remembers, Hal Call of the Mattachine Society chided DOB for publicly identifying itself as a lesbian organization rather than an organization for the discussion of ideas about sex variation. He warned that, as a result, Mattachine members might not feel comfortable attending the conference. "He said that . . . their organization had always said they were interested in [homosexuality], but they were not called a gay organization," Martin recalls. The president of DOB later drafted a letter to San Francisco's Mattachine Society suggesting that if Mattachine members dressed properly and conducted themselves with decorum at the conference they would surely not be taken for lesbians.[69]

The Daughters of Bilitis and the Mattachine Society also differed in their approaches to McCarthy-era politics and prohibitions. While DOB members were nervous about being perceived as political subversives, the Mattachine Society's "Aims and Principles" went so far as to explicitly reject any affiliation with the Communist Party, signaling the seriousness with which Mattachine understood its precarious relationship to the state.[70] The final paragraph of Mattachine's 1956 "General Aims" reads, "Although the Mattachine Society is a non-sectarian organization and is not affiliated with any political organization, it is, however, unalterably opposed to Communists and Communist activity and will not tolerate the use of its name or organization by or for any Communist group or front." Anti-communist rhetoric riddles the *Mattachine Review*'s first several volumes. While one might read these statements as a strategy for resisting the right-wing conflation of communism and homosexuality (or the legacy of Harry Hay's Communist Party–inspired organizational leadership), a patriotic concern for the obedience of law permeates the organization's foundations. A complementary organizational aim, for instance, reads, "The Society is not seeking to overthrow or destroy any of society's existing institutions, laws or mores, but to aid the assimilation of variants as constructive, valuable and responsible citizens."[71] The ideological grounds upon which the terms "constructive," "valuable," and "responsible" are employed comply with heterosexist fears of homosexual subversion and a converse trust in the righteousness of mainstream ideological and judicial systems.

The Daughters of Bilitis' statement of goals and principles, however, positions the meaning of homosexual "adjustment" on less certain ground, leaving their statements open to a greater degree of interpretation. In fact, their commitment to building a library and facilitating discussion groups signals a concern that lesbians develop their own strategies for engaging in a public discourse about homosexuality.[72] As Phyllis Gorman argues in her analysis of the organization, DOB was not simply an auxiliary to the Mattachine Society but had a unique ideological coherence.[73] The Daughters of Bilitis saw themselves as advocates of lesbian empowerment and, as a result, positioned their political struggles within the realm of mainstream American politics without having to entirely forfeit their lesbian-centered ideological base or capitulate to anticommunist rhetoric. In fact, Gorman argues that DOB's greatest purpose was its cultural work, providing "a safe space for lesbians to come together" and enabling a breadth of activities not previously part of "organized Lesbian culture."[74] Despite these important differences, both Mattachine and DOB regulated their members' behavior, particularly their gendered behavior, in order to project positive images and counter mainstream stereotypes that denied the legitimacy of homosexual subjectivity.

Gender, Sex, and Citizenship

The conflation of homosexuality and cross-gender behavior in western societies stretches back to at least the turn of the twentieth century. Late-nineteenth-century sexological categories identified "sexual inversion" as a complete reversal of one's sex role.[75] Although inverts would later be more commonly referred to as homosexuals, a clinically gender-free category of sexual behavior, it is not clear that same-sex sexual behavior ever lost its association with transgressive or inverted gender roles. George Chauncey argues that in turn-of-the-century New York City, gender-transgressive and working-class "fairies" functioned as the center of gay urban life.[76] Anthropologist Esther Newton suggests another line of reasoning in an article on "the mythic mannish lesbian." She argues that mannish women became an icon for lesbianism in elite English-speaking societies after the publication of Radclyffe Hall's *Well of Loneliness* in 1928. The gender-specific semiotics of "mannish lesbians" thus became culturally enmeshed in public representations of lesbian sexual desire. Indeed, as J. R. Roberts argues, "dyke" has its semantic roots in "dight," an Old English term that meant to dress, clothe, or adorn and which was later translated into both African American and Anglo-American vernacular to mean a masculine or aggressive lesbian.[77] In U.S. culture and society, cross-gender behavior was never more than a step away from same-sex sexuality.

As homosexual representation became a central issue for homophile activists, homophile organizations regulated their members' dress and behavior. The Daughters of Bilitis and the Mattachine Society attempted to distance their constituencies from practices that conflated gender transgression with homosexuality. They also distanced themselves from the activism and political contestations of communities of color.[78] Homophile activists believed that if lesbians looked and acted like middle-class white women and gay men looked and acted like middle-class white men, experts and professionals such as lawyers, doctors, ministers, and priests would be more likely to engage with homosexuals and take their concerns seriously. For example, DOB's statement of purpose advocated "a mode of behaviour [*sic*] and dress acceptable to society."[79] While DOB encouraged lesbians to wear dresses in public and questioned the utility of "dressing butch," Mattachine was, by necessity, engaged in a wider-ranging discourse about inappropriate public behavior. Concerned with popular stereotypes of gay men as a public nuisance and, worse, a threat to children, Mattachine not only advocated appropriate gender behavior but also condemned public sexual solicitation, public sex of any kind, and (especially) sex with minors. Mattachine's policies encouraged "behavior that is acceptable to society in general and compatible with recognized institutions of a moral and civilized society with respect for the sanctity of home, church and state."[80]

Nevertheless, disagreements about gender-transgressive behavior pepper both *The Ladder* and the *Mattachine Review*. In a 1956 issue of *The Ladder*, the president's message responds affirmatively to a letter that claims, "The kids in fly-front pants and with the butch haircuts and mannish manner are the worst publicity that we can get."[81] An article published several months later, "Transvestism—A Cross-cultural Survey," reiterates this theme through the lens of psychoanalysis. It traces a brief history of the causes of "female transvestism" and remarks that cross-dressing was once an important practice of gender resistance and female empowerment. Still, the article maintains that present-day (mid-1950s) cross-dressing was harmful to lesbian emancipation because "transvestism is the tag that labels the Lesbian." The article concludes that "truly self-confident people have no need to express themselves or barricade themselves by costume," simultaneously pathologizing the butch or masculine lesbian as psychologically underdeveloped while making invisible the costumes of heterosexual subjectivity and desire.[82] In the next issue of *The Ladder*, however, an irate reader responds that "transvestism is *not* necessarily coincident with homosexuality." In reference to the self-policing that occurs within subcultural communities, the reader continues, "The cult of conformity itself remains to be questioned. . . . Those who depart from the rules are punished for the 'crime' of not behaving like a typical Negro, professional worker or feminine woman. The homosexual world is as guilty as the rest, when they would confer the straitjacket of 'Butch-hood' upon its embryo members."[83] To

above: Drag performers, c. 1930s. (GLBT Historical Society, Wide Open Town History Project)

left: "Michelle" (right) and friend at the Beige Room, c. 1956. (Courtesy of José Sarria)

right: José Sarria, high school graduation photo, 1941. (Courtesy of José Sarria)

below: Opus One, 1951. (GLBT Historical Society, Wide Open Town History Project)

José Sarria and date, New Year's Eve 1957. (Courtesy of José Sarria)

Black Cat menu, 1950. (GLBT Historical Society, Wide Open Town History Project)

PRICE LIST

WHISKEY	
BAR WHISKEY	.35
CALL BLENDS	.40
STRAIGHTS, BONDS & SCOTCH	.50
CALL SCOTCH	.60
MIXED DRINKS & COCKTAILS	.50
WESTERN BEER	.25
EASTERN BEER	.35

FOOD	
CATBURGER	.30
CHEESEBURGER	.40
FISH & CHIPS	.50
ENCHILADA	.25
CHILI CON CARNE	.25

SUNDAY BREAKFAST

TOMATO JUICE

HOT CAKES

HAM & EGGS

TOAST, COFFEE

$1.00

City & County of
SAN FRANCISCO
City Election,
Tuesday, Nov. 7th
1961

Elect

JOSÉ JULIO
SARRIA

Supervisor

"Equality!"

left: José Julio Sarria for Supervisor poster, 1961. (Courtesy of José Sarria)

below: James MacGuiness, known as Hazel, pianist at the Black Cat, c. 1965. (Courtesy of José Sarria)

right: Drag queens inside bar, c. 1965. (GLBT Historical Society, Wide Open Town History Project)

below: "Gay Is Good but José Is Better": Easter float, c. 1968. (Courtesy of José Sarria)

below: José Sarria in fur coat, with Hector Navarro and "Roxanne," c. 1975. (Courtesy of José Sarria)

bottom: Three empresses: Empress Maxine, Empress Freda, and José Sarria, also known as Empress José, at the 1974 coronation sponsored by the Imperial Court system founded by Sarria and others in 1965. (Courtesy of José Sarria)

right: Finocchio's from Broadway, 1999. (Copyright Nan Alamilla Boyd)

below: Rikki Streicher (left) with friends at the Claremont Hotel in Oakland, c. 1945. (Courtesy of Mary Sager)

Reba Hudson in auto shop shirt, c. 1944. (Courtesy of Mary Sager)

Mona's 440 Club from street with Gladys Bentley banner, c. 1945. (GLBT Historical Society, Wide Open Town History Project)

above: Bar photo cover from Mona's, c. 1945. (Courtesy of Mary Sager)

right: Beverly Shaw singing at Mona's 440, c. 1945. (GLBT Historical Society, Wide Open Town History Project)

below: Kay Scott (right) and tourists at Mona's 440, c. 1945. (GLBT Historical Society, Wide Open Town History Project)

below: Male impersonators and performers pose at Mona's 440, c. 1945. Clockwise from top left: Butch Minton, Jan Jansen, Kay Scott, Jimmy Renard, Mickey, unknown, Beverly Shaw, Mike. (GLBT Historical Society, Wide Open Town History Project)

above right: Male impersonators and performers between sets at Mona's 440, c. 1945: from left to right, Kay Scott, Butch Minton, Jimmy Renard. (Courtesy of Mary Sager)

below right: Butch lesbians inside Mona's Candlelight, c. 1949: from left to right, unknown, Kay Caroll, Jeanne Sullivan, Tommy Vasu. (Courtesy of Mary Sager)

below: Butch lesbian "Nicki" in convertible in Golden Gate Park, c. 1945. (Courtesy of Mary Sager)

bottom: Fem-butch couple at Mona's 440, c. 1945. (Courtesy of Mary Sager)

left: Lesbian wedding, c. 1968. (GLBT Historical Society, Wide Open Town History Project)

below: Lesbian house party, c. 1968. (GLBT Historical Society, Wide Open Town History Project)

right: Mona Hood in 1991 with earlier (ca. 1940) photo of herself. (Copyright Nan Alamilla Boyd)

below: Reba Hudson, Mona Hood, and Rikki Streicher, 1991. (Copyright Nan Alamilla Boyd)

some, the regulation of gendered behavior often seemed as strong within lesbian communities as it did in the larger society.

The Daughters of Bilitis worked to negotiate the tension between mainstream notions of gender-appropriate behavior and the parameters of lesbian culture. In doing so, DOB wrapped a public discourse about the meaning of lesbianism around a manipulation of gendered symbols. As one contributor to *The Ladder* noted, "One of the problems that is paramount in the adjustment of the Lesbian is the acceptance of her 'femininity.'"[84] Still, debate about gender roles and the gendered signifiers of lesbian desire pervaded lesbian communities, even communities that were not based in bars. Mildred Dickemann, who never participated in DOB functions and rarely went to bars, interacted primarily with a group of "closeted" and mostly white teachers and professional women. Dickemann acknowledges that "everybody in those days felt themselves to one degree or another to be butch or fem." She explains that although "some people didn't adopt the dress so much," most middle-class lesbians "felt they had to feel that way [butch or fem] or were expected to feel that way so they could put themselves on a continuum someplace."[85] The relationship between gender and sexuality shaped the meaning of lesbian existence—both in how lesbians functioned among other lesbians and how they negotiated the world around them.

Given its impact on the everyday life of most lesbians, DOB's choice of gender as a site of social and political activism made sense. But this strategy often backfired, alienating DOB from the constituency it most wanted to reach. In 1959, for example, DOB participated in the legal defense of Mary's First and Last Chance Bar. Mary's was a lesbian bar (though gay men and others also frequented the place) in Oakland, and the Alcoholic Beverage Control Board (ABC) had ordered a revocation of its license on the grounds that homosexuals were regular patrons of the bar. The owners, Albert L. Vallerga and Mary Azar, contested the ABC's order, and for two years the case proceeded through municipal and state courts. During the proceedings, however, defense attorneys representing Mary's pitted the Daughters of Bilitis against the butch and cross-dressed women that frequented the bar. They held up DOB lesbians as an example of upstanding and law-abiding women, and in doing so, they positioned lesbian civil rights on the terms of DOB's gender-appropriate behavior.

The case against Mary's First and Last Chance Bar, known as *Vallerga v. Department of Alcoholic Beverage Control,* became a landmark in

California law—not because of the minor role that DOB played in the proceedings, but because the case reviewed the constitutionality of legislative attempts to control the ABC. *Vallerga* challenged Section 24200(e) of the California Business and Professions Code, which stated that the ABC could revoke the liquor license of a bar catering to "users of narcotics, prostitutes, pimps, panderers, or sexual perverts." Section 24200(e) had been passed by the California state legislature in 1955 partly in response to the 1951 decision in *Stoumen v. Reilly,* a decision that upheld the right of homosexuals to assemble in bars and taverns so long as "immoral acts" were not being committed. *Vallerga* functioned as a test of Section 24200(e) in that the case against Mary's First and Last Chance centered on evidence that the bar catered to homosexuals, a fact that the bar's owners did not dispute. Lawyers for *Vallerga* argued that Section 24200(e), a legislative act, moved unconstitutionally beyond (and seemed to overrule) *Stoumen.* The wording of Section 24200(e) suggested that the mere presence of "sexual perverts" constituted grounds for the revocation of a bar's liquor license, but this situation had already been protected by *Stoumen.* On 23 December 1959, after numerous appeals, the California Supreme Court ruled in favor of Mary's First and Last Chance, arguing that Section 24200(e) was indeed unconstitutional. Since ABC detectives had not noted any illegal or immoral acts on the premises but had grounded their revocation on the fact that the owners did not deny the presence of homosexuals, the state supreme court asked the ABC to rescind its revocation order against the bar.[86]

The fact that the ABC did not include in its statements to the court evidence of same-sex behavior[87] was an oversight on its part (and a mistake it would not soon repeat). The ABC had studied Mary's First and Last Chance Bar for over two years.[88] During their time at the bar, ABC detectives watched lesbians interact, dance, and kiss each other affectionately. Lesbians at the bar even solicited the female detectives working undercover. An ABC report noted:

> Helen Davis, a policewoman, was on the premises in May of 1956 with another policewoman, Marge Gwinn. Buddy, a female waitress, greeted the policewomen who were later joined by the lesbian, Shirleen. Shirleen told Marge, "you're a cute little butch." Shirleen later grabbed Marge and kissed her. Buddy the waitress just said to watch it and if they continued to do that they should go to the restroom. The next night nothing apparently happened. The following night Buddy joined the group again with a trio of sexual perverts. Shirleen was not the only girl who took a liking to Marge for Buddy had grown quite fond of Marge too. . . . On May 11, 1956 two females this time were observed by Agent Sockyer holding hands

> affectionately. The only thing normal about this pair was that one of the couple used the women [*sic*] restroom.[89]

Despite the presence of this document, the information that moved forward to the supreme court included only a few "isolated acts," the most weighty of which was evidence that "the majority of the female customers were dressed in mannish attire."[90] According to the supreme court, cross-dressing was not serious enough to constitute "immoral or illegal acts," the backbone of the state's anti-homosexual campaign.[91] Nevertheless, in an effort to counter this paltry evidence, attorney Morris Lowenthal (the spouse of the aforementioned Juliet Lowenthal and the attorney who had represented Sol Stoumen in *Stoumen v. Reilly*) prepared an *amicus curiae* brief in support of Vallerga's defense team. It is here that the Daughters of Bilitis enter the scene, carrying with them the weight of lesbian representation. Lowenthal's brief argues:

> In passing, it should be noted that it is a fact that *most* Lesbians do *not* dress in male attire and cannot be identified as Lesbians by their attire. . . . In fact, the Lesbian organization in San Francisco known as the Daughters of Bilitis, described elsewhere in this brief, is presently carrying on an educational program to discourage Lesbians from dressing in male attire and to educate Lesbians to the fact that it is not in their self-interest to so attire themselves and that it simply encourages repressive action or conduct against them. . . . It is very possible that in time such an educational program, in this area at least, will eliminate the questions raised by the particular attire of such patrons as those who frequented the Vallerga bar.[92]

In this document, not only does Lowenthal represent DOB as capable of pushing gender-transgressive lesbians out of view, but DOB lesbians surface as the legitimate bearers of civil rights. Because of their gender-appropriate behavior, they are entitled to the right to gather in bars, but no rights are claimed for gender-transgressive lesbians. Indeed, lesbian advancement was gained for homophile women as a reward for their work toward the education and potential "elimination" of butch or mannish lesbians.

The Daughters of Bilitis worked tirelessly to clean up and correct popular or stereotypical images of lesbians and homosexuals. They configured butch or mannish behavior as a kind of false consciousness, a misunderstanding of the true meaning of lesbianism. For instance, in their 1972 publication, *Lesbian/Woman,* Del Martin and Phyllis Lyon describe their relationship with Toni, a lesbian they met in a "rather raunchy gay bar in North Beach." Toni projected a butch image, with "hair short and slicked back, no makeup and dressed completely in men's clothes." Martin and Lyon insisted that Toni join DOB, and "as a result of the group's example, *its unspoken pressure,* she toned down her dress." Martin and Lyon recall their complete success in transforming Toni's gendered behavior into something more socially acceptable: "We met Toni for dinner before the theatre one night. There she was in all her glory, neatly turned out in dress, hat, gloves and high heels, *the very epitome of a middle class matron.*"[93] Just as DOB pushed for the assimilation of lesbians into mainstream society, it worked to project an upwardly mobile representation of the "Lesbian woman." Toni's transformation occurs in explicitly class-based terms. For the Daughters of Bilitis, gender operated as a powerful screen upon which they could project new public representations of "the Lesbian." But class-based notions of appropriate behavior clearly informed the meaning of gender and the path through which DOB encouraged lesbians to integrate into mainstream society. A homophile language about gender, as a result, remained inseparable from postwar constructions of class and citizenship.

The Mattachine Society similarly framed gender politics against a backdrop of class mobility. In the *Mattachine Review,* the organization's glossy monthly magazine, writers discussed gender-appropriate behavior in terms of "respectable" and "responsible" actions. Using themselves as models, they projected an image of the upstanding, lawful, and civic-minded homosexual. For example, in "An Open Letter to Senator Dirksen," the writer (name withheld) petitions the senator to rethink his statement that "the wreckers and destroyers, the security risks and homosexuals, the blabbermouths and drunks, the traitors and saboteurs" should be removed from government office.[94] The author's rebuttal, written in 1955, argues that homosexuals "share the American Dream": "We are not distinguishable from heterosexual people in any visible way . . . we are no more unreliable, unstable or dangerous than heterosexuals. . . . Our hearts are not less full of pride and honor at the sight of massed American flags because we are homosexual. We do not work less hard for America, or love her less, or support the Republican administration and policies less whole-heartedly because we are homosexual."[95] Written at the height of the McCarthy era, when concepts of work, citizenship, and patriotism overlapped, the construction of the responsible homosexual citizen relied on a heightened level of political conservatism. The image the Mattachine Society wanted to project left little room for political disagreement or debate.

The gendered quality of homosexual citizenship is more explicit in a 1958 *Mattachine Review* article entitled "Effeminacy v. Affectation."[96]

Here, the author distinguishes between effeminacy, a sympathetic and acceptable disposition shared by homosexuals and heterosexuals, and affectation, a neurotic condition that is "deliberately offensive" to both heterosexuals and right-minded homosexuals. The author claims that "earmarks of the 'affected' individual are inflection of voice, mincing steps, and broken wrists"—all gendered qualities. Affectation was only a problem, however, in that it made visible the sexual quality of homosexuality. It linked gender inversion to homosexuality, a visible (and pathological) somatic type. The author maintains that "it is pathetic that *this type of homosexual* should tend to perpetuate the popular stereotype," because society "must be allowed to see and learn about a great many average, responsible and reasonably well-adjusted homosexuals."[97]

By the mid-1960s, the Mattachine Society had evolved into a "norm-oriented" social reform movement, argues criminologist Roxanna Sweet in her 1968 study of San Francisco's homophile organizations.[98] While homophile activists by this time understood themselves to be part of a minority group, status hierarchies played a large role in the group's function. The group embraced an identification with dominant standards of normalcy and shunned "undesirables" such as effeminate men, overt homosexuals, and people of color. According to Sweet, homophile activists expressed particular disdain for "hair fairies":

> These are individuals who, while not dressing in female attire, use heavy facial makeup, wear bouffant hairdos, and exhibit many feminine characteristics (e.g., swiveling the hips, falsetto voices, holding cigarettes with bent wrists, etc.). They are perhaps the most openly rebellious and defiant of all homosexuals, wearing their sexual orientations like a lavender badge of courage. Most "hair-fairies" (also referred to as "street queens") use feminine pronouns and terms of reference among themselves (e.g., "she," "her," "that bitch," etc.). They often can be seen in large "packs" walking down the main street in the central shopping district of San Francisco.[99]

Homophile activists placed great emphasis on downplaying the stereotypes of effeminacy, perhaps to shed the association between homosexuality and mental illness, but as groups like the Mattachine Society placed respectability as their central goal, they drew their membership from the more conforming members of society. As Sweet's study of San Francisco's homophile movements concludes, "The members are not vitally concerned with aspects of law making and law enforcement [that] pertain to homosexuals not as high in their hierarchy of statuses—overt 'queens,' young male 'hustlers,' or homosexuals who are members of racial minority groups."[100] San Francisco's homophile organizations, as a result, reflected a membership that was, on the whole, white, middle-class, and native born, and members concerned themselves with the rights and privileges of their social and racial class.

Because the Daughters of Bilitis and the Mattachine Society encouraged assimilationist strategies of social change, they were the first to enter a public discourse as homosexuals and negotiate limited civic entitlements. They were also the first to effectively secure the advocacy of trusted civic leaders like ministers and psychologists. However, the "queer ladder of social mobility" that homophile activists and their advocates pursued secured entitlements on very limited terms.[101] Not only were the terms of homophile advancement gender-based, but they carried a perhaps less overt discourse about class and race that would, ultimately, alienate a large part of their constituency. DOB publications reveal that gender-based representations went hand in hand with class-based notions of social advancement. Similarly, Mattachine Society publications reveal that middle-class ideologies of individuality, patriotism, and respectability were foundational to the integration of the homosexual into mainstream society.

The Popularization of Homophile Attitudes

While the goals and principles of the Mattachine Society and the Daughters of Bilitis were not identical, between 1950 and 1965, both struggled to clean up the image of the homosexual, to project new images into the public sphere, and to educate dominant society about the existence of socially acceptable and law-abiding homosexuals. Both organizations sought to function as mediators between "public" heterosexual society and "private" homosexual subcultures, but they spent much more energy reaching into the public sphere than the queer world of bars, taverns, baths, and beaches. The Mattachine Society, for instance, was convinced that homosexuals could make a positive contribution to their cause through participation in the public sphere. They instructed variants not to "withdraw into an invert society of their own." To achieve "full assimilation" into mainstream society, Mattachine proposed a wide-ranging agenda that included "the education of the general public," vigilant law-abiding behavior, and cooperation with scientists.[102] The Mattachine Society and DOB were effective in realizing their goals, and education of the public became, in many ways, their most spectacular success. Through active solicitation, they encouraged a number of scholars and writers to voice their perspectives and thus popularize their ideas. Evelyn Hooker's studies of psychological well-being and Jess Stearn's popular sociology serve as particularly compelling examples of this phenomenon.

Evelyn Hooker's research followed on the heels of Alfred Kinsey's 1948 report, which revolutionized midcentury social theories of sex and sexuality. Early on, Kinsey had sought the aid of the Mattachine Society to find subjects. Kinsey had culled subjects from the early (Los Angeles–based) Mattachine Society for his initial research into the sexual behaviors of American men, and when Kinsey contacted the president of San Francisco's Mattachine Society in late 1953 to find subjects for a study of homosexuals who had run into trouble with the law, several participants quickly volunteered.[103] Kinsey's exhaustive and meticulous studies of sexual behavior found that a large percentage of white American men—up to 50 percent—had erotic responses to other men; over 30 percent had post-adolescent sexual experiences with men leading to orgasm; and over 12 percent had experienced exclusive same-sex behavior for at least a three-year period.[104] His 1953 study of female sexual behavior reported similarly shocking results.[105] These findings had a tremendous impact on gay and lesbian social movements. As homophile organizations like the Mattachine Society and the Daughters of Bilitis struggled to justify their existence, Kinsey's reports seemed to confirm that a great number of Americans—many more than ever imagined—suffered the weight of legal prohibition, social ostracism, and perhaps silent self-condemnation. Homophile activists realized the importance of their own work and became ever more cognizant of the positive impact of scientific research. As a result, they reached out to sympathetic researchers and volunteered as subjects for studies by reputable scientists such as Alfred Kinsey and Evelyn Hooker.

While Kinsey's studies reflected a quantitative approach to analyzing human sexual behavior, Evelyn Hooker's qualitative research sought to debunk psychological theories of homosexuality as a mental disease. In the mid-1940s, while teaching psychology at UCLA, Hooker began to socialize with a group of gay men who, in her mind, seemed to defy contemporary notions of homosexual maladjustment.[106] The men who became her friends seemed creative, intelligent, motivated, and emotionally fit—not at all the picture most psychological studies drew of homosexual men. After a short trip to San Francisco (with her husband and two gay friends) and an enjoyable visit to Finocchio's, Hooker was convinced that it was her scientific duty to study homosexuals. Her gay friends "made an urgent request that I conduct a scientific investigation of 'people like them.' By 'people like them,' they meant homosexuals who do not seek psychiatric help and who lead relatively stable, occupationally successful lives."[107] Soon thereafter, she applied for a grant from the National Institute of Mental Health to compare the psychological adjustment of exclusively homosexual and heterosexual men who were not under psychiatric care. Finding homosexual men to participate in the study was easy, Hooker recalls; she found recruits at a Los Angeles chapter of the Mattachine Society.[108] Finding exclusively heterosexual men to participate in her research project was much more difficult. They were often discouraged by the stigma of homosexual association, but after some effort she assembled a group of sixty subjects, thirty homosexual and thirty heterosexual men, and began her research.

For her project, Hooker administered a series of detailed psychological tests to each of the sixty men. Using the Rorschach (ink-blot), TAT (Thematic Apperception), and MAPS (Make-a-Picture Story) tests, she compiled a wealth of data. Fearful that her interpretation of the results might be biased, she challenged outside experts to read the data. Expert psychologists who had maintained that they could easily discern a homosexual response to personality tests were surprised to find that they could not correlate the respondent's sexuality with his social adjustment. Moreover, in the final analysis, just as many homosexual men fell into each category of social adjustment as did heterosexual men. Hooker's study revealed that the social adjustment of homosexual and heterosexual men was similar. Like the homophile movements that embraced her, Evelyn Hooker's research challenged the idea of homosexual pathology. By extension, her research challenged the idea of homosexual difference and asserted broad notions of hetero-homo sameness. More importantly, Hooker's research found that homosexuals were no less well adjusted than their heterosexual counterparts. "The most striking finding of the three judges who examined the projective materials was that many of the homosexuals were very well adjusted," Hooker reported.[109] Like the Mattachine Society, Hooker encouraged social scientists to admit the possibility of well-adjusted and emotionally healthy homosexual men.

Evelyn Hooker's relationship with the Mattachine Society was not simply ideological. Her social contacts with gay men in Los Angeles overlapped considerably with homophile organizations, and she used Mattachine members for her research. Although she initially refused to join Mattachine's board of directors, after she completed her research and reported its findings, she became an advisor to the Mattachine Society and published some of her subsequent research in the *Ladder* and *ONE Magazine*.[110] Hooker was part of a cohort of professionals and sympathetic outsiders who worked closely with homophile organizations to bring their message to a wider audience. While her research questions, strategies, and findings were certainly her own, she sympathized heavily with homophile goals and incorporated homophile ideologies into her own work. "Many homosexuals are beginning to think of themselves as a minority group," she noted in a published article, describing the problems of homosexuals and their struggle "against the prejudices of a dominant heterosexual majority."[111] But Hooker's advice often took a conservative tone. In an address to the Mattachine Society she warned that the organization faced a strategic dilemma: "It must either become a quiet-working cooperative organization, seeking to use processes of education, findings of scientists whose research the Society may facilitate, and the aid of agencies in the fields related to Mattachine to accomplish its program, OR attempt to require society as a whole to accept the minority through hostility and demands for integration. I am happy to see the Society has chosen the first pathway."[112]

The research of reputable scientists like Alfred Kinsey and Evelyn Hooker bolstered homophile confidence and fueled the belief that scientific research would pave the way for homosexual integration. Sympathetic scientists seemed capable of projecting the message of tolerance to large audiences, and homophile activists used their voices in media publications and publicity. Similarly, homophile activists often latched onto popular writers who, without the mantle of scientific research, espoused limited social tolerance and acceptance. One such writer was Jess Stearn, a journalist who in the early 1960s turned his eye to the subject of homosexuality.

In his 1964 exposé of what some viewed as an alarming growth of lesbianism in the United States, Jess Stearn reported that secretive or "lace-curtain" lesbians in San Francisco wore green on Thursdays as a veiled code of sexual identification.[113] They also surreptitiously fingered their right eyebrow to signal other lesbians in the know. Stearn's narrative, which describes these "indistinguishable" lesbians as "part of a vast, sprawling grapevine," suggests a depth and intricacy in lesbian culture in the United States that far exceeds that expressed on the pages of *The Ladder*. While many of Stearn's findings are dubious and unreliable, his text, *The Grapevine*, identifies many facets of lesbian existence, especially bar life, in the post–World War II era. However, like the testimony of Morris Lowenthal in the trial of Mary's First and Last Chance Bar, Stearn's text ultimately works to promote homophile ideologies and position the Daughters of Bilitis as a legitimate and socially acceptable lesbian constituency.

The Grapevine, written in a confidential, avuncular style, follows up on Stearn's impressionistic and less sympathetic expose of male homosexuality in the United States, *The Sixth Man,* published in 1962.[114] His inspiration for a book devoted entirely to lesbians came during the 1962 DOB conference where, as an invited speaker, Stearn took heavy criticism from a number of lesbians in the audience. "[They] wanted to challenge the picture I had drawn of the homosexual [in the *Sixth Man],*" he recalls, "and some were positively livid about the brief references I had made to the lesbian."[115] Despite their anger and antipathy, DOB members soon became Stearn's primary informants as well as the unspoken heroes of his chronicle of "the fourth sex."[116] Stearn corresponded frequently with Del Martin, engaged Martin and Lyon in social visits, and scheduled interviews with a number of DOB members in order to create sketches of lesbian attitudes and behaviors. While some members balked at Stearns's presence, Martin and Lyon were enthusiastic about his project. They even nominated him for the organization's annual SOB (Son of Bilitis) award in recognition for his service to the lesbian community.[117] As a result, the narrative reflects and reproduces information about lesbian subjectivity based on DOB's organizational goals. It celebrates appropriately gendered lesbians while it writes a sad story of degeneracy, debauchery, and pathological desire on the bodies of "mannish, hostile" lesbians.

The Grapevine nevertheless remains an important text because it is an early source of information about non-homophile lesbians. Lurid and detailed, it reveals the lives of "secret lesbians" and documents the experiences of "fallen women." The central drama of the text revolves around two questions: "How many lesbians are *really* out there?" and "What causes lesbianism?" Stearn's text thus reflects the concerns of a nervous readership that seemed all too aware of the increased visibility of homosexuality in postwar American cities. He explains that "the so-called emancipation of women, with the fairer sex taking a more active role in outside affairs, has a lot to do with the rise of homosexuality in general."[118] He also cites the rising aggressiveness of women, the absence of women from the home, and, most importantly, the shifting values of a society on the brink of nuclear disaster. "Two great wars and the threat of another holocaust had done much to unsettle the moral climate," he claims.[119] Stearn dubiously links feminism and the increased economic opportunities for women in the postwar era to what he considered an alarming rise of lesbianism in the United States. His analysis thus serves as a cautionary tale—it underscores a postwar domestic economy that worked to contain and limit female sexuality.[120]

Stearn's text responds to social fears about the proliferation of lesbians by identifying both the purported causes of lesbianism and the ways that overt lesbians might be more effectively managed or controlled. While Stearn's text maintains that the vast majority of lesbians lived "underground" and did not publicly proclaim their lesbianism, most of the book is dedicated to documenting the habits of overt or publicly visible lesbians. Not surprisingly, Stearn pits the DOB lesbian, who "would tend to be the thoughtful, public-spirited, respectable type," against the stereotypical "hostile figure with a short masculine haircut, coarse skin, nasty vocabulary, and rough male clothing."[121] These "glandular cases," repeatedly described by Stearn in the harshest terms ("course skins, lumpy faces, and deep voices"), could be found on street corners and in bars and cafes. They cunningly contributed to the increasing debauchery of society by leading fresh young women with an "inherent disposition to homosexuality" down the road to ruin. Indeed, *The Grapevine* reads like any number of popular case studies of sexual deviance in that it recounts over and over the transformation of "normally sexed" and potentially (re)productive women into social outcasts.[122]

One such case is Ellen, "a superb beauty of eighteen" who had, from Stearn's point of view, unfortunately fallen in with a stern "bleached-blond butch." At the time of their acquaintance, Ellen fascinated the narrator: "She was in a white shirt, tails flapping charmingly over the blue jeans encasing her smooth, slim hips. Her hair, of newly burnished gold, fell carelessly in lustrous waves over her shoulders. The open shirt revealed a marble-like throat and the gentle swell of virginal breasts. She had a clean, wind-swept look that made her seem sultry and unattainable at the same time." After spending a year with her butch, however, Ellen was completely corrupted and abused. Her fresh beauty had been replaced by course skin, dull eyes, unkempt hair, and dirty nails. Moreover, she had been forced into a drug addiction that "numbed Ellen's mind and broke her spirit." Her beauty gone, Ellen was now used by the butch as a prostitute. Stearn knowingly concludes that "it seemed a routine chronicle of another unhappy girl's downfall."[123]

Stearn's narrative reflects popular attitudes and concerns. While it demands increased vigilance in the social control of women's sexuality, Stearn's text identifies homophile activism as one solution to the "social problem" lesbianism represented. As a result, Stearn set a number of images of lesbians against each other: the hypersexual fallen woman, the gender-inappropriate butch, and the DOB lesbian. He positions the corrupting influences of "butches" and "dikes" against DOB members who worked to improve the image and appearance of publicly visible lesbians. Stearn therefore popularizes the idea of a class of socially acceptable lesbians by juxtaposing this image against public fears about weak and degenerate women who were unable to control or contain their sexuality. Stearn devotes the last chapter of his text to the Daughters of Bilitis, arguing that this organization is "more intent on reversing their own public image than on revamping society." Working to rehabilitate lesbians who have "withdrawn bitterly from society," Stearn notes that the Daughters of Bilitis are "making converts" by "sending out as emissaries of femininity girls who were as stereotyped as the next butch until they discovered the DOB."[124] Stearn thus serves as an expert mouthpiece through which DOB introduced a more public and, in many ways, sympathetic representation of lesbianism to a hostile and homophobic readership. But the use of outside experts often played into the fears and fantasies of dominant culture. At the same time that they projected a cleaned-up and/or upwardly mobile image of homophile activists, experts sometimes unwittingly perpetuated the denigration of queer and gender-transgressive homosexuals.

Homophile organizations like the Mattachine Society and the Daughters of Bilitis were able to articulate lesbian and gay community needs and expectations through their monthly publications and the voices of experts like ministers, lawyers, scientists, and, later, popular writers. Through these means, they were able to interject a homophile-generated discourse about homosexuality into mainstream society. The ideas they proposed worked to educate the public that homosexuals could function as socially responsible and productive members of society. Homophile activism also worked to help integrate and assimilate the homosexual into mainstream society. However, homosexual social responsibility and integration, as they were configured by homophile activists, became increasingly limited by gender, class, and race-specific ideologies and behaviors. Homophile activism also depended on a discourse of individual privacy rights—divorcing upwardly mobile activists from the collective and group-based activism of bars and taverns. Homophile activists, therefore, were able to negotiate limited social and legal entitlements for lesbians and gay men only as they denied or muted many of the signifiers of queer culture and community. However, as the next chapter will show, homophile activists were only one of the forces that emerged in San Francisco in the late 1950s and early 1960s. A series of public events translated the differences between homophile and bar-based activism into a compromised but coherent social movement—one less reliant on social uplift than a confrontation with the San Francisco police.

ORAL HISTORY

George Mendenhall

The great thing about that era was the secret society. It's no longer a secret society. Then, the word "gay" was not popularly known, and you could say on a bus, "I went to a gay party last night," and people wouldn't know what you were talking about. Today, the word "gay" can't be used in any other context. Back then, there was a lot of mystery, and I think the mystery was fun. We had our own words, our own dialogue, like "trade" and "butch." There was even a couple of gay books in the '60s which had glossaries in them so gay people across the nation would know what the words meant. I was surprised that the words people used on the east coast were not the same as those used on the west coast. "Ki-ki," for instance. You ever heard that term? It means having sex with someone who's also gay. Back in SIR days, "ki-ki" meant going to bed with your "sister," somebody that you pal around with, like a gay male who pals around with another gay male. It means having sex with somebody who, normally, you wouldn't be interested in. The two of you would be looking for the same thing. Maybe, a male who would insert. You're both looking for that, but you end up going to bed and doing it with each other because you don't make out. So they'd say, "They're ki-ki sisters!"

Through the 1950s and 1960s, I worked in a factory, American Can Company, making tin cans. For thirty-three years I did that. And, believe it or not, I used to do all my activism at night. I totally gave up my weekends for about ten years. I gave up a great deal of my life because I was very aggressively involved in the gay movement. But I still had time to have sex. [Laughs.] I was just very busy. Sometimes when I wrote for the gay paper—I wrote for *BAR* [*Bay Area Reporter*] for about seventeen years—I used to take days off from work to go to meetings so I could write articles about them, and I would lose very nice wages, a hundred dollars a day, which was a lot of money. It's a lot

George Mendenhall, interviewed by Nan Alamilla Boyd, tape recording, San Francisco, 13 November 1991, Wide Open Town History Project, GLBT Historical Society. This interview has been edited by the author.

of money now. [Laughs.] They used to constantly reprimand me for excessive absenteeism. They always used to ask me why, but I would say it's personal.

Of the thirty-three years I spent at American Can, the first fifteen were here in San Francisco at Third and Twentieth Street, and the last eighteen years were in Oakland. I was openly gay at work although I didn't wear gay liberation badges. I didn't wear the pink triangle to work, but in casual conversation if it came up, I revealed myself to people who I thought would accept me. It never caused me any problems. Occasionally, I had sex with somebody at work in an elevator, some butch guy who approached me. It didn't happen too often, but occasionally I'd stop the elevator between floors. People would be banging on the doors, and I'd be carrying on in the elevator. I looked for every opportunity. [Laughs.]

I got involved in SIR after hearing about José Sarria. This was in 1966. SIR started in 1964. Do you want me to give you a five-minute summary of the gay liberation movement up to 1964? Ok. Sometime in the 1950s the Mattachine Society started in Los Angeles. It came to San Francisco under Hal Call, and it was primarily people meeting in homes having little discussion groups. There was one annual meeting, and people used false names. They did that at SIR too. They used phony names because they were afraid the police might get a hold of their names through the organization's files. You see, bars were occasionally being raided, baths were occasionally being raided, and people were stopped on the street in drag. But I never used a false name. The top officers at SIR, the people who ran the organization, none of us used false names. Second-level people, regular volunteers, and people below that used false names.

In the 1960s, the Mattachine Society existed, and there was also the Council on Religion and the Homosexual at Glide Church. They met monthly, and they were trying to involve ministers in gay liberation. There was the Daughters of Bilitis, but it sort of came and went. They had an office for a while at Sixth and Market, right near SIR. Phyllis and Del, you know them? Phyl and Del ran that. I say on and off because they always had the *Ladder* publication, but most people didn't know about the Daughters of Bilitis. It didn't get much publicity. They didn't have a lot of members, but it was there for people who wanted some information or wanted to call a woman. They used false names at DOB too. Later, at a national convention, I was made a Son of Bilitis, one of a few, an honorary title, an "SOB," which I was very proud of.

There was also the Tavern Guild of San Francisco, which was basically a gay bar owners group, though they will tell you otherwise. It was not generally known to the gay community because it was always an in-house organization. About the same time there was also the League for Civil Education

[LCE]. It was run by Guy Strait, who died a few years ago. He started up that organization, and its purpose was to use pamphlets and meetings to educate people about their rights if they were arrested or accosted by the police, which wasn't infrequent. A lot of arrests were happening in the bars. LCE was around earlier, 1958 through 1963. I know the dates because Guy Strait was suspected of absconding with funds, and there was a scandal involved. Then the people involved in the League for Civil Education and some others got together in a private home and decided to start a new organization called the Society for Individual Rights, SIR. They were extremely ambitious. They decided to rent a large auditorium and offices at Sixth and Mission. It was very gutsy. With very little money they rented this place with ten thousand square feet and decided to have a very large agenda of programs.

SIR just took off. Its biggest fundraisers were drag shows where men played all the women's roles. The shows always played to capacity houses, and we did all of them. We did *Dolly* and *Gypsy*—we had a whole series of drag Broadway shows. The next biggest fundraisers at SIR were dances, because dancing was prohibited in gay bars. At the time, there were no consensual sex laws, and the police would not permit body contact. A couple of bars had dancing in back rooms on the weekends, but they were frequently raided. To get the ok for dances, SIR had a lot of meetings with the police. The police had a community relations officer assigned to the gay community, and his name was Eliot Blackstone. Eliot Blackstone had an affinity for all things gay. He was a big overweight guy, and butch. He was very close to the gay community, and he had a lot to do with the police department accepting dancing at SIR. So on Saturday nights, we would have lines all the way down the street. That people would stand in line on a public street to go into a gay establishment was unheard of at the time, but people were willing to do it to dance at SIR.

You see, the people at SIR were seen as respectable middle-class males, and we were considered the nice homosexuals of the city by the police department. We were the nice ones. We weren't hanging out in bars and we weren't having sex, right? [Laughs.] Not in steam baths anyway. Well we were, but the image we created was that we were very respectable. We had an office, and it was very beautifully painted, with flowers and all. Our offices were very nice and comfortable. We also had an endless variety of activities. We had a psychological Gestalt kind of group. We had a karate self-defense class. We had dances on Saturday nights. We had dinners one night a week. We had a bridge club. We had bowling. You name it, we had it. We called ourselves an umbrella organization. You could come in and say "I want to have a Parcheesi group," and we'd put it in the bulletin that we sent out occasionally, and we'd put signs up in the lobby. We also had a magazine that came out from day one called *Vector*, which I edited for a couple years. *Vector* became a slick and professional magazine. As a result, people began to know what was happening at SIR, and those that were daring enough to do it would go down there to find out what was happening.

My first experience going to SIR was to survey the entire street outside. That was Sixth Street, skid row, yet I looked at everybody's face on the street to make sure I didn't know anyone before I would slip in the door. [Laughs.] I wasn't the only one that did that. People were scared to death to be seen going into such a place. Some people would leave through the back door because they didn't want to be seen. But the police used to come up on Saturday nights in uniform and watch us dance, just because they'd never seen anything like that. They'd laugh. You know, it was just something we tolerated. And SIR went on and on and on. I was on the board of directors for six years, and I was extremely active. I was on several committees. After a while, I realized I was burning myself out. In fact, at one point I collapsed psychologically, and I was out of SIR for a year before I came back. I came back when I knew how to use the word "no," and I stopped volunteering for everything.

The reason SIR disintegrated—it started in 1964 and had a fairly short life because it ended about 1971—the reason it ended was that the gay liberation movement had started. There was a gay liberation movement going on in the Bay Area, and activists who had been politically involved in SIR moved into that. Also, the *Bay Area Reporter* was under way. Then the drags moved their shows out and started a separate organization. They started producing drag shows at Bimbo's nightclub in North Beach. The political committee became the Alice B. Toklas Club, for all practical purposes. They moved over there. And the bars got dancing. The ABC relaxed its rules, and the bars got dancing. That killed a major source of income for us, and we just couldn't pay the rent. The rent was like six hundred dollars a month, which was an awful lot of money for us to come up with every month. Although SIR, at its peak, had six hundred members and four hundred subscribers to its magazine, which is phenomenal even by today's standards, it began to dwindle very fast. Other organizations began to be formed, so there was just more awareness, more things going on, and the community didn't need SIR. SIR was an umbrella organization, and its umbrella collapsed because all the parts of it were moving on. And, in the middle of all this, we had a major fire that destroyed the entire floor that we were on. It destroyed everything we had.

So much happened in the six, seven years that SIR existed that it's hard to describe it all. There was so much activity, and people were relating to it. We had a lecture series with people like Melvin Belli and state legislators. Willie

Brown spoke there many times, as did Dianne Feinstein. City politicians became aware of gay politics for the first time through SIR. We had Mayor Joseph Alioto at the time, but he wouldn't speak to us or have anything to do with us. He wouldn't even allow us in his office, but Dianne Feinstein, before she was elected to office, came to SIR and asked for our support. I gave it to her in a big editorial in *Vector*—without the approval of the organization. We have been friends to this day for that reason. A lot of people who are still around today, like Terence Hallinan, were active in supporting SIR. That gave us prestige with the police. For example, there were raids at Macy's, and they arrested forty people in one week for restroom sex. SIR went down and picketed Macy's because Macy's refused to meet with us to discuss what they might do for the situation. We were asking that they make their public restroom less private. We suggested that they put some vents in the doors or somehow reconstruct the restroom so people couldn't have sex in the stalls. When Macy's wouldn't cooperate, we went to the police, and told them how we protested this. We told them that we're not for that kind of sex, but we also are very much against arresting large numbers of people for, what? Just to destroy their lives? At that time, the newspapers would run the names of people, and some papers would run the actual jobs that people had and their addresses. Phew. It's unbelievable. It's hard to believe that happened. But it did.

In 1964, at the same time SIR was founded, there was also a dance at California Hall. The gays, with the approval of the police department, were allowed to have a dance in a public hall. It was a big event because it was the first time it had happened. But after getting approval from Eliot Blackstone and others to do this without police problems, the police showed up with paddy wagons parked out front. They took photographs of people entering, and they questioned people. It was just a mess. Herb Donaldson, who is a municipal judge now, Cecil Williams, Reverend Chuck Lewis, who was the head of the Council on Religion and the Homosexual at that time, and other people were there. When the police attempted to enter, these people formed a barricade and some were arrested. It was an amazing event. I was there briefly, but when I saw all the police cars I took off. I was scared. What happened was there were arrests, and the next day the *Chronicle* ran headlines about what had happened. There was a front page editorial, which was unheard of, condemning it. The editorial attacked the police and called for the police to relate to the gay community. That's when we got a lot of supportive statements from the police saying that it should never have happened. They actually said the raid should never have happened. It was unheard of. The police apologized to the public for that event, and it gave us prestige. It gave us a lot of publicity. The newspaper coverage talked all about SIR and the Council on Religion and the Homosexual. After that event, there was a great deal of relating to the gay community. The newspapers began to form lists of people to call in the gay community whenever anything happened that was gay related, just to get a local angle. The newspapers became aware of gay organizations. It really opened the door for a lot of things, that event and the publicity it got. It made people aware of the gay community, and it woke up a lot of people to accept us that hadn't accepted us before.

5 | QUEER COOPERATION AND RESISTANCE

A Gay and Lesbian Movement Comes Together in the 1960s

> Younger kids come out to San Francisco, but they have no idea! It really was the bars that fought for their rights, the Tavern Guild and the bars. They're the ones that got this city as open as it is today. We kept fighting.
>
> *Charlotte Coleman, bar owner*

In the summer of 1964 *Life* magazine published an exposé titled "Homosexuality in America." Photographers captured the flamboyance of gay life, and journalists like Ernest Havemann described in lurid detail the concentration of homosexuals in American cities: "Do the homosexuals, like the Communists, intend to bury us?" Havemann asked.[1] Responding not simply to the rhetorical link between communism and homosexuality that McCarthy-era politics secured, Havemann's panicked statement articulated another threat: the growing population of homosexuals in urban areas. "Homosexuality—and the problem it poses—exists all over the U.S., but is most evident in New York, Chicago, Los Angeles, San Francisco, New Orleans and Miami."[2] According to *Life* magazine, big cities offered homosexuals important advantages such as social tolerance, political affiliation, and job opportunities. But cities also offered homosexuals the opportunity to socialize in bars, taverns, parks, and baths. "In the city of San Francisco, which rates as the 'gay capital,'" one article noted, "there are more than 30 bars that cater exclusively to a homosexual clientele."[3] In national media like *Life,* San Francisco stood out as uncommonly queer. Its concentration of gays and lesbians marked a high point in social tolerance.

How did San Franciscans feel about the number of homosexuals in their city? If opinion polls in the local newspapers are any indication, non-gay residents seemed alternately ambivalent and alarmed. They were at times proud of San Francisco's liberalism and at other times nervous or unsure about the role of homosexuals in the city. For instance, a 1961 "Question Man" column for the San Francisco *Chronicle* asked, "Why are there so many homosexuals living in S.F.?" A number of residents responded that the city's tolerance was simply part of its character. "We look at homosexualism [*sic*] with a more enlightened view," one respondent noted. Another quipped, "This is a liberal city that appeals to many types. Perhaps the homosexuals feel more secure and tolerated here."[4] In 1966, however, the city's newspapers registered a different attitude. A 1965 police report blamed the growth of the city's homosexual community on "liberal attitudes," and Sex Detail Inspector Rudy Nieto dubiously linked homosexuality to a dramatic increase in sex crimes.[5] When a 1966 news column posed the question, "Are There More Homosexuals Today?" respondents expressed a number of different concerns, mostly critical of the influx of homosexuals. One respondent, for instance, replied "Yes," noting, "It's because they're mentally sick. They follow you. It's embarrassing. You can't insult them. If you hit them, well, it's just like hitting a girl. If you slug them one, they'd throw you in jail." Another respondent similarly (if erroneously) complained, "Homosexuals [in San Francisco] register with the police. That way they're protected. If they make a pass at you and you hit them, they can prosecute you."[6] Both responses reveal fears that social tolerance and a seemingly hands-off legal policy encouraged the presence of queers in San Francisco. Nevertheless, while incorrect in the details, both responses register the larger truth that the role of the police had shifted in the early 1960s—from that of a protector of heterosexual prerogative (and violence against queers) to that of a mediator of lesbian and gay civil rights.

In the 1960s, a long and tenacious legal battle over the existence of gay bars culminated in the growth and increased visibility of San Francisco's queer and transgender communities. By 1962, California Supreme Court rulings (re)secured for homosexuals the legal right to assemble in bars and taverns, and gay bars proliferated. In fact, as part of its exposé, *Life* magazine projected sexy images of two San Francisco bars to its national readership. It captured the silhouetted interior of the Tool Box, a leather bar, and a raucous gathering at the Jumpin' Frog, a Polk Street tavern. The intimacy and camaraderie of these bars was hard to miss. With scores of men standing close in smoky, overcrowded spaces, both images seemed invitingly defiant, even celebratory—unconcerned with bar raids and police intimidation. Thus, while news coverage sought to expose the "problems" of urban homosexuality, it projected powerful new images to its readership and traced a richly differentiated social world. In San Francisco, as *Life* reported, one could find any number of gay bars. There were no-nonsense pickup bars with few stools and little conversation; upscale cocktail lounges in some of the city's best hotels; friendly neighborhood bars with explicitly homosexual entertainment; bottom-of-the-barrel Tenderloin bars where prostitutes, drag queens, and runaways mingled; and leather bars in the city's warehouse district where a cult of masculinity replaced homosexual effeminacy.[7] In fact, according to sociologist Wayne Sage, in the 1970s gay bars in urban areas were more likely to segregate according to age, sex, ethnicity, status, and character than small-town gay bars, where the common trait of homosexuality transcended a range of social and cultural differences.[8] The "problem" of urban homosexuality in the mid-1960s was not that the number of homosexuals had necessarily grown but that the public space occupied by homosexuals had expanded. Or, as *Life* magazine put it, the "secret world" occupied by homosexuals "grows open and bolder [and] society is forced to look at it."[9] The public visibility of gays and lesbians, by the mid-1960s, had become an urban phenomenon, and San Francisco stood at the center of this trend.

How did San Francisco become a center for gay urban life? Homophile activist Hal Call reasons that *Life* magazine's coverage and the images it projected began the migrant train that saturated the city's gay districts, cafes, and taverns.[10] While national media coverage certainly contributed to the growth and development of San Francisco's reputation as a gay town, several local events brought the city's homosexual populations into the limelight and secured a space for lesbian and gay community development. Between 1959 and 1961, six events changed the climate for queers in San Francisco: the mayoral election of 1959, the 1959 California Supreme Court decision in *Vallerga v. Department of Alcoholic Beverage Control,* the 1961 "gayola" police payoff scandal, José Sarria's 1961 bid for city supervisor, the August 1961 Tay-Bush raid, and the 1961 repeal of California's vagrancy law. These events, all of which occurred within a short period of time, stimulated the emergence of a public discourse about homosexuality in San Francisco. They functioned as a catalyst for the development of a more articulate, cooperative, and resistant gay and lesbian social movement. In fact, the constellation of events that occurred between 1959 and 1961 stimulated the formation of four new gay and lesbian organizations: the League for Civil Education (1961), the San Francisco Tavern Guild (1962), the Society for Individual Rights (1963), and the Council on Religion and the Homosexual (1964). While the membership in these organizations often overlapped—both with each other and with other homophile organizations—they stretched the boundaries of social and political affiliation. They challenged the assimilative ideology of the early Daughters of Bilitis and the San Francisco–based Mattachine Society, and they moved the concept of gay and lesbian political affiliation away from the stronghold of early homophile representation. In fact, the interpersonal dynamics at play in the establishment of these four organizations helped resolve the often fractious relationship between San Francisco's queer constituency and the reformist politic of 1950s homophile movements.

By New Year's Day 1965, when police descended on California Hall and disrupted a costume ball organized by the Council on Religion and the Homosexual, many of the differences between bar-based and homophile organizations had been resolved. By this time, a new climate of cooperation characterized San Francisco's gay, lesbian, and transgender communities. While the events and organizations described in this chapter did not galvanize a national movement in the way the Stonewall Riots were able to do, they brought a disparate community together, stimulated a public discourse about the role of homosexuals in the city, and negotiated limited legal protections for lesbians and gay men in San Francisco. Ironically, as John D'Emilio has noted, the political events that conspired to put San Francisco on the map as a gay capital also rendered it politically neutral by the time of Stonewall.[11] By 1965, San Francisco had gained, to a limited extent, the kinds of freedoms activists rallied for during the Stonewall Riots, and by 1969 San Francisco's gay and lesbian communities had lapsed into a more stable politics of reform. This chapter is less concerned with why queer political resistance in San Francisco did not spark a national movement than how San Francisco's homosexual populations were able to demand and negotiate limited political gains through the late 1950s and early 1960s. In particular, as this chapter describes the events that transpired between 1959 and 1961 and the organizations that emerged following those events, it highlights the often contentious relationship between bar-based culture and homophile politics that led to the solidification and stabilization of what has come to be known as San Francisco's gay and lesbian community.

THE EVENTS

The Election of 1959

George Christopher became San Francisco's mayor in 1956 after a landslide victory, and he promptly instituted a harsh anti-vice campaign. He appointed Frank Ahern and then, after Ahern's death, Tom Cahill as chief of police. Cahill quickly earned a reputation in San Francisco for his "S-Squad" tactics (S stood for a "strategy of saturation and selective enforcement"), whereby two to four nights a week, a squad of sixty-four undercover officers patrolled the city and interrogated anyone who looked suspicious. Cahill's forces targeted the city's homosexual bars and districts, and Cahill's men earned an unflattering reputation in these quarters. Arrests soared recklessly, but Christopher stood squarely behind Cahill despite a public outcry—even the city's district attorney complained that Chief Cahill employed "Gestapo" methods.[12] Christopher's administration faced a difficult challenge. While Christopher's anti-crime platform had earned him a landslide victory at the polls, his subsequent hard-ball tactics threatened one of San Francisco's most beloved qualities—its reputation as a wide-open town.

In 1959, when Christopher made a bid for reelection, his opponent, Russell Wolden, quickly took a lead in the polls. Wolden, the city assessor, was a pro-labor candidate who positioned himself as the Democratic choice even though he was not officially endorsed by the Democratic Party. Christopher, on the other hand, relied on the support of business leaders, and he projected a clean, all-American public image (signified, for instance, by his popular decision to lure the Giants and major league baseball to San Francisco). The campaign lumbered along until early October, just weeks before the election, when Wolden attempted to smear Christopher's anti-vice platform with the accusation that under Christopher's administration the city had become a haven for homosexuals. In a radio address to the city on 7 October 1959, Wolden flamboyantly charged, "I say San Francisco is not a closed town! And it is not a clean town! And I charge that conditions involving flagrant moral corruption do exist here which will revolt every decent person."[13] Wolden's address insisted that sexual perversion existed "in open and flagrant defiance of the law," and, he warned, he had evidence of over twenty bars or restaurants in San Francisco that catered to homosexuals. Wolden singled out the Mattachine Society as evidence of the city's immoral conditions: "So favorable is the official climate for the activities of these persons that last month at a convention in Denver, Colorado, an organization of sex deviates known as the Mattachine Society, whose national office is established in our city, actually passed a resolution praising Mayor Christopher by name for what the resolution described as the enlightened attitude of his Administration toward them."[14] In a press release the following day, Wolden challenged the grand jury to investigate his allegations and collect facts.[15]

Wolden's strategy to upbraid and challenge Christopher's reputation backfired for several reasons. First, Wolden's popularity (as a vote against Christopher) rode on public dissatisfaction with Christopher and Cahill's anti-vice campaign; therefore, to insist that Christopher was soft on crime eroded Wolden's own electoral strength. Second, Wolden seriously miscalculated the city's capacity to let homosexuality be an issue in the campaign. Because Wolden's accusation brought homosexuality to the front page of every city newspaper, it brought homosexuality into every home and office, offending Wolden supporters by forcing them to read about the vice that dared not speak its name. Finally, Wolden's campaign lost all credibility when informants revealed that the Mattachine resolution praising Christopher and Cahill was, in fact, instigated by a "behind-the-scenes operator" in the Wolden campaign, William Patrick Brandhove.[16] City newspapers rallied against Wolden, and the *Chronicle* issued a call for Wolden's withdrawal from the campaign, stating that, "Russell L. Wolden has put himself beyond the pale of decent politics by his effort to inject the shoddy issue of homosexuality into the mayoral campaign."[17]

Christopher was reelected by a substantial margin, but the effects of Wolden's smear campaign went far beyond his own failed political career. George Dorsey, Christopher's biographer, states that "for the first time in the history of the United States, homosexuality became the major issue in a big-city political campaign."[18] Wolden's tactics pushed homosexuality into mainstream politics and, in doing so, stimulated a shift in gay and lesbian political consciousness. In fact, one day after Wolden's radio address, the Mattachine Society filed a one-million-dollar slander suit against him, arguing that Wolden "wrongfully and maliciously . . . [declared that the Mattachine Society] exposed teenagers to contact with homosexuals."[19] The Mattachine Society manipulated the publicity that swirled around Wolden's campaign and flexed its political muscle. A Mattachine newsletter noted that the offices of the Mattachine Society were "deluged with telephone calls and visits from friends, well-wishers, curiosity-seekers and others" after Wolden's public comments.[20] The Daughters of Bilitis took the issue further, suggesting in a July 1960 issue of the *Ladder* that Wolden's campaign raised the possibility of a homosexual voting bloc. "The important issue here for homosexuals," insisted Del Martin, "is to register—and vote."[21] Wolden's accusations not only forced the mainstream press to focus unprecedented attention on homosexual issues, but, remarkably, his comments stimulated a gay and lesbian political consciousness to take root.[22]

Vallerga v. Department of Alcoholic Beverage Control

While the 1959 mayoral election brought the issue of homosexuality to big-city politics, *Vallerga v. ABC* brought new questions about homosexual civil rights to the California courts. *Vallerga* shifted a public discourse about homosexuality away from its medical moorings and onto a legal track that clarified the civil rights of lesbians and gay men. In late 1959, attorneys for the owners of Mary's First and Last Chance Bar appeared before the California First District Court of Appeal to challenge the 1955-enacted Section 24200(e) of the California Business and Professional Code, which stated that the State Alcoholic Beverage Control Board (ABC) could revoke the liquor license of a bar catering to "users of narcotics, prostitutes, pimps, panderers, or sexual perverts."[23] Section 24200(e) had been initiated by the state legislature in an attempt to undercut *Stoumen v. Reilly,* which maintained that bar owners could serve homosexual clientele as long as they were not committing "illegal or immoral acts."[24]

Vallerga was a success. It confirmed that section 24200(e) was unconstitutional, and it reestablished that the presence of homosexuals in a bar did not automatically imply the presence of sexual perverts. Gay men and lesbians could, again, gather legally in bars if they did not exhibit "immoral, indecent, disgusting or improper" behavior. However, because immoral, indecent, disgusting, or improper behaviors were ambiguously defined, the regulation of behavior remained open to interpretation. As historian Allan Bérubé notes, what the courts called "lewd behavior" was arbitrarily policed and might sometimes include "dress of the patrons, the manner in which they paired off, the use of the women's rest room by a woman wearing men's clothing, a woman kissing another woman, or a man kissing another man, caressing people of the same sex, or dancing with people of the same sex."[25] The *Vallerga* decision, handed down on Christmas Eve 1959, was an important victory for lesbian and gay civil rights in that it confirmed that bar owners could run establishments catering to well-behaved homosexuals, but it potentially widened the net within which the ABC could shut down bars where questionable ("lewd") behaviors were exhibited.

This case had a number of important implications. First, it furthered an ongoing dialogue about homosexual civil rights. Morris Lowenthal, for example, plaintiffs' attorney in *Vallerga* (as he had been in *Stoumen*), constantly relied on a legal strategy that foregrounded questions about civil rights. He claimed that bar owners were denied due process by the ABC, and he reasoned that bar owners could not be held legally responsible for determining the sexuality of their patrons. Furthermore, he argued that patrons (homosexual or not) had a constitutional right to assembly and service. "What is the owner to do?" he asked, "refuse service and deprive someone of his constitutional rights?"[26] On a more pernicious note, the case established that some homosexuals were more moral (and legal) than others. Court testimony suggested that well-behaved homosexuals were both non-sexual and gender-appropriate and argued, as previously mentioned, that these were the homosexuals who deserved civil rights. Also, because the *Vallerga* case was based on the activities of a lesbian bar, Mary's First and Last Chance, it placed lesbian political identities alongside those of gay men. It articulated that lesbian civil rights could be understood as analogous to those of gay men. Finally, the *Vallerga* case allowed homosexuals in San Francisco a modicum of political entitlement and a momentary respite from ABC pressure and police harassment. Norbert Falvey, ABC officer, stated that "the court decision meant the department henceforth 'cannot touch' a number of San Francisco taverns popular with male and female homosexuals."[27]

The "Gayola" Scandal

Perhaps the most important impact of *Vallerga* was that it bolstered the confidence of queer bar owners. Immediately following the court's decision, a number of bar owners brought charges against several San Francisco beat cops and one liquor board investigator for soliciting protection money. In fact, the Handlebar, whose liquor license was restored after *Vallerga,* was one of the first bars to report police payoffs to the city's district attorney's office in early 1960.[28] The ensuing "gayola" scandal, which started with confidential reports by the Handlebar, pushed the issue of homosexual civil rights back into the city's newspapers and resulted in the arrest of several San Francisco police officers.

The first arrest was made in February 1960, when SFPD Sergeant Waldo Reesink's supervisors arrested him for bribery after they recorded a conversation between Reesink and Leo Orrin, owner of the Handlebar.[29] By July, when Reesink stood trial, six other SFPD officers had been arrested on charges of soliciting and/or accepting bribes from gay bar owners for police "protection." While Reesink's case was something of a sleeper (he pleaded guilty to a lesser charge), the July–August trial of four San Francisco beat cops captured the public's attention and the media's sympathies.

The "gayola" trial was a month-long media frenzy. Both the *Chronicle* and *Examiner* ran daily columns, often with photos, explaining to readers the technicalities of the trial as well as the ins and outs of San Francisco's homosexual subcultures. The trial centered on payoffs made by the Castaway bar at 90 Market Street and Jack's Waterfront at 111 Embarcadero. Both bars were "known to police as a hangout for homosexuals," and both allegedly had been paying between $150 and $200 per month for several years in order to keep police surveillance and harassment to a minimum.[30] However, unlike in the Reesink case and the November trial of Lawrence Cardellini, a supervisor for the ABC who was caught with marked money in his pocket and arrested for bribery, the six police officers were indicted without hard evidence, on the basis of the accusations of several bar owners and managers.

Of the six officers named in the investigation, two were released and four, Sergeants Robert McFarland and Alfred Cecchi and Officers Edward Bigarani and Michael Sugrue, stood trial after pleading not guilty. Although Police Chief Cahill remained adamant that he would continue to "crack down and close" the city's homosexual bars, press commentary during the trial seemed uncommonly sympathetic to the gay bar owners, and the trial prolonged the break in Cahill's drive to "clean up the city." For instance, unfriendly mug shots served as the only visual representations of the indicted officers in the local papers, and the press curtly dismissed the defendants' position that bribery charges stemmed from "a conspiracy of bar owners" who were angered by constant harassment.[31] Throughout the trial, reporters cast the concerns of gay bar owners in a respectful light and at times ridiculed the demeanor of the accused police officers. *Examiner* reporter Ernest Lenn characterized Sergeant Alfred Cecchi as obstinately self-righteous: "Adamantly, as though refusing to tear up a traffic ticket, he held to his protestations of innocence."[32] Later, Lenn characterized Edward Bigarani as a buffoon. Bigarani peppered his statements with "What the hells" and played up a hard-boiled image, Lenn noted. "Like a dead-pan Damon Runyon character spouting from a Kinsey report, he recounted a series of run-ins at the bar."[33] It was also during the "gayola" trial that journalists started using the phrase "gay bar" rather than the more inflammatory "resorts for sex perverts" to identify the taverns in question.[34] The city's traditionally conservative newspapers, perhaps in an effort to chastise Cahill's leadership, stood on the side of the plaintiffs and agreed that police impropriety had gotten out of hand.

The most important aspect of the trial, however, was an expanded public discourse about homosexual civil rights. Allen Brown's "Question Man" column in the *Chronicle* posed a question at the Hall of Justice during the trial, and the responses Brown collected reveal a complex level of thinking about homosexual civil rights. Brown's question, "Should We Discourage Gay Bars?" elicited the following responses:

> Homosexuals do have a right to congregate.
>
> H. Wainwright, attorney for the defense
>
> Homosexuals do have rights, of course, and should not be coerced.
>
> N. Cohn, attorney for the defense
>
> It goes beyond the problem of whether homosexuals are people. That's established. . . . Homosexuals should be adult enough to mingle with others in places of entertainment without being conspicuous.
>
> J. MacInnis, attorney for the defense
>
> These people have to drink some place, and like any minority group they're entitled to equal accommodations. As long as they conduct themselves properly in a legal bar, I see nothing wrong with it. A gay bar is a public place, and if *non-homosexuals* don't like it, they can leave.
>
> M. Schneider, attorney for the defense [emphasis mine]
>
> The police method of handling the problem is not the proper one.
>
> A. Dresow, chief deputy public defender
>
> The bars are not desirable. . . . Still, you can't throw them out of town without some violation of law. They're entitled to equal protection.
>
> N. Deriman, assistant district attorney[35]

Despite their courtroom strategies, the city's defense attorneys unanimously agreed, at least in principle, to the concept of homosexual civil rights. More importantly, they framed these statements in a discourse about "minority rights" and equal protection that moved well beyond the platform of individual rights sustained by homophile activists. The articulation of civil rights based on the Fourteenth Amendment's equal protection clause gave gay and lesbian activists access to a new level of legal discourse, specifically, the discourse of group-based discrimination that would figure importantly in future gay and lesbian civil rights cases.[36]

José Sarria's City Supervisor Candidacy

José Sarria's fall 1961 bid for an elected seat on the city's Board of Supervisors was controversial and marginal at best, but it helped solidify the concept of homosexual political subjectivity and demonstrated the voting power of San Francisco's gay, lesbian, and transgender communities. Sarria's candidacy sprang from his popularity at the Black Cat, where he worked in drag as a cocktail waitress and later as a singer and entertainer. "That's how I began. . . . I was the entertainer . . . and I changed the character of the Black Cat. I became the Black Cat."[37] Sarria's performances were immensely popular, and while the Black Cat's Sunday afternoon stage shows helped Sarria launch his campaign, it was his personal history that enabled him to run for city office as an openly gay man, remarkably, on a platform that insisted "gay is good."[38]

Sarria was born in San Francisco in 1923 and spent his youth in the home of a wealthy Central American family that employed his Colombian-born mother as a governess.[39] Sarria's early awareness of himself as a privileged outsider emanated from this environment. "I had a good living, a good childhood," Sarria notes. "My mother wasn't rich, but I had everything."[40] Sarria remembers that because his mother's employer was very "social-minded," he had the opportunity to see a lot of "big entertainment." He recalls attending the opera and theater with his mother and godmother. Later, Sarria's mother worked for the O'Brien family, which had connections with San Francisco's police department. "That's how my mother was well known," Sarria explains, and through these "familial" relations, Sarria learned to maneuver, as an outsider, within the world of San Francisco's social and political elites.[41]

Sarria started cross-dressing at an early age. As a young adult he would sometimes dress as a girl "just to be crazy" and go out with his mother to one of San Francisco's bohemian restaurants or nightclubs. "We went to places like the Paper Doll, which was not gay gay gay as per se, but once in a while I would go as a girl."[42] Mostly, he cross-dressed for fun and had little trouble from his family or the law until 1952, when he was arrested for solicitation in the Oak Room. Sarria's arrest put an end to his plans to become a teacher—"sex offenders" were prohibited from teaching—so he experimented more seriously with cross-dressing.[43] He won second prize in a drag contest at Pearl's and went to work there and then at the Beige Room, hoping to eventually make his way to Finocchio's.[44]

Sarria never made it to Finocchio's, but he did make a name for himself at the Black Cat. Sarria explains that historically the Black Cat was not a gay bar but, rather, a bohemian bar that tolerated all sexual persuasions. Mixing biting political commentary into his often humorous and campy floor shows, Sarria dared the "bohemians" who frequented the Black Cat to identify themselves more openly as homosexuals. Sarria's popularity rested on his ability to humorously but directly address the lives of a closeted bargoing homosexual constituency. He was able to cajole a sizable number of homosexuals into a social and political consciousness. As activist George Mendenhall remembers:

> [The Black Cat] was my primary hangout. I was usually there every Sunday for . . . José Sarria's concerts. They were really operas, satirical operas, commenting on the Gay community and in a satirical and very comical way. The place was overflowing onto the street, and there were just lots of people laughing and cheering. There was really no Gay activism going on politically at all except for the Sunday Black Cat with José where he was very political in the way he handled things. I really identified with that. Fact is, some of the people who later went on to form the S.I.R. organization reflected back that they too were first exposed to politics at the Black Cat.[45]

Through the late 1950s, Sarria's Sunday afternoon operas became a forum for his social and political opinions and ambitions. Dressed in various stages of drag, he would read and comment on articles from local newspapers, sing opera, help serve brunch, and deliver notices from the local police. At the end of each performance, he would have everyone stand, hold hands, and sing "God Save Us Nellie Queens" to the tune of "God Save the Queen." In his performances and commentary, he insisted that "gay is good" and criticized the "double life," that is, being closeted.

In 1961, the eleven members of San Francisco's Board of Supervisors, the city and county's legislative body, were elected at large. (City elections have since converted to district elections, which in effect enabled Harvey Milk to win a seat on the board as an openly gay man representing the city's Castro Street [Eureka Valley] district in 1976.) Sarria faced a difficult prospect, running against political insiders and well-financed business leaders. Remarkably, with campaign funding of less than $500 and, except for one outside appearance, his campaigning limited to his weekend performances at the Black Cat, Sarria received 5,613 votes. District election winners received between 70,000 to 100,000 votes in 1961. While Sarria did not get elected to the board, the fact that he was able to launch a campaign as a Latino and an openly gay man shifted the political consciousness of the city's queer communities. It provided evidence of gay, lesbian, and transgender electoral strength and modeled the connections between white homosexuals and queers of color. "Victory was there," one commentator noted, "for he had run the gamut of the political circus without being smeared by a single opponent."[46]

Sarria's campaign can be seen as part of an ongoing and contentious dialogue between the public, the media, and the city's queer communities. Public information about the harassment of the city's queer communities was balanced against a shifting discourse about homosexuality that moved from questions about morality and public health to questions about civil rights. While the press waffled on the "problem" of homosexuality, activists like Sarria proposed a counterdiscourse, claiming that gay was good and that homosexuals constituted a potentially powerful political constituency. Some members of San Francisco's social and political elite were quicker to perceive and support Sarria's vision than others. Herb Caen, for example, deftly observed the transformation brewing in San Francisco's queer communities:

> The Grand Jury is showing more than casual interest in the apparently increasing number of homosexuals in San Francisco. . . . I say "apparently increasing" because of a long acquaintanceship with—and resultant skepticism about—the science of statistics. . . . Modern and more accurate diagnoses have changed medical statistics, for example; and I'm not sure whether something of the sort has not also brought the homosexuality problem into sharper focus. . . . Meanwhile the Gay Set, unimpressed, continues to act more and more like a political organization here. We had the recent business of a candidacy for Supervisor being organized out of a certain homosexually oriented bar. . . . Now The Boys are holding house parties to raise money.[47]

Caen's commentary documents a shift in the idea of homosexuality as a social or medical problem to that of cultural community and political constituency. Moreover, as Sarria's vision of a politically organized and socially effective community set the stage for future mobilization, it did so by engaging a previously untapped segment of the queer community, specifically the bargoing homosexuals who led a "double life."

The Tay-Bush Raid

"In the biggest action of its kind in the history of the department," the *San Francisco Chronicle* began its front page coverage, "police raided a small restaurant at Bush and Taylor streets early yesterday and jailed 101 suspected sex deviates."[48] The raid occurred at approximately 3:00 A.M. on Sunday, 14 August 1961, at the Tay-Bush Inn, a small cafe where, according to police reports, over fifty men were dancing to music from a small jukebox. While San Franciscans witnessed a number of dramatic police raids on taverns and nightclubs catering to homosexuals through the 1940s and 1950s, the raid on the Tay-Bush Inn stands out both in magnitude and significance.[49] Not only was it the largest raid on a gay bar in San Francisco's history, but it generated a great deal of attention from the press and, thus, continued to engage San Francisco's mayor, lawmakers, police department, and citizens in a dialogue about homosexuality.[50] In combination with the preceding events (the mayoral election, the *Vallerga* decision, the "gayola" scandal, and Sarria's candidacy), the media frenzy around the Tay-Bush raid propelled a discursive transition that increasingly considered the question of gay and lesbian civil rights, a transition that fundamentally altered the way San Francisco's police department would handle the "problem" of gay bars.

The Tay-Bush was an after-hours cafe that served beer and hamburgers to the "all-night" crowd after the bars closed. "What it was all about was going and listening to the jukebox and dancing. That's why it was there, and also eating and staying up until dawn and starting at the bars again," remembers Ethel Whitaker, who was at the Tay-Bush on the night of the raid:

> I was to meet these friends . . . so we took different cars, and when I got there [my friends] were already there. I came in, and I really had to go to the bathroom. I said to Jamie, "Order me a cheeseburger and I'll be right back." I go upstairs, there's only one bathroom, and there's about I'd say 150 people there and the room is about this big, thirty by thirty . . . it was pretty jam-packed. So I waited in line. The jukebox was really jumping, and you know, people are talking. I go into the bathroom, take my turn, come out and you could hear a pin drop. I said, "What's going on?" I was really surprised, you know what I mean, because I knew something had happened. . . . So as I descended the staircase: floodlights. I see all these floodlights and I hear these loudspeakers outside. I said, "Jamie, what's going on?" He says, "We're in a raid!" I said, "What?! What do we do?" He says, "I don't know!"[51]

According to newspaper reports, in a roundup "reminiscent of the old speakeasy days of prohibition," fourteen policemen corralled 103 Tay-Bush patrons into seven separate patrol wagons and herded them to the city jail.[52] The police were not able to capture everyone, and as newspaper reports added, "Most of them bolted, beat it around the corner and were gone."[53] Whitaker recalls, however, that "they were picking out the people there, like lawyers' daughters and sons, anyone who had any political clout here in San Francisco, [and] sending them on home." She remembers that the Tay-Bush was an extremely mixed crowd, but on 14 August, "the ones that didn't have any clout, they were putting us in the paddy wagons." So it is no surprise that Ethel Whitaker, a small, butch, African American woman, was detained and arrested. "I was one of them, so they searched me down. They supposedly thought I was a boy—I was small at that time, and one of the few that had an Afro."[54]

Journalist Herb Caen also commented that the police department's harassment policy was not directed at homosexuals in general but at certain segments of the city's homosexual populations: "Quick cut to a police raid on a cafe at Taylor and Bush. The Mayor is pleased. 'Something is being done!' Nothing is being done: the fashionable Ones don't give themselves away . . . they wear elegant clothes, smell of expensive cologne, live at good addresses and are left alone—as befits leading citizens who are merely Odd."[55] The "problem" of homosexuality in San Francisco was not one of morality, he reasoned, but access to public space, which meant wealthier homosexuals often escaped the city's dragnet. Caen continued "The only moral, if it's a question of morals: Don't be a poor One. Don't be a poor anything."[56] Still, a number of professionals found themselves behind bars on that Sunday morning, and they became the subject of public scrutiny and apprehension. A front page article in the *Examiner* claimed that the arrested "included actors, actresses, professional dancers, a State hospital psychologist, a bank department manager, an artist, and an Air Force purchasing agent."[57] The article zeroed in on these individuals, giving their names, ages, addresses, occupations, and employers. This special treatment—no other arrested persons were identified this way—punished middle-class or salaried workers for transgressing class boundaries. It highlights the midcentury anxiety that homosexuals, previously associated with working-class vice districts, were permeating the middle class.

By the end of the week, news coverage had softened its representation of homosexuals, and journalists began to use the Tay-Bush raid as a forum for discussing and criticizing the mayor's law-and-order policies.

An *Examiner* piece, for instance, tentatively suggested police impropriety and cast the mayor in a defensive light.[58] An accompanying photo, oversized and compelling, depicted a courtroom scene with scores of well-dressed men waiting nervously to enter their pleas. The following day, the *Examiner* firmly raised the question of civil rights, noting that the Mattachine Society, "a national organization dedicated to public education and the problems of homosexuality," had thrown its weight behind the case. The Mattachine Society found legal representation for the arrested, began a defense fund to fight the case, and promised to "take care of the cost of printing briefs in the event defendants are convicted and must appeal to a higher court." Moreover, the *Examiner* continued, "other established 'gay' places throughout the country have offered aid in a fight for the right of sexual deviates to meet in public without 'persecution' by police."[59] No longer acting as humiliated and defenseless individuals, the defendants represented a group or community wrongly accused. And as with the "gayola" scandal, the press seemed much more concerned with the problem of police corruption and harassment than the specter of homosexuality.

As civil rights battles waged across the south, confronting racial segregation and challenging white supremacy, San Franciscans seemed increasingly willing to address the fact of police repression and the possibility of homosexual civil rights. By mid-September, the city had dropped its charges against all but two of those arrested in the Tay-Bush raid, and the victory was more than symbolic. Under the auspices of a friendly attorney who agreed to represent Tay-Bush defendants, most of those charged had pleaded not guilty, and all but two had won their cases. This signaled to the city's police department that mass arrests based on a liberal interpretation of "lewd behavior" would not hold up in court. Furthermore, it encouraged gay men and lesbians to defend themselves in court rather than pleading no contest and paying large fines to avoid public exposure. Robert Johnson, the Tay-Bush proprietor who pleaded not guilty to charges of keeping a disorderly house (and won), admitted that his cafe was a "gathering spot for homosexuals" but insisted that this did not mean it was necessarily disorderly. "His position," one news article noted, "was that deviates have the same rights to meet publicly as any other person."[60] This attitude seemed to permeate the city. A *Chronicle* poll ("Should S.F. Close the Gay Clubs?") by the "Inquiring Photographer" revealed once again that the city's desire to protect "young people" from access to homosexual "immorality" could not be so easily separated from homosexual rights to assembly and equal access to public space.[61] Homosexuals in San Francisco came to be recognized as a community that was more and more capable of asserting its rights.

The Repeal of California's Vagrancy Law

While San Francisco's queer and gender-transgressive populations were subjected to a range of anti-homosexual policies that spanned the gamut of city, county, state, and federal law, anti-vagrancy law had the most dramatic impact on the everyday lives of homosexuals. Because vagrancy was a crime of status rather than behavior, its power lay in its arbitrary applications. Anyone, gay or straight, might be arrested on vagrancy charges at any time for the mere suspicion of antisocial or same-sex sexual behavior. Vagrancy law thus gave police a great deal of leverage in dispensing "sidewalk justice." It rendered individuals vulnerable to the capricious behavior of police and set the stage for police impropriety and payoffs. Through the midcentury, as law-and-order politics took the upper hand at city hall, San Francisco police stepped up their vagrancy arrests. But as civil rights increasingly came under the legal microscope, liberal lawyers, criminologists, and even San Francisco's district attorney decried the vague and arbitrary quality of vagrancy law. By 1958, more vagrancy arrests were being dismissed by the district attorney's office than prosecuted.[62] In September 1961, under increased pressure to update its laws and protect due process, California overturned its vagrancy laws, and San Francisco's gay and lesbian communities celebrated yet another victory in the tense battle against police harassment.

Vagrancy laws in the United States are derived from fourteenth-century British laws that restricted the migration of laborers and retained, in underpopulated areas, a cheap labor pool.[63] In the United States, vagrancy law focused on criminal behavior, and through the nineteenth century it functioned to control the use of public space. In the Reconstruction era, for instance, vagrancy law became important in restricting freed slaves from travel and public accommodations.[64] In the early twentieth century, vagrancy laws were disproportionately applied to urban crime; they were used to target prostitutes, pickpockets, derelicts, and skid-row dwellers. California's 1872 Vagrancy Law reflected both the anti-labor quality of early British law and its later applications. It defined a vagrant as "every person (except a California Indian) without visible means of living who has the physical ability to work, and who does not seek employment, nor labor when employment is offered him." Under these guidelines, California arrested scores of depression-era migrants who fled the poverty of the Dust Bowl for California's farmlands. But the state's vagrancy law had urban applications as well. It targeted "crimes of status," identifying specific types of people as vagrants and subjecting them to arrest simply for being in the wrong place at the wrong time. In San Francisco, for instance, an early 1956 "dragnet on vagrants" targeted pickpockets, drunks, drug users, prostitutes, pimps, shills, confidence men, and winos.[65] The drive was so successful that Oakland police complained that their city had experienced a "huge influx" of "undesirables" and hastened to organize its own anti-vagrancy drive.[66]

Through the 1950s, San Francisco police increasingly used vagrancy law to curb the use of public space by African Americans and homosexuals. While "common vagrants" were arrested and released on little or no bail, "thousand-dollar vagrants" had to post a $1,000 bond to secure their release. Of the 2,550 arrested in San Francisco in 1957 as "thousand-dollar vagrants," 55 percent were African American, a figure grossly disproportionate to the city's African American population.[67] Even if charges were subsequently dropped, those arrested had to forfeit the $100 deposit on bail bonds, which meant that a heavy tax was being extracted from "vagrants" for the simple use of public streets. In addition, arrest records (fingerprints and mug shots) were retained by state and federal authorities even when the accused was cleared of all wrongdoing. Because prior arrests would come into play if the individual was twice arrested, vagrancy law led to the increased criminalization of those populations targeted by the police.

A subsection of the state's vagrancy law targeted queers and members of other sexualized communities such as prostitutes. It identified vagrants as "every lewd or dissolute person, or every person who loiters in or about public toilets in public parks." In a 1958 seminar on civil rights, Ernest Besig, director of the San Francisco branch of the American Civil Liberties Union (ACLU), charged the SFPD with abuse and harassment, noting that it unfairly focused on the city's homosexual communities. Vagrancy statutes allowed police to round up individuals "for no reason," he noted, and a preponderance of arrests took place in the city's Grant Avenue and Polk Street areas, both heavily trafficked by gay men.[68] Lesbians were also targeted. In 1957, three San Francisco State College students were arrested for vagrancy in a bar because they were wearing "men's clothing."[69] To further its campaign against unlawful vagrancy arrests in San Francisco, the ACLU filed for damages against police officers responsible for dubious arrests. One case involved Alex Williams, who was arrested by plainclothes officer David Dillon as he left a San Francisco restaurant in the early morning of 4 December 1957. Booked as a "thousand-dollar vagrant," he spent the night in jail and faced municipal court charges the following day. When the district attorney's office dismissed the charges for lack of evidence, Williams, with the support of the ACLU, filed suit against Dillon, seeking $20,000 in damages.[70]

As a growing number of lawyers, professors, and elected officials joined the chorus of complaints against California's vagrancy law, the State Legislature moved to remake its archaic statute. In June 1961, Assembly Bill 874 passed both houses, and status-based vagrancy evolved into conduct-specific laws against such crimes as public drunkenness, sexual solicitation, and prostitution.[71] As he signed the law into effect, Governor Edmund G. Brown noted, "We are saying, 'It is what a man does, not who or where he is, that defines the crime.'"[72] Still, disorderly conduct laws continued to target homosexuals. An anti-loitering subsection included a provision directed against any person "who loiters in or about any toilet open to the public for the purpose of engaging in or soliciting any lewd or lascivious or any unlawful act."[73] But, as an ACLU newsletter acknowledged, the repeal of vagrancy law clamped down on police intimidation and harassment. It demanded that officers cite specific actions rather than target the status of individuals.[74]

The repeal of vagrancy law had a significant impact on the evolution of San Francisco's gay and lesbian civil rights movement in that it reduced the arbitrary detention or arrest of homosexuals, particularly those who wandered the public spaces of parks and beaches or frequented public toilets in search of sexual contacts and liaisons.[75] Before its repeal, vagrancy law had also wielded a tremendous amount of power over transgender populations that occupied the city's streets and parks, as well as bars and taverns. Despite its attachment to more sexually transgressive populations, vagrancy law was one area of struggle in which homophile and bar-based communities colluded. Anti-vagrancy articles peppered the homophile press, and bar-based cultures challenged the application of vagrancy law in court. Vagrancy law became a point of cooperation between homophile and bar-based communities because anyone who walked the streets, regardless of their sexual proclivities, gendered appearance, or state of inebriation, remained vulnerable to the capricious applications of the state's "vag-lewd" ordinances.

THE ORGANIZATIONS

The series of events described above—the mayoral election of 1959, *Vallerga v. ABC,* the "gayola" police scandal, Sarria's bid for supervisor, the Tay-Bush raid, and the repeal of California's vagrancy laws—brought homosexuality increasingly into the public eye. They generated a discourse about gay and lesbian civil rights that was difficult to ignore, and they worked to reframe the hostile relationship between San Francisco's queer communities and the police. By the end of 1961, San Francisco police had little power to control and dominate queer public space. The California Supreme Court had reaffirmed the legality of gay and lesbian bars, the chief of police had become increasingly wary of district-level payoffs, large-scale police raids had failed in the courts, lewd behavior (the lynchpin of anti-homosexual law) seemed no longer to include dancing and touching, and the state legislature repealed crimes of status in favor of conduct-specific infractions. More importantly, gay and lesbian communities began to assert a political presence in San Francisco. José Sarria's candidacy for city supervisor did much to raise the consciousness of bargoing queers, but his campaign also functioned to meld the concerns of San Francisco's bar-based and homophile communities. Where bar-based constituents had asserted collective rights (the right to association) and homophile communities had asserted individual rights (the right to due process), the emergence of a viable political constituency suggested an alternative approach to civil rights—a minority-based discourse based on equal protection law.

Moreover, while bar-based communities had asserted a rhetoric of difference, rejecting the desire to fit in, and homophile activists had asserted a rhetoric of homo-hetero sameness, the events between 1959 and 1961 softened the ideological differences between the two communities. In the early 1960s, homophile organizations became increasingly active in the interests of gay and lesbian bars, and bartenders and bar owners seemed more willing to support homophile activities. An article on police entrapment, reprinted in the *Mattachine Review,* for instance, clarifies a homophile position with regard to the practice of policing gay bars. "[W]ho declares that special pains must be made to arrest homosexuals? Who decided that 'gay bars' must have their licenses revoked? Do outraged citizens, political forces, church and clergy, or just a set of 'no faces' make this demand?"[76] An editorial warned that while the

Mattachine Society respected "good law enforcement" and opposed disorderly conduct, it would not stand for police taking the law into their own hands:

> Time and again the State Supreme Court has given the axe to state laws which have declared it illegal for homosexuals to congregate in a bar. It is NOT illegal, the court has said. Therefore Gay Bars are not illegal. Can a police official assume the authority to close such establishments as he sees fit in spite of what the courts have ruled? Or can the mayor assume such authority, in spite of his possible aim of having a record of strong "law" enforcement practices when he runs for higher political office in another year? And finally, we can see no legal basis for the Alcoholic Beverage Control Department to ignite its own crusading fire about something which the people and the courts do not oppose nor consider a threat to the community.[77]

In the 1960s homophile organizations took an increasingly defiant tone, not simply to defend the legal rights of homosexuals but to join queer communities in the struggle to define and protect the public territory of bars and taverns.

The spirit of cooperation between bar-based communities and homophile activists did not extend to the actual participation of bargoing queers in homophile activities and events. Many saw the Mattachine Society and the Daughters of Bilitis as too extreme, elite, or public for their liking. But the early 1960s saw the formation and development of four new organizations that, over time, drew a much larger constituency than the early homophile organizations. In 1961, Guy Strait and José Sarria founded the League for Civil Education. This organization was not terribly popular, nor was it economically strong, but its political ideology and organizational strategy set the stage for two much more influential organizations: the San Francisco Tavern Guild and the Society for Individual Rights (SIR). About the same time, Del Martin and Phyllis Lyon helped found the Council on Religion and the Homosexual (CRH). Branching off from their work in the Daughters of Bilitis, Martin and Lyon steered CRH toward a wide-ranging slate of social issues, including homelessness, gays in the military, employment discrimination, the needs of transsexuals, and police harassment. Mindful of the overlap between queer culture and social activism, CRH sponsored a New Year's Day costume ball in 1965. After it was raided, the Tavern Guild and SIR displayed a new quality of resistance that demonstrated the strength and power of a surprisingly coordinated and effective political constituency.

The League for Civil Education

The League for Civil Education began in March 1961 as the brainchild of Guy Strait and José Sarria. From its inception, LCE (pronounced "Elsie") stressed cooperation between gay bar owners, bartenders, homophile leaders, and the San Francisco police. In fact, along with bar and homophile representatives, two police officers, Lieutenant Scott and Inspector Tompkins, attended the first meeting. The topic of conversation addressed improved relations with police. "Cooperation with the police is possible and necessary," an LCE bulletin noted, and the presence of police went far in promoting this goal.[78] Scott and Tompkins were "courteous and interested" in LCE's goals, but they denied the existence of police entrapment or police discrimination against gay bargoers. The group then discussed the problem of sex in city parks, and when questioned about police interrogation practices, the officers reassured "Senator Strait" that no one would be arrested for failure to answer questions about their employment. Setting a conciliatory tone, LCE members agreed to discourage participation in "glory holes," and they pledged to "drive the hustlers" off Market Street so as to "make San Francisco an even better place to live."[79] To follow up, Guy Strait posted a letter to Chief of Police Cahill suggesting a short conference "to give us the opportunity to work with you."[80] Cahill never responded to Strait's letter, but the organization continued its efforts to buffer the gay community from police intimidation and harassment.

In addition to police negotiations, the League for Civil Education targeted voter registration and direct political action. The organization reasoned that if queers could register to vote in their "favorite watering spot," LCE could dramatically increase the gay community's political power. "We want all 70,000 of you to register and to vote," a bulletin noted.[81] Guy Strait and José Sarria even applied to San Francisco's registrar of voters as assistants, but they were denied sponsorship by both the Republican and Democratic parties (respectively).[82] Using language that went beyond the assimilative goals of the early homophile movements, the LCE made its desire for community involvement clear: "The League is for your protection. Your support is necessary. If you expect to have others do the things that need being done such as [the] election of public officials who are not bigots, stopping entrapment, discreet handling of blackmail threats, employment of attorneys to fight civil rights cases, the securing of a list of competent, reasonably priced legal counsel and so forth you are going to be very disappointed when you need help."[83]

In its first year, much of LCE's energy and political vision went into José Sarria's campaign for city supervisor. Strait and Sarria worked together to promote Sarria's candidacy as a kind of test balloon of queer electoral strength. But LCE also worked to promote the association of bar owners and bartenders in the city, and the organization hoped to provide everyday services "free from discrimination of any kind" in the form of job referrals, housing placement, and personal counseling. Still, the league's most important contribution was its work to protect gay men from police entrapment and arrest.[84]

After José Sarria resigned from LCE in March 1962, Guy Strait focused his attention on disseminating information about "hot spots" around town. Early on, LCE used informal news bulletins typed on a single sheet of paper. Penned by then secretary José Sarria, warnings and information took on a humorous quality: "Macy's still continues to be a source of revenue for attorneys defending silly queens who insist on going there to shop at the T room."[85] Later, under Guy Strait's guidance, LCE filled a biweekly newspaper with community gossip, bar happenings, party photos, and warnings about police action and arrests. Called the *LCE News,* Strait's journal featured useful instructions on how to avoid police entrapment and what to do in the case of arrest. Several issues included diagrams of popular downtown "T rooms" (or public toilets) and demonstrated how police tracked and trapped men who used these locations for sexual liaisons. Later, Strait's newspapers featured photos and descriptions of undercover cops under the titles "Have You Seen This Man?" and "How to Spot a Cop." The text reads, "Working as an undercover agent, Officer Buckman has no qualms about making phony arrests. He is to be treated with the respect of a asp [*sic*]. Do not talk to him and by all means do not walk to the door of any establishment in his company, nor precede him, or follow him out of any bar, or speak to him on the street unless he displays his badge first."[86] In effect, the League for Civil Education became a vehicle for information about the pleasures and dangers of gay male cruising.

Guy Strait's newspapers survived their organizational roots. The League for Civil Education folded in May 1964, when its board of directors walked out amid allegations of financial mismanagement, but long after LCE had ceased to exist, Strait's gossipy newspapers continued to churn out lively commentary on bar culture and police impropriety. In 1963, the *LCE News* changed its name to *The News,* perhaps to signal a break from the League for Civil Education. In 1964, the periodical's name changed again to *The Citizens News,* and it ran under this title until March 1967. Each volume, five in all, started with the city's late-October Halloween parties, highlighting the importance of drag and costume events to the city's queer communities. In other words, the annual calendar that marked time in the gay bars started with Halloween, and in an effort to address the queer community on its own terms, Strait's campy but news-filled periodicals did the same. In 1965 Strait began producing the *Cruise News and World Report,* a less serious publication aimed at a national readership. Ever mindful of police action and abuse, the Guy Strait newspapers were the first of their kind. With no intention of winning a Pulitzer Prize, they sacrificed style and aesthetics for gritty commentary that reached into the everyday lives of bar-going queers. Moreover, because Strait drew revenue from a range of business advertisements, he established a forum for gay and lesbian marketing and commerce. Also, because he distributed his papers directly to the bars and cafes that sustained his readership, he encouraged the politicization of a community at the center of what was becoming a gay and lesbian social movement.

The Tavern Guild of San Francisco

In early 1962, following on the heels of the "gayola" police payoff scandal and the Tay-Bush raid—and following the lead of LCE's initial work to bring bar owners under a political umbrella—an informal Tuesday afternoon drinking society comprised of gay bartenders and bar owners decided to band together. They met at the Suzy-Q, a gay bar on Polk Street, and called themselves the Tavern Guild of San Francisco (TGSF).[87] The original members reasoned that "the unjust and intolerable laws, the method of enforcing them, and the seriousness of their consequence gave this weekly drinking group purpose and determination to build an organization which collectively could fight the discriminatory acts against our community."[88] They elected Phil Doganiero, a popular Suzy-Q bartender, as the first president of the Tavern Guild and continued to meet weekly on Tuesday afternoons at alternating host bars to discuss the needs of San Francisco's gay bar community.[89]

The Tavern Guild had initially formed to bring business to alternating bars on typically slow Tuesday afternoons, and the original members stressed the importance of drinking—and gossip.[90] But within its first year, TGSF instituted a number of policies that helped protect bartenders, bar owners, and patrons from continued problems. It established a telephone networking system (a phone tree) to track San Francisco police and Alcoholic Beverage Control Board movement. If a bar was being harassed or raided, TGSF members would phone each other and quickly spread the news. TGSF also set up a bad-check list "to protect itself from its over-indulgent customers."[91] Because of the capricious flow of business and the quick reversal of fortune many bars experienced as a result of state pressure and police harassment, many businesses failed, and TGSF members found themselves unemployed. To remedy this situation, the Tavern Guild set up a loan fund for its unemployed members and worked to keep experienced bartenders employed.[92] By mid-July 1962, TGSF had composed a formal constitution that identified it as a nonprofit organization, but the 1964 constitution was much more explicit about the organization's goals:

> Believing in our democratic heritage and that ethical values are self-determined and limited only by every person's right to decide his own, we organize under this constitution for: The reaffirming of individual pride and dignity regardless of orientation; the elimination of . . . unjust laws concerning private relationships among consenting adults; the giving of real and substantial aid to members in difficulties; the promoting of better physical, mental, and emotional health; the creating of a sense of community; and, the establishing of an attractive social atmosphere and constructive outlets for members and friends.[93]

In many ways, the Tavern Guild functioned similar to turn-of-the-century fraternal or ethnic organizations.[94] By pulling together collective resources, TGSF was able to cushion the economic hardships of its members—mostly small business owners—while simultaneously protecting them from police harassment and/or the manipulations of organized crime.[95] The organization also functioned to express the goals of a hard-working and upwardly mobile but socially stigmatized business community. For example, TGSF members developed business practices that undercut the traumas of a freely competitive market. They fixed prices at reasonable rates and worked against unfriendly rumormongering that might quickly ruin a good business—a leaked story, for instance, that a particular bar was being watched by the ABC. In fact, according to TGSF member Charlotte Coleman, price-fixing was one of the most important original purposes of the Tavern Guild.[96] TGSF members also developed friendly relations with liquor distributors, touring their facilities and promoting their products at events. "We remember that Falstaff, Burgie/Schlitz and Hamm's have all invited us to their facilities, thus proving that in our business community the street has traffic both ways," Bill Plath remarked at a Tavern Guild event.[97] Charlotte Coleman remembers that beer distributors even supported gay bar owners during disputes with the law: "They were behind us to fight anything that went wrong because they were making a lot of money through us."[98] Finally, the Tavern Guild positioned itself as a benign and charitable organization. It raised money for gay, lesbian, and homophile organizations, including the Daughters of Bilitis, the Mattachine Society, the League for Civil Education, the Council on Religion and the Homosexual, and the Society for Individual Rights. Later, it contributed to other organizations and causes such as the American Civil Liberties Union, Youth for Service, the United Farm Workers, and the Civil Rights Movement. In 1965, the Tavern Guild helped raise funds to send at least two clergymen to Selma, Alabama, for Freedom Summer.[99]

The Tavern Guild succeeded as a popular and effective organization because it was able to combine grassroots politics and good business practices with a host of lively social activities. Also, TGSF officers developed innovative approaches to fundraising and community organizing. They hosted Monday night auctions to raise funds and increase patronage at rotating bars, and they organized annual fundraising events that promoted the guild. The Election Day Party was a popular event; Tavern Guild members celebrated inside one of their "closed" bars while the rest of the city sat out this historically dry day. The annual picnic, typically in Marin County, became famous for its drinking games and cruising.[100] Finally, the Tavern Guild sponsored an annual Halloween drag ball, the Beaux Arts Ball. Darryl Glied, third president of the guild and manager of the Jumpin' Frog bar on Polk Street, organized the first ball in 1963; the event became so large that it eventually outgrew the Tavern Guild and incorporated itself as a separate entity.[101]

The Beaux Arts Ball was symbolic of the Tavern Guild's ability to draw from and support vastly different subcultures than San Francisco's homophile organizations could reach. The Beaux Arts Ball became the centerpiece for San Francisco's drag community, and until 1970 the city's "Empress" was elected annually at this event. While TGSF members argued about gender-appropriate appearance and behavior, they did not back away from or deny the support of San Francisco's drag and transgender communities. In fact, they often saw it as a measure of success. "Our annual Hallowe'en ball is now a tradition," Bill Plath reminded the association at a Tavern Guild meeting, "Last year's designation of an 'Empress' drew some spirited reactions among our various associated groups, but it also resulted in a cooperative effort to stage a New Years Ball that went absolutely unharassed a few months ago.

This tells us that times are changing, and our work has an effect."[102] As TGSF developed more social and political power, the group positioned the right to public association as the cornerstone of a gay and lesbian civil rights agenda, and it applied this right to any and all communities that gathered in the public space of gay bars and taverns.

The Tavern Guild "was a great thing in the end because it got the government—the ABC and the police department—to leave us alone a little bit because we showed some strength," argues bar owner Charlotte Coleman in an oral history interview.[103] While much of this strength was derived from the sheer popularity of bar-related socializing, fundraising was an important aspect of the guild's success. Money garnered from the variety of TGSF events allowed its members to protect their own legal and financial interests, contribute to a multitude of causes, and most importantly, intervene in evolving gay politics in San Francisco. Tavern Guild activist Rickie Streicher comments, "The Tavern Guild was probably singly the reason why bars achieved a success politically. Because a buck is the bottom line at all times. And the bars had commanded an enormous amount of money in terms of the city. So when they began to invite politicians to their meetings, the politicians realized that here's an organized group and that, number one, they have money and, number two, they have votes."[104]

Through its philanthropy and large community events, the Tavern Guild was able to draw a political constituency out of San Francisco's bar-based queer community. However, one of the Tavern Guild's most important functions was its ability to communicate with and influence San Francisco's homophile movements. Through that influence, the Tavern Guild shaped an evolving notion of what constituted the gay and lesbian community. No other city in the United States was able to so effectively link bar-based communities to homophile activism. "We are told that a name such as Mattachine is still 'persona non grata' in cities such as New York," Plath reported, and homophile organizations such as ONE "have only a grudging acceptance in the gay bar community of Los Angeles."[105] In San Francisco, however, the lines of communication between organized gay bar owners, bartenders, and homophile activists remained open. This meant that homophile publications were distributed in bars through the 1960s, homophile activists participated in bar-based events and activities, and homophile leaders took ever more seriously the needs of San Francisco's queer and transgender communities.

The Society for Individual Rights

On 26 May 1964, the board of directors of the League for Civil Education sat in the home of Jim Foster, a board member, and discussed the future of the organization. A failed fundraising drive and financial mismanagement had saddled the organization with thousands of dollars of debt, and after three years of singlehanded leadership, Guy Strait stepped down from his post as president. Despite Strait's urging, the board refused to assume LCE's debts, and no one stepped up to take over the group's leadership. Amid accusations of fiscal irresponsibility, a majority of board members voted to dissolve LCE and walked across the street to the home of Bill Plath, another board member, where they discussed the formation of a new organization.[106] Called the Society for Individual Rights, or SIR, the new organization took on many of the aims of the League for Civil Education, but its structure was broadened to encompass a larger group of members and a wider slate of activities than either LCE or the Mattachine Society. As Bill Plath recalls, "[LCE] was very much a one-man organization. [It was] run by Guy. He had a board of directors and there were people that were, oh, the officers of the corporation and all that, but he was—it was his outfit. . . . [Just as] Hal Call was the building force [of the Mattachine Society], Guy was of LCE. Hal's whole concept of membership [was] you just send us the money and we'll do the work. This was the big difference between Mattachine and SIR. SIR was an active membership organization."[107]

By July 1964, the Society for Individual Rights had written its constitution, and by September it was incorporated as a nonprofit in the State of California. In January 1965, after six months of active recruitment, SIR's membership of roughly three hundred surpassed that of all other gay and lesbian organizations in San Francisco. "This is shocking and somewhat surprising to those of us who helped formulate S.I.R. and its policies," then president Bill Beardemphl confessed. "The 'professional homosexuals' in the homophile field had created a false concept of a job accomplished and criticized us by saying we were only doing that which already had been done."[108] Almost immediately, SIR drew a flood of new members to its doors. By membership standards alone, it indeed charted new territory in gay and lesbian organizing.[109]

How was SIR different from the organizations that preceded it? First, SIR projected a bold language of social activism that was more in sync with civil rights organizations like SNCC, the Student Non-Violent Coordinating Committee, or CORE, the Congress on Racial Equality, than homophile organizations like the Mattachine Society. For instance, on page one of the first issue of the organization's monthly magazine, *Vector,* president Bill Beardemphl articulated the organization's vision: "SIR is an organization formed from within the Community working for the Community. By trying to give the individual a sense of dignity before himself and within his Society, it answers the question of how we can maintain our self-respect. SIR is dedicated to [the] belief in the worth of the homosexual and adheres to the principle that the individual has the right to his own sexual orientation." Using the language of dignity, self-respect, and self-worth, Beardemphl stressed that social change depended on political organizing, and he urged the organization's members to defend their rights. He outlined the organization's agenda of political action, adequate and responsible legal counsel, cooperation with churches, education in citizenship rights, and the desire "to provide our people with an honorable social fabric." Noting the strengths and failures of other organizations, Beardemphl promised that SIR would not fall into "inwardness," personality conflicts, or dictatorial control. Instead, SIR would pursue an open and democratic structure so as to "produce the most potent weapon possible in our fight for the elimination of sexual puritanism, social-political apathy, and personal irresponsibility. This weapon is fraternity."[110]

SIR's early leadership adopted a powerful tone, but the organization's success rested in its committee structure. Or, in the words of activist Larry Littlejohn, SIR made room for "everybody's idea about what the organization should be."[111] The organization's constitution required that members elect a president, vice president, and board of directors, but leadership also came from elected committee chairs who worked autonomously to plan activities and organize events. In February 1965, for instance, members recognized eight committees: Political, Community Service, Membership, Publications, Religious, Legal, Social, and *Vector* (the organization's monthly magazine). While the Community Service Committee worked to educate members about public health dangers such as venereal disease and the Membership Committee worked to expand the organization's rosters, the Political Committee took on such tasks as reaching out to elected officials and encouraging gay people to vote. Later, it organized candidates' nights and advertised the concept of a gay voting bloc. "We put out the word that there were ninety thousand gay votes to be had in San Francisco, and that those people would vote as a block [*sic*]," Nancy May, the first chair of the Political Committee, remembers. "We actually made [the numbers] up. . . . We thought it was probably true, but had no way of finding out."[112] Through the 1960s, candidates' nights gained momentum, and by the late 1960s, several candidates for public office (and incumbents) appealed to the gay community for support. In this way, SIR's Political Committee set the foundation for lesbian and gay political organizations such as San Francisco's Alice B. Toklas and Stonewall Democratic Clubs. The Political Committee also claims partial responsibility for Dianne Feinstein's 1969 election as president of San Francisco's Board of Supervisors, the position from which she launched her hugely successful political career.[113]

As the Political Committee worked to make itself known to city hall, SIR's Legal Committee worked to protect its members from harassment and arrest. Legal Committee meetings were often attended by attorneys such as Herb Donaldson and Evander Smith, who were willing to give free legal advice, and *Vector* ran a regular column where attorneys answered legal questions. The Legal Committee also published a pocket-sized pamphlet that gave instructions on what to do in the case of arrest. The "Pocket Lawyer" insisted that when confronted by a police officer, one must not resist. Instead, one should ask to see the officer's identification, make a note of the officer's badge number, and "deny everything." Most importantly, one should not disclose one's place of employment. "Although you must give your name and an address, DO NOT TELL ANYONE WHERE YOU WORK. The ONLY exception to this will be your bail bondsman. Answer ALL other statements or questions about you as follows: 'I DENY THAT' [or] 'MAY I CALL MY LAWYER.'"[114] SIR lawyers reasoned that most cases would not be prosecuted unless the individual disclosed harmful information at the time of arrest. "Ninety percent of all convictions are obtained between the time of arrest and the arrival of the bail-bondsman," Legal Committee Chair Evander Smith warned.[115] Lawyers also knew that police often contacted the employer of the accused, so even if cases were never prosecuted, the risk of being fired was high for those who disclosed their place of employment.

Perhaps the most important committee that SIR developed, and the one that had the highest level of member participation, was the Social Committee. Social Committee members hit on the idea of selling tickets to private dances, and because dancing was not typically allowed in bars, SIR dances attracted a tremendous amount of attention. According to SIR founder Bill Plath,

> Up until that time it was against the law for same-sex dancing. There was no law against that as such, but there was a law against lewd and lascivious dancing. And the police chose to assume that any two people of the same gender dancing was "lewd and lascivious" and that's all there was to it. SIR held a dance in the basement of California Hall that was wild. It was just incredible. The crowd had assembled and assembled and assembled—bands take a long time to get set up, you know, they're messing around—and all of a sudden they hit a Dixieland number and there was a roar and everybody hit the dance floor. It was wild! Really exciting. That broke the presupposition that it was lewd and lascivious, and we held regular dances at the SIR Center.[116]

Because SIR dances often sold out and the Social Committee sold tickets to members ahead of time, access to dances was a tremendous incentive for new members to join the organization.[117] In addition to dances, the Social Committee staged elaborate drag shows and popular theatrical productions such as *The Boyfriend, Little Mary Sunshine, Once upon a Mattress,* and *A Funny Thing Happened on the Way to the Forum,* which, according to Bill Plath, planted a fertile seed for the emergence of gay and lesbian theater companies such as San Francisco's Theater Rhinoceros. The Social Committee also organized a slate of activities such as bowling nights, tennis matches, hiking expeditions, a softball league, card games, discussion groups, and camping trips. Almost every night of the week there was a social event planned, and team activities like the bowling league continued to draw a heavy turnout well after SIR had ceased to exist.[118]

In May 1965, the SIR board of directors proposed to its membership that the organization open a community center to house all of its activities and events. They imagined that the center would serve the entire "homosexual community" and function as a clearinghouse for any gay and lesbian organizations.[119] By early 1966, SIR had raised over $2,500 for its building fund, and in a March 1966 fundraising letter to its membership, SIR president Bill Beardemphl set the opening date for 17 April 1966. Located at 83 Sixth Street, just south of Market Street, the center boasted office space, a boardroom, library, kitchen, and a public assembly area large enough to hold 500 people. Publicity fliers announced, "The Center itself will become a symbol of our unity and will show that we not only desire but are able to function effectively and responsibly in the larger community."[120]

SIR functioned as an active organization for about seven years, and while its list of social and political accomplishments is impressive, its most important contribution was to bring together the disparate communities that framed queer life in San Francisco. "SIR unified the community," Bill Plath notes. "It brought a cohesiveness to it."[121] Larry Littlejohn concurs: "[SIR] included every interest the Gay people had, and it worked real well and got a lot of people together at one time."[122] Almost everyone, it seems, participated at one time or another in a SIR activity or event, and because the spirit of cooperation was explicit, it allowed SIR leadership to shape and articulate the concept of shared community. In a letter to SIR members, for instance, Bill Beardemphl stressed the need for "the community" to vote as one voice in an upcoming election. "We are in agreement. Even the Mattachine and the *Citizens News,* who always are miles apart, agree on this. The Bars agree, the DOB agrees. Our straw poll has overwhelmingly shown that *the whole gay community,* when it becomes informed, agrees on these issues."[123] As a collective, SIR peaceably bridged the gap between the assimilationist politics of the Mattachine Society and the more radical politics of Guy Strait's bar-based journalism. As a result, SIR helped shift the discourse from that of individual rights to collective social action. Using the language of equal protection, SIR sounded more like the early African American Civil Rights Movement than the early homophile movement:

> Committed to the proposition that "responsible action by responsible people in responsible ways" will best serve both the members of S.I.R. and society at large, S.I.R. has undertaken to present the true image of the homosexual to the community. Contrary to the dire predictions of hostile commentators, neither S.I.R., nor its voice, VECTOR, is proselytizing to obtain converts; rather, the attempt is to present the homosexual as he is—by far and large a responsible and moral member of his community and one seeking only the equal protection of the laws guaranteed to all Americans by the 14th Amendment to the Constitution of the United States.[124]

Through a wide range of social and political activities and a commitment to cooperative participation, SIR was able to shape the notion of a "gay community" into an effective political tool.

The Council on Religion and the Homosexual

The final organization under consideration in this chapter gained its importance not because it ushered in a new era of political organizing but because it galvanized, through a single event, the attention of a mass movement and focused the political intentions of organizations like SIR and the San Francisco Tavern Guild. The Council on Religion and the

Homosexual (CRH) started as a retreat undertaken by fifteen clergymen and fifteen representatives of the homophile community who met for three days at the White Memorial Retreat House of the United Church of Christ in Mill Valley, California. Guy Strait noted in a short article entitled "The Growing Language" that in 1964 the word "homophile" was gaining currency as meaning "the social movement devoted to the improvement of the status of the homosexual, and to groups, activities, and literature associated with the movement." No longer restricted to the work of the Mattachine Society and the Daughters of Bilitis, in the early 1960s, the word "homophile" began to take on a wider meaning, at least in San Francisco.[125] In any case, from 31 May to 2 June 1964, with members of many religious backgrounds and persuasions in attendance, participants at the White Memorial Retreat House considered the relationship between homosexuals and the church. Formal presentations and small-group discussions addressed topics such as the views clergy had of homosexuals, the views homosexuals had of "churchmen," homosexuals and the law, and biblical and/or theological issues. At the end of the weekend, most participants agreed that the church had let down the homosexual through a lack of understanding, and they sought to somehow remedy the situation. In order to continue and widen the conversation, the Council on Religion and the Homosexual was born.[126]

Promising to promote an understanding of homosexuality in its broadest variation, CRH encouraged the participation of lesbian and gay activists, among them Hal Call and Donald Lucas of the Mattachine Society, Del Martin and Phyllis Lyon of the Daughters of Bilitis, Guy Strait of the *Citizens News,* Darryl Glied of the Tavern Guild, and Bill Beardemphl and Mark Forrester of the Society for Individual Rights. In effect, the Council on Religion and the Homosexual functioned as a forum for lesbian and gay leadership in San Francisco. It was an issue-based organization that held the attention and cooperation of the range of activists and organizations. Certainly there were many ministers involved, notably Reverends Ted McIlvenna and Cecil Williams, but the active participation of the leaders of each of San Francisco's lesbian and gay organizations marked a new era of cooperation. To lend their support, in late 1964 six lesbian and gay organizations agreed to cosponsor a fundraising event for CRH. "Never before have all six groups united in concert to promote a community project," Hal Call announced in a December 1964 newsletter.[127]

CRH secured the somewhat run-down California Hall at 625 Polk Street for the event, and board members planned a costume ball with a Mardi Gras theme to be held on New Year's Day. Co-sponsoring organizations would each sell tickets for the event at a one-dollar kickback for their efforts, but most organizations promised more than monetary support. The Mattachine Society and the *Citizens News* promised to advertise the event, the Tavern Guild would man the bar, and SIR promised to take responsibility for decorating the hall. The *Citizens News* announced, "Tickets are for sale in many of the bars in San Francisco, plus many of the organizations. The donation for the affair is $5.00. This is a private affair and to keep it this way no tickets are to be available at the door or on the day of the ball . . . [and] since the fire department has put a 1500 person limit on this dance hall there will not be any more than 1500 tickets sold. Those planning to attend *must* get their tickets early."[128] At five dollars a ticket, with the promise of up to 1,500 tickets, San Francisco's gay, lesbian, and homophile organizations promised to give CRH a sizeable jump on fundraising.

Prior to the ball, ministers and lawyers for CRH met with police officers from the city's Sex Crimes detail. They explained that the event was a fundraiser for a church-based organization and discussed potential problems. Officers questioned the ministers about their interest in homosexuals, and after "strained negotiations," CRH members left with the understanding that police would not interfere with the private event.[129] A few hours before the ball, however, Hal Call and Don Lucas at the Mattachine Society received a call from police, who threatened to arrest anyone wearing a mask or in costume. Knowing that there was no legal grounds for arrests of this sort, CRH board members decided to go ahead with the event, and they called on CRH lawyers Herbert Donaldson and Evander Smith to advise them in the event of arrests. By nightfall, as the ball was set to begin, police congregated at the entrance to California Hall. They blocked off the intersection, diverted traffic, set up kleig lights, and ordered police photographers to record the face of everyone entering the dance hall.[130] Homophile coverage noted that there were dozens of police officers at the ball—thirty-five in uniform and fifteen in plainclothes.[131] At a subsequent trial, Inspector Rudy Nieto noted that he brought fourteen officers to the scene, one policewoman and two police photographers. When asked by Judge Leo Friedman why he brought so many officers, Nieto responded (to much laughter in the courtroom), "We went to inspect the premises."[132]

At the New Year's Day Ball, police clearly intended to intimidate the crowd rather than regulate lawful behavior, and with such a visible police presence, only 600 of the promised 1,500 ticket-holders braved the police gauntlet and made it inside the hall. Police shuffled about outside the hall, taking photographs, and later demanded entrance so as to "make inspections." Police entered the hall, looked around and wandered back outside. When they attempted entrance again, lawyers Herbert Donaldson and Evander Smith resisted, asking for a warrant. Ironically, the only arrests police made (despite threats) were of the lawyers who challenged them as they entered the premises and of Nancy May, who was working the ticket counter at the entrance.[133] And while those arrested suffered a tremendous amount of stress from the event—all feared the loss of their jobs and possible fines—the most noteworthy outcome seemed to be the response of CRH ministers who, along with their wives, had worked to organize the event. The day after the incident, seven ministers lined up for a press conference at San Francisco's Glide Memorial Church and accused the police of "intimidation, broken promises and obvious hostility." Using strong language, the ministers described the event to journalists, questioned police tactics, and calmly explained their interest in the Council on Religion and the Homosexual. An accompanying photo pictured a stern-looking bunch of collared ministers, arms folded, with anger and disappointment written on their faces.[134]

The ball at California Hall on 1 January 1965 galvanized the community in ways no other event had previously been able to. The outrage expressed by a group of Protestant ministers seemed to mirror and intensify the tensions brewing between San Francisco's gay and lesbian communities and the police. And the police, ultimately, suffered a humiliating blow. According to activist Larry Littlejohn, "[It was] probably the most dramatic, large scale exhibition of the police trying to show that they were going to force their morality on the city, and they looked so foolish doing it that the editorial comment in the papers was all very negative and most people . . . realized that Gay people were in fact being oppressed by the police department."[135] Mayor John F. Shelley demanded a full report from Police Chief Thomas Cahill, and news coverage fell decidedly on the side of those who had been in attendance at the ball. "Ministers who sponsored the New Year's dance for homosexuals said they cleared it first with Cahill," one news article reported, "[they] hired private police to keep order, and were having no problems until police arrived."[136] In the days following the dance, letters to the editor published in San Francisco newspapers ran almost twelve to one protesting police harassment at the event.[137] "I wish to protest the actions of the San Francisco Police Department in their unjustified and harassing attack on the Mardi Grass [*sic*] Ball held at the California Hall January 1," one letter began. In another, Mr. and Mrs. G. R. Mon stated that they had attended the "Masquerade Ball" and were dismayed and angry at the unwarranted display of police power. "We support the enforcement of law and order, but not [the] harassment of any minority groups."[138] Finally, the mid-February trial of those arrested at the dance returned an indictment of the police rather than the defendants. During the proceedings, Judge Leo Friedman seemed unwilling to accept the testimony of the police. He challenged Inspector Rudy Nieto's assertion that police had arrived "just to inspect the premises" and wondered why, then, the police took so many photographs. Nieto responded that the police department "wanted pictures of these people because some of them might be connected to national security."[139] The next day, Judge Friedman halted the proceedings after the state had presented its case and demanded that the jury return a not guilty verdict. "It's useless to waste everybody's time following this to its finale," he stated.

Police harassment at California Hall changed the course of the Council on Religion and the Homosexual. While the group continued to be interested in an ongoing dialogue between ministers and homosexuals, the topic of conversation shifted from theology to police harassment and abuse. As part of a series of pamphlet-sized publications, ministers affiliated with CRH published "A Brief of Injustices: An Indictment of Our Society in Its Treatment of the Homosexual." In this pamphlet, they declared that "we have discovered that there is very little justice for the homosexual," and they listed in lengthy description ten "great injustices," including unfair laws, ineffective legal counsel, police intimidation, police entrapment, discriminatory employment practices, violence, and alienation from the public space of bars and taverns.[140] The ministers associated with CRH rode the tide of public opinion and expressed a level of outrage that helped focus the aim of organizations like SIR. The incident at the New Year's Day Ball had, then, a number of important consequences. It boosted membership in both the Society for Individual Rights and the San Francisco Tavern Guild. (SIR saw its membership rosters swell from three hundred to over a thousand in 1965.)[141] It hastened the development of an organization called Citizen's Alert, which functioned as a hotline for police abuse in the city.[142] (Del

Martin and Phyllis Lyon were instrumental in organizing this service.) It necessitated that the chief of police appoint a liaison to the gay, lesbian, and transgender communities.[143] And it forced police to retreat from the project of harassment and intimidation that had, for so long, held San Francisco's queer communities in its grip.

The 1965 ball functioned as a turning point in San Francisco's queer history, not because of what it accomplished on its own, which was considerable, but because the event, much like New York City's 1969 Stonewall Riots, concentrated the political energies of organizations already in place while it mobilized new constituencies into action. Because the ball was a cooperative event that brought together homophile activists and bargoing queers, and because it produced such a compelling cohort of spokespersons, the event hastened the politicization of bar-based populations who were fed up with the harassment and mistreatment that had relegated them to second-class citizenship. With the rhetoric of the Civil Rights Movement ringing in their ears, bargoing queers joined homophiles in a political movement that sought equal rights just as decidedly as it defended the pleasure of being queer.

CONCLUSION

Marketing a Queer San Francisco

Each year at the end of June, San Francisco fills with gay, lesbian, bisexual, and transgender (GLBT) tourists. The Castro Theater in San Francisco's gay neighborhood screens a week-long lesbian- gay-themed film festival, the city flies multicolored gay pride flags from poles stretching the length of Market Street, and crowds of up to half a million gather for the annual Gay and Lesbian Pride Parade on the last Sunday in June. June is a lucrative month for gay-owned businesses. Gay bars, restaurants, and hotels fill to capacity, and stores catering to gay tourists do a brisk trade in pride rings, necklaces, and T-shirts. While gay tourism is good for gay businesses, the revenue generated from gay tourism reaches beyond the GLBT community. Of the 4.2 million hotel guests who made San Francisco a destination in 1999, 4.6 percent dined in the Castro district at least once, bringing almost $10 million in revenue to the city in restaurant business alone.[1] As was the case in the postwar years, the ability of the GLBT community to draw tourist dollars to the city affects its strength in relation to city politics. In the 1940s and 1950s, San Francisco's tourist economy gave gay bars a foothold in San Francisco's North Beach district. Currently, as gay tourism draws millions of dollars to San Francisco each year, gay, lesbian, and transgender community representatives from San Francisco serve both elected and appointed positions within municipal, state, and federal government offices. The ability of the GLBT community to draw revenue from its culture and use that revenue to assert progressive political change underscores one aspect of this study. Through the gradual and sporadic success of gay and lesbian bars—not simply as social and cultural institutions but as small businesses—queer community activists have been able to implement and fund civil rights campaigns that resulted in increased voter participation, civic awareness, and improved relations with the police.

The relationship between San Francisco's tourist economy and the emergence of vibrant and publicly visible queer communities is only part of the story, however. Tourism was the backdrop for the development of lesbian and gay cultures and communities in San Francisco's North Beach district, but before long, new cultures and communities spun off and began to take up space in different areas of the city, outside the purview of mainstream tourism. Through the 1960s, gay men opened bars, socialized, and began to cruise Polk Street, which by the late 1960s was an important artery of San Francisco's queer culture and community. In the 1970s, the streets and alleys near Polk Street were known for their dance bars and drug scene, but drag bars and a culture of prostitution remained an important part of Polk Street's allure. Similarly, as lesbians moved away from North Beach in the 1950s and 1960s, an increasing number of lesbian bars, coffee shops, and bookstores opened their doors on or near Valencia Street in the Mission District. One exception was Rikki Streicher's popular lesbian bar Maud's. Maud's opened in 1964, and because it was located in Cole Valley, just up the street from the city's Haight-Ashbury district, Maud's bridged the gap between San Francisco's lesbian community and its hippie generation. Maud's remained a central gathering spot for a new and countercultural generation of lesbians for over twenty years. Meanwhile, south of Market Street, in small cross streets like Dorr Alley and, later, on Folsom Street, San Francisco's leather and S and M community began to make itself more visible. Like San Francisco's lesbian communities, the leather district, or what Gayle Rubin has called the "miracle mile," escaped the specter of mainstream tourism until recently, when the city's Folsom Street fair began to grow in popularity.[2] Finally, in the late 1970s, with Harvey Milk's successful bid for city supervisor and the political response to his assassination, the Castro district emerged as a center of gay life in the city.[3] Through the 1980s and 1990s, "the Castro" became a phenomenon, a city within a city where gay, lesbian, bisexual, and transgender residents gradually began to outnumber other residents. As the numbers of gay people who lived in or visited the Castro increased, new businesses opened. Along with gay bars and restaurants, there were gay travel agents, gay bookstores, gay florists, gay groceries, gay clothing shops, and gay shoe stores. There was even, for a brief time, a gay bank. With the security of majority status (at least within the district) and the traffic of tens of thousands, a new level of commercialization has descended on the city's gay, lesbian, bisexual, and transgender communities.

Today, large corporations with familiar brand names are eager to capitalize on gay dollars and gay spending power. While this phenomenon—niche marketing to gay and lesbian shoppers—promises to open up new modes of visibility (and presumed social acceptance), the large-scale and corporate commercialization of queer culture threatens to transfer the control of representations of gay, lesbian, bisexual, and transgender people from the hands of activists and community members to large corporations. When beer companies, for example, place ads in gay magazines, the images they choose reflect corporate assumptions about gay life. Whether corporate images accurately reflect gay life is less significant than the fact that corporate sponsorship will always assert the interests of capitalism. The images are positive when they increase product sales.[4] In the 1950s, early homophile activists struggled to control gay and lesbian representations. Homophile activists believed that the projection of "positive" or socially acceptable images was a fundamental component of the battle for civil rights. To break through the wall of silence that trapped lesbians and gay men in negative stereotypes and to help project new images of lesbian and gay life into mainstream culture, homophile activists solicited the help of esteemed outsiders such as scientists, doctors, and ministers. Later, bar-based activists like Guy Strait took up the project of representation from a different angle. Strait's newspapers directed their messages at San Francisco's queer community; his campy satire and political commentary helped bring bargoing queers to a new level of social consciousness. Through the 1950s and 1960s, activists set the project of visibility and questions about representation at the center of their program for social change. The early homophile desire for visibility—any kind of media attention—often worked toward normativity, social acceptance, and tolerance, but it identified an important venue for social change that others, later, took in different directions.

In this book I have attempted to illustrate the ways in which marketplace activity—the small businesses of gay and lesbian bars and restaurants—has served the interests of queer community development. Through the 1940s and 1950s gay bars and restaurants functioned as community centers. They enabled a distinct and publicly visible community to emerge on the fringes of society. Later, as bars funneled their profits back into the community in the form of legal challenges and court cases protesting harassment by local police, Alcoholic Beverage Control Board officers, and military police, bars became a space for the articulation of community-based political goals such as the right to assembly. In no way does this argument attempt to deny the manipulations of marketplace activity—bar owners certainly had much more power to articulate a political agenda than bar patrons. However, this argument suggests that the public space of gay bars, the social and cultural forms that developed inside bars, became important to the articulation of gay and lesbian civil rights. As bars matured into spaces, like the Black Cat, where ideas like gay pride became fundamental to their culture, gay bars emerged as important players in the social and political movement for civil rights. The culture inside gay bars, therefore, became a fertile ground for the assertion of social movement activism on its own terms. Bar culture expressed the interests of bargoing queers, and these interests often found a political expression that functioned as a counterpoint to the rights articulated by formal civil rights organizations such as the Mattachine Society and the Daughters of Bilitis. Homophile organizations were vitally important to the development of a gay and lesbian civil rights agenda in the city of San Francisco, but they were not the only voice articulating a project of social change. In San Francisco, the unfolding of a gay and lesbian civil rights movement involved actors from both bar-based communities and homophile organizations.

The assertion that both bar-based communities and homophile organizations articulated a civil rights agenda in San Francisco does not mean that bar culture and homophile activism did not overlap. They did. In fact, it was the spaces of overlap that propelled the movement for civil rights forward in the early 1960s. These spaces created the opportunity for cooperative resistance and the consolidation of resources. But through the 1950s, the terms upon which bar-based communities asserted their civil rights were different than the terms upon which homophile organizations asserted theirs. Bar-based communities engaged in a battle for public space, and in doing so, they fought state discrimination and police harassment by asserting their rights to public association and accommodation. Through legal challenges to police and liquor control agencies, bar owners, bartenders, and patrons asserted their rights as a collective, a social group. Homophile organizations, on the other hand, fought for civil rights protections based on the assertion of individual rights. Homophile organizations sought to accommodate and assimilate homosexuals into mainstream society and insisted that homosexuals obey laws and represent themselves in conventional ways. Bar-based and homophile activism also differed in their conception of queer culture and community. Bar-based activists pursued a politic of difference that sought to protect queer space and the differences inherent in queer life from outside harassment. Homophile activists focused much of their energy on projecting the notion of hetero-homo sameness, a politic of sameness. These differing ideas about the meaning of homosexuality and the role of queer society manifest themselves in questions about gender-appropriate dress and behavior. In fact, the question of gender-transgression or the gendered qualities of queer life became a significant point of difference between the two social groups in the late 1950s and early 1960s.

In both gay bars and homophile organizations gender expression functioned as a flag or signifier of same-sex sexuality. Many gay and lesbian bars, particularly those that early on marketed themselves to tourists, staged gender-transgressive performances as part of the expression of queer cultural difference. However, at the same time that gays and lesbians began to assert their civil rights through bars and homophile organizations, a transgender movement began to take shape. In the 1950s, individuals like Christine Jorgensen articulated a transsexual identity and, in doing so, brought a new level of consciousness to the gender-transgressive function of queer culture and society.[5] Transsexuals, Jorgensen and others argued, were not always gay or lesbian. A person's gender identity may be incongruous with their biological sex, but their sexuality may still be heterosexual. In the 1950s, as a result, transgender activism became an overlapping but often distinct aspect of queer cultural resistance. In this way, the gender-transgressive behavior that became vital to the expression of a culture of resistance in San Francisco's gay bars and nightclubs can be seen as an important aspect of both lesbian and gay community development and the early rumblings of a transgender culture and community. Indeed, as historians like Susan Stryker and Joanne Meyerowitz have shown, San Francisco was at the forefront of transgender community activism and resistance in the 1950s and 1960s.[6] It is not surprising, then, that the language of early gay and lesbian civil rights contained a significant amount of commentary about the meaning of gender-transgressive behavior and the overlap between gay, lesbian, and transgender activism. Organizations like the Mattachine Society and the Daughters of Bilitis, for instance, distanced themselves from gender-transgressive images and often worked to clarify the differences between presumed gender-normal gays and lesbians and transgendered "others." Organizations like SIR, the Society for Individual Rights, also questioned the value of transgender representations—most notably in the struggle over José Sarria's leadership. Still, through the 1960s transgender entertainments remained central to lesbian and gay bar culture, and, despite their reservations, organizations like SIR were able to translate the gender-transgressive culture of queer bars into organized social movement activism.

Essentially, this book argues that in the early stages of San Francisco's gay and lesbian civil rights movement, the politics of everyday life were every bit as important as the politics of organized social movement activism. Along with homophile movement activism, the culture of gay, lesbian, and transgender bars and nightclubs contributed significantly to the form and function of a resistant queer social movement. In fact, in its prideful assertion of difference, bar culture transmitted the progressive idea of minority rights (or rights based in the Fourteenth Amendment's equal protection clause) to the larger lesbian and gay movement for social change. Initially, gay and lesbian bar owners resisted prohibitions against serving a homosexual clientele simply to protect their livelihood—the quintessentially American "right to make a buck." However, as the harassment of gay and lesbian bars continued, bar owners shifted their strategy. Leaning on the Bill of Rights, lawyers representing the interests of bar owners, bartenders, and patrons argued that homosexuals should not be denied access to public accommodation. In this way, bar-based communities asserted their fundamental right to association and assembly. Because these arguments resonated with other minority-based civil rights campaigns, most notably the African American Civil Rights Movement, legal challenges to the harassment of gay and lesbian bars were successful in securing limited civil rights for queers. Moreover, some bar-based activists like José Sarria and Rikki Streicher asserted the idea that bar culture could be a strong foundation for social movement activism. In its fundamental differences from mainstream society, gay and lesbian culture was strong. It was the strength of difference and the historic projection of a unique sexual culture that enabled—and continues to enable—queer life in San Francisco to forcefully assert gay, lesbian, bisexual, and transgender civil rights.

APPENDIX A

Map of North Beach Queer Bars and Restaurants, 1933–1965

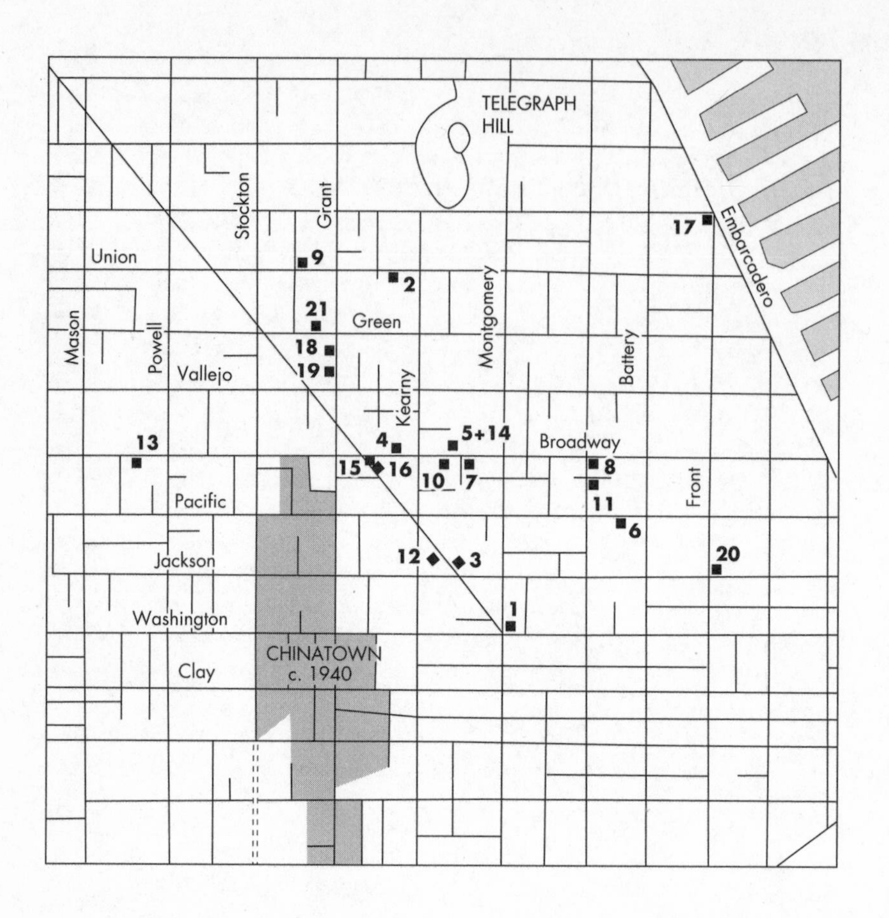

TELEGRAPH HILL
Embarcadero
Stockton
Grant
Union
Mason
Powell
Green
Montgomery
Battery
Vallejo
Kearny
Broadway
Pacific
Front
Jackson
Washington
Clay
CHINATOWN c. 1940
1
2
3
4
5+14
6
7
8
9
10
11
12
13
15
16
17
18
19
20
21

NORTH BEACH QUEER BARS AND RESTAURANTS, 1933–1965 (PARTIAL LIST)

	Name	Address	Years
1.	Black Cat	710 Montgomery	1933–1963
2.	Mona's (original)	431 Union Street	1934–1935
3.	Mona's Barrel House	140 Columbus	1936–1938
4.	Finocchio's	506 Broadway	1937–1999
5.	Mona's 440	440 Broadway	1939–1948
6.	Artist's Club	345 Pacific Street	1946–1949
7.	Mona's Candlelight	473 Broadway	1948–1957
8.	299 Club	299 Broadway	1948–1952
9.	Paper Doll	524 Union Street	1949–1961
10.	Chi Chi Club	467 Broadway	1949–1956
11.	Gordon's	840 Sansome Street	1949–1970
12.	Opus One	141 Columbus	1951–1959
13.	Beige Room	831 Broadway	1951–1958
14.	Ann's 440	440 Broadway	1952–1962
15.	Tommy's Place	529 Broadway	1952–1954
16.	12 Adler Place	12 Adler Place	1952–1954
17.	Tin Angel	987 Embarcadero	1954–1960
18.	Miss Smith's Tea Room	1353 Grant Avenue	1954–1960
19.	Copper Lantern	1335 Grant Avenue	1955–1965
20.	The Front	600 Front Street	1958–1961
21.	Anxious Asp	528 Green Street	1958–1967

APPENDIX B

List of Interviewees

Laura Atkinson, 13 December 1991
Joe Baron (pseud.), 21 July 1991, 4 August 1991
Lois Beeby, 7 April 1992
Gerald Belchick, 23 July 1991
Dante Benedetti, 10 July 1992
Garry Bernhardt, 15 August 1991
Marilyn Braiger, 2 December 1991
Harold Call, 14 August 1992
Peg Cellarius, 21 August 1991
Charlotte Coleman, 13 July 1992
Donald Currie, 6 December 1991
Thelma Davis, 21 November 1991
Mildred Dickemann, 18 October 1991
Ruth Frederick, 23 July 1992
Cheryl M. Gonzales, 1 February 1992
Maria Gonzalez (pseud.), 4 November 1992
Roma Guy, 20 July 1991
Patricia Healey, 23 July 1992
James L. Heig, 25 March 1992
Ramona "Mona" Hood, 25 July 1992
Reba C. Hudson, 29 May 1992, 10 July 1992, 25 July 1992
Jim (pseud.), 11 January 1992
Monika Kehoe, 24 July 1991
Patricia Kemper, 19 August 1991
Matthew C. Little Moon, 25 October 1991
Phyllis Lyon, 2 December 1992
Del Martin, 2 December 1992
Francisco Mattos, 8 June 1992
George Mendenhall, 13 November 1991
Kenneth Najour, 16 July 1992
Bill Plath, 4 August 1992
José Julio Sarria, 15 April 1992, 20 May 1992
Angelo Sotto (pseud.), 29 August 1991
Joseph St. Amand, 2 August 1991
Rikki Streicher, 22 January 1992, 4 March 1992, 25 July 1992
M. J. Talbot, 8 June 1992
Sharon Tracy, 9 October 1991
Kate Ullman, 9 October 1991
Ethel Whitaker (pseud.), 30 August 1992
Lee Y. Woo, 13 March 1992
Merle Woo, 15 May 1992
Edward Young, 8 June 1992

Notes

INTRODUCTION

Epigraph: Larry Littlejohn, interviewed by Scott Bishop, tape recording, San Francisco, 27 April 1990, Scott Bishop Papers, Gay, Lesbian, Bisexual, Transgender Historical Society of Northern California (hereafter GLBT Historical Society).

1. Howard S. Becker and Irving Louis Horowitz, "The Culture of Civility," in Howard S. Becker, ed., *Culture and Civility in San Francisco* (Chicago: Aldine, 1971), 6.

2. There are several wonderful essays (and longer projects in process) but few book-length historical studies. Susan Stryker and Jim Van Buskirk's introduction to San Francisco's queer history, *Gay by the Bay: A History of Queer Culture in the San Francisco Bay Area* (San Francisco: Chronicle Books, 1996), is an exception. See also John D'Emilio, *Sexual Politics, Sexual Communities: The Making of a Homosexual Minority in the United States, 1940–1970* (Chicago: University of Chicago Press, 1983); Martin Dennis Meeker, Jr., "Come Out West: Communication and the Gay and Lesbian Migration to San Francisco, 1940s–1960s" (Ph.D. diss., University of Southern California, 2000). Essays on San Francisco's gay, lesbian, and queer history include Les Wright, "San Francisco," in David Higgs, ed., *Queer Sites: Gay Urban Histories since 1600* (London: Routledge, 1999), 164–189; Gayle S. Rubin, "The Miracle Mile: South of Market and Gay Male Leather, 1962–1997," in James Brook, Chris Carlsson, and Nancy J. Peters, eds., *Reclaiming San Francisco: History, Politics, Culture* (San Francisco: City Lights Books, 1998), 247–272; Allan Bérubé, "The History of Gay Bathhouses," in Dangerous Bedfellows, ed., *Policing Public Sex: Queer Politics and the Future of AIDS Activism* (Boston: South End Press, 1996), 187–220; John D'Emilio, "Gay Politics and Community in San

Francisco since World War II," in Martin Duberman, Martha Vicinus, and George Chauncey, Jr., eds., *Hidden from History: Reclaiming the Gay and Lesbian Past* (New York: Penguin, 1989), 456–473.

3. Robert W. Cherny, "Patterns of Toleration and Discrimination in San Francisco: The Civil War to World War I," *California History* 73 (Summer 1994): 131–142; William Issel, "Liberalism and Urban Policy in San Francisco from the 1930s to the 1960s," *Western Historical Quarterly* 22, no. 4 (November 1991): 431–450.

4. Mexico and the United States ended the Mexican-American war with the signing of the Treaty of Guadalupe-Hidalgo on 2 February 1848. Oscar Lewis, *San Francisco: Mission to Metropolis,* 2nd ed. (San Diego: Howell-North Books, 1980), 1–37; William Issel and Robert W. Cherny, *San Francisco 1865–1932: Politics, Power, and Urban Development* (Berkeley: University of California Press, 1986), 8–18; Antonia I. Castenada, "Sexual Violence in the Politics and Policies of Conquest," in Adela de la Torre and Beatríz Pezquera, eds., *Building with Our Hands: New Directions in Chicana Studies* (Berkeley: University of California Press, 1993), 15–33.

5. James Marshall's discovery of gold at Sutter's Mill on 24 January 1848 preceded the signing of the Treaty of Guadalupe-Hidalgo by nine days.

6. Issel and Cherny, *San Francisco 1865–1932,* 23–24.

7. Issel and Cherny, *San Francisco 1865–1932,* 15. Jay Monaghan, *Chile, Peru, and the California Gold Rush of 1849* (Berkeley: University of California Press, 1973).

8. Issel and Cherny, *San Francisco 1865–1932,* 23.

9. Issel and Cherny, *San Francisco 1865–1932,* 24.

10. Issel and Cherny, *San Francisco 1865–1932,* 14.

11. Monaghan, *Chile, Peru, and the California Gold Rush;* Abraham Nasatir, "Chileans in California during the Gold Rush Period and the Establishment of the Chilean Consulate," *California Historical Quarterly* 53, no. 1 (Spring 1974): 52–70.

12. Monaghan, *Chile, Peru, and the California Gold Rush,* 137.

13. Susan Lee Johnson, *Roaring Camp: The Social World of the California Gold Rush* (New York: W. W. Norton, 2000), 81–87. See also Paul M. Ong, "Chinese Labor in Early San Francisco: Racial Segmentation and Industrial Expansion," *Amerasia* 8, no. 1 (1981): 69–92.

14. Many abolitionist newspapers, often wary of the promises of freedom in the American west, noted the fact that in California Blacks could earn great sums of money outside of service occupations. However, San Francisco had not originally welcomed African Americans. The California constitution of 1851 did not extend suffrage rights to African Americans, and it prohibited the testimony or use of Black witnesses in court cases involving white people. The 1852 legislature even considered a bill to prohibit Black immigration. African Americans nevertheless migrated in significant numbers to California, and by 1860, there were 4,086 African Americans living in California. Rudolph M. Lapp, *Blacks in Gold Rush California* (New Haven: Yale University Press, 1977), 12–48, 94–108; Philip Montesano, "San Francisco Black Churches in the Early

1860's: Political Pressure Group," *California Historical Quarterly* 52, no. 2 (Summer 1973): 145–152.

15. Herbert Asbury, *The Barbary Coast: An Informal History of the San Francisco Underworld* (New York: Knopf, 1933), 32–38; Stephen Longstreet, *The Wilder Shore: A Gala Social History of San Francisco's Sinners and Spenders, 1849–1906* (Garden City, NY: Doubleday, 1968), 258.

16. Asbury, *Barbary Coast,* 101; Lance S. Davidson, "Shanghaied! The Systematic Kidnapping of Sailors in Early San Francisco," *California Historical Quarterly* 64, no. 1 (Winter 1985): 11.

17. For information on San Francisco's mid-nineteenth-century and vigilante history, see Robert Senkewicz, *Vigilantes in Gold Rush San Francisco* (Stanford, CA: Stanford University Press, 1985); Lewis, *San Francisco,* 58–78. See also David Beesley, "Communists and Vigilantes in the Northern Mines," *California Historical Quarterly* 64, no. 2 (Spring 1985): 143. For fictionalized accounts of San Francisco's vigilante period (1850–1859), see Richard Summers, *Vigilante* (New York: Duell, Sloan, and Pearce, 1949); Stanton A. Coblentz, *Villains and Vigilantes* (New York: A. S. Barnes & Co., 1936; rpt. 1957).

18. Article 1 of the Vigilance Committee constitution of 1851, cited in Lewis, *San Francisco,* 61.

19. Martin Meeker explores the relationship between print media and queer migrations ("sexual migrations") to San Francisco in "Come Out West."

20. The term "homophile" was chosen by the early Mattachine Society to avoid the clinical and pathological connotations the term "homosexual" carried in the early 1950s. For more information, see Stuart Timmons, *The Trouble with Harry Hay, Founder of the Modern Gay Movement* (Boston: Alyson, 1990), 148–149.

21. Benedict Anderson, *Imagined Communities* (New York: Verso, 1991), 5–7.

22. D'Emilio, *Sexual Politics,* 192–195. It would not be until the 1970s that the gay community began to be called the "gay and lesbian community." Later, the words "bisexual" and "transgender" were added to the titles of San Francisco's same-sex and/or queer organizations in order to recognize the connections between gay, lesbian, bisexual, and transgendered people.

23. See Michael Warner, "Introduction," in Michael Warner, ed., *Fear of a Queer Planet: Queer Politics and Social Theory* (Minneapolis: University of Minnesota Press, 1993).

24. On the queer aspects of interracial sex, see Judy Tzu-Chun Wu, "Was Mom Chung a 'Sister Lesbian'? Asian American Gender Experimentation and Interracial Homoeroticism," *Journal of Women's History* 13, no. 1 (2001): 58–82. See also Henry Yu, "Mixing Bodies and Cultures: The Meaning of America's Fascination with Sex between 'Orientals' and 'Whites,'" in Martha Hodes, ed., *Sex, Love, Race: Crossing Boundaries in North American History* (New York: New York University Press, 1999), 444–463; Peggy Pascoe, "Miscegenation Law, Court Cases, and Ideologies of 'Race' in Twentieth-Century America," *Journal of American History* 83, no. 1 (June 1996): 44–69.

25. On the relationship between queer theory and the social construction of

sex, sexuality, and sexual identities, see Judith Butler, *Bodies that Matter: On the Discursive Limits of "Sex"* (New York: Routledge, 1991); Warner, ed., *Fear of a Queer Planet*; Jennifer Terry and Jacqueline Urla, eds., *Deviant Bodies* (Bloomington: Indiana University Press, 1995); Steven Seidman, ed., *Queer Theory/Sociology* (Cambridge, MA: Blackwell, 1996).

26. For a discussion of the concept of a "gay community," see Steven O. Murray, "Components of Gay Community in San Francisco," in Gilbert Herdt, ed., *Gay Culture in America: Essays from the Field* (Boston: Beacon Press, 1992), 107–146.

27. Sarah Thornton, "General Introduction," in Ken Gelder and Sarah Thornton, eds., *The Subcultures Reader* (New York: Routledge, 1997), 2.

28. Thornton, "General Introduction," 2.

29. Allan Bérubé, *Coming Out under Fire: The History of Gay Men and Women in World War Two* (New York: Free Press, 1990).

30. D'Emilio, "Gay Politics and Community in San Francisco," 456–473.

31. D'Emilio, *Sexual Politics*; Marc Stein, *City of Sisterly and Brotherly Loves: Lesbian and Gay Philadelphia, 1945–1972* (Chicago: University of Chicago Press, 2000).

32. D'Emilio, *Sexual Politics,* 2.

33. Stryker and Van Buskirk, *Gay by the Bay,* 29–49.

34. George Chauncey, *Gay New York: Gender, Urban Culture and the Making of the Gay Male World, 1890–1940* (New York: Basic Books, 1994).

35. Elizabeth Lapovsky Kennedy and Madeline D. Davis, *Boots of Leather, Slippers of Gold: The History of a Lesbian Community* (New York: Routledge, 1993), 390, n. 3. See also Eric Hobsbawm, *Primitive Rebels: Studies in Archaic Forms of Social Movement in the Nineteenth and Twentieth Centuries* (New York: Praeger, 1963).

36. D'Emilio, *Sexual Politics,* 2.

37. Kennedy and Davis, *Boots of Leather,* 378.

38. Kennedy and Davis, *Boot of Leather,* 2.

39. Marc Stein makes a similar argument in *City of Sisterly and Brotherly Loves.* See also Vicki Eaklor, "Learning from History: A Queer Problem," *Journal of Gay, Lesbian, and Bisexual Identity* 3, no. 3 (1998): 195–211.

40. Chauncey, *Gay New York.*

41. Chauncey, *Gay New York,* 23.

42. Chauncey, *Gay New York,* 23.

43. Daniel Bell, *The End of Ideology: On the Exhaustion of Political Ideas in the Fifties* (New York: Free Press, 1960), 117.

CHAPTER 1

Epigraph: Herbert Asbury, *The Barbary Coast: An Informal History of the San Francisco Underworld* (New York: Knopf, 1933), 285–286.

1. Asbury, *Barbary Coast,* 280–283.

2. *San Francisco Call,* 20 October 1908, p. 2.

3. Asbury, *Barbary Coast,* 283–284; *San Francisco Call,* 20 October 1908,

p. 1; *San Francisco Call,* 21 October 1908, p. 1. See also Walton Bean, *Boss Reuf's San Francisco: The Story of the Union Labor Party, Big Business, and the Graft Prosecution* (Berkeley: University of California Press, 1952).

4. "Dive Men Officials for Cook," *San Francisco Call,* 20 October 1908, p. 1.

5. Anna Sommer, "The Barbary Coast," *The News,* 6 February 1934.

6. Madeline Powers, *Faces Along the Bar: Lore and Order in the Workingman's Saloon, 1870–1920* (Chicago: University of Chicago Press, 1998); Jon M. Kingsdale, "The 'Poor Man's Club': Social Functions of the Urban Working-Class Saloon," *American Quarterly* 25 (December 1973): 472–489.

7. Kenneth D. Rose, "Wettest in the West: San Francisco and Prohibition in 1924," *California History* 65, no. 4 (December 1986): 285–295.

8. Howard M. Bahr, ed., *Disaffiliated Man: Essays and Bibliography on Skid Row, Vagrancy, and Outsiders* (Toronto: University of Toronto Press, 1970), 15, 20–21.

9. For a detailed analysis of the city's South of Market district as a predominantly single men's quarter, see Alvin Averbach, "San Francisco's South of Market District, 1885–1950: The Emergence of a Skid Row," *California Historical Quarterly* 52, no. 3 (1973): 197–223.

10. Oscar Lewis, *San Francisco: Mission to Metropolis,* 2nd ed. (San Diego: Howell-North Books, 1980), 144–146.

11. Lewis, *San Francisco,* 70.

12. Will Irwin, quoted by William Hogan, "Fabulous Frisco," *Saturday Review* 39 (May 1956): 17; Hamilton Basso, "San Francisco," *Holiday* 14, no. 3 (September 1953): 32. See also Douglas Henry Daniels, *Pioneer Urbanites: Social and Cultural History of Black San Francisco* (Philadelphia: Temple University Press, 1980), 144–160.

13. Stephen Longstreet, *The Wilder Shore: A Gala Social History of San Francisco's Sinners and Spenders, 1849–1906* (Garden City, NY: Doubleday, 1968), 262–63. See also Asbury, *Barbary Coast,* 280–283.

14. Asbury, *Barbary Coast,* 98–124.

15. Asbury, *Barbary Coast,* 232–277; Longstreet, *Wilder Shore,* 253–265; Lucius Beebe and Charles Clegg, *San Francisco's Golden Era* (Berkeley: Howell-North, 1960), 126–127. See also Curt Gentry, *The Madams of San Francisco; An Irreverent History of the City by the Golden Gate* (New York: Ballantine Books, 1964); Sally Stanford, *The Lady of the House* (New York: G. P. Putnam's Sons, 1966).

16. Asbury, *Barbary Coast,* 291–293.

17. Robert C. Toll, *On with the Show! The First Century of Show Business in America* (New York: Oxford University Press, 1976), 239–245; Thomas Bolze, "Female Impersonation in the United States, 1900–1970" (Ph.D. diss., State University of New York at Buffalo, 1994), 31; M. Alison Kibler, *Rank Ladies: Gender and Cultural Hierarchy in American Vaudeville* (Chapel Hill: University of North Carolina Press, 1999), 111–116; Sharon Ullman, *Sex Seen: The Emergence of Modern Sexuality in America* (Berkeley: University of California Press, 1997), 49; Laurence Senelick, "Boys and Girls Together: Sub-

cultural Origins of Glamour Drag and Male Impersonation on the Nineteenth-Century Stage," in Lesley Ferris, ed., *Crossing the Stage: Controversies on Cross-Dressing* (London: Routledge, 1993), 84–85.

18. Bolze, "Female Impersonation," 24–39.

19. David R. Roediger, *The Wages of Whiteness: Race and the Making of the American Working Class* (New York: Verso, 1991), 115–122. See also Robert Toll, *On with the Show!* 81–110.

20. Roediger, *Wages of Whiteness,* 121; Toll, *On with the Show!* 240.

21. Eric Lott, *Love and Theft: Blackface Minstrelsy and the American Working Class* (New York: Oxford University Press, 1993), 53–55, 160–164.

22. Bolze, "Female Impersonation," 33; Marybeth Hamilton, "'I'm the Queen of the Bitches': Female Impersonation and Mae West's *Pleasure Man,*" in Lesley Ferris, ed., *Crossing the Stage: Controversies on Cross-Dressing* (London: Routledge, 1993), 109–110; Toll, *On with the Show!* 239–242.

23. Ullman, *Sex Seen,* 45–61; Hamilton, "'I'm the Queen,'" 109–112; Toll, *On with the Show!* 239–264.

24. Toll, *On with the Show!* 276–77.

25. David Nasaw, *Going Out: The Rise and Fall of Public Amusements* (New York: Basic Books, 1993), 1–9.

26. Kibler, *Rank Ladies,* 15–54.

27. Nasaw, *Going Out,* 23–27.

28. Nasaw, *Going Out,* 27.

29. Kibler, *Rank Ladies,* 54.

30. Ullman, *Sex Seen,* 49–51; Toll, *On with the Show!* 239–263; Hamilton, "'I'm the Queen,'" 109–110.

31. Ullman, *Sex Seen,* 51. See also C. J. Bulliet, *Venus Castina: Famous Female Impersonators Celestial and Human* (New York: Bonanza Books, 1928; rpt. 1956). Many thanks to Don Romesberg for this reference.

32. Toll, *On with the Show!* 247.

33. Bulliet, *Venus Castina,* 261–266. See also Laurence Senelick, "Lady and the Tramp: Drag Differentials in the Progressive Era," in Laurence Senelick, ed., *Gender in Performance: The Presentation of Difference in the Performing Arts* (Hanover, NH: University Press of New England, 1992), 26–27.

34. Senelick, "Lady and the Tramp," 27.

35. Paul D. Hardman, "Walter Bothwell Browne," *California Voice,* 20 May 1983, pp. 16–17.

36. Bothwell Browne clippings file, Performing Arts Library and Museum (PALM), San Francisco. According to Paul Hardman ("Walter Bothwell Brown"), Browne also ran a dance studio at 364 Hayes Street.

37. For a photo of Brown's performance of the "Champagne Ballet," see *The Evening Post,* 2 April 1904, in the Bothwell Browne clippings file, PALM. See also Jim Wood, "Second Look," *San Francisco Examiner* (hereafter *Examiner*), 26 March 1979.

38. *Los Angeles Examiner,* 24 May 1913, quoted in Ullman, *Sex Seen,* 59.

39. Hardman, "Walter Bothwell Browne."

40. Ullman, *Sex Seen,* 52.

41. Bolze, "Female Impersonation," 100–116.

42. Toll, *On with the Show!* 252.

43. Senelick, "Lady and the Tramp," 29.

44. *Variety,* 24 April 1909, quoted in Ullman, *Sex Seen,* 54.

45. Quoted in Toll, *On with the Show!* 253.

46. Kathy Peiss, *Cheap Amusements: Working Women and Leisure in Turn-of-the-Century New York* (Philadelphia: Temple University Press, 1986).

47. Joanne Meyerowitz, "Sexual Geography and Gender Economy: The Furnished-Room Districts of Chicago, 1890–1930," in Vicky L. Ruiz and Ellen Carol DuBois, eds., *Unequal Sisters: A Multicultural Reader in U.S. Women's History,* 2nd ed. (New York: Routledge, 1994), 186–202.

48. On modernism and the changing meanings of sex and sexuality, see Jennifer Terry, *An American Obsession: Science, Medicine, and Homosexuality in Modern Society* (Chicago: University of Chicago Press, 1999). See also George Chauncey, "From Sexual Inversion to Homosexuality: Medicine and the Changing Conceptualization of Female 'Deviance,'" *Salmagundi* 58–59 (Fall 1982 / Winter 1983): 114–146; George Chauncey, *Gay New York: Gender, Urban Culture, and the Making of the Gay Male World, 1890–1940* (New York: Basic Books, 1994), 47–63.

49. Eric Lott explains the psychosexual dynamic of minstrel impersonators, and this analysis might easily be applied to the female impersonators who frequented the turn-of-the-century vaudeville stage. Lott, *Love and Theft,* 159–168. See also C. J. Bulliet's analysis of the (homo)erotic quality of female impersonation in *Venus Castina,* 9–12.

50. Toll, *On with the Show!* 250; Ullman, *Sex Seen,* 55–61; Bolze, "Female Impersonation," 51–56.

51. Toll, *On with the Show!* 255; Bolze, "Female Impersonation," 55; Ullman, *Sex Seen,* 58–59. Unlike Eltinge, Browne never married, and he seemed less interested in subverting the association between female impersonation, gender transgression, and sexual deviancy. When vaudeville shut its doors to impersonators, Browne continued his career as a San Francisco dance instructor and lived out his years in the company of his nieces, Dorothy and Flavilla Browne, who were also well-known dancers. Hartman, "Walter Bothwell Browne."

52. Senelick, "Boys and Girls Together," 85.

53. Senelick, "Lady and the Tramp," 33.

54. Senelick, "Boys and Girls Together," 88.

55. To Marybeth Hamilton, the distinction between female impersonators and fairy impersonators lies in the fact that unlike female impersonators, fairy impersonators transported a queer cultural style to the stage. "The thrill of an Eltinge, billed as a 'female illusionist,' lay quite explicitly in his skills of performance—his ability to conjure himself across what spectators believed to be an immutable gender divide. The thrill of the fairy impersonator, in contrast lay in the fact that he was not, technically, performing at all." While Hamilton's comments raise important questions about the naturalness of cross-gender behavior, I use the phrase "fairy impersonator" to signify class or location in the entertainment hierarchy, rather than degrees of gender performance. Fairy performers were often located in lower-paying venues and more likely to be associ-

ated with the presumed base motivations of the working class—like sexual deviancy. Also, although some performers seemed to be performing themselves, the performance of gender that impersonators exploited always carried a sexual quality, no matter how well performers (like Eltinge) managed to distance themselves from the stigma of sexual deviancy. Hamilton, *When I'm Bad I'm Better: Mae West, Sex, and American Entertainment* (New York: HarperCollins, 1995), 145.

56. Bolze, "Female Impersonation," 58. Because Savoy passed as a woman at times, his "impersonations" might also be recognized as part of a fledgling transgender culture and community. In any case, Savoy's connection to sex- and gender-transgressive communities—his history as a "fairy impersonator"—fueled his later success on the vaudeville stage. See Nan Alamilla Boyd, "Bodies in Motion: Lesbian and Transsexual Histories," in Martin Duberman, ed., *A Queer World* (New York: New York University Press, 1996); Don Romesberg, "Don't Fence Me In: Transgendering Western History" (unpublished manuscript, c. 2000, author's copy).

57. Senelick, "Lady and the Tramp," 37.

58. Senelick, "Lady and the Tramp," 37.

59. Bolze, "Female Impersonation," 59.

60. Bolze, "Female Impersonation," 3; Hamilton, *When I'm Bad I'm Better,* 144–149. See also Esther Newton's brilliant and pathbreaking study of female impersonators, *Mother Camp: Female Impersonators in America* (Chicago: University of Chicago Press, 1972).

61. Senelick, "Boys and Girls Together," 87.

62. Lou Rand (Hogan), "The Golden Age of Queens," unpublished manuscript, Len Evans Collection, GLBT Historical Society, chap. 1, p. 2.

63. Hamilton, "'I'm the Queen,'" 116.

64. Bulliet, *Venus Castina,* 265.

65. Bulliet, *Venus Castina,* 7.

66. Gendered pronouns present a problem. In an attempt to communicate to the reader without confusion and remain respectful of the pronouns chosen by historical subjects and/or their biographers (if this information exists), I use pronouns as carefully as possible. In this case, Ruby's choice to pass as a woman in public suggests the use of a female pronoun. In the case of Lou Rand, who uses both male and female pronouns in his/her autobiography, I follow Rand's lead, using male or female pronouns as Rand does. For a longer discussion of the use of gendered pronouns in transgendered history, see Boyd, "Bodies in Motion"; Romesberg, "Don't Fence Me In."

67. Bulliet, *Venus Castina,* 252, 256.

68. Rand, "The Golden Age of Queens," chap. 1, p. 4.

69. Rand, "The Golden Age of Queens," chap. 1, p. 5; chap. 2, p. 2.

70. Ullman, *Sex Seen,* 60.

71. Rand, "The Golden Age of Queens," chap. 4, p. 4.

72. Rand, "The Golden Age of Queens," chap. 6, p. 7

73. Chauncey, *Gay New York,* 168.

74. Chauncey, *Gay New York,* 331–354. See also Bolze, "Female Impersonation," 197; Hamilton, "'I'm the Queen.'"

75. Bolze, "Female Impersonation," 197.
76. Kibler, *Rank Ladies,* 87.
77. Hamilton, *When I'm Bad I'm Better,* 144.
78. Paula Baker, "The Domestication of Politics: Women and American Political Society, 1780–1920," *American Historical Review* 89 (1984): 620–647.
79. On women's anti-prostitution efforts in San Francisco, see Brenda Elaine Pillors, "The Criminalization of Prostitution in the United States: The Case of San Francisco, 1854–1919" (Ph.D. diss., University of California, Berkeley, 1982). On white women's anti-prostitution work among San Francisco's Chinese community, see Peggy Pascoe, *Relations of Rescue: The Search for Moral Authority in the American West, 1874–1939* (New York: Oxford University Press, 1990). On the importance of household and women's influence on men's voting patterns in San Francisco during the Progressive Era, see Phillip J. Ethington, "Recasting Urban Political History: Gender, the Public, the Household, and Political Participation in Boston and San Francisco during the Progressive Era," *Social Science History* 16 (Summer 1992): 301–333.
80. Asbury, *Barbary Coast,* 232–277.
81. Gentry, *Madams of San Francisco,* 44–45.
82. Gentry, *Madams of San Francisco,* 34, 77. On masquerade balls, see also Jacqueline Baker Barnhart, *The Fair but Frail: Prostitution in San Francisco, 1849–1900* (Reno: University of Nevada Press, 1986), 29.
83. Neil Larry Shumsky discusses accusations that a city-run "municipal crib" housed over a hundred prostitutes in a crowded and dirty brothel. "Vice Responds to Reform: San Francisco, 1910–1914," *Journal of Urban History* 7, no. 1 (November 1980): 39.
84. Lucie Cheng Hirata, "Free, Indentured, Enslaved: Chinese Prostitutes in Nineteenth-Century America," *Signs* 5, no. 1 (Autumn 1979): 3–29; Pillors, "Criminalization of Prostitution," 89–123. See also Bensen Tong, *Unsubmissive Women: Chinese Prostitutes in Nineteenth-Century San Francisco* (Norman: University of Oklahoma Press, 1994).
85. Asbury, *Barbary Coast,* 232–277.
86. Barnhart, *Fair but Frail,* 32.
87. Neil Larry Shumsky and Larry M. Springer, "San Francisco's Zone of Prostitution, 1880–1934," *Journal of Historical Geography* 7, no. 1 (1981): 78–79.
88. Shumsky and Springer, "San Francisco's Zone of Prostitution," 71–89; Neil Larry Shumsky, "Tacit Acceptance: Respectable Americans and Segregated Prostitution, 1870–1910," *Journal of Social History* 19 (Summer 1986): 665–679.
89. Lucie Cheng Hirata, "Free, Indentured, Enslaved"; Shumsky, "Tacit Acceptance"; Pillors, "Criminalization of Prostitution," 121–123; Merritt Barnes, "'Fountainhead of Corruption': Peter P. McDonough, Boss of San Francisco's Underworld," *California History* 58, no. 2 (Summer 1979): 143–153.
90. Ethington, "Recasting Urban Political History"; Pillors, "Criminalization of Prostitution," 125–145. See also Egal Feldman, "Prostitution, the Alien Woman and the Progressive Imagination, 1910–1915," *American Quarterly* 19 (Summer 1967): 192–206.

91. Megumi Dick Osumi, "Asians and California's Anti-Miscegenation Laws," in Nobuya Tsuehida, ed., *Asian and Pacific American Experiences: Women's Perspectives* (Minneapolis: University of Minnesota Press, 1982), 6–7. See also Ivan Light, "The Ethnic Vice Industry, 1880–1944," *American Sociological Review* 42 (1977): 464–479. On the connection between anti-prostitution efforts and public fears of racial mixing and/or miscegenation, see Kevin Mumford, *Interzones: Black-White Sex Districts in Chicago and New York in the Early Twentieth Century* (New York: Columbia University Press, 1997), 93–117. On miscegenation law more generally, see Peggy Pascoe, "Miscegenation Law, Court Cases, and Ideologies of 'Race' in Twentieth-Century America," *Journal of American History* 83, no. 1 (June 1996): 44–69.

92. Pillors, "Criminalization of Prostitution," 90–117; Tong, *Unsubmissive Women.*

93. Shumsky, "Vice Responds to Reform," 31–47; Pillors, "Criminalization of Prostitution."

94. Bean, *Boss Reuf's San Francisco,* 298; Shumsky, "Vice Responds to Reform," 38.

95. Shumsky, "Vice Responds to Reform," 37–43. See also Asbury, *Barbary Coast,* 299–314; Bean, *Boss Reuf's San Francisco;* Pillors, "Criminalization of Prostitution," 157; Barnes, "'Fountainhead of Corruption,'" 147.

96. Shumsky, "Vice Responds to Reform," 44; Pillors, "Criminalization of Prostitution," 148.

97. Pillors, "Criminalization of Prostitution," 162.

98. Asbury, *Barbary Coast,* 307; Pillors, "Criminalization of Prostitution," 161–169.

99. Shumsky, "Tacit Acceptance," 669.

100. Shumsky and Springer, "San Francisco's Zone of Prostitution," 85–87.

101. Shumsky and Springer, "San Francisco's Zone of Prostitution," 86.

102. Pillors, "Criminalization of Prostitution," 155–156.

103. Rand, "The Golden Age of Queens," chap. 2, p. 2.

104. Rand, "The Golden Age of Queens," chap. 2, p. 2 (ellipses in original). On prostitution payoffs in the Tenderloin, see Barnes, "'Fountainhead of Corruption,'" 147.

105. Rose, "Wettest in the West."

106. Gilman M. Ostrander, *The Prohibition Movement in California, 1848–1933* (Berkeley: University of California Press, 1957), 174.

107. The state's Harris Act was passed before the federal Volstead Act of 1920, and it defined alcoholic beverages as anything containing more than 0.5 percent alcohol, outlawing beer and wine along with harder liquors. Anti-Prohibition forces rallied to allow beer and wine sales in California, and the Harris law was overturned by popular referendum in 1920. In 1922 the Wright Act replaced the Harris Act to guide the enforcement of Prohibition in California. The Wright Act simply incorporated the terms of the Volstead Act without stipulating alcohol percentage or the legality of beer and wine. Ostrander, *Prohibition Movement,* 152–161.

108. Ostrander, *Prohibition Movement,* 150.

109. Ostrander, *Prohibition Movement,* 63–65. In 1906, 58 percent of churchgoing San Franciscans attended Catholic churches and 15 percent attended Protestant churches. In Los Angeles, 56 percent of the population was Protestant. On the development of Protestantism in the San Francisco Bay Area, see Douglas Firth Anderson, "'We Have Here a Different Civilization': Protestant Identity in the San Francisco Bay Area, 1906–1909," *Western Historical Quarterly* 23, no. 2 (May 1992): 199–221.

110. Gunther Barth, *Instant Cities: Urbanization and the Rise of San Francisco and Denver* (New York: Oxford University Press, 1975), 145–150.

111. Barth, *Instant Cities.*

112. Ostrander, *Prohibition Movement,* 81–82.

113. On the impact of free lunches and treating, see Powers, *Faces Along the Bar,* 75–133.

114. Ostrander, *Prohibition Movement,* 77–81.

115. *The Pacific,* 20 July 1892, cited in Ostrander, *Prohibition Movement,* 76.

116. Ostrander, *Prohibition Movement,* 74–75.

117. Ostrander, *Prohibition Movement,* 108.

118. Ostrander, *Prohibition Movement,* 134.

119. Rose, "Wettest in the West," 286, 290.

120. Ostrander, *Prohibition Movement,* 174.

121. Ostrander, *Prohibition Movement,* 173.

122. Michael Kazin, "The Great Exception Revisited: Organized Labor and Politics in San Francisco and Los Angeles, 1870–1940," *Pacific Historical Review* 55 (1986): 371–402; Barnes, "'Fountainhead of Corruption.'"

123. Ostrander, *Prohibition Movement,* 185.

124. Robert Sylvester, *No Cover Charge: A Backward Look at the Night Clubs* (New York: Dial Press, 1956), 299.

125. Bolze, "Female Impersonation," 227. See also Allan Bérubé, *Coming Out under Fire: The History of Gay Men and Women in World War Two* (New York: Free Press, 1990), 72–74.

126. Chauncey, *Gay New York,* 131–154.

127. In 1890, with 3,117 liquor licenses distributed in San Francisco (at a ratio of 1 for every 96 residents) and over 2,000 "blind pigs," or speakeasies, city authorities estimated San Francisco's annual liquor revenue at almost $10 million. During Prohibition, liquor revenue was driven underground. Repeal came in 1933; by 1935, the revenue for the entire state of California was just over $10 million, the same as it had been in the city of San Francisco alone prior to Progressive Era legislation and the post-Prohibition reorganization of liquor sales and authority. See Asbury, *Barbary Coast,* 123–124; Leonard Harrison and Elizabeth Laine, *After Repeal* (New York: Harper & Brothers, 1936), 144.

128. Harrison and Laine, *After Repeal,* 48, 54–56, 84–87.

129. California was one of four states that held exclusive state-administered authority over the distribution of liquor licenses rather than allowing local municipalities to participate in the licensing process. The others were Connecticut, Delaware, and South Carolina. Harrison and Laine, *After Repeal,* 48.

130. Humbert S. Nelli, "American Syndicate Crime: A Legacy of Prohibition," in David E. Kyvig, ed., *Law, Alcohol, and Order: Perspectives on National Prohibition* (Westport, CT: Greenwood Press, 1985), 123–137.

131. By 1935, California had issued 73,189 liquor licenses, more than any other state. Harrison and Laine, *After Repeal,* 58.

132. J. W. Erlich, *A Life in My Hand: An Autobiography* (New York: G. P. Putnam's Sons, 1965), 87. On the absence of Mafia in San Francisco, see Nelli, "American Syndicate Crime."

133. Chauncey, *Gay New York,* 347.

134. Kazin, "The Great Exception Revisited."

135. Organized labor in San Francisco actively excluded Chinese workers. In fact, one of the successes of organized labor was the institutionalization of Chinese exclusion in California. See Michael Kazin, *Barons of Labor: The San Francisco Building Trades and Union Power in the Progressive Era* (Urbana: University of Illinois Press, 1987). On San Francisco's labor movement, see also Thomas R. Clark, "The Voting Behavior of the San Francisco Working Class, 1912–1916," *California History* 66, no. 3 (September 1987): 197–208; Jules Tygiel, "Where Unionism Holds Undisputed Sway: A Reappraisal of San Francisco's Union Labor Party," *California History* 62, no. 3 (Fall 1983): 196–214.

136. Barnes, "'Fountainhead of Corruption,'" 149.

137. Kazin, "The Great Exception Revisited," 393–396.

138. On the general strike, see John Kogel, "The Day the City Stopped," *California History* 63, no. 3 (Summer 1984): 213–222; David F. Selvin, "An Exercise in Hysteria: San Francisco's Red Raids of 1934," *Pacific Historical Review* 58 (August 1989): 361–374.

139. Barnes, "'Fountainhead of Corruption,'" 150.

140. On the heels of the Atherton Report, McDonough's bail bond license was revoked, and despite protests from a wide-ranging set of "friends," McDonough's appeal was never granted. Barnes, "'Fountainhead of Corruption,'" 151–152.

141. Eric Garber, "Finocchio's: A Gay Community Landmark," *San Francisco Bay Area Gay and Lesbian Historical Society Newsletter* 3, no. 4 (June 1988): 1, 4–5; Stuart Timmons, *The Trouble with Harry Hay, Founder of the Modern Gay Movement* (Boston: Alyson, 1990), 46–47; Li-Kar, Finocchio's undated playbill, Ephemera Collection, GLBT Historical Society.

142. Jesse Hamlin, "What a Drag: Finocchio's to Close," *San Francisco Chronicle* (hereafter *Chronicle*), 4 November 1999.

143. Joseph Finocchio, quoted in Eric Garber, "Finocchio's," 1.

144. "Police Raiders Arrest Ten in SF Night Club," *Chronicle,* 20 June 1936; "Singers Jailed 30 Days for Naughty Tunes," *Chronicle,* 22 June 1936, p. 25.

145. *Chronicle,* 9 September 1937, p. 1.

146. Li-Kar, undated Finocchio's playbill, Ephemera Collection, GLBT Historical Society.

147. "Joseph Finocchio Dies," *Los Angeles Times,* 16 January 1986, Metro section, p. 2.

148. Nasaw, *Going Out,* 64.

149. *San Francisco Life* 7, no. 1 (December 1938): 8–9.

150. Richard Reinhardt, *Treasure Island: San Francisco's Exposition Years* (San Francisco: Scrimshaw Press, 1973); Richard Reinhardt, "The Other Fair," *American Heritage* 40, no. 4 (May/June 1989): 42–53.

151. *San Francisco Life* 15, no. 6 (June 1947).

152. Frank Kay, "I Get Around: Nite Club Review: Finocchio's," c. 1938. Eric Garber Collection, GLBT Historical Society. Note that the epigraph that appeared with this review states, "Finocchio's: Where Korea's night life is reproduced in Aphroditic form."

153. *San Francisco Life* 8, no. 15 (December 1940): 25.

154. John Stanley, "Finocchio's: A Reputable Bastion of a Bizarre Art," *Chronicle,* 8 January 1967, Datebook section, pp. 7–8. On closing night, 27 November 1999, Finocchio's featured a host of artists, including Alejandro Cruz, aka Alejandra the Puerto Rican Bombshell. Jesse Hamlin, "Strutting into History: Laughter Gives Way to Tears as Finocchio's Ends 63-Year Drag-Show Run," *Chronicle,* 29 November 1999, section D, p. 1.

155. Elizabeth Drorbaugh, "Sliding Scales: Notes on Stormé DeLarverié and the Jewel Box Revue, the Cross-Dressed Woman on the Contemporary Stage, and the Invert," in Lesley Ferris, ed., *Crossing the Stage: Controversies on Cross-Dressing* (London: Routledge, 1993), 120–143.

156. Silke Tudor, "Night Crawler," *San Francisco Weekly,* 1 December 1999.

157. Jack Lord and Lloyd Hoff, *Where to Sin in San Francisco,* 5th ed. (San Francisco: Richard F. Guggenheim, 1948), 145.

158. Jack Lord and Jenn Shaw, *Where to Sin in San Francisco,* 4th ed. (San Francisco: N.p., 1945), 93.

159. As cited in Eric Garber, "Finocchio's," 4.

160. "Black Cat Cafe Will Celebrate Anniversary," *Chronicle,* 8 November 1913, p. 14.

161. "12 Supervisors Threaten Rolph," *Examiner,* 31 January 1917, p. 5.

162. Michael R. Gorman, *The Empress Is a Man: Stories from the Life of José Sarria* (New York: Harrington Park Press, 1998), 124.

163. "Cafe Owners Bar Girls' Escape" and "Cafes Quiet; Business Fair," *Examiner,* 31 January 1917.

164. "Police Clamp Lid on Cafes; Oust Dancers," *Examiner,* 8 January 1921, p. 1; "Black Cat, Pup Dances Banned," *Examiner,* 26 April 1921, p. 1.

165. Jack Lord and Lloyd Hoff, *Where to Sin in San Francisco,* 5th ed. (San Francisco: Richard F. Guggenheim, 1948), 101.

166. "Cleanup Begun at Night Spots; Cafes Warned," *Examiner,* 15 June 1949, p. 1; "3 in Cafe Raid Convicted," *Examiner,* 16 June 1949, p. 19.

167. Announcement, Senior Armed Forces Disciplinary Control Board, Western Area, 1 February 1951. "Military, Off-Limits and Out-of-Bounds," 1947–1957. Alcoholic Beverage Control Subject Files, California State Archives (CSA), F3718:341–342.

168. Gorman, *The Empress Is a Man,* 123–135.

169. José Sarria, interviewed by Nan Alamilla Boyd, tape recording, San Francisco, 15 April 1992 and 20 May 1992, Wide Open Town History Project, GLBT Historical Society.

170. José Sarria, interviewed by Nan Alamilla Boyd, tape recording, San Francisco, 15 April 1992 and 20 May 1992, Wide Open Town History Project, GLBT Historical Society.

171. Sherri Cavan, "Interaction in Home Territories," *Berkeley Journal of Sociology* 4 (1963): 17–32.

172. Cavan, "Interaction in Home Territories." Cavan notes that "challenges to territorial definitions" were often unsuccessful because there were fewer resources with which non-gay outsiders could defend themselves. There was no moral high ground, little social support, and defensive challenges often increased the outsider's stigma as the watched rather than the watcher. Men in larger groups often posed the most serious challenge, but interactions often terminated with the outsider "accepting the position which the indigenous group has defined him in."

173. José Sarria, interviewed by Nan Alamilla Boyd, tape recording, San Francisco, 15 April 1992, Wide Open Town History Project, GLBT Historical Society.

174. José Sarria, quoted in Gorman, *The Empress Is a Man,* 162.

175. Nancy Achilles, "The Development of the Homosexual Bar as an Institution," in John H. Gagnon and William Simon, eds., *Sexual Deviance* (New York: Harper and Row, 1967), 228–244; Barbara A. Weightman, "Gay Bars as Private Places," *Landscape* 24, no. 1 (1980): 9–14.

176. Donald Webster Cory, *The Homosexual in America: A Subjective Approach* (New York: Greenberg, 1951), 120.

177. Guy Strait, "What Is a 'Gay Bar'?" *Citizens News* 4, no. 5 (December 1964): 6.

178. Thomas Jacob Noel, "Gay Bars and the Emergence of the Denver Homosexual Community," *Social Science Journal* 15, no. 2 (April 1978).

CHAPTER 2

Epigraph: Reba Hudson, interviewed by Nan Alamilla Boyd, tape recording, San Francisco, 29 May 1992, Wide Open Town History Project, GLBT Historical Society.

1. Mona Hood, handwritten notes, July 1992 (in author's possession). Referencing Henri Murger's *Scènes de la Vie de Bohème,* late-nineteenth-century artists in San Francisco often called themselves bohemians and mimicked the style of Parisian writers and artists. Later, a group of self-proclaimed bohemians clustered near the intersections of Pacific, Washington, Jackson, and Montgomery, where low-rent studios were plentiful. Nancy J. Peters, "The Beat Generation and San Francisco's Culture of Dissent," in James Brook, Chris Carlsson, and Nancy J. Peters, eds., *Reclaiming San Francisco: History, Politics, Culture* (San Francisco: City Lights Books, 1998), 199–202.

2. Mona Hood, interviewed by Nan Alamilla Boyd with Rikki Streicher and

Reba Hudson, tape recording, Santa Rosa, CA, 25 July 1992, Wide Open Town History Project, GLBT Historical Society.

3. *San Francisco Life* 4, no. 2 (January 1936): 29; 4, no. 3 (February 1936): 46; 4, no. 4 (March 1936): 48; 4, no. 5 (April 1936): 48; 4, no. 6 (May 1936): 54.

4. "Cops Moan Low down over Mona's," *San Francisco Chronicle* (hereafter *Chronicle*), 30 March 1938, p. 15. Actually, police arrested Mona's sister, Sybil Hale, who said she was Mona. "Time Flies, Mona Moans," *Chronicle*, 7 March 1938, p. 1; "And Mona Wasn't Arrested," *Chronicle*, 8 March 1938, p. 1; "Sister of Mona, Barmen Fined," *Chronicle*, 17 March 1938, p. 13.

5. Charlie Murray opened the 440 in 1939 and soon thereafter brought in Mona as a partner. The club was called Mona's 440 from 1940 to 1948. Mona Hood, interviewed by Nan Alamilla Boyd with Rikki Streicher and Reba Hudson, tape recording, Santa Rosa, CA, 25 July 1992, Wide Open Town History Project, GLBT Historical Society; *San Francisco Life* 9, no. 10 (October 1941): 26; Mona Hood, handwritten notes, July 1992 (in author's possession).

6. Jack Lord and Jenn Shaw, *Where to Sin in San Francisco*, 1st ed. (San Francisco: Richard F. Guggenheim, 1939), 56–57.

7. A note on the use of the term "lesbian": While many women engaged in same-sex behaviors and activities, not all of these women called themselves lesbians. In fact, it was not until the 1960s that a sizeable cohort of women in San Francisco began to use the term "lesbian" to identify themselves. In oral histories with women who participated in San Francisco's queer community in the 1940s and 1950s, most remember that they called themselves "gay women," but some identified as "bohemian" and others, depending on class, race, and ethnicity, called themselves (or others) "dykes," "butches," "studs," "girls," and "fems." So as not to confuse the reader with a variety of terms, I use the term "lesbian" throughout this chapter to refer to women who engaged in same-sex behaviors and participated in San Francisco's queer and transgender cultures.

8. Reba Hudson, interviewed by Nan Alamilla Boyd, tape recording, San Francisco, 29 May 1992, Wide Open Town History Project, GLBT Historical Society. Mona's 440 is also described in Lonnie Coleman's short story "Bird of Paradise," in *Ship's Company* (New York: Dell, 1957), 126–127. Many thanks to Allan Bérubé for referring me to this source.

9. Longtime San Franciscan Clyde Evans (who was the lover of writer Clarkson Crane for forty-seven years) recalls a lesbian speakeasy that he visited in the late 1920s near Fisherman's Wharf, one or two streets from the bay. It was filled with lesbians who, he recalls, were very well dressed. Telephone conversation with former GLBT Historical Society archivist Willie Walker, 12 July 2002.

10. Manuel Castells, *The City and the Grassroots: A Cross-Cultural Theory of Urban Social Movements* (Berkeley: University of California Press, 1983), 138–164; Manuel Castells and Karen Murphy, "Cultural Identity and Urban Structure: The Spatial Organization of San Francisco's Gay Community," in Norman I. Fainstein and Susan S. Fainstein, eds., *Urban Policy under Capitalism*, vol. 22, *Urban Affairs Annual Reviews* (Beverly Hills, CA: Sage Publications, 1982); Deborah Goreman Wolf, *The Lesbian Community* (Berkeley: University of California Press, 1979), 71–105.

11. Castells, *The City and the Grassroots,* 140.

12. Wolf, *Lesbian Community,* 71–105.

13. For more recent studies of lesbian visibility and invisibility, see Moira Rachel Kenney, *Mapping Gay L.A.: The Intersection of Place and Politics* (Philadelphia: Temple University Press, 2001), 111–150; Marc Stein, *City of Sisterly and Brotherly Loves: Lesbian and Gay Philadelphia, 1945–1972* (Chicago: University of Chicago Press, 2000), 84–112; Yolanda Retter, "Lesbian Spaces in Los Angeles, 1970–90," in Gordon Brent Ingram, Anne-Marie Bouthillette, and Yolanda Retter, eds,. *Queers in Space* (Seattle: Bay Press, 1997), 325–337; Anne-Marie Bouthillette, "Queer and Gendered Housing: A Tale of Two Neighbourhoods in Vancouver," in Gordon Brent Ingram, Anne-Marie Bouthillette, and Yolanda Retter, eds., *Queers in Space* (Seattle: Bay Press, 1997), 213–232; Tamar Rothenberg, "'And She Told Two Friends': Lesbians Creating Urban Social Space," in David Bell and Gill Valentine, eds., *Mapping Desire* (London: Routledge, 1995), 165–181; Gill Valentine, "Out and About: Geographies of Lesbian Landscapes," *International Journal of Urban and Regional Research* 19, no. 1 (March 1995): 96–111; Maxine Wolfe, "Invisible Women in Invisible Places: Lesbians, Lesbian Bars, and the Social Production of People/Environment Relationships," *Architecture and Behavior* 8, no. 2 (1992): 137–158; Sy Adler and Johanna Brenner, "Gender and Space: Lesbians and Gay Men in the City," *International Journal of Urban and Regional Research* 16, no. 1 (March 1992): 24–34.

14. For an analysis of how the public sphere mediates the state and society, see Jürgen Habermas, *The Structural Transformation of the Public Sphere* (Cambridge, MA: MIT Press, 1989).

15. Warren Susman, "Did Success Spoil the United States? Dual Representation in Postwar America," in Lary May, ed., *Recasting America: Culture and Politics in the Age of Cold War* (Chicago: University of Chicago Press, 1989), 19–37.

16. Jackson Lears, "A Matter of Taste: Corporate Cultural Hegemony in a Mass-Consumption Society," in Lary May, ed., *Recasting America: Culture and Politics in the Age of Cold War* (Chicago: University of Chicago Press, 1989), 38–57; William Chafe, *The Unfinished Journey: America since World War II* (New York: Oxford University Press, 1989), 54–145.

17. Chafe, *Unfinished Journey,* 97–101; George Lipsitz, *Class and Culture in Cold War America: A Rainbow at Midnight* (New York: Prager, 1981).

18. The Taft-Hartley Act required compulsory mediation between labor and management prior to a proposed strike. It suspended National Labor Relations Board protections during unionization efforts, and it discouraged sympathy strikes and jurisdictional strikes. In effect, it mandated government arbitration so as to insure "orderly and effective labor-management negotiations." Lipsitz, *Class and Culture,* 124.

19. Lipsitz, *Class and Culture,* 170.

20. Lears, "A Matter of Taste," 51–54; Lipsitz, *Class and Culture,* 173–190; Warren Susman, *Culture as History: The Transformation of American Society in the Twentieth Century* (New York: Pantheon, 1984).

21. Alan Nadel, *Containment Culture: American Narratives, Postmodernism, and the Atomic Age* (Durham: Duke University Press, 1995).

22. Elaine Tyler May, *Homeward Bound: American Families in the Cold War Era* (New York: Basic Books, 1988). See also Robert J. Corber, *Homosexuality in Cold War America: Resistance and the Crisis of Masculinity* (Durham: Duke University Press, 1997).

23. J. Edgar Hoover, "An Open Letter from the Director of the FBI," *This Week Magazine,* 27 October 1957, p. 10. See also J. Edgar Hoover, "Let's Wipe Out the Schoolyard Sex Racket!" in *This Week Magazine,* 25 August 1957.

24. Herb Caen, "Mr. San Francisco," *Chronicle,* Sunday Punch, 9 September 1979, p. 1.

25. "25 Years Ago Today: S.F. High School Girl Swam in from 'Rock,'" *San Francisco News,* 17 October 1958.

26. Herb Caen, "It's News to Me," *Chronicle,* 28 February 1940, p. 11. See also Mona Hood Scrapbook, Ephemera Collection, GLBT Historical Society.

27. *San Francisco Life* 9, no. 9 (September 1941): 22.

28. *San Francisco Life* 9, no. 10 (October 1941): 26.

29. *San Francisco Life* 10, no. 3 (March 1942): 24; 9, no. 10 (October 1941): 26.

30. *San Francisco Life* 9, no. 9 (September 1941): 22.

31. Pat Bond, interviewed by Allan Bérubé, tape recording, San Francisco, 18 May 1981, World War II Project Records, GLBT Historical Society.

32. Pat Bond, *One Act Play: Bush St. Incident,* 1981, Pat Bond Collection, GLBT Historical Society. Pat Bond was an entertainer in San Francisco through the 1970s and 1980s, and she performed a number of one-woman shows that explored historical themes relating to lesbian life. Her most famous production was based on the life of Gertrude Stein *(Gertrude Stein in Pieces, Patricia Bond in Stitches),* but she also performed as Lorena Hickock and Lizzie Borden. She was featured in Peter Adair's documentary *Word Is Out* (1977). These lyrics and the following appear in autobiographical work set in San Francisco in the early 1950s.

33. Pat Bond, "The Only Gay Bar in Town," c. 1981, Pat Bond Collection, GLBT Historical Society.

34. *San Francisco Life* 10, no. 4 (April 1942): 26.

35. Erik Cohen, "A Phenomenology of Tourist Experiences," *Sociology* 13, no. 2 (May 1979): 179–202.

36. Andy and Ted Marefos, brothers, ran the Chi-Chi Club from 1949 to 1956 at 467 Broadway. It featured both female and male impersonators and served a queer and tourist clientele. Rikki Streicher, interviewed by Nan Alamilla Boyd, tape recording, San Francisco, 22 January 1992, Wide Open Town History Project, GLBT Historical Society; Eric Garber, "A Historical Directory of Lesbian and Gay Establishments in the San Francisco Bay Area," c. 1992, p. 43 (unpublished data in author's possession). See also Queer Sites Database, GLBT Historical Society.

37. Mona Hood, interviewed by Nan Alamilla Boyd with Rikki Streicher and Reba Hudson, tape recording, Santa Rosa, CA, 25 July 1992, Wide Open Town History Project, GLBT Historical Society.

38. *San Francisco Life* 9, no. 8 (August 1941); Rikki Streicher, interviewed by Nan Alamilla Boyd, tape recording, San Francisco, 22 January 1992, Wide Open Town History Project, GLBT Historical Society.

39. Reba Hudson, interviewed by Nan Alamilla Boyd, tape recording, San Francisco, 10 July 1992, Wide Open Town History Project, GLBT Historical Society.

40. Rikki Streicher, interviewed by Nan Alamilla Boyd, tape recording, San Francisco, 22 January 1992, Wide Open Town History Project, GLBT Historical Society.

41. Beverly Shaw, "Just Between Us Girls," *In the Life* 2 (Fall 1983): 4.

42. Shaw, "Just Between Us Girls," 4; Mona Hood, who remained in contact with Beverly Shaw long after she left Mona's, recalls that when Shaw died she was buried in her tuxedo with "things the way she wanted." Mona Hood, interviewed by Nan Alamilla Boyd with Rikki Streicher and Reba Hudson, tape recording, Santa Rosa, CA, 25 July 1992, Wide Open Town History Project, GLBT Historical Society.

43. *San Francisco Life* 10, no. 7 (July 1942): 30.

44. Eric Garber, "Gladys Bentley: The Bulldagger Who Sang the Blues," *OUT/LOOK* 1, no. 1 (Spring 1988): 52–61.

45. On Bentley in Harlem, see Pearl Bailey, *The Raw Pearl* (New York: Harcourt, Brace, World, 1968), 20; Willie Smith, *Music on My Mind: The Memoirs of an American Pianist* (Garden City, NY: Doubleday, 1964), 159; Langston Hughes, *The Big Sea* (New York: Hill & Wang, 1963; rpt. 1940), 225–227. These sources were culled from the Gladys Bentley files in the Eric Garber Collection, GLBT Historical Society.

46. *Los Angeles Times,* 21 February 1940.

47. *San Francisco Life* 10, no. 7 (July 1942): 30.

48. Reba Hudson, interviewed by Nan Alamilla Boyd, tape recording, San Francisco, 29 May 1992, Wide Open Town History Project, GLBT Historical Society.

49. *San Francisco Life* 11, no. 2 (February 1943): 21.

50. On urbanism and sexuality, see Lawrence Knopp, "Sexuality and Urban Space: A Framework for Analysis," 149–161, and other essays in David Bell and Gill Valentine, eds., *Mapping Desire* (London: Routledge, 1995). On international sex tourism, see Malcolm Crick, "Representations of International Tourism in the Social Sciences: Sun, Sex, Sights, Savings, and Servility," *Annual Review of Anthropology* 18 (1989): 307–344; Julia O'Connell Davidson, "Sex Tourism in Cuba," *Race & Class* 38, no. 1 (1986): 39–48. On U.S. urban tourism, see Christopher M. Law, *Urban Tourism: Attracting Visitors to Large Cities* (London: Mansell, 1993); John A. Jakle, *The Tourist: Travel in Twentieth-Century North America* (Lincoln: University of Nebraska Press, 1985), 245–262. For a sociological analysis of the impetus behind midcentury travel and tourism, see Dean MacCannell, *The Tourist: A New Theory of the Leisure Class* (New York: Schocken, 1976).

51. Laurence Senelick, "The Evolution of the Male Impersonator on the Nineteenth-Century Popular Stage," *Essays in Theatre* 1, no. 1 (November 1982): 31–44.

52. Mona Hood, interviewed by Nan Alamilla Boyd with Rikki Streicher and Reba Hudson, tape recording, Santa Rosa, CA, 25 July 1992, Wide Open Town History Project, GLBT Historical Society.

53. Mona Hood, interviewed by Nan Alamilla Boyd with Rikki Streicher and Reba Hudson, tape recording, Santa Rosa, CA, 25 July 1992, Wide Open Town History Project, GLBT Historical Society.

54. On the psychology of sex tourism, see Cohen, "Phenomenology."

55. On race tourism and ethnic tourism, see Wayne Martin Mellinger, "Toward a Critical Analysis of Tourism Representations," *Annals of Tourism Research* 21, no. 4 (1994): 756–779; Patrician Jasen, "Native People and the Tourist Industry in Nineteenth-Century Ontario," *Journal of Canadian Studies* 28, no. 4 (Winter 1994): 5–23; Martha Norkunas, *The Politics of Public Memory: Tourism, History, and Ethnicity in Monterey, California* (Albany: SUNY Press, 1993).

56. Connie Young Yu, "A History of San Francisco Chinatown Housing," *Amerasia* 8, no. 1 (1981): 93–109; Chalsa M. Loo and Connie Young Yu, "Heartland of Gold: A Historical Overview," in Chalsa M. Loo, *Chinatown: Most Time, Hard Time* (New York: Praeger, 1991), 31–56; Victor G. Nee and Brett de Bary Nee, eds., *Longtime Californ': A Documentary Study of an American Chinatown* (Stanford, CA: Stanford University Press, 1972), xi-xxvii; Thomas W. Chinn, *Bridging the Pacific: San Francisco Chinatown and Its People* (San Francisco: Chinese Historical Society of America, 1989); Judy Yung, *Unbound Feet: A Social History of Chinese Women in San Francisco* (Berkeley: University of California Press, 1995).

Chinatown was not completely closed off from tourist trade, however. In the late 1880s, both Oscar Wilde and Sarah Bernhardt toured Chinatown during visits to the city. Lois Foster Rodecape, "'Quand Même': A Few California Footnotes to the Biography of Sarah Bernhardt," *California Historical Society Quarterly* 20, no. 2 (June 1941): 126–146; Lois Foster Rodecape, "Gilding the Sunflower: A Study of Oscar Wilde's Visit to San Francisco," *California Historical Society Quarterly* 19, no. 2 (June 1940): 97–112.

57. "S.F. Vice Raids Net 62 in Lottery Dens," *San Francisco Call-Bulletin*, 7 March 1938; "Jail 52 More in Vice Raids," *San Francisco Call-Bulletin*, 8 March 1938.

58. Ivan Light, "From Vice District to Tourist Attraction: The Moral Career of American Chinatowns, 1880–1940," *Pacific Historical Review* 43 (1979): 367–394.

59. Anthony Lee, "Another View of Chinatown: Yun Lee and the Chinese Revolutionary Artists' Club," in James Brook, Chris Carlsson, and Nancy J. Peters, eds., *Reclaiming San Francisco: History, Politics, Culture* (San Francisco: City Lights Books, 1998), 163–182. See also Light, "From Vice District to Tourist Attraction," 385.

60. *San Francisco Life* 7, no. 2 (January 1939): 31. For other references to Chinatown, see *San Francisco Life* 7, no. 5 (April 1939): 31–32; 7, no. 15 (October 1939): 27–29.

61. *San Francisco Life* 7, no. 17 (November 1939): 25.

62. *San Francisco Life* 7, no. 3 (February 1939): 31; 7, no. 1 (December 1938): 29.

63. *San Francisco Life* 7, no. 1 (December 1938): 29.

64. *San Francisco Hotel Greeters Guide,* undated clipping, courtesy of Willie Walker. On Charlie Low's Forbidden City, see Chinn, *Bridging the Pacific,* 217–220; see also Arthur Dong's documentary film *Forbidden City U.S.A.* (DeepFocus Productions, 1989).

65. Merle Woo, interviewed by Nan Alamilla Boyd, tape recording, San Francisco, 15 May 1992, Wide Open Town History Project, GLBT Historical Society.

66. San Francisco's World Fair (the Golden Gate International Exposition) ran from 19 February 1939 to 2 September 1940. On the impact of world fairs on tourism in American cities, see Jakle, *The Tourist,* 252–254; Warren Susman, "The People's Fair: Cultural Contradictions of a Consumer Society," in Helen A. Harrison, ed., *Dawn of a New Day: The New York World's Fair, 1939–1949* (New York: 1980).

67. Richard Reinhardt, *Treasure Island: San Francisco's Exposition Years* (San Francisco: Scrimshaw Press, 1973), 81. On San Francisco's investment in tourist industry revenues, see William Issel and Robert W. Cherny, *San Francisco, 1865–1932: Politics, Power, and Urban Development* (Berkeley: University of California Press), 152–54; John B. McGloin, *San Francisco: The Story of a City* (San Rafael, CA: Presidio Press, 1978), 376–379. On the economic impact of urban tourism more generally, see Chris Ryan, *Recreational Tourism: A Social Science Perspective* (London: Routledge, 1991), 65–94; Colin Michael Hall and John M. Jenkins, *Tourism and Public Policy* (London: Routledge, 1995); Law, *Urban Tourism.*

68. Pardee Lowe, "Chinatown's Last Stand," *Survey Graphic* 25 (1936): 88.

69. *San Francisco Life* 9, no. 8 (August 1941): 30.

70. *San Francisco Life* 10, no. 10 (October 1942): 26.

71. *San Francisco Life* 11, no. 1 (January 1943): 21.

72. Cohen, "Phenomenology," 186–193; Crick, "Representations of International Tourism"; David Engerman, "Research Agenda for the History of Tourism: Towards an International Social History," *American Studies International* 32, no. 2 (October 1994): 3–31.

73. Robert F. Reid-Pharr, "The Spectacle of Blackness," *Radical America* 24, no. 4 (April 1993).

74. Esther Newton, *Mother Camp: Female Impersonators in America* (Chicago: University of Chicago Press, 1972).

75. "Gold Rush: '39 Tourists Brought State $80,251,626," *Chronicle,* 4 March 1940, p. 13.

76. Charlotte Coleman, interviewed by Nan Alamilla Boyd, tape recording, San Francisco, 13 July 1992, Wide Open Town History Project, GLBT Historical Society.

77. Rikki Streicher, interviewed by Nan Alamilla Boyd, tape recording, San Francisco, 22 January 1992, Wide Open Town History Project, GLBT Historical Society; Charlotte Coleman, interviewed by Nan Alamilla Boyd, tape recording, San Francisco, 13 July 1992, Wide Open Town History Project, GLBT Historical Society; Joe Baron (pseud.), interviewed by Nan Alamilla Boyd, tape

recording, San Francisco, 21 July 1991, Wide Open Town History Project, GLBT Historical Society.

78. Sherri Cavan, *Liquor License: An Ethnography of Bar Behavior* (Chicago: Aldine Publishing, 1966).

79. When it first opened, the Paper Doll was a predominantly lesbian bar, with Mona Sargent as its hostess and several lesbian waitresses. After 1954, when Dante Benedetti bought the club, it became more of a gay bar. Charlotte Coleman, interviewed by Nan Alamilla Boyd, tape recording, San Francisco, 13 July 1992, Wide Open Town History Project, GLBT Historical Society; Rikki Streicher, interviewed by Nan Alamilla Boyd, tape recording, San Francisco, 22 January 1992, Wide Open Town History Project, GLBT Historical Society; Mona Hood, interviewed by Nan Alamilla Boyd with Rikki Streicher and Reba Hudson, tape recording, Santa Rosa, CA, 25 July 1992, Wide Open Town History Project, GLBT Historical Society; Reba Hudson, interviewed by Nan Alamilla Boyd, tape recording, San Francisco, 10 July 1992, Wide Open Town History Project, GLBT Historical Society.

80. Joseph St. Amand, interviewed by Nan Alamilla Boyd, tape recording, San Francisco, 2 August 1991, Wide Open Town History Project, GLBT Historical Society; Pat Healey and Ruth Frederick, interviewed by Nan Alamilla Boyd, tape recording, Sebastopol, CA, 23 June 1992, Wide Open Town History Project, GLBT Historical Society; Dante Benedetti, interviewed by Nan Alamilla Boyd, tape recording, San Francisco, 10 July 1992, Wide Open Town History Project, GLBT Historical Society.

81. Jack Lord and Lloyd Hoff, *Where to Sin in San Francisco,* 5th ed. (San Francisco: Richard F. Guggenheim, 1948), 112–113.

82. Garber, "Historical Directory," 6; Reba Hudson, interviewed by Nan Alamilla Boyd, written notes (in author's possession), San Francisco, 17 July 1997.

83. Located at 345 Pacific Street, the Artist's Club ran from 1946 to 1949. Reba Hudson remembers that the Artist's Club was a lesbian hangout because Connie Smith worked there. Reba Hudson, interviewed by Nan Alamilla Boyd, written notes (in author's possession), San Francisco, 1 July 1997. Miss Smith's Tea Room was located at 1353 Grant Avenue. It was raided and temporarily closed in 1956. Garber, "Historical Directory," 133.

84. Cited in Garber, "Historical Directory," 133; Charlotte Coleman, interviewed by Nan Alamilla Boyd, tape recording, San Francisco, 13 July 1992, Wide Open Town History Project, GLBT Historical Society; Joseph St. Amand, interviewed by Nan Alamilla Boyd, tape recording, San Francisco, 2 August 1991, Wide Open Town History Project, GLBT Historical Society; Rikki Streicher, interviewed by Nan Alamilla Boyd, tape recording, San Francisco, 4 March 1992, Wide Open Town History Project, GLBT Historical Society.

85. The Copper Lantern was located at 133 Grant Avenue, and it ran from 1955 to 1962. Garber, "Historical Directory," 53; Rikki Streicher, interviewed by Nan Alamilla Boyd, tape recording, San Francisco, 4 March 1992, Wide Open Town History Project, GLBT Historical Society. See also "4 S.F. Bars Accused in Vice Drive," *San Francisco Examiner* (hereafter *Examiner*), 28 August 1956.

86. Garber, "Historical Directory," 7; Jane Chamberlin, *The Great and Notorious Saloons of San Francisco* (Santa Barbara: Capra Press, 1982), 86.

87. The Front was located at 600 Front Street, on the corner of Front and Jackson, in San Francisco's produce district, at the far edge of Broadway's tourist strip. According to Charlotte Coleman, the Front was "a women's bar and we had entertainment now and then. We just had beer and wine, but in those days that wasn't so bad. We had a great time down there." For a time, the Front served food, and Janet Roger ran Coleman's concession. After she quit, in late 1959, Roger opened Our Club at 1342 Pacific Street, another popular "women's bar." Charlotte Coleman, interviewed by Nan Alamilla Boyd, tape recording, San Francisco, 13 July 1992, Wide Open Town History Project, GLBT Historical Society; Ethel Whitaker, interviewed by Nan Alamilla Boyd, tape recording, San Francisco, 30 August 1992, Wide Open Town History Project, GLBT Historical Society; Marilyn Braiger, interviewed by Nan Alamilla Boyd, tape recording, Berkeley, 2 December 1991, Wide Open Town History Project, GLBT Historical Society. See also Susan Darm, "Lesbians Over 60," *Deneuve* 1, no. 3 (September/October 1991): 14–18.

88. Jennifer Terry, "Anxious Slippages between 'Us' and 'Them': A Brief History of the Scientific Search for Homosexual Bodies," David G. Horn, "This Norm Which Is Not One: Reading the Female Body in Lombroso's Anthropology," and Carol Groneman, "Nymphomania: The Historical Construction of Female Sexuality," in Jennifer Terry and Jacqueline Urla, eds., *Deviant Bodies* (Bloomington: Indiana University Press, 1995), 129–169, 109–128, 219–249. See also Lucy Bland and Laura Doan, eds., *Sexology in Culture: Labeling Bodies and Desires* (Chicago: University of Chicago Press, 1998).

89. Richard von Krafft-Ebing, "Congenital Sexual Inversion in Women," *Psychopathia Sexualis* (1886; rpt. New York: Pioneer Publications, 1953), 395–443; Havelock Ellis, "Sexual Inversion in Women," *Studies in the Psychology of Sex* (1901; rpt. New York: Random House, 1936), vol.1, pt. 4, 195–263; George W. Henry, *Sex Variants: A Study of Homosexual Patterns* (New York: Paul B. Hoeber, 1948), 730–918. See also George Chauncey, Jr., "From Sexual Inversion to Homosexuality: Medicine and the Changing Conceptualization of Female Deviance," *Salmagundi* 58–59 (Fall 1982 / Winter 1983): 114–146; Jeffrey Weeks, *Sexuality and Its Discontents* (London: Routledge and Kegan Paul, 1985), particularly his chapter on sexology, "'Nature Had Nothing to Do with It': The Role of Sexology," 61–95; Sander Gilman, "Black Bodies, White Bodies: Toward an Iconography of Female Sexuality," in Henry Louis Gates, Jr., ed., *"Race," Writing, and Difference* (Chicago: University of Chicago Press, 1985), 223.

90. Krafft-Ebing, *Psychopathia Sexualis,* 398.

91. Jess Stern, *The Grapevine* (Garden City, NY: Doubleday, 1964).

92. John O'Day, *Confessions of a Hollywood Call Girl* (Los Angeles: Sherbourne Press, 1964), 85.

93. May, *Homeward Bound.*

94. Donna Penn, "The Sexualized Woman: The Lesbian, the Prostitute, and the Containment of Female Sexuality in Postwar America," in Joanne Meyero-

witz, ed., *Not June Cleaver: Women and Gender in Postwar America, 1945–1960* (Philadelphia: Temple University Press, 1994), 358–381.

95. Important exceptions are Joan Nestle, "Lesbians and Prostitutes: An Historical Sisterhood," in *Restricted Country* (Ithaca, NY: Firebrand Books, 1987), 157–177, and the writings by lesbians in Frederique Delacoste and Priscilla Alexander, eds., *Sex Work: Writings by Women in the Sex Industry* (Pittsburgh: Cleis Press, 1987), 21–28, 62–69, 150–154.

96. Jacqueline Baker Barnhart, *The Fair but Frail: Prostitution in San Francisco, 1849–1900* (Reno: University of Nevada Press, 1986), 16.

97. Jay Monaghan, *Chile, Peru, and the California Gold Rush of 1849* (Berkeley: University of California Press, 1973).

98. White women, particularly Frenchwomen, were the highest priced prostitutes and were therefore more likely to start their own businesses. Barnhart, *Fair but Frail,* 40–56; Stephen Longstreet, *The Wilder Shore: A Gala Social History of San Francisco's Sinners and Spenders, 1849–1906* (New York: Doubleday, 1968), 271–273; Yung, *Unbound Feet,* 26–37.

99. Longstreet, *Wilder Shore,* 226–232, 256–280; Sally Stanford, *The Lady of the House* (New York: G. P. Putnam's Sons, 1966); Curt Gentry, *The Madams of San Francisco: An Irreverent History of the City by the Golden Gate* (New York: Ballantine Books, 1964).

100. Lucie Cheng Hirata, "Free, Indentured, Enslaved: Chinese Prostitutes in Nineteenth-Century America," *Signs* 5, no. 1 (Autumn 1979): 3–29.

101. White slavery, as Frederick Grittner defines it, was the entrapment of white women "by means of coercion, trick, or drugs by a non-white or non-Anglo-Saxon man for purposes of sexual exploitation." Frederick K. Grittner, *White Slavery: Myth, Ideology, and American Law* (New York: Garland Publishing, 1990), 5.

102. Ruth Rosen, *The Lost Sisterhood: Prostitution in America, 1900–1918* (Baltimore: Johns Hopkins University Press, 1982).

103. California's Red Light Abatement Act was upheld by the state's supreme court in 1917. The Barbary Coast, San Francisco's historic vice district, was shut down on 14 February 1917, when the local police blockaded the district and emptied its prostitution houses. Herbert Asbury, *The Barbary Coast: An Informal History of the San Francisco Underworld* (New York: Knopf, 1933), 299–314. See also Brenda Elaine Pillors, "The Criminalization of Prostitution in the United States: The Case of San Francisco, 1854–1919" (Ph.D. dissertation, University of California, Berkeley, 1982); Neil Larry Shumsky and Larry M. Springer, "San Francisco's Zone of Prostitution, 1880–1934," *Journal of Historical Geography* 7, no. 1 (1981), 85.

104. Reynolds, *Economics of Prostitution,* 60.

105. *Chronicle,* 13 March 1942, p. 1; 17 November 1942, p. 1; 18 November 1942, p. 9; 24 November 1942, p. 9.

106. *Chronicle* 24 November 1942, p. 9; 21 May 1954, p. 3.

107. "Straight" was a term used by both prostitutes and lesbians to mean either non-prostitutes or non-lesbians. "In the life" was also a phrase both prostitutes and lesbians, particularly lesbians of color, used to describe their partic-

ipation in either sexual subculture. Both "straight" and "in the life," initially part of a culture of sex work, have more recently emerged as part of a queer or homosexual lexicon.

108. Cavan, *Liquor License,* 200–204.

109. Cavan, *Liquor License,* 205–233; Helen Branson, *Gay Bar* (San Francisco: Pan Graphic Press, 1957).

110. Reynolds, *Economics of Prostitution,* 37, 61.

111. Gordon's Restaurant opened in 1949 and remained a popular gay nightspot until 1970. Originally opened by Gordon Jones and William Bowman, who had worked together at the Paper Doll, Gordon's changed ownership in the late 1960s. Garber, "Historical Directory," 91.

112. Charlotte Coleman, interviewed by Nan Alamilla Boyd, tape recording, San Francisco, 13 July 1992, Wide Open Town History Project, GLBT Historical Society.

113. Reba Hudson, interviewed by Nan Alamilla Boyd, tape recording, San Francisco, 29 May 1992, Wide Open Town History Project, GLBT Historical Society.

114. Herb Caen, *Chronicle,* 8 January 1961, p. 19.

115. "Eight Women Held in Raid," *Chronicle,* 16 June 1949, p. 1.

116. Charlotte Coleman, interviewed by Nan Alamilla Boyd, tape recording, San Francisco, 13 July 1992, Wide Open Town History Project, GLBT Historical Society; Marilyn Braiger, interviewed by Nan Alamilla Boyd, tape recording, Berkeley, 2 December 1991, Wide Open Town History Project, GLBT Historical Society.

117. James Sobredo, "From Manila Bay to Daly City: Filipinos in San Francisco," in James Brook, Chris Carlsson, and Nancy J. Peters, eds., *Reclaiming San Francisco: History, Politics, Culture* (San Francisco: City Lights Books, 1998), 273–286.

118. Reba Hudson, interviewed by Nan Alamilla Boyd, tape recording, San Francisco, 29 May 1992, Wide Open Town History Project, GLBT Historical Society.

119. Reba Hudson, interviewed by Nan Alamilla Boyd, tape recording, San Francisco, 29 May 1992, Wide Open Town History Project, GLBT Historical Society.

120. Reba Hudson, interviewed by Nan Alamilla Boyd, tape recording, San Francisco, 29 May 1992, Wide Open Town History Project, GLBT Historical Society.

121. Sucheta Mazumdar, "General Introduction: A Women-Centered Perspective on Asian American History," in Asian Women United of California, eds., *Making Waves: An Anthology of Writings by and about Asian American Women* (Boston: Beacon Press, 1989), 3–5.

122. Mazumdar, "General Introduction." See also Lucie Cheng Hirata, "Free, Indentured, Enslaved," 402–434; Ronald Takaki, *Strangers from a Different Shore: A History of Asian Americans* (Boston: Little-Brown, 1989).

123. For an analysis of prostitution in Honolulu during World War II, see Beth Bailey and David Farber, "Hotel Street: Prostitution and the Politics of War," *Radical History Review* 52 (1992): 52–77.

124. Nestle, "Lesbians and Prostitutes."

125. Marilyn Braiger, interviewed by Nan Alamilla Boyd, tape recording, Berkeley, 2 December 1991, Wide Open Town History Project, GLBT Historical Society.

126. Charlotte Coleman, interviewed by Nan Alamilla Boyd, tape recording, San Francisco, 13 July 1992, Wide Open Town History Project, GLBT Historical Society.

127. Cheryl Gonzales, interviewed by Nan Alamilla Boyd, tape recording, San Francisco, 2 February 1992, Wide Open Town History Project, GLBT Historical Society.

128. Reba Hudson, interviewed by Nan Alamilla Boyd, tape recording, San Francisco, 29 May 1992, Wide Open Town History Project, GLBT Historical Society; Rikki Streicher, interviewed by Nan Alamilla Boyd, tape recording, San Francisco, 22 January 1992, Wide Open Town History Project, GLBT Historical Society.

129. "San Francisco Police Raid Reveals Lack of Knowledge of Citizen's Rights," *Ladder* 1, no. 2 (November 1956): 5.

130. Del Martin and Phyllis Lyon, interviewed by Nan Alamilla Boyd, tape recording, San Francisco, 2 December 1992, Wide Open Town History Project, GLBT Historical Society.

131. John D'Emilio, *Sexual Politics, Sexual Communities: The Making of a Homosexual Minority in the United States, 1940–1970* (Chicago: University of Chicago Press, 1983), 76; Corber, *Homosexuality in Cold War America*; May, *Homeward Bound*, 94–95; Chafe, *Unfinished Journey*, 108.

132. Chamberlin, *Great and Notorious Saloons*.

133. Mildred Dickemann, interviewed by Nan Alamilla Boyd, tape recording, Richmond, CA, 18 October 1991, Wide Open Town History Project, GLBT Historical Society.

134. Ernest Lenn, "Liquor, Drug Sale at Tommy's Place Told by 2 Girls," *Examiner*, 21 December 1954, p. 1.

135. "S.F. Teen-age Girls Tell of 'Vice Academy': Youths Describe 'Recruiting' at Bar, Narcotics Parties," *Chronicle*, 10 September 1954, p. 1, and photos p. 5.

136. San Francisco Police Department, "The Organization Structure of the San Francisco Police Department and the Scope of Its Responsibility," 1952. See also William N. Eskridge, Jr., "Privacy Jurisprudence and the Apartheid of the Closet, 1946–1961," *Florida State University Law Review* 24 (1997): 703–838. For an analysis of the emergence and ideological impact of "sex crimes" in American culture, see Estelle B. Freedman, "'Uncontrolled Desires': The Response to the Sexual Psychopath, 1920–1960," *Journal of American History* 74 (1987): 83–106.

137. J. Edgar Hoover, "Warning to U.S. Teen-Agers," *This Week Magazine*, 27 October 1957, p. 10.

138. Partly in response to a statewide panic linking homosexuality to sexual violence against children, the University of California conducted a three-year study on sex crimes in California. The resulting report, summarized in *Time* magazine, concluded that in 1953 "investigators could find no evidence of a

great wave of sex crime, or that 'sex fiends' were everywhere on the prowl." The report also insisted on making a distinction between violent sex crimes and "socially offensive but nondangerous" sex offenses. *Time,* 2 March 1953, p. 42. See also Freedman, "'Uncontrolled Desires.'"

139. "Police Jail, Warn Sex Deviates in Full Scale Drive," *Examiner,* 27 June 1954, p.1; "Raids Continue on S.F. Sex Deviates," *Examiner,* 28 June 1954, p. 1.

140. "Needed: A Cleanup," *Examiner,* 28 June 1954, p. 12.

141. "Police Jail, Warn Sex Deviates in Full Scale Drive," *Examiner,* 27 June 1954, p. 1.

142. "Raids Here Lauded," *Examiner,* 29 June 1954, p. 1.

143. "Military Aids S.F. Drive on Sex Deviates," *Examiner,* 1 July 1954, p. 1. See also Ernest Lenn, "Military Agency to Clamp Down on Vice Spots," *Examiner,* 28 July 1954, p. 1; "Will Drive on Deviates Fizzle Out Again?" *Examiner,* 11 September 1954, p. 10. The military's ability to control vice in civilian areas derives from laws passed by Congress during World War II that allowed Army and Navy police to patrol and regulate the off-base recreational activities of their enlistees. For more information on wartime vice control and its aftermath, see Allan Bérubé, *Coming Out under Fire: The History of Gay Men and Women in World War Two* (New York: Free Press, 1990), 98–127.

144. Allan Bérubé also makes this point in his unpublished article "'Resorts for Sex Perverts': A Political History of Gay Bars in San Francisco," 1985 (author's copy).

145. "Grand Jury Sets Action on Vice as Probe Spreads," *Examiner,* 11 September 1954.

146. "Will Drive on Deviates Fizzle Out Again?" *Examiner,* 11 September 1954.

147. Ernest Lenn, "Sex Deviate Ring Here," *Examiner,* 24 September 1954.

148. Lenn, "Sex Deviate Ring Here," *Examiner,* 24 September 1954; "Grand Jury Sets Action on Vice as Probe Spreads," *Examiner,* 11 September 1954." See also United States Congress, Committee on the Judiciary, *Hearings before the Subcommittee to Investigate Juvenile Delinquency,* 24 and 27 September and 4–5 October 1954 (Washington, DC: U.S. Government Printing Office, 1955). See especially "Testimony of Capt. John Keily, Juvenile Bureau," 258–285, and "Testimony of Russell Wood, Patrolman," 433–440.

149. "Grand Jury Sets Action on Vice as Probe Spreads," *Examiner,* 11 September 1954."

150. "Schoolgirls' Vice, Dope Revealed in S.F. Bar Raid: Man Held as Corrupter of Youths," *Chronicle,* 9 September 1954; "S.F. Teen-age Girls Tell of 'Vice Academy': Youths Describe 'Recruiting' at Bar, Narcotics Parties," *Chronicle,* 10 September 1954.

151. "S.F. Teen-age Girls Tell of 'Vice Academy': Youths Describe 'Recruiting' at Bar, Narcotics Parties," *Chronicle,* 10 September 1954.

152. "S.F. Teen-age Girls Tell of 'Vice Academy': Youths Describe 'Recruiting' at Bar, Narcotics Parties," *Chronicle,* 10 September 1954.

153. "Bar Facing Ban in Dope, Sex Ring for Minor Girls," *Examiner,* 10 September 1954.

154. "Schoolgirls' Vice, Dope Revealed in S.F. Bar Raid: Man Held as Corrupter of Youths," *Chronicle,* 9 September 1954.

155. Although Eleanor ("Tommy") Vasu was not arrested in response to the raid on Tommy's Place, she was convicted of the unlawful sale of heroin in August 1969 and served five years at Tehachapi State Prison in Vacaville, California. California Department of Corrections, case records, in author's possession.

156. Reba Hudson, interviewed by Nan Alamilla Boyd, tape recording, San Francisco, 29 May 1992, Wide Open Town History Project, GLBT Historical Society.

157. United States Congress, Committee on the Judiciary, *Hearings before the Subcommittee to Investigate Juvenile Delinquency,* 24 and 27 September and 4–5 October 1954 (Washington, DC: U.S. Government Printing Office, 1955), 261. Ellipses added.

158. "New Arrests in Bar Drive," *San Francisco Call-Bulletin,* 11 September 1954.

159. "S.F. Vice 'At Low Ebb,' Delinquency Quiz Told," *Chronicle,* 6 October, 1954.

160. "Grand Jury Sets Action on Vice as Probe Spreads," *Examiner,* 11 September 1954; "New Arrests in Bar Drive," *San Francisco Call-Bulletin,* 11 September 1954.

161. "Senators, S.F. Jury Map Study of Delinquency," *Chronicle,* 30 September 1954, p. 5; "Drink, Vandalism Chief Teen Problems," *Chronicle,* 1 October 1954, p. 10.

162. Lenn, "Sex Deviate Ring Here," *Examiner,* 24 September 1954.

163. United States Congress, Committee on the Judiciary, *Hearings before the Subcommittee to Investigate Juvenile Delinquency,* 24 and 27 September and 4–5 October 1954 (Washington, DC: U.S. Government Printing Office, 1955), 434–435.

164. "From the Editor's Notebook . . ." San Francisco Mattachine *Newsletter,* no. 16 (September 1954).

165. Lenn, "Sex Deviate Ring Here," *Examiner,* 24 September 1954.

166. District Attorney Thomas C. Lynch, quoted in Lenn, "Sex Deviate Ring Here," *Examiner,* 24 September 1954, p. 10.

167. "Juvenile Delinquency Hearings Reveal Legality of M.S. [Mattachine Society]; Cite Liquor, Dope, Newspapers as Prime Contributing Factors," San Francisco Mattachine *Newsletter,* no. 17 (October 1954).

168. Carolyn Anspacher, "Tommy's Bar Called Perverts' Haven," *Chronicle,* 21 December 1954, p. 2.

169. "Vice Academy Boss Sentenced to San Quentin," *Chronicle,* 24 December 1954, p. 9; Reba Hudson, interviewed by Nan Alamilla Boyd, tape recording, San Francisco, 29 May 1992, Wide Open Town History Project, GLBT Historical Society.

CHAPTER 3

Epigraph: "Needed: A Cleanup," *San Francisco Examiner* (hereafter *Examiner*), 28 June 1954, p. 12.

1. Lou Rand, *Rough Trade* (Los Angeles: Argyle Books Company, 1964), 75.

2. Rand, *Rough Trade,* 48.

3. Rand, *Rough Trade,* 76.

4. Charles Wollenberg, *Golden Gate Metropolis: Perspectives on Bay Area History* (Berkeley: Institute of Governmental Studies, 1985), 243.

5. Roger W. Lotchin, "California Cities and the Hurricane of Change," *Pacific Historical Review* 63 (August 1994): 397.

6. Historian Gerald Nash argues that World War II transformed California from a colony of east coast industrial capitalism to a "burgeoning manufacturing complex" in that war jobs enabled new employment opportunities, government investments in military bases and manufacturing expanded the structural base of California's economy, and rapid population growth transformed the cultural and political institutions of the region. Marilynn S. Johnson disagrees with Nash's thesis, arguing that economic growth in cities like Richmond and Oakland was temporary, but she agrees that the social and political effects of war were profound and permanent. Roger Lotchin, on the other hand, sees little relative change in either the economic development of California's urban areas or the social and political culture of West Coast cities. War may have accelerated economic change and created a culture of local identification, but continuities far outweighed discontinuities. See Gerald Nash, *The American West Transformed: The Impact of the Second World War* (Bloomington: University of Indiana Press, 1985); Gerald Nash, *World War II and the West: Reshaping the Economy* (Lincoln: University of Nebraska Press, 1990); Marilynn S. Johnson, *The Second Gold Rush: Oakland and the East Bay in World War II* (Berkeley: University of California Press, 1993); Roger W. Lotchin, *Fortress California, 1910–1961: From Warfare to Welfare* (New York, 1992). See also Roger W. Lotchin, ed., "Special Issue: Fortress California at War: San Francisco, Los Angeles, Oakland, and San Diego, 1941–1945," *Pacific Historical Review* 63, no. 3 (August 1994).

7. Wollenberg, *Golden Gate Metropolis,* 244.

8. For a lengthy analysis of the economic impact of World War II on Bay Area industry, see Nash, *World War II and the West;* Johnson, *Second Gold Rush.*

9. Wollenberg, *Golden Gate Metropolis,* 251.

10. African American workers constituted anywhere from 10 to 40 percent of shipyard workers in the Bay Area. Alonzo Smith and Qunitard Taylor, "Racial Discrimination in the Workplace: A Study of Two West Coast Cities during the 1940s," *Journal of Ethnic Studies* 8 (1980): 42; Wollenberg, *Golden Gate Metropolis,* 248.

11. Albert Broussard, "Strange Territory, Familiar Leadership: The Impact of World War II on San Francisco's Black Community," *California History* 65 (March 1986): 18–25; Marilynn S. Johnson, "War as Watershed: The East Bay and World War Two," *Pacific Historical Review* 63, no. 3 (August 1994): 320. On Japanese relocation, see Donald Tervo Hata, Jr., and Nadine Ishitani Hata, *Japanese Americans and World War II* (St. Charles, MI: Forum Press, 1974); Roger Daniels, "The Decision to Relocate the North American Japanese: Another Look," *Pacific Historical Review* 51 (1982): 71–77.

12. Analyzing the convergence of "the city and the sword," Roger W. Lotchin argues that since 1919, when U.S. Secretary of the Navy Josephus Daniels transferred half of the naval fleet to the Pacific Coast, San Francisco had been under the influence of military policy, competing for "naval booty" with Los Angeles and San Diego. Roger W. Lotchin, "The Metropolitan-Military Complex in Comparative Perspective: San Francisco, Los Angeles, and San Diego, 1919–1941," *Journal of the West* 18 (July 1979): 19–30.

13. Allan Bérubé, "Marching to a Different Drummer: Lesbian and Gay GIs in World War II," in Martin Duberman, Martha Vicinus, and George Chauncey, Jr., eds., *Hidden from History: Reclaiming the Gay and Lesbian Past* (New York: Penguin, 1989), 383–394.

14. John D'Emilio, "Gay Politics and Community in San Francisco since World War II," in Martin Duberman, Martha Vicinus, and George Chauncey, Jr., eds., *Hidden from History: Reclaiming the Gay and Lesbian Past* (New York: Penguin, 1989), 458.

15. Allan Bérubé, *Coming Out under Fire: The History of Gay Men and Women in World War Two* (New York: Free Press, 1990), 113.

16. The *Guild Dictionary of Homosexual Terms* (Washington, DC: Guild Press, 1965) defines trade as "(n.): Generic for the male of masculine type and body build, usually heterosexual, who takes the positive, leading, inserter role in sexual relations with the homosexual, and who does not make (or may pretend so) any identification with homosexuality. (v.): TO DO FOR TRADE. Homosexual relations with any heterosexual male for the purposes of this male's sexual gratification only. Syn.: PIECE OF TRADE" (p. 45). It defines "rough trade" as "(n.): (1) Uncultured, crudely spoken male, potentially dangerous, as opposed to TRADE, which is not. (2) A heterosexual who has sex with a homosexual" (p. 39).

17. Bérubé, *Coming Out under Fire,* 117.

18. Bérubé, *Coming Out under Fire,* 126. See also John D'Emilio, *Sexual Politics, Sexual Communities: The Making of a Homosexual Minority in the United States, 1940–1970* (Chicago: University of Chicago Press, 1983), 23–33.

19. Bérubé, *Coming Out under Fire,* 121. Bérubé notes that the military only used the May Act twice during the war years, in Tennessee and North Carolina.

20. Bérubé, *Coming Out under Fire,* 121.

21. Letter from Furber M. Libby of the Armed Forces Services, 12 August 1944. Alcoholic Beverage Control Board Subject Files, California State Archives (hereafter ABC Files, CSA), F3718:343a.

22. Allan Bérubé, *Coming Out under Fire,* 123.

23. "Taverns Put 'Off Limits,'" *Examiner,* 5 July 1942, p. 6.

24. The Silver Rail was located at 972 Market Street in the Tenderloin. It was quite large, extending from its entrance on Market Street all the way to Turk Street. Eric Garber, "A Historical Directory of Lesbian and Gay Establishments in the San Francisco Bay Area," c. 1992, p. 187 (unpublished data in author's possession). See also Queer Sites Database, GLBT Historical Society.

25. The Old Adobe was owned and operated by Mark Gartman, who also owned Jack's Baths, a popular gay bathhouse. Garber, "Historical Directory," 27, 145.

26. "State Warns 50 Taverns They Must Oust 'B' Girls," 1942, GLBT Historical Society, clippings file.

27. Letters from the Joint Army-Navy Disciplinary Control Board to the Fifty Eight Club, Sea Cave Cafe, Saw Dust Inn, and Skippy's, 13 June 1945. ABC Files, CSA, F3718:341–342.

28. Letter from the State Board of Equalization to Jerome Norwitt, 23 October 1950. ABC Files, CSA, F3718:341–342.

29. Bérubé, *Coming Out under Fire,* 123–127.

30. Bérubé, *Coming Out under Fire,* 125–126.

31. "New Military Unit Ordered to Clamp Down on S.F. Bars," *Examiner,* 28 July 1954.

32. Bérubé, *Coming Out under Fire,* 261–265. See also Bérubé, "Marching to a Different Drummer"; Allan Bérubé and John D'Emilio, "The Military and Lesbians during the McCarthy Years," in Estelle B. Freedman, Barbara C. Gelpi, Susan L. Johnson, and Kathleen M. Weston, eds., *The Lesbian Issue: Essays from "Signs"* (Chicago: University of Chicago Press, 1984), 279–295; William N. Eskridge, Jr., "Privacy Jurisprudence and the Apartheid of the Closet, 1946–1961," *Florida State University Law Review* 24 (1997): 703–838.

33. Bérubé, *Coming Out under Fire,* 255.

34. Bérubé, *Coming Out under Fire,* 256. See also Leisa Meyer, *Creating GI Jane: Sexuality and Power in the Women's Army Corps during World War II* (New York: Columbia University Press, 1996), 166–168.

35. On the postwar dismissal of lesbians from the military, see Meyer, *Creating GI Jane,* 176–179.

36. Bérubé, *Coming Out under Fire,* 261.

37. Eskridge, "Privacy Jurisprudence," 737–38. The military's 1949 policy classified homosexuals into three levels of crime and punishment: 1) Those who engaged in coercive sex or sex with minors would be court-martialed; 2) those who engaged in homosexual acts would be given dishonorable discharges; and 3) those who confessed homosexual tendencies would be retained or discharged at the recommendation of the personnel board.

38. Even though the raw numbers of undesirable discharges were higher during wartime, the percentage of GIs discharged for homosexuality tripled in the 1950s. Bérubé, *Coming Out under Fire,* 262.

39. Bérubé, *Coming Out under Fire,* 264.

40. Robert J. Corber, *Homosexuality in Cold War America: Resistance and the Crisis of Masculinity* (Durham: Duke University Press, 1997), 8. On HUAC and the culture of McCarthyism, see Ellen Schrencker, *Many Are the Crimes: McCarthyism in America* (Princeton, NJ: Princeton University Press, 1998).

41. Subcommittee on Investigations of the Senate Committee on Expenditures in the Executive Department, "Interim Report: Employment of Homosexuals and Other Sex Perverts in Government," 8 (1950). Cited in Eskridge, "Privacy Jurisprudence," 738–739.

42. Cited in Eskridge, "Privacy Jurisprudence," 738–739.

43. Gerard Sullivan, "Political Opportunism and the Harassment of Homosexuals in Florida, 1952–1965," *Journal of Homosexuality* 37, no. 4 (1999): 58–59.

44. Eskridge, "Privacy Jurisprudence," 742.

45. Minutes, Senior Armed Forces Disciplinary Control Board meeting, 23 May 1951. ABC Files, CSA, F3718:341–342.

46. Minutes, Senior Armed Forces Disciplinary Control Board meeting, 23 May 1951, p. 9. ABC Files, CSA, F3718:341–342.

47. Minutes, Senior Armed Forces Disciplinary Control Board meeting, 23 May 1951, p. 13. ABC Files, CSA, F3718:341–342.

48. On the function of gender in cold war America, see Elaine Tyler May, *Homeward Bound: American Families in the Cold War Era* (New York: Basic Books, 1988). See also Joanne Meyerowitz, ed., *Not June Cleaver: Women and Gender in Postwar America, 1945–1960* (Philadelphia: Temple University Press, 1994); Corber, *Homosexuality in Cold War America.*

49. On women workers fired after the war, see Sherna Berger Gluck, *Rosie the Riveter Revisited: Women, the War, and Social Change* (Boston: Twayne Publishers, 1987); Karen Tucker Anderson, "Last Hired, First Fired: Black Women Workers during World War II," *Journal of American History* 69, no. 1 (1982): 82–97. On the role of women in the military, see Meyer, *Creating GI Jane;* Bérubé, *Coming Out under Fire.*

50. Meyer, *Creating GI Jane,* 148–178.

51. Bérubé and D'Emilio, "The Military and Lesbians during the McCarthy Years," 280.

52. Bérubé, *Coming Out under Fire* 262; Bérubé and D'Emilio, "The Military and Lesbians during the McCarthy Years," 280.

53. In 1944 Congress passed the Serviceman's Readjustment Act, which entitled World War II veterans to benefits that included federally subsidized home loans, college loans, farm and business loans, unemployment benefits including allowances and training and placement, burial allowances, subsidized life insurance, disability pensions, and hospital care including physical rehabilitation. Bérubé, *Coming Out under Fire,* 229–230.

54. D'Emilio, "Gay Politics and Community in San Francisco," 456–473.

55. Sullivan, "Political Opportunism and the Harassment of Homosexuals." See also Eskridge, "Privacy Jurisprudence," 727–733.

56. "Sad Day on Montgomery Street," *San Francisco Chronicle* (hereafter *Chronicle*), 15 October 1949, p. 9.

57. Joan W. Howarth, "First and Last Chance: Looking for Lesbians in Fifties Bar Cases," *Review of Law and Women's Studies* 5 (1995): 155.

58. Quoted in Arthur S. Leonard, "The Gay Bar and the Right to Hang Out Together," in *Sexuality and the Law: An Encyclopedia of Major Legal Cases* (New York: Garland Publishing, 1993), 191.

59. *Stoumen v. Reilly* 234 P.2d 969 (Cal. 1951). See also Howarth, "First and Last Chance," 155.

60. *Stoumen v. Reilly* 234 P.2d 969 (Cal. 1951); Ernest Lenn, "Police War on Dives," *Examiner,* 4 August 1954, p. 1; Howarth, "First and Last Chance," 155.

61. *Stoumen v. Reilly* 234 P.2d 969 (Cal. 1951).

62. Leonard, "The Gay Bar," 191–195.

63. The distinction between homosexuality as a state of being (status) and

homosexuality as an act (conduct) led to tricky legal territory, as Joan W. Howarth argues: "As soon as the lesbian has done anything to identify herself as a lesbian, that conduct strips her of her pure identity as a human being and marks her as immoral and unfit." See Howarth, "First and Last Chance," 170. See also William Eskridge, "Privacy Jurisprudence."

64. Minutes, Senior Armed Forces Disciplinary Control Board, 23 May 1951, p. 8. ABC Files, CSA, F3718:341–342.

65. Most notably, see D'Emilio, *Sexual Politics,* 177–182. See also Catherine Stimpson, "The Beat Generation and the Trials of Homosexual Liberation," *Salmagundi* 58–59 (Fall 1982 / Winter 1983): 373–392. Stimpson argues that the Beats were the incarnation of Donald Webster Cory's 1951 call for leadership in the public assertion of a homosexual minority. "Until the world is able to accept us on an equal basis as human beings entitled to the full rights of life," Cory argued, "we are unlikely to have any great numbers willing to become martyrs by carrying the burden of the cross." Donald Webster Cory, *The Homosexual in America: A Subjective Approach* (New York: Greenberg, Publishers, 1951), p. 14. Stimpson theorizes that the Beat poets, in their writings about sex and sexuality, valorized the homosexual as a rebel and proclaimed the legitimacy of unconventional desire. The Beats, she argues, helped "generate a reinterpretation of homosexuality" by "creating a community of naming that stripped censored materials of some of the psychic burdens; brought those materials into public speech; and cheered what public speech had previously reviled" (Stimpson, "Beat Generation," 390–391).

66. Stimpson, "Beat Generation," 377. An example from Jack Kerouac, *On the Road:* "The car belonged to a tall, thin fag who was on his way home to Kansas and wore dark glasses and drove with extreme care; the car was what Dean called a 'fag Plymouth,' it had no pickup and no real power. 'Effeminate car!' whispered Dean in my ear." Cited in Oliver Harris, "Queer Shoulders, Queer Wheel: Homosexuality and Beat Textual Politics," in Cornelis A. Van Minnen, Jaap van der Bent, and Mel van Elteren, eds., *Beat Culture: The 1950s and Beyond* (Amsterdam: VU University Press, 1999), 233–237.

67. Harris, "Queer Shoulders, Queer Wheel."

68. For an overview of Beat culture, community, and writings, see Steven Watson, *The Birth of the Beat Generation: Visionaries, Rebels, and Hipsters, 1944–1960* (New York: Pantheon Books, 1995); Nancy J. Peters, "The Beat Generation and San Francisco's Culture of Dissent," in James Brook, Chris Carlsson, and Nancy J. Peters, eds., *Reclaiming San Francisco: History, Politics, Culture* (San Francisco: City Lights Books, 1998), 199–216.

69. D'Emilio, *Sexual Politics,* 181. Much has been published on the censorship of Ginsberg's *Howl.* For a journalistic account from the period, see "Trade Winds," *Saturday Review* 40 (October 1957); "Big Day for Bards at Bay," *Life* 43 (9 September 1957): 105–108. See also Watson, *Birth of the Beat Generation,* 251–253.

70. Allan Ginsberg, *Howl,* in Ann Charters, ed., *The Portable Beat Reader* (New York: Viking Press, 1992), 64.

71. Allan Brown, "Life and Love Among the Beatniks," *Chronicle,* 15 June 1958, p. 4.

72. Marilyn Braiger, interviewed by Nan Alamilla Boyd, tape recording, Berkeley, 2 December 1991, Wide Open Town History Project, GLBT Historical Society.

73. George Mendenhall, interviewed by Nan Alamilla Boyd, tape recording, San Francisco, 13 November 1991, Wide Open Town History Project, GLBT Historical Society.

74. Gerald Belchick, interviewed by Nan Alamilla Boyd, tape recording, San Francisco, 23 July 1991, Wide Open Town History Project, GLBT Historical Society.

75. Rickie Streicher, interviewed by Nan Alamilla Boyd, tape recording, San Francisco, 22 January 1992, Wide Open Town History Project, GLBT Historical Society. The phrase "lesbian bar" became more common in the 1960s.

76. Burt Gerrits, interviewed by Allan Bérubé, tape recording, San Francisco, 9 February 1980, World War II Project Records, GLBT Historical Society.

77. Guy Strait, "What Is a 'Gay Bar'?" *Citizens News* 4, no. 5 (December 1964): 6–7. On the development of a queer lexicon, see *The Guild Directory of Homosexual Terms,* which defines "ki ki" as "[a] homosexual who desires sexual relations exclusively with homosexuals of his own type and proclivity" (p. 26).

78. Nancy Achilles, "The Development of the Homosexual Bar as an Institution," in John H. Gagnon and William Simon, eds., *Sexual Deviance* (New York: Harper and Row, 1967), 233–239.

79. According to court testimony, a Paper Doll bartender warned a patron (who later turned out to be an undercover cop) not to go outside with a person suspected of being an undercover cop. "The bartender said that several arrests had been made the night before; it would be all right as long as he [the patron] did not leave the premises." *Benedetti v. Dept. Alcoholic Beverage Control* 187 Cal. App. 2d 213 (1960); 9 *California Reporter,* 525.

80. Pat Bond, interviewed by Allan Bérubé, tape recording, San Francisco, 18 May 1981, World War II Project Records, GLBT Historical Society.

81. In the post-*Stoumen* era, the behaviors that rendered gay bar-goers subject to arrest expanded beyond the fact of assembly and began to include behaviors such as physical gestures, touching, and speech. Sexualized speech, common in all bars, soon became evidence of lewd and thus deviant behavior, and conversations that suggested sexual attraction or desire became grounds for suspicion and potential arrest.

82. Pat Bond, interviewed by Allan Bérubé, tape recording, San Francisco, 18 May 1981, World War II Project Records, GLBT Historical Society.

83. Joe Baron (pseud.), interviewed by Nan Alamilla Boyd, tape recording, San Francisco, 24 August 1991, Wide Open Town History Project, GLBT Historical Society.

84. In testimony at a liquor board hearing, an ABC agent described the Handlebar, a gay bar on California Street that ran from 1956 to 1961, as having "a sort of curtain hanging, shielding the door from the premises when you enter. Then you have a bar along the west side of the wall as you enter the premises on your left. And then there is another bar located at the east side of the

premises towards the rear." *Orrin v. Alcoholic Beverage Control Appeals Board, et al.* ABC Files, CSA, F3718:391.

85. Pat Healey and Ruth Frederick, interviewed by Nan Alamilla Boyd, tape recording, Sebastopol, CA, 23 June 1992, Wide Open Town History Project, GLBT Historical Society.

86. Barbara Weightman, "Gay Bars as Private Places," *Landscape* 24, no. 1 (1980): 10.

87. See Leonard, "The Gay Bar"; Howarth, "First and Last Chance"; Eskridge, "Privacy Jurisprudence."

88. Minutes, Senior Armed Forces Disciplinary Control Board meeting, 23 May 1951, pp. 8, 11. ABC Files, CSA, F3718:341–342.

89. "State Agents Crackdown on Late Clubs," *Examiner,* 30 September 1954, p. 1.

90. Letters between Col. C. V. Cadwell, Chairman of the Senior Armed Forces Disciplinary Control Board, and George M. Stout, A. Whitaker, and E. J. Clark, State Liquor Administrators, California State Board of Equalization, 4 April 1951, 11 April 1951, 23 April 1951, 23 April 1951, 17 August 1951; letter from Lt. Col. Franklin E. Winnie, Armed Forces Disciplinary Control Board, to E. J. Clark, 4 September 1951. ABC Files, CSA, F3718:341–342.

91. Internal memo from Don Marshall, San Francisco District Liquor Control Administrator, State Board of Equalization, to E. J. Clark, Senior Armed Forces Disciplinary Control Board, San Francisco, 8 January 1952. ABC Files, CSA F3718:341–342.

92. "S.F. Vice 'At Low Ebb,' Delinquency Quiz Told," *Chronicle,* 6 October 1954.

93. The Board reviewed only 1,318 liquor-related offenses in fiscal year 1952–1953, for the entire state of California, and of that total, 908 licenses were suspended, 64 revoked, and 346 cases were dismissed. "Disposition by the Board of Charges of Violations of the Alcoholic Beverage Control Act against Alcoholic Beverage Licenses, by Nature of Charge, 1952–53," *Annual Report of the State Board of Equalization* (Sacramento, 30 June 1953).

94. Letter from Don Marshall, San Francisco District Liquor Control Administrator, State Board of Equalization, to E. J. Clark, Senior Armed Forces Disciplinary Control Board, San Francisco, 14 December 1954. ABC Files, CSA F3718:341–342.

95. Eskridge, "Privacy Jurisprudence," 766–771.

96. Fred C. Franke, ABC Special Agent, Supplemental Report on the Senior Armed Forces Disciplinary Control Board meeting, 30 March 1955. ABC Files, CSA, F3718:341–342.

97. Burt Gerrits, interviewed by Allan Bérubé, tape recording, San Francisco, 9 February 1980, World War II Project Records, GLBT Historical Society.

98. Henry Diekow (Baroness Von Dieckoff), "Bag-a-Drag by the Bay," 31 July 1952, Dieckoff Papers, GLBT Historical Society.

99. Burt Gerrits, interviewed by Allan Bérubé, tape recording, San Francisco, 9 February 1980, World War II Project Records, GLBT Historical Society. Despite the misogynistic tone of the bar's humor, the Beige Room was also popular with lesbians, and women on leave from military service often found their

way to the Beige Room for Sunday afternoon dances. Pat Healey and Ruth Frederick, interviewed by Nan Alamilla Boyd, tape recording, Sebastopol, CA, 23 June 1992, Wide Open Town History Project, GLBT Historical Society.

100. Misspellings and typos have been corrected. Grammar, punctuation, and the use of uppercase type reflect the original. Henry Diekow (Baroness Von Dieckoff), "Bag-a-Drag by the Bay," 7 June 1951, Dieckoff Papers, GLBT Historical Society.

101. Herb Caen's columns ran under a number of different titles, including "San Franciscaen," "Don't Call It Frisco," and "Baghdad-by-the-Bay."

102. "Police Jail, Warn Sex Deviates in Full Scale Drive," *Examiner,* 27 June 1954, p. 1.

103. Henry Diekow (Baroness Von Dieckoff), "Bag-a-Drag by the Bay," 15 December 1951, Dieckoff Papers, GLBT Historical Society.

104. Henry Diekow (Baroness Von Dieckoff), "Bag-a-Drag by the Bay," 31 October 1954, Dieckoff Papers, GLBT Historical Society.

105. Dante Benedetti, interviewed by Nan Alamilla Boyd, tape recording, San Francisco, 10 July 1992, Wide Open Town History Project, GLBT Historical Society. Many interviewees remember the food at the Paper Doll. It was "the best food in San Francisco," an interviewee asserts. "I'm sure if you talk to anyone they'd back me up on that." Pat Healey and Ruth Frederick, interviewed by Nan Alamilla Boyd, tape recording, Sebastopol, CA, 23 June 1992, Wide Open Town History Project, GLBT Historical Society.

106. Tom Redmon, interviewed by Len Evans, San Francisco, 17 May 1984, GLBT Historical Society; Garber, "Historical Directory," 66, 91, 153.

107. Pat Healey and Ruth Frederick, interviewed by Nan Alamilla Boyd, tape recording, Sebastopol, CA, 23 June 1992, Wide Open Town History Project, GLBT Historical Society.

108. Rikkie Streicher, interviewed by Nan Alamilla Boyd, tape recording, San Francisco, 4 March 1992, Wide Open Town History Project, GLBT Historical Society.

109. Garber, "Historical Directory," 43; Burt Gerrits, interviewed by Allan Bérubé, tape recording, San Francisco, World War II Project Records, GLBT Historical Society.

110. Charlotte Coleman, interviewed by Nan Alamilla Boyd, tape recording, San Francisco, 13 July 1992, Wide Open Town History Project, GLBT Historical Society.

111. Letter from George H. White, District Supervisor for the U.S. Treasury Department's Bureau of Narcotics, to Russell S. Munro, Director, Department of Alcoholic Beverage Control, 31 August 1955. ABC Files, CSA, F3718:291.

112. Herb Caen, quoted in Garber, "Historical Directory," 201.

113. Garber, "Historical Directory," 53.

114. "Needed: A Cleanup," *Examiner,* 28 June 1954, p. 12.

115. "Police Jail, Warn Sex Deviates in Full Scale Drive," *Examiner,* 27 June 1954, p. 1.

116. "Raids Continue on S.F. Sex Deviates," *Examiner,* 28 June 1954, p. 1.

117. "Military Aids S.F. Drive on Sex Deviates," *Examiner,* 1 July 1954, p. 1. The names and addresses of bars under investigation were printed in the

newspaper, purportedly to alert the public to stay away, but this information also advertised these places to readers interested in visiting queer nightspots. The Crystal Bowl was at 1032 Market, Lena's Burger Basket was at 1747 Post, the 1228 Club could be found at 1228 Sutter, Kip's Bar was at 70 Eddy Street, and the Rocket Club, listed as a "haven for female homosexuals," could be found at 236 Leavenworth.

118. Lenn, "Police War on Dives," *Examiner,* 4 August 1954, p. 1.

119. Lenn, "Police War on Dives," *Examiner,* 4 August 1954, p. 1. Ann Dee, who fronted Ann's 440, was also a manager of the 181 Club.

120. Garber, "Historical Directory," 147–148.

121. Ernest Lenn, "Sex Deviate Ring Here," *Examiner,* 24 September 1954; Ernest Lenn, "State Acts in S.F. Teen-Age Vice Problem," *Examiner,* 25 September 1954; Ernest Lenn, "Grand Jury to Dig into 'Teen Crime,'" *Examiner,* 28 September 1954; Ernest Lenn, "Sex Deviate Problem in S.F. Detailed," *Examiner,* 29 September 1954.

122. "Will Drive on Deviates Fizzle Out Again?" *Examiner,* 11 September 1954.

123. Letter from Russell S. Munro, Director, Department of Alcoholic Beverage Control, to California Governor Goodwin J. Knight, 20 May 1957. ABC Files, CSA, F3718:99.

124. The newly structured ABC brought English-only and citizenship requirements to the board, and it changed the name of local investigators from "officers" to "agents," perhaps reflecting the FBI-like tactics of its employees. On English-only requirements for ABC employment, see letter from Frank Fullenwider, 13 June 1955, ABC Files, CSA, F3718:46. On the requirement that liquor license holders be U.S. citizens, see letter from Bion Gregory, 20 December 1962, ABC Files, CSA, F3718:50–58. On structural changes to the organization, including the title of workers, see letter from Russell S. Munro, 11 July 1955, ABC Files, CSA, F3718:171. On the carrying of firearms, see Frank Fullenwider, memo to Russell Munro, 20 July 1956, ABC Files, CSA, F3718:161.

125. Letter from Russell S. Munro to San Francisco Mayor George Christopher, 6 February 1956, ABC Files, CSA, F3718:291; letter from Russell S. Munro to Col. George R. White of the U.S. Bureau of Narcotics, 26 August 1955, ABC Files, CSA, F3718:291; letter from Russell S. Munro to California Governor Goodwin J. Knight, 20 May 1957, ABC Files, CSA, F3718:99.

126. Ernest Lenn, "State Fights Bar Hangouts of Deviates," c. 25 May 1955, GLBT Historical Society, clippings file.

127. Frank Fullenwider, "Statement to the Press," 9 June 1955, ABC Files, CSA, F3718:111.

128. Eskridge, "Privacy Jurisprudence," 723–724.

129. Leonard, "The Gay Bar."

130. Howarth, "First and Last Chance," 157, n. 15.

131. Ernest Lenn, "Police Order Renews Drive on Sex Deviates," *Examiner,* 26 May 1955, p. 8.

132. Lenn, "Police Order Renews Drive on Sex Deviates," *Examiner,* 26 May 1955, p. 8.

133. Leonard, "The Gay Bar," 190; Eskridge, "Privacy Jurisprudence," 719–720.

134. Frank Fullenwider, memo to Russell Munro, 27 July 1956, ABC Files, CSA, F3718:161.

135. Evidence from undercover cops was less reliable if it came from a single witness, so agents worked in pairs or small groups. On procedural protections with regard to undercover cops, see Eskridge, "Privacy Jurisprudence," 785–788. According to a news article, evidence that might become important to an ABC or municipal court hearing included "men dancing with one another; men wearing lipstick; men making indecent overtures or proposals to other men; instances of degenerate acts being practiced on the premises." Lenn, "State Fights Bar Hangouts of Deviates," c. 25 May 1955, GLBT Historical Society, clippings file.

136. Testimony of Jay D. Caldis, *Orrin v. Alcoholic Beverage Control,* ABC Appeals Board Hearing, 9 January 1960, p. 9. ABC Files, CSA, F3718:391.

137. Testimony of Alexander A. Ralli, *Orrin v. Alcoholic Beverage Control,* ABC Appeals Board Hearing, 9 January 1960, p. 34. ABC Files, CSA, F3718:391.

138. Testimony of Alexander A. Ralli, *Orrin v. Alcoholic Beverage Control,* ABC Appeals Board Hearing, 9 January 1960, p. 10. ABC Files, CSA, F3718:391. Through the late 1950s, the number of arrests for sex offenses, particularly "lewd and indecent acts," showed a marked increase. "Arrests By Charge and Age," San Francisco Police Department Annual Reports, 1951–1957.

139. The Superior Court decided against Orrin, and Krueger appealed to the First District Court of Appeals, which agreed with the Superior Court's decision. The California Supreme Court denied a hearing, and the case closed in April 1961. The Handlebar's license was revoked, and the bar went out of business.

140. On the legality of undercover agents and police decoys, see Eskridge, "Privacy Jurisprudence," 785–88.

141. *Nickola v. Munro* 328 P. 2d 271 (Cal. 1958).

142. *Nickola v. Munro* 328 P. 2d 271 (Cal. 1958). See also the Reporter's Transcript for *Falvey v. Nickola,* 21 May 1956.

143. *Nickola v. Munro* 328 P. 2d 271 (Cal. 1958). See also the Reporter's Transcript for *Falvey v. Nickola,* 21 May 1956.

144. *Nickola v. Munro* 328 P. 2d 271 (Cal. 1958).

145. *Nickola v. Munro* 328 P. 2d 271 (Cal. 1958).

146. "Peninsula Raiders Net 90 at Alleged Sex Deviate Hangout," *Chronicle,* 20 February 1956, p. 3; "Sex Deviate Case—30 Forfeit Bail," *Chronicle,* 2 March 1956, p. 9.

147. Vagrancy was a catchall offense that, in this case, included citations for "being lewd and dissolute persons and committing acts outraging public decency." See Ernest Besig, "Alleged Homosexuals Victims of Lawless Mass Arrests," *ACLU News,* reprinted in *Mattachine Review* 2, 2nd special issue (March 1956): 5–6. See also "American Civil Liberties Union Acts to Appeal California's Lewd Vagrancy Law after Convictions Resulting from Mass Raids and Arrests," *Mattachine Review* 2, no. 3 (June 1956): 3–4.

148. "Peninsula Raiders Net 90 at Alleged Sex Deviate Hangout," *Chronicle,* 20 February 1956, p. 3; "Sex Deviate Case—30 Forfeit Bail," *Chronicle,* 2 March 1956, p. 9.

149. "Sharp Park Police Case on Appeal," *ACLU News* 21, no. 12 (December 1956): 4. Some judges "admonished prosecutors for trying to gain convictions on the basis of defendants' homosexual status rather than their conduct," but this was rare. "The principle that status ought not be a crime was unevenly applied in urbanized jurisdictions with large homosexual subcultures and substantial vice squads." Eskridge, "Privacy Jurisprudence," 788.

150. "Bar Appeals License Loss in 'Perversion,'" c. 15 February 1957, GLBT Historical Society, clippings file.

151. Michael Riordan, quoted in George Dorsey, *Christopher of San Francisco* (New York: Macmillan, 1962), 108. Emphasis in original.

152. Dorsey, *Christopher,* 106–120.

153. George Christopher, interviewed by Scott Bishop, tape recording, San Francisco, 6 February 1990, Scott Bishop Papers, GLBT Historical Society.

154. Dorsey, *Christopher,* 110–111.

155. On Christopher's dealings with the police department, particularly his warnings against corruption, see Scott Bishop's interview with Thomas Cahill, former San Francisco chief of police. In this interview, Cahill discusses Christopher's 1956 appointment of Police Commissioners Mellon, Bissinger, and McKinnon, who were, according to Cahill, "strictly business, strictly honest, and [with] integrity beyond question." Thomas Cahill, interviewed by Scott Bishop, tape recording, San Francisco, 8 February 1990, Scott Bishop Papers, GLBT Historical Society.

156. Dorsey, *Christopher,* 115.

157. George Christopher, quoted in Dorsey, *Christopher,* 116. Emphasis in original.

158. Stan Delaplane, "Pete McDonough," *Chronicle,* 10 July 1947, quoted in Merritt Barnes, "'Fountainhead of Corruption': Peter P. McDonough, Boss of San Francisco's Underworld," *California Historical Quarterly* 58, no. 2 (Summer 1979): 147.

159. Barnes, "'Fountainhead of Corruption,'" 142–153.

160. Roger Rapoport, *California Dreaming: The Political Odyssey of Pat and Jerry Brown* (Berkeley: Nolo Press, 1982). This citation is listed in Stephen G. Bloom, "San Francisco's Worst Kept Secret: The Untold Story of Millionaire Abortion Queen Inez Brown Burns," *Californians* 13, no. 2 (1996). On the mafia and organized crime, see E. J. Hobsbawm, "The Mafia as a Social Movement," in R. Serge Denisoff and Charles H. McCaghy, eds., *Deviance, Conflict and Criminality* (Chicago: Rand McNally & Co., 1973), 191–206.

161. *Examiner,* 11 May 1952, p. 1.

162. Stephen G. Bloom, "San Francisco's Worst Kept Secret: The Untold Story of Millionaire Abortion Queen Inez Brown Burns," *Californians* 13, no. 2 (1996).

163. Dorsey, *Christopher,* 114; Bloom, "San Francisco's Worst Kept Secret."

164. Dante Benedetti, interviewed by Nan Alamilla Boyd, tape recording,

San Francisco, 10 July 1992, Wide Open Town History Project, GLBT Historical Society.

165. Dante Benedetti, interviewed by Nan Alamilla Boyd, tape recording, San Francisco, 10 July 1992, Wide Open Town History Project, GLBT Historical Society.

166. "State Moves to Shut 4 S.F. Bars," *Examiner,* 28 August 1956, p. 27.

167. *Benedetti v. Department of Alcoholic Beverage Control,* 187 Cal. App. 2d 213 (1960); 9 *California Reporter,* 525. Evidence against the Paper Doll also included the testimony that Benedetti was knowledgeable of the fact that the Paper Doll was a gay bar. An undercover ABC agent testified that Dante Benedetti told him that the place was a "gay joint" and that he (Dante) and the cook were the only "straight" persons in the place. "Owner Says Paper Doll 'Gay' Joint," *Chronicle,* 4 December 1956, p. 22.

168. Ernest Lenn, "License Ban on Sex Deviate Bars Upheld," *Examiner,* 30 November 1957, p. 1.

169. "New Liquor Law Invalid, Bar Owner Tells Hearing," *Examiner,* 28 November 1956, p. 28; "State Closes Case against Black Cat," *Chronicle,* 30 November 1956, p. 18.

170. William Thomas, "Homosexual Rights in Bars Argued," *Chronicle,* 19 September 1957, p. 11.

171. Thomas, "Homosexual Rights in Bars Argued," *Chronicle,* 19 September 1957, p. 11.

172. The Black Cat didn't close without a party. On 31 October 1963, it staged its final Halloween party—without alcohol. "'Black Cat' Hangs On to Its Last Life," *Chronicle,* 25 October 1963, p. 3; "The Black Cat Clings to Life," *Chronicle,* 30 October 1963, p. 27; Merla Zellerbach, "Rights, Liberties and the Black Cat Closing," *Chronicle,* 30 October 1963, p. 41; Bill Yaryan, "Black Cat's Dry Halloween," *Chronicle,* 1 November 1963, p. 2; Ernest Lenn, "Hexed . . . So Black Cat Goes on Milk at Last," *Examiner,* 1 November 1963, p. 37.

CHAPTER 4

Epigraph: "Aims and Principles," *Mattachine Review* 2, special issue (January 1956).

1. *Last Call at Maud's,* directed by Paris Poirier, 1993, video. See also Kelly Anderson, "Out in the Fifties: The Daughters of Bilitis and the Politics of Identity" (M.A. thesis, Sarah Lawrence College, 1994), 27.

2. *Last Call at Maud's.*

3. Rikki Streicher, interviewed by Nan Alamilla Boyd, tape recording, San Francisco, 22 January 1992, Wide Open Town History Project, GLBT Historical Society.

4. Rikki Streicher, interviewed by Nan Alamilla Boyd, tape recording, San Francisco, 22 January 1992, Wide Open Town History Project, GLBT Historical Society.

5. Marc Stein makes a similar argument about the "strategies of respect-

ability" deployed by Philadelphia homophiles in the 1960s. See *City of Sisterly and Brotherly Loves: Lesbian and Gay Philadelphia, 1945–1972* (Chicago: University of Chicago Press, 2000), 211–219.

6. The Mattachine Society was founded in Los Angeles in 1950, but by 1953 its original leadership had collapsed and the organization began to shift its headquarters to San Francisco. Martin Meeker notes that the society's headquarters shifted between 1953 and 1957, but I set the date of transition somewhat sooner, in 1955, when the Mattachine Society in San Francisco began publishing the *Mattachine Review*. Meeker, "Behind the Mask of Respectability: Reconsidering the Mattachine Society and Male Homophile Practice, 1950s and 1960s," *Journal of the History of Sexuality* 10, no. 1 (January 2001): 79.

7. I use the term "mainstream society" interchangeably with "middle-class culture" and "dominant society" to denote the social, legal, and political system that privileged or enfranchised race- and class-specific social groups (specifically, native-born U.S. citizens of white European descent) in the United States during the post–World War II era.

8. John D'Emilio argues that the founding of Mattachine marks the beginning of an unbroken chain of homosexual organizing in the United States. D'Emilio, *Sexual Politics, Sexual Communities: The Making of a Homosexual Minority in the United States, 1940–1970* (Chicago: University of Chicago Press, 1983), 58. Stuart Timmons notes that at least Harry Hay and perhaps other founding members of the Mattachine Society had heard of the Chicago Society for Human Rights, a short-lived homosexual emancipation organization that petitioned the state of Illinois for a nonprofit charter in December 1924. Although it is not clear that Hay's knowledge of the Chicago Society for Human Rights influenced his founding of the Mattachine Society, this information connects the two organizations and suggests that an unbroken chain of homosexual organizing in the United States may extend back to the 1920s. Timmons, *The Trouble with Harry Hay, Founder of the Modern Gay Movement* (Boston: Alyson, 1990), 145. For more information about the Chicago Society for Human Rights, see Jonathan Katz, *Gay American History* (New York: Crowell Company, 1976), 385–397.

9. There are notable exceptions, of course. In the lesbian pulp genre, Gale Wilhelm, Valerie Taylor, and Paula Christian produced a number of novels that either challenged the typical pulp genre representation of lesbianism or interjected important information about lesbian or gay community issues into their texts. Gale Wilhelm, *We Too Are Drifting* (New York: Lion Books, 1951) and *The Strange Path* (New York: Berkley Publishing, c. 1938; originally published as *Torchlight to Valhalla*); Paula Christian, *Edge of Twilight* (Greenwich, CT: Fawcett Publications, 1959) and *Another Kind of Love,* (Greenwich, CT: Fawcett Publications, 1961); Valerie Taylor, *Whisper Their Love* (Greenwich, CT: Fawcett Publications, c. 1957) and *Journey to Fulfillment* (New York: Tower Publications, 1964). See also Michèle Aina Barale, "When Jack Blinks: Si(gh)ting Gay Desire in Ann Bannon's *Beebo Brinker,*" in Henry Abelove, Michèle Aina Barale, and David Halperin, eds., *The Lesbian and Gay Studies Reader* (New York: Routledge, 1993), 604–615.

10. "The state" operated as a complex web of social, cultural, legal, and political structures that enforced or regulated individual and group behavior through both repressive practices (i.e., police action) and non-repressive or ideological practices (i.e., education, art, religion). See Louis Althusser, "Ideology and Ideological State Apparatuses," in *Lenin and Philosophy* (New York: Monthly Review, 1972); see also Stuart Hall, "Culture, the Media and the 'Ideological Effect,'" in James Curran, Michael Gurevitch, and Janet Woollacott, eds., *Mass Communication and Society* (London: Open University Press, 1977); Stuart Hall, "Race, Articulation and Societies Structured in Dominance," in UNESCO, ed., *Sociological Theories: Race and Colonialism* (Paris: UNESCO, 1980).

11. Jürgen Habermas, "The Public Sphere," in Chandra Mukerji and Michael Schudson, eds., *Rethinking Popular Culture: Contemporary Perspectives in Cultural Studies* (Berkeley: University of California Press, 1991), 389–404.

12. R. S. Rood, M.D., "Atascadero State Hospital," *Mattachine Review* 1, no. 3 (May/June 1955): 10–11.

13. Don Jackson, "Dachau for Queers," in Len Richmond and Gary Noguera, eds., *The Gay Liberation Book* (San Francisco: Ramparts Press, 1973), 42–49; William N. Eskridge, Jr., "Privacy Jurisprudence and the Apartheid of the Closet, 1946–1961," *Florida State University Law Review* 24 (1997): 716. See also Estelle B. Freedman, "'Uncontrolled Desires': The Response to the Sexual Psychopath, 1920–1960," *Journal of American History* 74 (1987): 83–106.

14. On homosexuals in the military during World War II, see Allan Bérubé, *Coming Out Under Fire: The History of Gay Men and Women in World War Two* (New York: Free Press, 1990). For a mid-1950s account of the discharge of homosexuals from State Department jobs, see "Fair Employment Practices and the HOMOSEXUAL," *Mattachine Review* 2, no. 2 (April 1956): 41–42. For a much more thorough account of postwar municipal, state, and federal policy toward homosexuals, see Eskridge, "Privacy Jurisprudence," 703–838.

15. For a discussion of discursive space, see George Lipsitz, *Time Passages* (Minneapolis: University of Minnesota Press, 1990), 99–109.

16. As for the "privacy" of homes, homosexuals enjoyed no such privilege. The illegality of same-sex activity rendered homosexuals subject to heightened levels of police and state scrutiny. See Eskridge, "Privacy Jurisprudence."

17. Maurice Leznoff and William A. Westley, "The Homosexual Community," *Social Problems* 3 (1956): 257–63.

18. Timmons, *The Trouble with Harry Hay,* 95–138; D'Emilio, *Sexual Politics,* 58–61.

19. D'Emilio, *Sexual Politics,* 65.

20. D'Emilio, *Sexual Politics,* 75–87; Eric Marcus, *Making History: The Struggle for Gay and Lesbian Equal Rights, 1945–1990* (New York: HarperCollins, 1992), 34–36, 62–63; Timmons, *The Trouble with Harry Hay,* 172–180. See also "A Brief History of the Mattachine Society," *Mattachine Review* 1, no. 2 (March/April 1955): 39.

21. D'Emilio, *Sexual Politics,* 78–80.

22. Harry Hay, Chuck Rowland, and Bob Hull resigned for different reasons. Rowland claims that the newly structured Mattachine was unworkable, while Hay and Hull, because of their CP affiliations, knew that Mattachine could not risk an investigation. See Timmons, *The Trouble with Harry Hay,* 177–179; Marcus, *Making History,* 35–36.

23. D'Emilio, *Sexual Politics,* 75–87; Timmons, *The Trouble with Harry Hay,* 172–180; Marcus, *Making History,* 34–35, 59–69. Hal Call, interviewed by Nan Alamilla Boyd, tape recording, San Francisco, 14 August 1992, Wide Open Town History Project, GLBT Historical Society. For a biographical sketch of Hal Call, see "Faces Behind the Names," *Mattachine Review* 4, no. 6 (June 1958): 28–29.

24. "A 'Do-It-Yourself' Kit for Organizational Publications," *Mattachine Review* 2, special issue (January 1956): 5–9; Meeker, "Behind the Mask," 101–105.

25. Call's pseudonyms included Wes Knight and John Logan. Hal Call, interviewed by Nan Alamilla Boyd, tape recording, San Francisco, 14 August 1992, Wide Open Town History Project, GLBT Historical Society.

26. Hal Call, interviewed by Nan Alamilla Boyd, tape recording, San Francisco, 14 August 1992, Wide Open Town History Project, GLBT Historical Society.

27. "A 'Do-It-Yourself' Kit for Organizational Publications," *Mattachine Review* 2, special issue (January 1956): 6.

28. Hal Call, interviewed by Nan Alamilla Boyd, tape recording, San Francisco, 14 August 1992, Wide Open Town History Project, GLBT Historical Society.

29. "Aims and Principles," *Mattachine Review* 2, special issue (January 1956): 12–13.

30. "Aims and Principles," *Mattachine Review* 2, special issue (January 1956): 12–13; "Daughters of Bilitis—Purpose," *Ladder* 1, no. 1 (October 1956): 4.

31. The Daughters of Bilitis and the Mattachine Society commonly referred to homosexuals as "sex variants" or simply "variants," positioning homosexuals "as a variation on the Kinsey scale of human sexuality." See Phyllis Lyon and Del Martin, "Reminiscences of Two Female Homophiles," in Ginny Vida, ed., *Our Right to Love: A Lesbian Resource Book* (Englewood Cliffs, NJ: Prentice-Hall, 1978), 126.

32. Del Martin uses the terms "white collar" and "blue collar" in her description of the formation of the Daughters of Bilitis. Del Martin and Phyllis Lyon, interviewed by Nan Alamilla Boyd, tape recording, San Francisco, 2 December 1992, Wide Open Town History Project, GLBT Historical Society. See also Kelly Anderson, "Out in the Fifties," where she notes that the eight original members included "two white lesbian mothers, one Chicana, one Filipina, two white working-class lesbians, and two white 'pink-collar' lesbians" (p. 7).

33. Del Martin and Phyllis Lyon, interviewed by Nan Alamilla Boyd, tape recording, San Francisco, 2 December 1992, Wide Open Town History Project, GLBT Historical Society. Del Martin describes the formation of the Daughters

of Bilitis as a kind of "privatization" of the lesbian community and as an alternative to bars.

34. For more information on Pierre Louÿs's poetry and its uses by the Daughters of Bilitis, see Gretchen Schultz, "Daughters of Bilitis: Literary Genealogy and Lesbian Authenticity," *GLQ: A Journal of Lesbian and Gay Studies* 7, no. 3 (2001): 377–389.

35. Minutes, San Francisco Chapter of the Daughters of Bilitis, 21 September 1955 and 2 October 1955, Lyon-Martin Papers, GLBT Historical Society.

36. Minutes, San Francisco Chapter of the Daughters of Bilitis, 9 November 1955, Lyon-Martin Papers, GLBT Historical Society.

37. ONE, Inc. was an off-shoot of the original Mattachine Society. Initially founded as the publications arm of Mattachine, it grew into an educational institute and, later, an archive for homophile activities. Several of Mattachine's founding members joined ONE when Mattachine–Los Angeles disintegrated and shifted its focus to San Francisco.

38. Lisa Ben wrote and distributed nine issues of *Vice Versa* in 1947 and 1948, and although *The Ladder* reprinted several pieces from *Vice Versa* no direct relationship existed between the two journals. Del Martin and Phyllis Lyon, interviewed by Nan Alamilla Boyd, tape recording, San Francisco, 2 December 1992, Wide Open Town History Project, GLBT Historical Society; Katz, *Gay American History,* 336, 635; Marcus, *Making History,* 5–15; D'Emilio, *Sexual Politics,* 101–107.

39. Manuela Soares, "The Purloined *Ladder:* Its Place in Lesbian History," *Journal of Homosexuality* 34, no. 3–4 (1998): 27–49.

40. Del Martin and Phyllis Lyon, interviewed by Nan Alamilla Boyd, tape recording, San Francisco, 2 December 1992, Wide Open Town History Project, GLBT Historical Society.

41. Minutes, San Francisco Chapter of the Daughters of Bilitis, 19 October 1955, Lyon-Martin Papers, GLBT Historical Society.

42. This information is from the Daughters of Bilitis' statement of purpose, which was published on page 1 of every issue of *The Ladder.*

43. Minutes, San Francisco Chapter of the Daughters of Bilitis, 4 January 1956, Lyon-Martin Papers, GLBT Historical Society.

44. San Francisco Mattachine *Newsletter,* no. 7 (December 1953); no. 14 (July 1954); no. 27 (August 1955); no. 50 (July 1957).

45. "They See How Mattachine Works," San Francisco Mattachine *Newsletter,* no. 50 (July 1957).

46. San Francisco Mattachine *Newsletter,* no. 30 (November 1955); *Mattachine Review* 1, no. 3 (May/June 1955): 19.

47. Minutes, San Francisco Chapter of the Daughters of Bilitis, 30 July 1957, Lyon-Martin Papers, GLBT Historical Society.

48. Eskridge, "Privacy Jurisprudence," 759–761.

49. "Censorship of the Newsstands," San Francisco Area Council *Newsletter* 79 (December 1959).

50. Curtis Dewees, "On the Suppression of Homosexual Literature," *Mattachine Review* 4, no. 8 (August 1958): 14–16; "Editorial: Perversion of Free-

dom," *Ladder* 5, no. 2 (November 1960): 4–5. For a longer discussion of the Mattachine Society's anti-censorship activism, see Meeker, "Behind the Mask," 100–105.

51. "Censorship vs. Sex Study," *Ladder* 2, no. 7 (April 1958): 14–15; "Editorial: The Curse of Censorship," *Ladder* 4, no. 4 (January 1960): 4.

52. Marvin Cutler, ed., *Homosexuals Today: A Handbook of Organizations and Publications* (Los Angeles: ONE, 1956), 22.

53. Cutler, *Homosexuals Today,* 25–29.

54. "Let's Kill Idle Rumors about Mattachine Aims. . ." *Mattachine Review* 1, no. 3 (May/June 1955): back cover.

55. "A Report from the Legal Director, Mattachine Society," San Francisco Mattachine *Newsletter,* no. 31 (December 1955).

56. Eskridge, "Privacy Jurisprudence," 707.

57. In 1958, Del Martin cheered a front-page article on homosexuality in the *San Francisco Chronicle.* Del Martin, "Public Press Goes Wild!" *Ladder* 3, no. 2 (November 1958): 6–7. On Mattachine Society investments in public visibility, see Meeker, "Behind the Mask."

58. Eskridge, "Privacy Jurisprudence," 755; D'Emilio, *Sexual Politics,* 124; Hal Call, interviewed by Nan Alamilla Boyd, tape recording, San Francisco, 14 August 1992, Wide Open Town History Project, GLBT Historical Society.

59. Eskridge, "Privacy Jurisprudence," 716–717.

60. In 1958, Section 290 of the State of California Penal Code was challenged in the State District Court of Appeal. Section 290 required that convicted sex offenders register with police any change of address. The challenge, led by attorney Kenneth Zwerin, clarified that sex offenders who failed to register a change of address would not be tried for a public offense if they had successfully finished their probation. "Sex Law Clarified," *Ladder* 2, no. 9 (June 1958): 20. For more on the "sex crimes panic" of the postwar era, see Freedman, "'Uncontrolled Desires.'"

61. Meeker also argues that the Mattachine Society should not be characterized as an organization hostile to or alienated from bar culture, but its support of bar culture, as Meeker documents, was minimal through the 1950s. Indeed, during this period the only significant support the Mattachine Society lent to bar-based cultures was the printing services it provided to Morris Lowenthal, attorney for the Black Cat. It was not until the late 1950s and early 1960s that the Mattachine Society began to cooperate more fully with bar-based activists and infuse energy into bar culture. Meeker, "Behind the Mask."

62. Eskridge, "Privacy Jurisprudence," 771. See also Roxanna Sweet, "Political and Social Action in Homophile Organizations" (D. Criminology diss., University of California, Berkeley, 1968).

63. Lyon and Martin, "Reminiscences," 126.

64. Luther Allen, "Morality v. the Mores," *Mattachine Review* 2, no. 4 (August 1956): 28–31. See also Luther Allen, "Homosexuality, Morality and Religion," *Mattachine Review* 2, no. 1 (February 1956) and 2, no. 3 (June 1956).

65. Over time, the dialogue between homophile activists and ministers dropped the language of sexuality and focused on the issue of civil rights. As a

result, ministers became much more important to homophile activism. In the mid-1960s, for example, the homophile-inspired Council on Religion and the Homosexual, which included a handful of prominent San Francisco ministers, spearheaded a campaign against police harassment. See Sweet, "Political and Social Action."

66. "Aims and Principles," *Mattachine Review* 2, special issue (January 1956); "Daughters of Bilitis—Purpose," *Ladder* 1, no. 1 (October 1956). For a discussion of the similarities between DOB and Mattachine goals and principles from the perspective of the Mattachine Society, see "Where Are We Headed?" San Francisco Mattachine *Newsletter,* no. 58 (March 1958): 2–9.

67. In the minutes of the San Francisco chapter of the Daughters of Bilitis, the word "lesbian" makes its first appearance in November of 1955. Prior to that time, the recording secretary used the words "gay," "deviate," and "variant" to describe the group's members and function.

68. Del Martin and Phyllis Lyon, interviewed by Nan Alamilla Boyd, tape recording, San Francisco, 2 December 1992, Wide Open Town History Project, GLBT Historical Society.

69. Del Martin and Phyllis Lyon, interviewed by Nan Alamilla Boyd, tape recording, San Francisco, 2 December 1992, Wide Open Town History Project, GLBT Historical Society.

70. The Board of Directors of the Daughters of Bilitis decided in February 1956 to make an anti-communist statement in its printed material, but this language was never incorporated into the organization's Statement of Purpose. Minutes, San Francisco Chapter of the Daughters of Bilitis, 29 February 1956, Lyon-Martin Papers, GLBT Historical Society.

71. "Aims and Principles," *Mattachine Review* 2, special issue (January 1956).

72. "Daughters of Bilitis—Purpose," *Ladder* 1, no. 1 (October 1956).

73. Phyllis Gorman, "The Daughters of Bilitis: A Description and Analysis of a Female Homophile Social Movement Organization, 1955–63" (M.A. thesis, Ohio State University, 1985), 6, 54.

74. Phyllis Gorman, "Daughters of Bilitis," 49. In the tradition of DOB publications and correspondence, Gorman capitalizes the word "lesbian."

75. For a discussion of the evolution of sexological understandings of same-sex sexual relations, particularly its relation to the concept of gender inversion, see Jeffrey Weeks, *Sexuality and Its Discontents* (London: Routledge and Kegan Paul, 1985), 61–126; George Chauncey, "From Sexual Inversion to Homosexuality: Medicine and the Changing Conceptualization of Female Deviance," *Salmagundi* 58–59 (Fall 1982 / Winter 1983): 114–146. See also Lucy Bland and Laura Doan, eds., *Sexology in Culture: Labeling Bodies and Desires* (Chicago: University of Chicago Press, 1998).

76. George Chauncey, *Gay New York: Gender, Urban Culture and the Making of the Gay Male World, 1890–1940* (New York: Basic Books, 1994).

77. Esther Newton, "The Mythic Mannish Lesbian: Radclyffe Hall and the New Woman," *Signs* 9, no. 4 (Summer 1984); J. R. Roberts, "In America They Call Us Dykes," *Sinister Wisdom* (1978): 3–11.

78. Sweet, "Political and Social Action," 61–65, 90–92, 223.

79. For a late-1970s explanation of early DOB organizational strategies, see Lyon and Martin, "Reminiscences," 124–128.

80. "Aims and Principles," *Mattachine Review* 2, special issue (January 1956); "Daughters of Bilitis—Purpose," *Ladder* 1, no. 1 (October 1956).

81. D. Griffin (pseud. Del Martin), "The President's Message," *Ladder* 1, no. 2 (November 1956): 2.

82. Barbara Stephens, "Transvestism—A Cross-cultural Survey," *Ladder* 1, no. 9 (June 1957): 10–14.

83. B.S., San Leandro, "Readers Respond," *Ladder* 1, no. 10 (July 1957): 28–29.

84. Betty Simmons, "On Accepting Femininity," *Ladder* 2, no. 2 (November 1957): 12–13.

85. Mildred Dickemann, interviewed by Nan Alamilla Boyd, tape recording, Richmond, CA, 18 October 1991, Wide Open Town History Project, GLBT Historical Society.

86. Arthur S. Leonard, "The Gay Bar and the Right to Hang out Together," in *Sexuality and the Law: An Encyclopedia of Major Legal Cases* (New York: Garland Publishing, 1993), 190–196. See also Del Martin, "Oh, Bitter Dicta! A Case Won—And Lost," *Ladder* 4, no. 5 (February 1960): 5–9, 19–20.

87. The illegality of same-sex behavior (such as kissing, touching, and dancing) was based on a liberal interpretation of state anti-sodomy laws that prohibited both sodomy and solicitation. While some behaviors, like kissing, seemed more obviously sexual (and potentially solicitous), it was generally up to the courts to decide when specific behaviors crossed into illegal territory. Leonard, "The Gay Bar"; Eskridge, "Privacy Jurisprudence."

88. ABC lawyers felt certain that the fact that the bar owners admitted to running a homosexual bar was evidence enough in itself to prove the bar's immoral character and thus illegality. Leonard, "The Gay Bar," 194.

89. Respondent's Memorandum of Application of Kershaw v. Department of Alcoholic Beverage Control at 2–3, *Vallerga v. Department of Alcoholic Beverage Control,* No. 282,411 (Cal. Super. Ct. 1957), cited in Joan W. Howarth, "First and Last Chance: Looking for Lesbians in Fifties Bar Cases," *Review of Law and Women's Studies* 5, no. 153 (1995): 166–167.

90. Leonard, "The Gay Bar," 194.

91. On case law pertaining to cross-dressing, see William N. Eskridge, Jr., and Nan D. Hunter, *Sexuality, Gender, and the Law* (Westbury, NY: The Foundation Press, 1997), 1129–1139.

92. Morris Lowenthal, Juliet Lowenthal, Karl D. Lyon as Amici Curiae on behalf of the appellants in *Vallerga v. Munro*. Reprinted in Del Martin, "The 'Gay' Bar—Whose Problem Is It?" *Ladder* 4, no. 3 (December 1959): 23–24. Emphasis in the original.

93. Del Martin and Phyllis Lyon, *Lesbian/Woman* (San Francisco: Glide Publications, 1972), 72–75. Emphasis added.

94. Reproduced in the *Mattachine Review* 1, no. 1 (January/February 1955) from *Hollywood Citizen,* 23 September 1954.

95. "An Open Letter to Senator Dirksen," *Mattachine Review* 1, no. 1 (January/February 1955).

96. Randolfe Wicker, "Effeminacy v. Affectation," *Mattachine Review* 4, no. 10 (October 1958): 4–6.

97. Wicker, "Effeminacy v. Affectation," 6. Emphasis in the original.

98. Sweet, "Political and Social Action."

99. Sweet, "Political and Social Action," 78–79.

100. Sweet, "Political and Social Action," 223.

101. "A Queer Ladder of Social Mobility" is the subtitle of the chapter "Crime as an American Way of Life" in Daniel Bell's *The End of Ideology: On the Exhaustion of Political Ideas in the Fifties* (New York: Free Press, 1960). This phrase works as a particularly compelling metaphor for looking at the emergence of San Francisco's homophile movements in that Bell's analysis of crime in the fifties and his dismissal of Marxist ideology have an uncanny similarity to the history of lesbian and gay homophile organizing in San Francisco.

102. "Let's Kill Idle Rumors about Mattachine Aims . . ." *Mattachine Review* 1, no. 3 (May/June 1955): back cover; "Aims and Principles," *Mattachine Review* 2, special issue (January 1956): 12–13; "Editorial," *Mattachine Review* 3, no. 3 (March 1957): 2; "What Does Mattachine Do?" *Mattachine Review* 3, no. 4 (April 1957): 19–23.

103. "Dr. Kinsey Begins Interviews for 'Sex and the Law' Material through S.F. Mattachine Society," San Francisco Mattachine *Newsletter,* no. 6 (November 1953): 1.

104. Alfred C. Kinsey, *Sexual Behavior in the Human Male* (Philadelphia: W. B. Saunders, 1948).

105. Alfred C. Kinsey, *Sexual Behavior in the Human Female* (Philadelphia: W. B. Saunders, 1953); D'Emilio, *Sexual Politics,* 33–37.

106. Evelyn Hooker, "Male Homosexuals and Their 'Worlds,'" in Judd Marmor, ed., *Sexual Inversion: The Multiple Roots of Homosexuality* (New York: Basic Books, 1965), 92–93.

107. Hooker, "Male Homosexuals."

108. Evelyn Hooker, interviewed as part of a video entitled *Changing Our Minds: The Story of Dr. Evelyn Hooker,* directed by Richard Schmiechen, 1992.

109. Evelyn Hooker, "What Is a Criterion?" *Journal of Projective Techniques* 23 (1959): 279.

110. "Research Experts Report on Homosexual Studies," *Ladder* 3, no. 1 (October 1958): 19–21; Evelyn Hooker, "Summary of Paper," *Ladder* 4, no. 6 (March 1960): 10–11; D'Emilio, *Sexual Politics,* 73–74; *Changing Our Minds.*

111. Hooker, "Male Homosexuals," 103.

112. Evelyn Hooker, "Society Is at Crossroads, Declares Research Advisor," San Francisco Mattachine *Newsletter,* no. 16 (September 1954): 1.

113. Jess Stearn, *The Grapevine* (Garden City, NY: Doubleday, 1964), 5, 179.

114. Jess Stearn, *The Sixth Man* (New York: McFadden, 1961). For a discussion of popular sociology addressing homosexuality in the postwar years, see

Jeffrey Escoffier, *American Homo: Community and Perversity* (Berkeley: University of California Press, 1998), 86–93.

115. Stearn, *The Grapevine,* 2.

116. Stearn identifies lesbians as "the fourth sex" because "if there is a third sex [the male homosexual], there is certainly a fourth, for the female homosexual is no more like the male homosexual than she is like other women." *The Grapevine,* 10.

117. While the relationship between Stearn and Martin remained trusting and mutually flattering through the early 1960s, his portraits of some interviewees resulted in angry recriminations and threats of legal action. See Jess Stearn correspondence file, Lyon-Martin Papers, GLBT Historical Society.

118. Stearn, *The Grapevine,* 59.

119. Stearn, *The Grapevine,* 59.

120. See Elaine Tyler May, *Homeward Bound: American Families in the Cold War Era* (New York: Basic Books, 1988).

121. Stearn, *The Grapevine,* 3, 270.

122. For a much more in-depth study of the transmission of sexological case studies into popular culture, see Jennifer Terry, *An American Obsession: Science, Medicine, and Homosexuality in Modern Society* (Chicago: University of Chicago Press, 1999). See also Lisa Duggan, *Sapphic Slashers: Sex, Violence, and American Modernity* (Durham: Duke University Press, 2001).

123. Stearn, *The Grapevine,* 39–41.

124. Stearn, *The Grapevine,* 248–297.

CHAPTER 5

Epigraph: Charlotte Coleman, interviewed by Nan Alamilla Boyd, tape recording, San Francisco, 13 July 1992, Wide Open Town History Project, GLBT Historical Society.

1. Ernest Havemann, "Scientists Search for the Answers to a Touchy and Puzzling Question: Why?" *Life,* 26 June 1964, 76.

2. Paul Welch, "The 'Gay' World Takes to the City Streets," *Life,* 26 June 1964, 68.

3. Welch, "The 'Gay' World," 68.

4. Dave Larsen, "The Question Man: Why Are There So Many Homosexuals Living in S.F.?" *San Francisco Chronicle* (hereafter *Chronicle*), 2 October 1961.

5. Mike Culbert, "90,000 S.F. Perverts—Startling Police Report," *San Francisco News Call,* 18 March 1965, p. 3.

6. O'Hara, "The Question Man: Are There More Homosexuals Today?" *Chronicle,* 10 August 1966, p. 42.

7. Welch, "The 'Gay' World," 68–74.

8. Wayne Sage, "Inside the Colossal Closet," *Human Behavior* 4, no. 8 (August 1975): 16–23.

9. "Homosexuality in America," *Life,* 26 June 1964, 66.

10. Hal Call, interviewed by Nan Alamilla Boyd, tape recording, San Francisco, 14 August 1992, Wide Open Town History Project, GLBT Historical Society.

11. John D'Emilio, "Gay Politics, Gay Community: San Francisco's Experience," in *Making Trouble: Essays on Gay History, Politics, and the University* (New York: Routledge, 1992), 74–94. This essay was originally published in *Socialist Review* 55 (January/February 1981): 77–104. See also D'Emilio, *Sexual Politics, Sexual Communities: The Making of a Homosexual Minority in the United States, 1940–1970* (Chicago: University of Chicago Press, 1983).

12. George Dorsey, *Christopher of San Francisco* (New York: Macmillan Co., 1962), 175–178. See also William Keller, "Police Abuses Denied by Cahill," *Chronicle,* 16 November 1958.

13. Russell Woldon, as quoted by Dorsey in *Christopher,* 187.

14. Russell Woldon, as quoted by Dorsey in *Christopher,* 187.

15. Russell L. Wolden, "Statement to the Press," issued by the Wolden for Mayor Media Headquarters, 8 October 1959.

16. George Draper, "Praise of Mayor's Policy on Deviates Engineered by Ex-Police Informer," *Chronicle,* 9 October 1959. John D'Emilio also discusses the mayoral election of 1959 and the Wolden/Brandhove connection in *Sexual Politics.* See also Cate C. Corcoran, "The Homophile Movement in Print," (undergraduate thesis, University of California, Santa Cruz, 1992).

17. *Chronicle* editorial, quoted in Dorsey, *Christopher,* 189.

18. Dorsey, *Christopher,* 187.

19. "Wolden Sued for Slander," *Chronicle,* 9 October 1959.

20. "Mattachine Society in the News," San Francisco Mattachine *Newsletter* (November 1959).

21. Del Martin, "Editorial: The Homosexual Vote," *Ladder* 4, no. 10 (July 1960): 4–5.

22. Ideas contained in this section emerged out of numerous conversations with Allan Bérubé and Willie Walker. Many thanks to Allan Bérubé for sharing his unpublished manuscript "'Resorts for Sex Perverts': A Political History of Gay Bars in San Francisco," 1985.

23. Section 24200(e) of the California Business and Professional Code (1955), cited by Del Martin in "The 'Gay' Bar—Whose Problem Is It?" *Ladder* 4, no. 3 (December 1959): 5. See also Arthur S. Leonard, "The Gay Bar and the Right to Hang Out Together," in *Sexuality and the Law: An Encyclopedia of Major Legal Cases* (New York: Garland Publishing, 1993), 190–196.

24. *Stoumen v. Reilly,* cited by Martin, "The 'Gay' Bar—Whose Problem Is It?" Sol Stoumen, owner of the Black Cat, fought a number of expensive court battles in an effort to protect his right to serve alcohol to homosexuals. It is estimated that Stoumen's expenses for *Stoumen v. Reilly* exceeded $38,000. D'Emilio, *Sexual Politics,* 186–188.

25. Bérubé, "'Resorts for Sex Perverts,'" 12.

26. Morris Lowenthal, quoted by Ron Fimrite in "Why 'Gay' Bars Get in Trouble," *Chronicle,* 29 May 1960.

27. Del Martin, "Oh, Bitter Dicta! A Case Won—And Lost," *Ladder* 4,

no. 5 (February 1960): 5; Fimrite, "Why 'Gay' Bars Get in Trouble," *Chronicle*, 29 May 1960.

28. D'Emilio, *Sexual Politics*, 182–3.

29. "Cop Sergeant Pleads Guilty in Gay Bar Bribery Case," *Chronicle*, 12 July 1960.

30. A San Francisco police officer probably earned less than $400 a month. Cardellini earned $473.47 a month for his work at the state liquor board, so a payoff of $200 was substantial.

31. Ernest Lenn, "Bar Owner Testified of Payoffs," *San Francisco Examiner* (hereafter *Examiner*), 26 July 1960; "Cop 'Helped Self,' Bribe Trial Told," *Chronicle*, 26 July 1960.

32. Ernest Lenn, "Cecchi Objects to Cop Trial Queries," *Examiner*, 6 August 1960.

33. Ernest Lenn, "Comedy Note Struck in Bar Bribe Trial," *Examiner*, 9 August 1960.

34. Bérubé, "'Resorts for Sex Perverts,'" 13.

35. Allen Brown, "The Question Man," "Should We Discourage Gay Bars?" *Chronicle*, 6 August 1960.

36. William N. Eskridge, Jr., and Nan D. Hunter, *Sexuality, Gender, and the Law* (Westbury, NY: The Foundation Press, 1997).

37. José Sarria, interviewed by Nan Alamilla Boyd, tape recording, San Francisco, 15 April 1992, Wide Open Town History Project, GLBT Historical Society.

38. Guy Strait, "The Nightingale," *The News* 3, no. 6 (23 December 1963).

39. José Sarria, interviewed by Nan Alamilla Boyd, tape recording, San Francisco, 15 April 1992, Wide Open Town History Project, GLBT Historical Society. See also Michael R. Gorman, *The Empress Is a Man: Stories from the Life of José Sarria* (New York: Harrington Park Press, 1998), 25–32. Sarria's Nicaraguan father, Julio Sarria, had little involvement in his son's upbringing.

40. José Sarria, interviewed by Nan Alamilla Boyd, tape recording, San Francisco, 15 April 1992, Wide Open Town History Project, GLBT Historical Society.

41. José Sarria, interviewed by Nan Alamilla Boyd, tape recording, San Francisco, 15 April 1992, Wide Open Town History Project, GLBT Historical Society; Gorman, *The Empress Is a Man*, 35.

42. José Sarria, interviewed by Nan Alamilla Boyd, tape recording, San Francisco, 15 April 1992, Wide Open Town History Project, GLBT Historical Society.

43. Gorman, *The Empress Is a Man*, 137–141.

44. Pearl's was located at 466 Twelfth Street in Oakland and operated from 1940 to 1955 as "a drag place owned by a tuxedo-wearing, cigar-smoking dyke named Pearl." The Beige Room, located at 831 Broadway in San Francisco (1951–1958), was an elegantly decorated nightclub that featured female impersonators such as T. C. Jones, Lynne Carter, and Kenneth Marlowe. Finocchio's, San Francisco's infamous nightclub featuring female impersonators, operated at 506 Broadway from 1937 to 1999. See Eric Garber, "A Historical Directory of Lesbian and Gay Establishments in the San Francisco Bay Area," c. 1992 (un-

published data in author's possession). See also Queer Sites Database, GLBT Historical Society.

45. George Mendenhall, interviewed by Scott Bishop, tape recording, San Francisco, 23 April 1990, Scott Bishop Papers, GLBT Historical Society.

46. Guy Strait, "The Nightingale," 4.

47. Herb Caen, *Chronicle,* 10 May 1962.

48. "Big Sex Raid—101 Arrested in Tiny Restaurant," *Chronicle,* 14 August 1961.

49. The February 1956 raid on Hazel's, a homosexual tavern in San Mateo County, resulted in eighty-seven arrests. See articles in the *Chronicle* and *Examiner,* 20 February 1956. See also articles in the *Mattachine Review* 2, 2nd special issue (March 1956) and 2, no. 3 (June 1956).

50. Allan Bérubé identifies the Tay-Bush raid as part of the post-"gayola" crackdown, whereby city police retaliated against resistant gay bars. Bérubé, "'Resorts for Sex Perverts.'" See also "Big Sex Raid," *Chronicle,* 14 August 1961; "A Gay Cafe Party—89 Men, 14 Women Held," *Examiner,* 14 August 1961; "103 S.F. Revelers Arrested in Raid," *Oakland Tribune,* 14 August 1961.

51. Ethel Whitaker (pseud.), interviewed by Nan Alamilla Boyd, tape recording, San Francisco, 30 August 1992, Wide Open Town History Project, GLBT Historical Society.

52. "Big Sex Raid," *Chronicle,* 14 August 1961.

53. "Big Sex Raid," *Chronicle,* 14 August 1961.

54. Ethel Whitaker (pseud.), interviewed by Nan Alamilla Boyd, tape recording, San Francisco, 30 August 1992, Wide Open Town History Project, GLBT Historical Society.

55. Herb Caen, *Chronicle,* 20 August 1961.

56. Herb Caen, *Chronicle,* 20 August 1961.

57. "A Gay Cafe Party—89 Men, 14 Women Held," *Examiner,* 14 August 1961.

58. "Vice Raid Justified—Mayor," *Examiner,* 15 August 1961.

59. "Vice Case to Test Public 'Tolerance,'" *Examiner,* 16 August 1961.

60. "Vice Case to Test Public 'Tolerance,'" *Examiner,* 16 August 1961.

61. "The Inquiring Photographer: Should S.F. Close the Gay Clubs?" *Examiner,* 4 September 1961.

62. Charles Raudebaugh, "Lynch Criticizes Vagrancy Law Use, Wants Revision," *Chronicle,* 30 July 1958, p. 1.

63. William J. Chambliss, "A Sociological Analysis of the Law of Vagrancy," in R. Serge Denisoff and Charles H. McCaghy, *Deviance, Conflict and Criminality* (Chicago: Rand McNally and Co., 1973), 256–270.

64. Amy Dru Stanley, *From Bondage to Contract: Wage Labor, Marriage, and the Market in the Age of Slave Emancipation* (Cambridge University Press, 1998).

65. "Dragnet on for All 'Vagrants,'" *Chronicle,* 12 January 1956.

66. "S.F. Too 'Hot'—Hoods Head for Oakland," *Chronicle,* 11 February 1956.

67. Raudebaugh, "Lynch Criticizes Vagrancy Law Use, Wants Revision," *Chronicle,* 30 July 1958, p. 1.

68. Keller, "Police Abuses Denied by Cahill," *Chronicle,* 16 November 1958.

69. "ACLU Clashes with San Francisco Police on Vagrancy Arrests," *Ladder* 1, no. 9 (June 1957): 19.

70. "Damage Suits Filed in 2 'Vag' Arrest Cases," c. 1958, GLBT Historical Society, clippings file.

71. "Governor Signs Bill Repealing Vagrancy Law," *ACLU Newsletter,* undated, GLBT Historical Society, clippings file.

72. "Police Here Drop Vagrancy Arrests," *Chronicle,* 2 June 1961.

73. "Police Here Drop Vagrancy Arrests," *Chronicle,* 2 June 1961.

74. "Governor Signs Bill Repealing Vagrancy Law," *ACLU Newsletter,* undated, GLBT Historical Society, clippings file.

75. On the use of public toilets for same-sex sexual liaisons, see Laud Humphreys, *Tearoom Trade: Impersonal Sex in Public Places* (Chicago: Aldine Publishing, 1970). On the importance of public sex to the evolution of gay culture and community, see Bérubé, "'Resorts for Sex Perverts.'"

76. "Calling Shots: 'Homosexuals' Arrested by 'Special Police,'" *Mattachine Review* 7, no. 2 (November 1961): 5.

77. "Calling Shots: 'Homosexuals' Arrested by 'Special Police,'" *Mattachine Review* 7, no. 2 (November 1961): 5.

78. Bulletin, League for Civil Education, c. 21 March 1961, José Sarria Papers, LCE documents, GLBT Historical Society.

79. Bulletin, League for Civil Education, 2 April 1961, José Sarria Papers, LCE documents, GLBT Historical Society.

80. Guy Strait, letter to Chief of Police Cahill, 31 March 1961, José Sarria Papers, LCE documents, GLBT Historical Society.

81. Bulletin, League for Civil Education, 2 April 1961, José Sarria Papers, LCE documents, GLBT Historical Society.

82. Guy Strait, letter to the California State Attorney General, José Sarria Papers, LCE documents, GLBT Historical Society.

83. Bulletin, League for Civil Education, 15 April 1961, José Sarria Papers, LCE documents, GLBT Historical Society.

84. "Purposes of the League for Civil Education," undated, José Sarria Papers, LCE documents, GLBT Historical Society.

85. Bulletin, League for Civil Education, 15 April 1961, José Sarria Papers, LCE documents, GLBT Historical Society.

86. "Have You Seen This Man?" *Citizens News* 3, no. 15 (May 1964). See also "How to Spot a Cop," *Citizens News* 4, no. 10 (March 1965): 3.

87. See Nan Alamilla Boyd, "Shopping for Rights: Gays, Lesbians, and Visibility Politics," *Denver University Law Review* 75, no. 4 (1998): 1361–1373.

88. "Lest We Forget, a Thumbnail History of the TGSF," Tavern Guild of San Francisco (TGSF) Records, GLBT Historical Society. See also Bill Plath, "The Tavern Guild: A Record of Accomplishment," transcript of an address delivered to the membership of the Tavern Guild, 5 April 1966, TGSF Records, GLBT Historical Society. See also Bob Ross, "Tavern Guild of San Francisco," *Gay Pride* 2 (Winter 1972–1973).

89. During the first year of operation, bar owners and bartenders who participated in organizing the Tavern Guild worked or had worked at the Handle Bar (1959–1960), 1438 California Street; Lupe's Echo (1952–1954), 545 Post Street; Keno's (1950–1956), 47 Golden Gate Avenue; Chili's (1954), 141 Embarcadero; Coffee Don's (1950s–1960s), Pine Street at Leavenworth; the Sea Cow (1954–1956) and the Cross Roads (1956–1963), both at 109 Steuart Street; Cal's (1957–1962), 782 O'Farrell Street; Dolan's Supper Club (1940s–1956), 406 Stockton; the Paper Doll (1940s–1961), 524 Union Street; the Beige Room (1951–1958), 831 Broadway; and the Suzy-Q (1960–1962), 1741 Polk Street. Many of these establishments had been closed by the ABC or the SFPD's Vice Squad. "Lest We Forget, a Thumbnail History of the TGSF"; Garber, "Historical Directory."

90. Tom Stuart, letter to José Sarria, 12 November 1970, José Sarria Papers, GLBT Historical Society; Darryl Glied, letter to José Sarria, 17 November 1970, José Sarria Papers, GLBT Historical Society.

91. "Lest We Forget, a Thumbnail History of the TGSF," 3.

92. "Lest We Forget, a Thumbnail History of the TGSF"; Plath, "The Tavern Guild: A Record of Accomplishment." See also Minutes, Tavern Guild of San Francisco, 18 December 1962, TGSF Records, GLBT Historical Society.

93. "Constitution of the Tavern Guild of San Francisco," 17 July 1962, TGSF Records, GLBT Historical Society.

94. For information about the fraternal and ethnic organizations that aided the economic mobility of late-nineteenth and early-twentieth century immigrants to the United States, see John Bodnar, Roger Simon, and Michael Weber, *Lives of Their Own* (Urbana: University of Illinois Press, 1983); Oliver Zunz, *The Changing Face of Inequality* (Chicago: University of Chicago Press, 1982).

95. Plath, "The Tavern Guild: A Record of Accomplishment."

96. Charlotte Coleman, interviewed by Nan Alamilla Boyd, tape recording, San Francisco, 13 July 1992, Wide Open Town History Project, GLBT Historical Society.

97. Plath, "The Tavern Guild: A Record of Accomplishment."

98. Charlotte Coleman, interviewed by Nan Alamilla Boyd, tape recording, San Francisco, 13 July 1992, Wide Open Town History Project, GLBT Historical Society.

99. Plath, "The Tavern Guild: A Record of Accomplishment," 2. See also TGSF *Newsletter,* 26 March 1965, TGSF Records, GLBT Historical Society.

100. "Lest We Forget, a Thumbnail History of the TGSF," 4.

101. "Lest We Forget, a Thumbnail History of the TGSF," 4. See also "Tavern Guild's Beaux Arts Costume Ball at the Hilton," *Town Talk* 1, no. 4 (October 1964) and "Guild's Beaux Arts Costume Ball a Brilliant Success," *Town Talk* 1, no. 5 (November 1964). *Town Talk* was a newsletter published by Hal Call from July 1964 to February 1966. A copy of this publication can be found at the GLBT Historical Society.

102. Plath, "The Tavern Guild: A Record of Accomplishment."

103. Charlotte Coleman, interviewed by Nan Alamilla Boyd, tape recording, San Francisco, 13 July 1992, Wide Open Town History Project, GLBT Historical Society.

104. Rikki Streicher, interviewed by Nan Alamilla Boyd, tape recording, San Francisco, 22 January 1992, Wide Open Town History Project, GLBT Historical Society. Rikki Streicher was the owner and manager of Maud's, a lesbian bar featured in the Paris Poirier documentary *Last Call at Maud's*. Streicher participated in the Tavern Guild through the late 1960s and the 1970s.

105. Plath, "Tavern Guild: A Record of Accomplishment," 2.

106. "L.C.E. Is No More," *Citizens News* 3, no. 17 (8 June 1964): 1, 4. See also Bill Plath, interviewed by Nan Alamilla Boyd, tape recording, San Francisco, 4 August 1992, Wide Open Town History Project, GLBT Historical Society.

107. Bill Plath, interviewed by Nan Alamilla Boyd, tape recording, San Francisco, 4 August 1992, Wide Open Town History Project, GLBT Historical Society.

108. Bill Beardemphl, "On Leadership," *Vector* 1, no. 2 (January 1965): 2.

109. Eric Marcus, *Making History: The Struggle for Gay and Lesbian Equal Rights, 1945–1990* (New York: HarperCollins, 1992), 145.

110. Bill Beardemphl, "S.I.R.'s Statement of Policy," *Vector* 1, no. 1 (December 1964): 1.

111. Larry Littlejohn, interviewed by Scott Bishop, tape recording, San Francisco, 27 April 1990, Scott Bishop Papers, GLBT Historical Society.

112. Nancy May, interviewed by Marcus in *Making History,* 139–140.

113. See the reprint of a 1969 *Vector* article, "S.I.R.'s Political Campaign Sweeps Feinstein into Presidency," in the *Bay Area Reporter,* 12 July 1972.

114. Evander Smith, "In Case of Arrest: The S.I.R. Pocket Lawyer," Society for Individual Rights Legal Committee, Ephemera Collection, GLBT Historical Society.

115. Smith, "In Case of Arrest."

116. Bill Plath, interviewed by Nan Alamilla Boyd, tape recording, San Francisco, 4 August 1992, Wide Open Town History Project, GLBT Historical Society.

117. Bill Plath, interviewed by Nan Alamilla Boyd, tape recording, San Francisco, 4 August 1992, Wide Open Town History Project, GLBT Historical Society.

118. May in Marcus, *Making History,* 139.

119. "Community House Proposed," *Vector* 1, no. 6 (May 1965): 1.

120. Letter to members from the SIR Board of Directors, 17 March 1966, José Sarria Papers, GLBT Historical Society.

121. Bill Plath, interviewed by Nan Alamilla Boyd, tape recording, San Francisco, 4 August 1992, Wide Open Town History Project, GLBT Historical Society.

122. Larry Littlejohn, interviewed by Scott Bishop, tape recording, San Francisco, 27 April 1990, Scott Bishop Papers, GLBT Historical Society.

123. Bill Beardemphl, "Gold Sheet," c. November 1966, José Sarria Papers, GLBT Historical Society. My emphasis.

124. Bill Beardemphl, "Editorial," *Vector* 1, no. 3 (February 1965): 6.

125. *Citizens News* 4, no. 4 (December 1964).

126. Donald S. Lucas, "The Homosexual and the Church" (San Francisco: Mattachine Society Publications, 1966).

127. "New Year's Ball Planned as Church Council Benefit," *Town Talk* 1, no. 6 (December 1964). The six groups were the Mattachine Society, the Daughters of Bilitis, the Society for Individual Rights, Strait & Associates (the *Citizens News*), the Tavern Guild of San Francisco, and the Coits.

128. "New Year's Ball," *Citizens News* 4, no. 5 (December 1964): 1.

129. Herbert Donaldson and Evander Smith in Marcus, *Making History,* 152–153; "Police Action at the Ball: The Law, the Action and the Reaction," *Citizens News* 4, no. 7 (January 1965): 2; Donovan Bess, "Angry Ministers Rip Police," *Chronicle,* 2 January 1965.

130. Donaldson and Smith in Marcus, *Making History,* 153.

131. "Police Action at the Ball: The Law, the Action and the Reaction," *Citizens News* 4, no. 7 (January 1965): 2; "What Really Happened," *Town Talk* 1, no. 8 (January 1965): 1.

132. "Witness Breaks Up a Courtroom," *Chronicle,* 11 February 1965.

133. May in Marcus, *Making History,* 141–46; Smith and Donaldson in Marcus, *Making History,* 152–165; "What Really Happened," *Town Talk* 1, no. 8 (January 1965) .

134. Bess, "Angry Ministers Rip Police," *Chronicle,* 2 January 1965.

135. Larry Littlejohn, interviewed by Scott Bishop, tape recording, San Francisco, 27 April 1990, Scott Bishop Papers, GLBT Historical Society.

136. "Shelley Asks Cops' Side of Dance Hassle," *Chronicle,* 5 January 1965, p. 22.

137. Hal Call, "Strumpet's Gall," *Town Talk* 1, no. 8 (January 1965): 1.

138. Letters to the editor, San Francisco *Chronicle,* 8 January 1965, p. 42.

139. "Witness Breaks Up a Courtroom," *Chronicle,* 11 February 1965.

140. Council on Religion and the Homosexual, Inc., "A Brief of Injustices: An Indictment of Our Society in Its Treatment of the Homosexual," *Citizens News* 4, no. 16 (May 1965).

141. May in Marcus, *Making History,* 145; Bill Plath, interviewed by Nan Alamilla Boyd, tape recording, San Francisco, 4 August 1992, Wide Open Town History Project, GLBT Historical Society.

142. Del Martin and Phyllis Lyon, interviewed by Nan Alamilla Boyd, tape recording, San Francisco, 2 December 1992, Wide Open Town History Project, GLBT Historical Society.

143. Members of the Gay and Lesbian Historical Society of Northern California, "MTF Transgender Activism in the Tenderloin and Beyond, 1966–1975: Commentary and Interview with Eliot Blackstone," *GLQ: A Journal of Lesbian and Gay Studies* 4, no. 2 (1998): 349–372.

CONCLUSION

1. These figures are conservative in that they do not account for out-of-town visitors who lodged with friends or lodged outside of San Francisco. They also do not account for leisure visitors from the Bay Area. A less conservative figure

might estimate San Francisco's annual revenue from gay tourism (again, in restaurant business) to be close to $30 million, since hotel-based tourism only accounts for one-third of the visitor volume. If one takes into account the other ways gay tourism generates revenue (i.e., hotels, shopping, souvenirs, and local transportation), the numbers increase significantly. For instance, a report from the San Francisco Convention and Visitors Bureau estimates that in 1999, the typical visitor to San Francisco staying in a hotel spent $233 per person, per day. This would bring the estimated expenditures of hotel-based gay tourists to $44 million in 1999. "Tourism Works for San Francisco," San Francisco Convention and Visitors Bureau (2000); "An Inside Look at the San Francisco Visitor," San Francisco Convention and Visitors Bureau (June 2000).

2. Gayle S. Rubin, "The Miracle Mile: South of Market and Gay Male Leather, 1962–1997," in James Brook, Chris Carlsson, and Nancy J. Peters, eds., *Reclaiming San Francisco: History, Politics, Culture* (San Francisco: City Lights Books, 1998), 247–272.

3. Randy Shilts, *Mayor of Castro Street: The Life and Times of Harvey Milk* (New York: St. Martin's Press, 1982).

4. Alex Chasin, *Selling Out: The Gay and Lesbian Movement Goes to Market* (New York: Palgrave, 2000). See also Nan Alamilla Boyd, "Shopping for Rights: Gays, Lesbians, and Visibility Politics," *Denver University Law Review* 75, no. 4 (1998): 1361–1373.

5. Joanne Meyerowitz, "Sex Change and the Popular Press: Historical Notes on Transsexuality in the United States, 1930–1955," *GLQ: A Journal of Lesbian and Gay Studies* 4, no. 2 (1998): 159–188.

6. Members of the Gay and Lesbian Historical Society of Northern California, "MTF Transgender Activism in the Tenderloin and Beyond, 1966–1975: Commentary and Interview with Elliot Blackstone," *GLQ: A Journal of Lesbian and Gay Studies* 4, no. 2 (1998): 349–372.

Index

Text: 9.25/13 Futura Book; 10/13 Sabon
Display: Futura; Sabon
Indexer: Sharon Sweeney
Compositor: G&S Typesetters, Inc.
Printer: Edwards Brothers, Inc.